The Concise Wadsworth Handbook

Laurie G. Kirszner
University of the Sciences in Philadelphia

Stephen R. Mandell
Drexel University

THOMSON
WADSWORTH

Australia   Canada   Mexico   Singapore   Spain   United Kingdom   United States

The Concise Wadsworth Handbook
Laurie G. Kirszner, Stephen R. Mandell

Publisher: *Michael Rosenberg*
Senior Acquisitions Editor: *Dickson Musslewhite*
Development Editor: *Karen R. Smith*
Senior Technology Project Manager:
Cara Douglass-Graff
Executive Marketing Manager: *Carrie Brandon*
Executive Advertising Project Manager:
Brian Chaffee
Senior Project Manager, Editorial Production:
Lianne Ames
Manufacturing Manager: *Marcia Locke*
Associate Permissions Editor: *Chelsea Junget*

Production Service: *Susan McIntyre, Nesbitt Graphics, Inc.*
Text Designer: *Nesbitt Graphics, Inc.*
Photo Manager: *Sheri Blaney*
Photo Researcher: *Sharon Donahue*
Cover Designer: *Brian Salisbury*
Cover Printer: *Transcontinental Printing, Inc.*
Compositor: *Nesbitt Graphics, Inc.*
Printer: *Transcontinental Printing, Inc.*

For more information about our products, contact us at:
Thomson Learning Academic Resource Center
1-800-423-0563
For permission to use material from this text or product, submit a request online at http://www.thomsonrights.com.
Any additional questions about permissions can be submitted by email to thomsonrights@thomson.com.

Library of Congress Control Number: 2004111049

Student Edition: 1-4130-1030-X(Spiral)
Student Edition: 1-4130-3275-3(Paperbound)
Instructor's Edition: 1-4130-1552-2

Thomson Higher Education
25 Thomson Place
Boston, MA 02210-1202
USA

Asia (including India)
Thomson Learning
5 Shenton Way
#01-01 UIC Building
Singapore 068808

Australia/New Zealand
Thomson Learning Australia
102 Dodds Street
Southbank, Victoria 3006
Australia

Canada
Thomson Nelson
1120 Birchmount Road
Toronto, Ontario M1K 5G4
Canada

UK/Europe/Middle East/Africa
Thomson Learning
High Holborn House
50–51 Bedford Road
London WC1R 4LR
United Kingdom

How to Use This Book

As writers, you already know that to express your ideas clearly, you need to understand the basic principles of grammar, mechanics, and style. As writers in the digital age, however, you also have to be acquainted with the electronic tools that you will need to navigate the Internet and to find information (both electronic and print) in the library. We wrote *The Concise Wadsworth Handbook* with these needs in mind. The result is a book that you can depend on to give you useful, no-nonsense, practical advice about writing.

The Concise Wadsworth Handbook is a complete reference for the college writer. Not only does it explain and illustrate the writing process, but it also offers guidance on grammar, style, punctuation, and mechanics and includes extensive sections on research and MLA and APA documentation styles. In addition, a unique section—Part 2, "Developing Strategies for Academic Success"—contains chapters on reading for college, writing essay exams, writing for the workplace, and designing effective documents and Web sites.

We have taken pains to make *The Concise Wadsworth Handbook* inviting, useful, clear, and—most of all—easy to use. To achieve these goals, we incorporated distinctive design features throughout the text—icons, close-up boxes, checklists, and marginal cross-references and navigational aids—to help you locate information quickly. Familiarizing yourself with the following page, which explains and illustrates these design features, will help you get the most out of this book.

Throughout *The Concise Wadsworth Handbook* we have made every effort to address the challenges that real writers face in the twenty-first century and to provide you with clear explanations and sound advice. The result, we hope, is a book that you can rely on—and one that you will use with ease and, perhaps, even with pleasure.

Laurie Kirszner
Steve Mandell
November 2004

The Concise Wadsworth Handbook: Design Features

- *Computer tips* highlight specific ways in which technology can help you throughout the writing, revising, and editing processes. Each computer tip includes the URL for the book's companion Web site <http://kirsznermandell.wadsworth.com>, which contains a wealth of online resources.

- *Numerous checklists* summarize key information to help you review and assess your work.

- *Close-up boxes* provide an in-depth look at some of the more perplexing writing-related issues you will encounter.

- *Specially designed documentation directories*—including one icon that designates print sources and a different icon that designates electronic sources—make it easy for you to locate models for various kinds of sources, including those found online from library subscription services such as InfoTrac® and LexisNexis™. *Chapter 46, "MLA Documentation Style,"* and *Chapter 47, "APA Documentation Style,"* include the most up-to-date documentation and format guidelines from the Modern Language Association and the American Psychological Association, respectively. In addition, annotated diagrams of sample works-cited and reference list entries clearly illustrate the elements of proper documentation.

See 1a
- *Marginal cross-references* throughout the book allow you to turn directly to other sections that treat related topics.

ESL 48d
- *Marginal ESL cross-references* throughout the book direct you to sections of Part 8, "Bilingual and ESL Writers," where concepts are presented as they apply specifically to second-language writers.

- *ESL tips* are woven throughout the text to explain concepts in relation to the unique experiences of bilingual students.

Exercise 8.1
- *Numerous exercises* throughout the text allow you to practice at each stage of the writing, revising, and editing processes. Answers are provided in the back of the book for items marked with a ▶.

Acknowledgments

We thank the following reviewers for their advice, which helped us develop the *Wadsworth Handbook* series:

Joan K. Anderson, *Southeastern Louisiana University*
Sherine Azzam, *Joliet Junior College*
James M. Baskin, *Joliet Junior College*
Jennifer Beech, *University of Tennessee, Chattanooga*
Cheryl D. Bohde, *McLennan Community College*
Ethel L. Bonds, *Virginia Western Community College*
Sarah K. Burns, *Virginia Western Community College*
Suzanne Campbell, *Southeastern Louisiana University*
Diane Rose Carr, *Midlands Technical College*
Cindy L. Casper, *Norwalk Community College*
Camille Colatosti, *Davenport University*
Dean R. Cooledge, *University of Maryland, Eastern Shore*
James Crawford, *Walters State Community College*
Paul G. Crawford, *Southeastern Louisiana University*
Michel de Benedictis, *Miami-Dade Community College, Kendall*
Jason De Polo, *North Carolina A&T State University*
Michael D. Donnelly, *Temple University*
Anne Maric Drew, *US Naval Academy*
John Duffy, *University of Notre Dame*
Niko Endres, *Western Kentucky University*
Sharynn Etheridge-Logan, *Tennessee State University*
Kathryn B. Everett, *Texas A&M University*
William G. Feeler, *Midland College*
Robert Felgar, *Jacksonville State University*
Jason D. Fichtel, *Joliet Junior College*
Samuel B. Garren, *North Carolina A&T State University*
Janet Garufis, *University of California, Santa Barbara*
Casey Gilson, *Broward Community College, North*
Joe Glaser, *Western Kentucky University*
Marina Gore, *Hudson Valley Community College*
Tim Gustafson, *University of Minnesota*
Sarah H. Harrison, *Tyler Junior College*
Cynthia Haynes, *University of Texas, Dallas*
Wade Heaton, *Southeastern Louisiana University*

Carolyn Hendon, *Tyler Junior College*
Jeff Hoogeveen, *Lincoln University*
Gloria Horton, *Jacksonville State University*
H.R. Houston, *Tennessee State University*
Elizabeth Howells, *Armstrong Atlantic State University*
Marcia Huntington, *Everett Community College*
Lauren S. Ingraham, *University of Tennessee, Chattanooga*
Beverly J. Jamison, *South Carolina State University*
Peggy Jolly, *University of Alabama, Birmingham*
Rachel Jorden, *Hudson Valley Community College*
Richard Keenan, *University of Maryland, Eastern Shore*
Elon Kulii, *North Carolina A&T State University*
Ronald M. Kyhos, *US Naval Academy*
Elizabeth A. Latshaw, *Auburn University*
Elisabetta LeJeune, *Southeastern Louisiana University*
Lin Marklin, *Kellogg Community College*
Manuel Martinez, *Santa Fe Community College*
David Martins, *California State University, Chico*
Matthew Marx, *University of Nebraska, Omaha*
Nellie McCrory, *Gaston College*
Susan McDermott, *Hudson Valley Community College*
Robert Milde, *Eastern Kentucky University*
Samantha A. Morgan-Curtis, *Tennessee State University*
Kevin Morris, *Greenville Technical College*
Roxanne F. Munch, *Joliet Junior College*
Kathryn Lee Neal, *York Technical College*
Brian Nerney, *Metropolitan State University*
Charlene Pate, *Point Loma Nazarene University*
John Pennington, *St. Norbert College*
Mark Rankin, *The Ohio State University*
Ellen Raphaeli, *Northern Virginia Community College*
Carole A. Raybourn, *Morehouse College*
Teresa P. Reed, *Jacksonville State University*
William E. Rivers, *University of South Carolina, Columbia*
Barbara JoAnn Seabrook, *University of Maryland, Eastern Shore*
Cary D. Ser, *Miami-Dade Community College, Kendall*
Linda S. Smith, *Midlands Technical College*
Kristy Leanne Starks-Winn, *University of Tennessee, Chattanooga*

Philip J. Stucky, *Harold Washington College*
Jill Swiencicki, *California State University, Chico*
Gina Thompson, *East Mississippi Community College, Golden Triangle*
Tom Treffinger, *Greenville Technical College*
William Vaughn, *Central Missouri State University*
Ted Walkup, *Clayton College & State University*
Jeff Wiemelt, *Southeastern Louisiana University*

At Wadsworth, we thank Michael Rosenberg, Publisher, who provided the guidance and support that made *The Concise Wadsworth Handbook* possible. He assembled an editorial team whose commitment, enthusiasm, and personal involvement made this book a pleasure to work on, and for this we are very grateful.

At this point, we would like to single out Karen Smith, who is, without a doubt, the best development editor we have ever worked with. Insightful, intelligent, well organized, astute, and unflappable, the awe-inspiring Karen remained in control in all situations—no matter how difficult. We predict great things for her.

Also at Wadsworth, we would like to thank Dickson Musslewhite, Senior Acquisitions Editor; Lianne Ames, Production Project Manager; Sheri Blaney, Photography Manager; Carrie Brandon, Executive Marketing Manager; and Marcia Locke, Manufacturing Manager. We would also like to thank Susan McIntyre, Project Manager, and the staff of Nesbitt Graphics Inc., who worked hard and did a great job.

Once again, we would like to thank our families—Mark, Adam, and Rebecca Kirszner and Demi, David, and Sarah Mandell. They were and still are the people we care about the most. Finally, we would like to thank each other for making this book a collaboration in the truest sense.

Successful students have *learned* to be successful: they have developed specific strategies for success, and they apply those strategies to their education. If you take the time, you can learn the habits of successful students and apply them to your own college education and, later on, to your career.

1. Learn to Manage Your Time Effectively

College makes many demands on your time. It is hard, especially at first, to balance studying, coursework, family life, friendships, and a job. But if you don't take control of your schedule, it will take control of you; if you don't learn to manage your time, you will always be behind, struggling to catch up.

Fortunately, there are two tools that can help you manage your time: a **personal organizer** and a **monthly calendar.** Carry your organizer with you at all times, and post your calendar in a prominent place (perhaps above your desk or next to your phone). Remember to record *in both places* school-related deadlines, appointments, and reminders (every due date, study group meeting, conference appointment, and exam) and outside responsibilities, such as work hours and medical appointments. (Be sure to record tasks and dates as soon as you learn of them.)

You can also use your organizer to help you plan a study schedule, as illustrated in Figure 1 on page 2. You do this by blocking out times to study or to complete assignment-related tasks—such as a library database search for a research paper—in addition to appointments and deadlines. (It is a good idea to make these entries in pencil so you can adjust your schedule as new responsibilities arise.)

Remember: your college years can be a very stressful time, but although some degree of stress is inevitable, it can be kept in check. If you are organized, you will be better able to handle the pressures of a college workload.

2. Put Studying First

To be a successful student, you need to understand that studying is something you do *regularly*, not right before an exam. You also need to know that studying does not mean just memorizing facts; it also means reading, rereading, and discussing ideas until you understand them.

October 2004

4 Monday	Thursday 7
Library orientation-noon	Work 3-5
*Call for appt. at tutoring center before chem test (Thurs before work?)	

5 Tuesday	Friday 8
Email Dr. G for conference appt.	Chem exam 10am!
Work 3-5	
Computer lab: first draft of English Paper	Home

6 Wednesday	Saturday 9
first draft of English paper due	Dentist 10 a.m.
	Sunday 10
8 p.m.-Meet w/ study group for chem exam	back to school ⟶

Figure 1 Sample organizer pages for one week.

To make studying a regular part of your day, set up a study space that includes everything you need (supplies, good light, a comfortable chair) and does not include anything you do not need (clutter, distractions). Then, set up a tentative study schedule. Try to designate at least two hours each day to complete assignments due right away, to work on those due later on, and to reread class notes. When you have exams and papers, you can adjust your schedule accordingly.

Successful students often form **study groups,** and you should use this strategy whenever you can—particularly in a course you find challenging. A study group of four or five students who meet regularly (not just the night before an exam) can make studying more focused and effective as well as less stressful. By discussing concepts with your classmates, you can try out your ideas and get feedback, clarify complex concepts, and formulate questions for your instructor.

Checklist: Doing Collaborative Work

Working **collaboratively**—in a study group, for example—requires some degree of organization. To get the most out of collaborative work, you need to set some ground rules for the group you are working with.

☐ Meet regularly.
☐ Decide in advance who will be responsible for particular tasks.
☐ Set deadlines.
☐ Listen when someone else is speaking.
☐ Don't reject other people's ideas and suggestions without considering them very carefully.
☐ Have one person take notes to keep a record of the group's activities.
☐ Take stock of problems and progress at regular intervals.
☐ Be mindful of other students' learning styles and special needs.

3. Be Sure You Understand School and Course Requirements

To succeed in school, you need to know what is expected of you—and, if you are not sure, to ask.

When you first arrived at school, you probably received a variety of orientation materials—a student handbook, library handouts, and so on—that set forth the rules and policies of your school. Read these documents carefully (if you have not already done so). If you do not understand something, ask your peer counselor or your adviser for clarification.

You also need to know the specific requirements of each course you take. Each course syllabus explains the instructor's policies about attendance and lateness, assignments and deadlines, plagiarism, and classroom etiquette. In addition, a syllabus may explain penalties for late assignments or missed quizzes, explain how assignments are graded, tell how much each assignment is worth, or note additional requirements, such as field work or group projects. Requirements vary significantly from course to course, so read each syllabus (as well as any supplementary handouts) carefully.

ESL Tip

If you did not attend high school in the United States, some of your instructors' class policies and procedures may seem strange to you. To learn more about the way US college classes are run, read the syllabus for each of your courses and talk to your instructors about your concerns. You may also find it helpful to talk to older students with cultural backgrounds similar to your own.

4. Be an Active Learner in the Classroom

Education is not about sitting passively in class and waiting for information and ideas to be given to you. It is up to you to be an active participant in your own education.

First, take as many small classes as you can. Small classes enable you to interact with other students and with your instructor. If a large course has recitation sections, be sure to attend these regularly, even if they are not required. Also, be sure to take classes that require writing. Good writing skills are essential to your success as a student (and as a college graduate entering the workforce), and you will need all the practice you can get.

Take responsibility for your education by attending class regularly and arriving on time. Listen attentively, and take careful, complete notes. (Try to review these notes later with other students to make sure you have not missed anything important.) Do your homework on time, and keep up with the reading. When you read an assignment, interact with the text (for example, underlining the text and making marginal annotations) instead of just looking at what is on the page. If you have time, read beyond the assignment, looking on the Internet and in books, magazines, and newspapers for related information.

Finally, participate in class discussions: ask and answer questions, volunteer opinions, and give helpful feedback to other students. By participating in this way, you learn to consider other points of view, to test your ideas, and to respect the ideas of others.

ESL Tip

Especially in small classes, US instructors usually expect students to participate in class discussion. If you feel nervous about speaking up in class, you might start by expressing your support of a classmate's opinion.

5. Be an Active Learner Outside the Classroom

Taking an active role in your education is also important outside the classroom. Do not be afraid to approach your instructors; take advantage of their office hours, and keep in touch with them by email. Get to know your major adviser well, and be sure he or she knows who you are and where your academic interests lie. Make appointments, ask questions, and explore possible solutions to problems: this is how you learn.

In addition, become part of your school community. Read your school newspaper, check the Web site regularly, join clubs, and apply for internships. This participation can help you develop new interests and friendships as well as enhance your education.

Finally, participate in the life of your community outside your school. Try to arrange an **internship,** a job that enables you to gain practical experience. (Many businesses, nonprofit organizations, and government agencies offer internships [paid or unpaid] to qualified students.) Take service learning courses, if they are offered at your school, or volunteer at a local school or social agency. As successful students know, education is more than just attending classes.

6. Take Advantage of College Services

Colleges and universities offer students a wide variety of support services. For example, if you are struggling with a particular course, you can go to the tutoring service offered by your school's academic support center or by an individual department. If you need help with writing or revising a paper, you can make an appointment with the writing lab, where tutors will give you advice. If you are having trouble deciding on what courses to take or what to major in, you can see your academic adviser. If you are having trouble adjusting to college life, your peer counselor or (if you live in a dorm) your resident adviser may be able to help you. Finally, if you have a personal or family problem you would rather not discuss with another student, you can make an appointment at your school's counseling center, where you can get advice from professionals who understand student problems.

ESL Tip

Many ESL students find using the writing lab (sometimes called a writing center) very helpful. Most writing labs provide assistance with assignments for any course, and they often assist with writing job application letters and résumés. Many writing labs have tutors who specialize in working with ESL students.

Many other services are available—for example, at your school's computer center, job placement service, and financial aid office. Your academic adviser or instructors can tell you where to find the help you need, but it is up to you to make the appointment.

7. Use the Library

Because so much material is available on the Internet, you may think your college library is outdated or even obsolete. But learning to use the library is an important part of your education. See 42a–c

First, the library can provide a quiet place to study—something you may need if you have a large family or noisy roommates. The library also contains materials that cannot be found online—rare books, special collections, audiovisual materials—as well as electronic databases that contain material you will not find on the free Internet.

Finally, the library is the place where you have access to the expert advice of your school's reference librarians. These professionals can answer questions, guide your research, and point you to sources that you might never have found on your own.

8. Use Technology

Technological competence is essential to success in college. For this reason, it makes sense to develop good word-processing skills and to be comfortable with the <u>Internet</u>. You should also know how to send and receive email from your university account as well as how to attach files to your email. Beyond the basics, you should learn how to manage the files you download, how to evaluate Web sites, and how to use the electronic resources of your library. You might also find it helpful to know how to scan documents (containing images as well as text) and how to paste these files into your documents.

If you do not have these skills, you need to locate campus services that will help you get them. Workshops and online tutorials may be available through your school library or campus computing services, and individual assistance on software and hardware use is available in computer labs.

Part of being technologically savvy in college involves being aware of the online services your campus has to offer. For example, many campuses rely on customizable information-management systems called **portals.** Not unlike commercial services, such as Yahoo! or America Online, a portal requires you to log in with a user ID and password to access services such as locating and contacting your academic adviser and viewing your class schedule and grades.

Finally, you need to know not only how to use technology to enhance a project—for example, how to use *PowerPoint* for an oral presentation or *Excel* to make a <u>table</u>—but also *when* to use technology (and when not to).

9. Make Contacts—and Use Them

One of the most important things you can do for yourself is to make academic and professional contacts that you can use during college and after you graduate.

Your first contacts are your classmates. Be sure you have the names, phone numbers, and email addresses of at least two students in each of your classes. These contacts will be useful to you if you miss class, if you need help understanding your notes, or if you want to start a study group.

You should also build relationships with students with whom you participate in college activities, such as the college newspaper or the tutoring center. These people are likely to share your goals and interests, and so you may want to get feedback from them as you choose a major, consider further education, and make career choices.

Finally, develop relationships with your instructors, particularly those in your major area of study. One of the things cited most often in studies of successful students is the importance of **mentors,** experienced individuals whose advice you trust. Long after you leave college, you will find these contacts useful.

10. Be a Lifelong Learner

Your education should not stop when you graduate from college. To be a successful student, you need to be a lifelong learner.

Get in the habit of reading newspapers; know what is happening in the world outside school. Talk to people outside the college community so that you don't forget there are issues that have nothing to do with courses and grades. Never miss an opportunity to learn: try to get in the habit of attending plays and concerts sponsored by your school or community and lectures offered at your local library or bookstore.

And think about the life you will lead after college. Think about who you want to be and what you have to do to get there. This is what successful students do.

Close-up: Ten Habits to Avoid

1. **Procrastination**   You should not procrastinate, no matter how tempting it is to postpone studying for a test, writing a paper, making a writing lab appointment, or setting up a meeting with your adviser. Being able to manage time is a skill that almost all good students have. Remember, if you put off your work until the last minute, your responsibilities will eventually overwhelm you.
2. **Lateness**   To avoid penalties that will hurt your grades, you should hand in assignments on time. You should also make sure that you take an exam on the day it is given. (Some instructors give a more difficult make-up exam to those who miss a scheduled test.) Finally, be sure to complete all your semester's coursework on time; request an Incomplete grade only in an emergency.
3. **Cuts**   Even if an instructor allows a certain number of unexcused absences, you should not miss class unless you absolutely have to. If you do miss a class, contact a classmate to find out what you missed. Don't email your instructor and ask, "Did I

(continued)

miss anything?" (The answer to this question is, "Of course you did.") If you will miss a number of classes because of a personal emergency, let your instructors know immediately. Most instructors will try to accommodate you if you keep them informed.

4. **Poor Communication**   Regular communication with your course instructors (as well as with lab assistants and recitation instructors) is vital to your success in college. Good communication will ensure that you understand what is expected of you and know how to achieve it.

5. **Focus on Grades**   Focusing on your grades instead of on your education is a poor strategy for academic success. Instead of asking your instructors (or even yourself), "What do I have to do to get an A?" ask, "How can I improve my understanding of the material?"

6. **Poor Health Habits**   Eat healthy, regular meals; exercise when you can; avoid drugs and alcohol.

7. **Poor Sleep Habits**   Resist the temptation to study (or party) all night. Try to go to sleep and wake up at about the same time each day rather than staying up late and sleeping until noon on the weekends.

8. **Inappropriate Behavior**   Show proper decorum in the classroom and in instructor conferences. Be polite and respectful, listen when others speak, and don't interrupt. In class, remove your hat, raise your hand when you want to speak, and watch your language.

9. **Negative Attitudes**   Try not to see one poor grade or negative instructor comment as the beginning of a trend that spells failure. Listen to criticism, learn from your mistakes, and take steps to improve.

10. **Overscheduling**   Be realistic when you plan your schedule. Don't sign up for more courses than you can handle or agree to take on more projects than you can reasonably hope to complete. In addition, don't work so many hours at your job that you have no time to study. Take breaks when you need to; schedule some downtime, and use it.

PART 1

Writing Essays

Everyone who sets out to write confronts a series of choices. Some choices are based on fairly obvious factors, such as how much you know about your subject and how much time you have. Others are determined by more subtle and far-reaching considerations, such as your purpose for writing and the audience you are addressing. In the writing you do in school, on the job, and in your personal life, your understanding of purpose and audience is essential, influencing the choices you make about content, emphasis, organization, style, and tone.

1a   Determining Your Purpose

In simple terms, your **purpose** for writing is what you want to accomplish. For instance, your purpose may be to *reflect*, to express private feelings, as in the introspective or meditative writing that appears in personal journals, diaries, and memoirs. Or your purpose may be to *inform*, to convey factual information as accurately and as logically as possible, as in the informational or expository writing that appears in reports, news articles, encyclopedias, and textbooks. At other times, your purpose may be to *persuade*, to convince your readers, as in advertising, proposals, editorials, and some business communications. Finally, your purpose may be to *evaluate*, to make a judgment about something, as in a recommendation report or a comparative analysis.

(1) Writing to Reflect

In diaries and journals, writers explore ideas and feelings to make sense of their experiences; in autobiographical memoirs and in personal letters, they communicate their emotions and reactions to others.

> At the age of five, six, well past the time when most other children no longer easily notice the difference between sounds uttered at home and words spoken in public, I had a different experience. I lived in a world magically compounded of sounds. I remained a child longer than most; I lingered too long, poised at the edge of language—often frightened by the sounds of *los gringos*, delighted by the sounds of Spanish at home. I shared with my family a language that was startlingly different from that used in the great city around us. (Richard Rodriguez, *Aria: A Memoir of a Bilingual Childhood*)

(2) Writing to Inform

In newspaper articles, writers report information, communicating factual details to readers; in reference books, instruction manuals, textbooks, and the like, as well as in catalogs, cookbooks, and government-sponsored Web sites, writers provide definitions and explain concepts or processes, trying to help readers see relationships and understand ideas.

> Most tarantulas live in the tropics, but several species occur in the temperate zone and a few are common in the southern U.S. Some varieties are large and have powerful fangs with which they can inflict a deep wound. These formidable-looking spiders do not, however, attack man; you can hold one in your hand, if you are gentle, without being bitten. Their bite is dangerous only to insects and small mammals such as mice; for man it is no worse than a hornet's sting. (Alexander Petrunkevitch, "The Spider and the Wasp")

(3) Writing to Persuade

In proposals and editorials, as well as in advertising, writers try to convince readers to accept their position on an issue.

> Testing and contact tracing may lead to a person's being deprived of a job, health insurance, housing and privacy, many civil libertarians fear. These are valid and grave concerns. But we can find ways to protect civil rights without sacrificing public health. A major AIDS-prevention campaign ought to be accompanied by intensive public education about the ways the illness is *not* transmitted, by additional safeguards on data banks and by greater penalties for those who abuse HIV victims. It may be harsh to say, but the fact that an individual may suffer as a result of doing what is right does not make doing so less of an imperative. (Amitai Etzioni, "HIV Sufferers Have a Responsibility")

(4) Writing to Evaluate

In reviews of books, films, or performances and in reports, critiques, and program evaluations, writers assess the validity, accuracy, and quality of information, ideas, techniques, products, procedures, or services, perhaps assessing the relative merits of two or more things.

> Kingston, Jamaica-based reggae label Phase One never got the credit it deserved for bridging the gap between dub and vocal reggae, but *We Are Getting Bad: The Sound of Phase One* might remedy the oversight. Phase One vocal groups like the Chantells and the Untouchables are backed by production as eerie as anything done by better-known auteurs. And the Untouchables' version of "Sea of Love" provides one of the most unexpected payoffs since the Human League covered "Reach Out (I'll Be There)." (Ethan Brown, "The War at Home," *New York* magazine)

Although writers do write to reflect, to inform, to persuade, and to evaluate, these purposes are certainly not mutually exclusive, and writers may have other purposes as well. And, of course, in any piece of writing a writer may have a primary aim and one or more secondary purposes; in fact, a writer may even have different purposes in different sections—or different drafts—of a single document.

Checklist: Determining Your Purpose

Is your purpose:

- ☐ to express emotions?
- ☐ to inform?
- ☐ to persuade?
- ☐ to explain?
- ☐ to amuse or entertain?
- ☐ to evaluate?
- ☐ to discover?
- ☐ to analyze?
- ☐ to debunk?
- ☐ to draw comparisons?
- ☐ to make an analogy?
- ☐ to define?
- ☐ to criticize?
- ☐ to motivate?

- ☐ to satirize?
- ☐ to speculate?
- ☐ to warn?
- ☐ to reassure?
- ☐ to take a stand?
- ☐ to identify problems?
- ☐ to suggest solutions?
- ☐ to identify causes?
- ☐ to predict effects?
- ☐ to reflect?
- ☐ to interpret?
- ☐ to instruct?
- ☐ to inspire?

Exercise 1.1

The primary purpose of the following article from the *New York Times* is to present information. Suppose you were using the information in an orientation booklet aimed at students entering your school, and your purpose was to persuade students of the importance of maintaining a good credit rating. How would you change the original article to help you achieve this purpose? Would you reorder any details? Would you add or delete anything?

What Makes a Credit Score Rise or Fall?

By JENNIFER BAYOT

Your financial decisions can affect your credit score in surprising ways. Two credit-scoring simulators can help consumers understand the potential impact.

The Fair Isaac Corporation, which puts out the industry-standard FICO scores, offers the myFICO simulator. A consumer with a score of 707 (considered good) and three credit cards would be likely to add or lose points from his score by making various financial moves. Following are some examples:

- By making timely payments on all his accounts over the next month or by paying off a third of the balance on his cards, he could add as many as 20 points.

- By failing to make this month's payments on his loans, he could lose 75 to 125 points.
- By using all of the credit available on his three credit cards, he could lose 20 to 70 points.
- By getting a fourth card, depending on the status of his other debts, he could add or lose up to 10 points.
- By consolidating his credit card debt into a new card, also depending on other debts, he could add or lose 15 points.

The other simulator, the What-If, comes from CreditXpert, which designs credit management tools and puts out its own, similar credit score. A consumer with a score of 727 points (also considered good) would be likely to have her score change in the following ways:

- Every time she simply applied for a loan, whether a credit card, home mortgage or auto loan, she would lose five points. (An active appetite for credit, credit experts note, is considered a bad sign. For one thing, taking on new loans may make borrowers less likely to repay their current debts.)
- By getting a mortgage, she would lose two points.
- By getting an auto loan or a new credit card (assuming that she already has several cards) she would lose three points.
- If her new credit card had a credit limit of $20,000 or more, she would lose four points, instead of three. (For every $10,000 added to the limit, the score drops a point.)
- By simultaneously getting a new mortgage, auto loan and credit card, she would lose seven or eight points.

1b   Identifying Your Audience

When you are in the early stages of a writing project, staring at an empty computer screen or a blank sheet of paper, it is easy to forget that what you write will have an audience. But except for diaries and private journals, you always write for an **audience,** a particular reader or group of readers. In this sense, writing is a public rather than a private activity.

(1) Writing for an Audience

At different times, in different roles, you address a variety of audiences.

- As a citizen, consumer, or member of a community, civic, political, or religious group, you may respond to pressing social, economic, or political issues by writing letters to a newspaper, a public official, or a representative of a special interest group.
- In your personal life, you may write notes and email messages to friends and family.

- As an employee, you may write letters, memos, and reports to your superiors, to staff members you supervise, or to coworkers; you may also be called on to address customers or critics, board members or stockholders, funding agencies or the general public.

See 4c2

- As a student, you write essays, reports, and other papers addressed to one or more instructors, and you may also participate in peer review, writing evaluations of classmates' essays and writing responses to their comments about your own work.

See 6c

As you write, you shape your writing in terms of what you believe your audience needs and expects. Your assessment of your readers' interests, educational level, biases, and expectations determines not only the information you include but also what you emphasize and how you arrange your material.

(2) The College Writer's Audience

See Ch. 6

Writing for Your Instructor As a student, you usually write for an audience of one: the instructor who assigns the paper. Instructors want to know what you know and whether you can express what you know clearly and accurately. They assign written work to encourage you to use critical thinking skills, so the way you organize and express your ideas can be as important as the ideas themselves.

See Chs. 46–47

As a group, instructors have certain expectations. Because they are trained as careful readers and critics, your instructors expect accurate information, standard grammar and correct spelling, logically presented ideas, and a reasonable degree of stylistic fluency. They also expect you to define your terms and to support your generalizations with specifics. Finally, every instructor also expects you to draw your own conclusions and to provide full and accurate documentation for ideas that are not your own.

If you are writing in an instructor's academic field, you can omit long overviews and basic definitions. Remember, however, that outside their areas of expertise, most instructors are simply general readers. If you think you may know more about a subject than your instructor does, be sure to provide background, and to supply the definitions, examples, and analogies that will make your ideas clear.

Writing for Other Students Before you submit a paper to an instructor, you may have an opportunity to participate in **peer review**, sharing your work with your fellow students and responding in writing to their work. In both these cases, you need to see your classmates as an audience whose needs you must take into account.

- **Writing Drafts** If you know that other students will read a draft of your paper, you need to consider how they might react to your ideas. For example, are they likely to agree with you? To be shocked or offended by your paper's language or content? To be confused, or even mystified, by any of your references? Even if your readers are your own age, you cannot assume that they share your cultural frame of reference. It is therefore very important that you maintain an appropriate tone and use moderate language in your paper and that you explain any historical, geographical, or cultural references that might be unfamiliar to your audience.

- **Writing Comments** When you respond in writing to other students' papers, you need to take into account how this audience will react to your comments. Here too, your tone is important: you want to be as encouraging (and as polite) as possible. In addition, keep in mind that your purpose is not to show how clever you are but to offer constructive comments that can help your classmate write a stronger essay.

Checklist: Audience Concerns for Peer-Review Participants

- ☐ **Know your audience.** To be sure you understand what the student writer needs and expects from your comments, read the paper several times before you begin writing your response.

- ☐ **Focus on the big picture.** Don't get bogged down on minor problems with punctuation or mechanics or become distracted by a paper's proofreading errors.

- ☐ **Look for a positive feature,** zeroing in on what you think is the paper's greatest strength.

- ☐ **Be positive throughout.** Try to avoid words like *weak*, *poor*, and *bad*; instead, try using a compliment before delivering the "bad news": "Paragraph 2 is very well developed; can you add this kind of support in paragraph 4?"

- ☐ **Show respect.** It is perfectly acceptable to tell a student that something is confusing or inaccurate, but don't go on the attack.

- ☐ **Be specific.** Avoid generalizations like "needs more examples" or "could be more interesting"; instead, try to offer helpful, focused suggestions: "You could add an example after the second sentence in paragraph 2"; "Explaining how this process operates would make your discussion more interesting."

- ☐ **Don't give orders.** Ask questions, and make suggestions.

- ☐ **Include a few words of encouragement,** emphasizing the paper's strong points.

> ### Checklist: Identifying Your Audience
>
>
> ☐ Who will read your paper?
> ☐ What are your audience's needs? Expectations? Biases? Interests?
> ☐ Does your audience need you to supply definitions? Overviews? Examples? Analogies?
> ☐ What does your audience expect in terms of document design? Format? Documentation style? Method of collecting and reporting data? Use of formulas and symbols or specialized vocabulary?

Exercise 1.2

Look again at the article in Exercise 1.1 on pages 12–13. This time, try to decide what audience or audiences it seems to be aimed at. Then, consider what (if anything) might have to be changed to address the needs of each of the following audiences:

- College students
- Middle-school students
- The elderly
- People with limited English skills
- People who do not live in the US

Chapter 2   Planning an Essay

2a Understanding the Writing Process

Writing enables you to discover ideas, make connections, and see from new perspectives. In this sense, writing is a demanding, creative process of thinking and learning—about yourself, about others, and about your world. In another sense, writing is a tool that empowers you: it enables you to participate in the ongoing dialogue among people who communicate in letters, emails, memos, petitions, reports, articles, editorials, and books.

> ### Close-up: The Writing Process
>
> The writing process includes the following stages:
> **Planning:** Consider your purpose, audience, and tone; choose your topic; discover ideas to write about.

> **Shaping:** Decide how to organize your material.
> **Drafting:** Write your first draft.
> **Revising:** "Re-see" what you have written; write additional drafts.
> **Editing:** Check grammar, spelling, punctuation, and mechanics.
> **Proofreading:** Check for typographical errors.

The neatly defined stages listed above communicate neither the complexity nor the flexibility of the writing process. These stages actually overlap: as you look for ideas, you begin to shape your material; as you shape your material, you begin to write; as you write a draft, you reorganize your ideas; as you revise, you continue to discover new material. Moreover, these stages may be repeated again and again throughout the writing process.

During your college years and in the years that follow, you will develop your own version of the writing process and use it whenever you write, adapting it to the audience, purpose, and writing situation at hand.

2b   Analyzing Your Assignment

Planning your essay—thinking about what you want to say and how you want to say it—begins well before you actually start recording your thoughts in any organized way. This planning is as important a part of the writing process as the writing itself. During this planning stage, you determine your <u>purpose</u> for writing, identify your <u>audience</u>, and decide on an appropriate tone. Then, you go on to focus on your assignment, choose and narrow your topic, and gather ideas.

See
Ch. 1

Before you begin writing, be sure you understand the exact requirements of your assignment, and keep those guidelines in mind as you write and revise. Don't assume anything; ask questions, and be sure you understand the answers.

Checklist: Analyzing Your Assignment

- ☐ Has your instructor assigned a specific topic, or can you choose your own?
- ☐ What is the word or page limit?
- ☐ How much time do you have to complete your assignment?
- ☐ Will you get feedback from your instructor? Will you have an opportunity to participate in <u>peer review</u>?
- ☐ Does your assignment require research?

See
4c2

(continued)

See
Ch. 46

Analyzing your assignment (continued)

☐ What format (for example, <u>MLA</u>) are you supposed to follow?
Do you know what its conventions are?
☐ If your assignment has been given to you in writing, have you
read it carefully and highlighted key words?

2c Choosing and Narrowing a Topic

If your instructor allows you to choose a topic, choose one you know
something about—or, at least, one you want to learn about. Perhaps
a class discussion or reading assignment will suggest a topic; maybe
you have seen a movie or television program or had a conversation
(or an argument) about a topic you could explore.

Most of the time your instructor will steer you toward a topic by
giving you an assignment that specifies a length, format, and general
subject; gives a list of general subjects from which to choose; or
poses a question for you to answer.

> Write a two-page critical analysis of a film. (Specifies length, for-
> mat, and general subject)

> Write an essay explaining the significance of one of these court
> decisions: *Marbury* v. *Madison, Baker* v. *Carr, Brown* v. *Board of Ed-
> ucation, Roe* v. *Wade.* (Gives list of general subjects from which to
> choose)

> How did the boundaries of Europe change after World War I?
> (Poses a question)

Even if your instructor gives you a very specific assignment, however, you may not be able to start writing immediately. First, you
must determine whether the topic this assignment suggests is narrow
enough for your purpose, your audience, and your page limit. If it is
not, you will need to narrow it further.

Narrowing a Topic

Course	Assignment	Topic
American History	Analyze the effects of a social program on one segment of American society.	How did the GI Bill of Rights affect American service-women?
Psychology	Write a three- to five-page paper assessing one method of treating depression.	Animal-assisted therapy for severely depressed patients

Course	Assignment	Topic
Composition	Write an essay about a problem you have encountered since coming to college.	My problems using a computer

Exercise 2.1

List ten possible essay topics about your childhood. Your purpose is to give your audience—your composition instructor and possibly members of your <u>peer-review</u> group—a vivid sense of what some aspect of your childhood was like. Then, choose the one topic that you feel best qualified to write about, and write a few sentences explaining why you selected it.

See 4c2

2d Finding Something to Say

Once you have a topic, you can begin to collect ideas for your paper, using one (or several) of the strategies discussed in the pages that follow.

ESL Tip

Some ESL students spend little time generating ideas for their writing because they are primarily concerned about writing grammatically correct sentences. But remember, the purpose of writing is to convey ideas. If you want to find material to write about, you will need to devote plenty of time to the activities described in this section.

(1) Reading and Observing

The best way to find material to write about is to open your mind to new ideas. As you read textbooks, magazines, and newspapers and browse the Internet, be on the lookout for ideas that relate to your topic, and make a point of talking informally with friends or family about it.

Films, television programs, interviews, telephone calls, letters, emails, and questionnaires can also provide material. But be sure your instructor permits such research—and remember to <u>document</u> ideas that are not your own to avoid committing <u>plagiarism</u>.

See Chs. 46–47

See Ch. 45

(2) Keeping a Journal

Many professional writers keep **journals** (print or electronic), writing in them regularly whether or not they have a specific project in mind. Journals, unlike diaries, do more than simply record personal experiences and reactions. In a journal, you explore ideas, ask questions, and draw conclusions. You might, for example, analyze your position on a political issue, try to solve an ethical problem, or trace the evolution of your ideas about an academic assignment. You can also record quotations that have special meaning to you or make notes about your reactions to important news events, films, or conversations. A good journal is a scrapbook of ideas that you can leaf through in search of new material and new ways of looking at old material. The important thing is to write regularly—every day if possible—so that when a provocative idea comes along, you won't miss the opportunity to record it.

Kimberly Romney, a student in a first-year composition class, decided to write about the problems she had in college when she was expected to use a computer for her coursework. Her journal entry appears below.

Journal Entry

```
     I'm not really comfortable writing about my own poor
computer skills, but I have to admit it's a good topic for
a paper about a problem I have. What I really want to focus
on, though, is the ways in which computer illiteracy is a
big problem not just for me but for many college students.
I don't want to write about the hours it took me to
register for classes online or the fact that it took me an
hour to figure out how to email my professor and then save
that email to a disk. I don't want this paper to be about
me and my problems. What I want to do is write about the
difficulties students with low computer skills have and
mention a few things about my own life to illustrate these
general ideas.
```

(3) Freewriting

Freewriting is another strategy that can help you discover ideas. When you freewrite, you write nonstop about anything that comes to mind, moving as quickly as you can. Give yourself a set period of time—say, five minutes—and don't stop to worry about punctuation, spelling, or grammar, or about where your mind is wandering. This strategy encourages your mind to make free associations; thus, it helps you to discover ideas you probably aren't even aware you have. When your time is up, look over what you have written, and underline, bracket, or star the most promising ideas. You can then use each of these ideas as the center of a focused freewriting exercise.

When you do **focused freewriting,** you zero in on your topic. Here too you write without stopping to reconsider or reread, so you have no time to be self-conscious about style or form, to worry about the relevance of your ideas, or to count how many words you have and panic about how many more you think you need. At its best, focused freewriting can suggest new details, a new approach to your topic, or even a more interesting topic. Kimberly's freewriting and focused freewriting exercises appear below.

Freewriting (Excerpt)

This isn't so bad because I finally don't have to worry about typing perfectly. I can make mistakes, and I won't have to stop writing and then correct myself. That's how I feel using computers: anxious. We had a few computers at my high school, but we didn't have to take a computer class, or even a typing class. Maybe we should have! When I got to college, I felt like such an idiot. Everyone else seemed to have no trouble using the Internet for research, creating <u>PowerPoint</u> presentations, and creating their own Web sites for class projects. All of a sudden I was expected to use computers to register, for research, and to communicate with my professors. It was horrible! Most other students didn't ever have to ask a question about computers. It's like there are two groups when you get to college: the people who are computer literate and those who aren't.

Focused Freewriting (Excerpt)

The first day of orientation we were told to use the computers to register. It's not like I'd never used a computer before or seen the Internet. Still, I had to raise my hand and get the proctor in the computer room to come help me click on the right icon. And then I had to ask a

lot of questions to figure out how to access two Web sites
at the same time so that I could look at both the online
course catalog and the registration program. Meanwhile,
most of the other students were already finished and on
their way to dinner. When I asked if I could get a copy of
the course schedule on paper, the proctor told me that the
university had recently gone "paperless." I realized then
and there that I was going to have to do a lot of extra
work to make myself computer literate.

(4) Brainstorming

One of the most useful ways to accumulate ideas is by brainstorming
(either on your own or in a group). This strategy enables you to recall pieces of information and to see connections among them.

When you **brainstorm,** you list all the points you can think of
that seem pertinent to your topic, recording ideas—comments,
questions, single words, symbols, or diagrams—as quickly as you
can, without pausing to consider their relevance or trying to understand their significance. Kimberly's brainstorming notes appear
below.

Brainstorming Notes

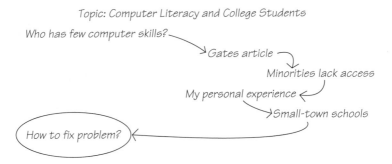

(5) Clustering

Clustering—sometimes called *webbing* or *mapping*—is similar to
brainstorming. As with brainstorming, you don't need to worry
about writing complete sentences, and you jot ideas down quickly,
without pausing to evaluate their usefulness or to analyze their logical relationships to other ideas. However, clustering encourages you
to explore your topic in a more systematic (and more visual) manner.

Begin your cluster diagram by writing your topic in the center of a sheet of paper. Then, surround your topic with related ideas as they occur to you, moving outward from the general topic in the center and writing down increasingly specific ideas and details as you move toward the edges of the page. Following the path of one idea at a time, you create a diagram (often lopsided rather than symmetrical) that arranges ideas on spokes or branches radiating out from the center (your topic). Kimberly's cluster diagram appears below.

Cluster Diagram

Topic: Computer Literacy and College Students

Understanding basic word processing   Minorities

Internet savvy   Small-town students

Assumptions that all are computer literate   Me: problems

$$\text{(College Students and Computers)}$$

Ways of fixing the problem

Programs at school

High school?

http://kirsznermandell.wadsworth.com

Computer Tip: Generating Ideas

You can use your computer to help you find material to write about.

When you **freewrite,** try turning down the brightness of the monitor, leaving the screen blank to eliminate distractions and encourage spontaneity. When you reread what you have written, you can boldface or underline important ideas (or highlight them in color).

When you **brainstorm,** type your notes randomly. Later, after you print them out, you can add more notes and graphic elements (arrows, circles, and so on) by hand to indicate parallels and connections.

(6) Asking Journalistic Questions

Journalistic questions offer an orderly, systematic way of finding material to write about. Journalists are trained to ask the questions *Who? What? Why? Where? When?* and *How?* to ensure that they have explored all angles of a story, and you can use these questions to make sure you have considered all aspects of your topic. Kimberly's list of journalistic questions appears below.

Journalistic Questions

- <u>Who</u> stereotypes college students? <u>Who</u> is familiar with computers and the Internet and <u>who</u> is not?
- <u>What</u> are some of the assumptions people make about college students? <u>What</u> is computer illiteracy? <u>What</u> kinds of programs exist to help those who are computer illiterate at the college level?
- <u>When</u> did computers become essential for college students?
- <u>Where</u> are students most likely to learn computer skills?
- <u>Why</u> is familiarity with the Internet so important in college? <u>Why</u> is there a gap between those who are computer savvy and those who are not?
- <u>How</u> can we bridge this gap?

(7) Asking In-Depth Questions

If you have time, you can ask a series of more focused questions about your topic. These in-depth questions not only can give you a great deal of information but also can suggest ways for you to eventually shape your ideas into paragraphs and essays.

In-Depth Questions	
What happened? When did it happen? Where did it happen?	Suggest <u>narration</u> (an account of your first day of school; a summary of Emily Dickinson's life)
What does it look like? What does it sound like, smell like, taste like, or feel like?	Suggest <u>description</u> (of the Louvre; of the electron microscope; of a Web site)
What are some typical cases or examples of it?	Suggests <u>exemplification</u> (three infant day-care settings; four popular fad diets)

How did it happen? What makes it work? How is it made?	Suggest process (how to apply for financial aid; how a bill becomes a law)
Why did it happen? What caused it? What does it cause? What are its effects?	Suggest cause and effect (the events leading to the Korean War; the results of global warming; the impact of a new math curriculum on slow learners)
How is it like other things? How is it different from other things?	Suggest comparison and contrast (of the popular music of the 1970s and 1980s; of two paintings)
What are its parts or types? Can they be separated or grouped? Do they fall into a logical order? Can they be categorized?	Suggest division and classification (components of the catalytic converter; kinds of occupational therapy; kinds of dietary supplements)
What is it? How does it resemble other members of its class? How does it differ from other members of its class?	Suggest definition (What is Marxism? What is photosynthesis? What is a MOO?)

An excerpt from Kimberly's list of in-depth questions appears below.

In-Depth Questions (Excerpt)

What causes the gap between those who are computer savvy and those who are not? Differences in family income, parents' education level, quality of public education, regional differences.

What are the effects of the gap? Differences in achievement in college, performance on the job; differences in access to information; differences in earning power.

Exercise 2.2

List all the sources you encounter in one day (specific people, books, magazines, Web sites, and so on) that could provide you with useful

information for the essay you are writing. Exchange lists with a classmate, and add two sources to his or her list.

Exercise 2.3

Make a cluster diagram and brainstorming notes for the topic you selected in Exercise 2.1. If you have trouble thinking of material to write
about, try freewriting. Then, write a journal entry assessing your
progress and evaluating the different strategies for finding something
to say. Which strategy worked best for you? Why?

Exercise 2.4

Using the question strategies described on pages 24–25 to supplement
the work you did in Exercises 2.2 and 2.3, continue generating material for a short essay on your topic from Exercise 2.1.

Chapter 3 Shaping Your Material

After you have gathered material for your essay and begun to see the
direction your ideas are taking, you start to sift through these ideas
and choose those you can use in your essay. As you do this, you begin
to shape your material into a thesis-and-support essay.

3a Understanding Thesis and Support

Your **thesis** is the main idea of your essay, the central point your
essay supports. The concept of **thesis and support**—stating the
thesis and then supplying information that explains and develops
it—is central to much of the writing you will do in college.

As the following diagram illustrates, the essays you will write will
See
5e2–3 consist of an introductory paragraph, which opens your essay and
states your thesis; a concluding paragraph, which closes your essay
and gives it a sense of completion, perhaps restating your thesis; and
a number of **body paragraphs,** which provide the support for your
thesis statement.

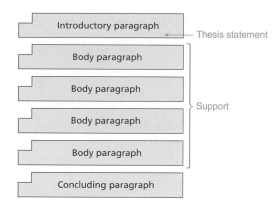

3b Developing a Thesis

(1) Stating Your Thesis

An effective **thesis statement** has four characteristics.

1. **An effective thesis statement clearly communicates your essay's main idea.** It tells readers what your essay's topic is and suggests what you will say about it. Thus, your thesis statement reflects your essay's <u>purpose</u>.

See 1a

2. **An effective thesis statement is more than a general subject, a statement of fact, or an announcement of your intent.**

Stating Your Thesis

Subject	Statement of Fact	Announcement
The Military Draft	The United States currently has no military draft.	In this essay, I will reconsider our country's need for a draft.

Thesis statement Once the military draft may have been necessary to keep the armed forces strong; however, today's all-volunteer force has eliminated the need for a draft.

3. **An effective thesis statement is carefully worded.** Because it communicates your paper's main idea, your thesis statement should be clearly and accurately worded. Your thesis statement—usually expressed in a single concise sentence—should be direct and straightforward, including no vague or abstract language,

overly complex terminology, or unnecessary details that might confuse or mislead readers.

Moreover, effective thesis statements should not include phrases such as "I hope to demonstrate" and "It seems to me," which weaken your credibility by suggesting that your conclusions are tentative or are based solely on opinion rather than on reading, observation, and experience.

4. **Finally, an effective thesis statement suggests your essay's direction, emphasis, and scope.** Your thesis statement should not make promises that your essay will not fulfill. It should suggest how your ideas are related, in what order your major points will be discussed, and where you will place your emphasis, as the following thesis statement does.

Effective Thesis Statement

```
Widely ridiculed as escape reading, romance novels are
becoming increasingly important as a proving ground
for many never-before-published writers and, more
significantly, as a showcase for strong heroines.
```

This thesis statement is effective because it tells readers that the essay to follow will focus on two major new roles of the romance novel: providing markets for new writers and (more important) presenting strong female characters. It also suggests that the essay will briefly treat the role of the romance novel as escapist fiction. As the diagram below shows, this effective thesis statement also indicates the order in which the various ideas will be discussed.

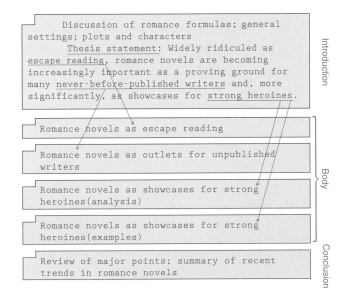

Close-up: Avoiding Vague Wording

Try to avoid vague, wordy phrases—*centers on, deals with, involves, revolves around, has a lot to do with, is primarily concerned with*, and so on. Be direct and forceful.

```
                                          is
The real problem in our schools does not
revolve around the absence of nationwide
goals and standards; the problem is primarily
concerned with the absence of resources with
which to implement them.
```

Checklist: Stating Your Thesis

☐ Does your thesis statement clearly communicate your essay's main idea? Does it suggest the approach you will take toward your material? Does it reflect your essay's purpose?

☐ Is your thesis statement more than a subject, a statement of fact, or an announcement of your intent?

☐ Is your thesis statement carefully worded?

☐ Does your thesis statement suggest your essay's direction, emphasis, and scope?

(2) Revising Your Thesis Statement

At this point, the thesis statement that you develop is only tentative. As you write and rewrite, you may think of new ideas and see new connections. As a result, you may modify your essay's direction, emphasis, and scope several times, and if you do so, you must reword your thesis statement to reflect these modifications.

Notice how the following thesis statement changed as the writer moved through successive drafts of the essay.

Revising Your Thesis Statement

Tentative Thesis Statement (rough draft)	Revised Thesis Statement (final draft)
Professional sports can easily be corrupted by organized crime.	Although supporters of legalized sports betting argue that organized crime cannot make inroads into professional sports, the way in which underworld figures compromised the 1919 World Series suggests the opposite.

3c Using a Thesis Statement to Shape Your Essay

The wording of your thesis statement often suggests not only a possible order and emphasis for your essay's ideas, but also a specific pattern of development—*narration, description, exemplification, process, cause and effect, comparison and contrast, division and classification,* or *definition.* These familiar <u>patterns of development</u> may also shape individual paragraphs of your essay.

See
5d

Using a Thesis Statement to Shape Your Essay

Thesis Statement	Pattern of Development
As the months went by and I grew more and more involved with the developmentally delayed children at the Learning Center, I came to see how important it is to treat every child as an individual.	Narration
Looking around the room where I spent my childhood, I realized that every object I saw told me I was now an adult.	Description
The risk-taking behavior that has characterized the past decade can be illustrated by the increasing interest and involvement in such high-risk sports as mountain biking, ice climbing, sky diving, and bungee jumping.	Exemplification
Armed forces basic training programs take recruits through a series of tasks designed to build camaraderie as well as skills and confidence.	Process
The gap in computer literacy between rich and poor has had many significant social and economic consequences.	Cause and Effect
Although people who live in cities and people who live in small towns have some similarities, their views on issues like crime, waste disposal, farm subsidies, and educational vouchers tend to be very different.	Comparison and Contrast

Thesis Statement	Pattern of Development
The section of the proposal that recommends establishing satellite health centers is quite promising; unfortunately, however, the sections that call for the creation of alternative educational programs, job training, and low-income housing are seriously flawed.	Division and Classification
Until quite recently, most people assumed that rape was an act perpetrated by a stranger, but today's wider definition encompasses acquaintance rape as well.	Definition

Exercise 3.1

Analyze each of the following items, and explain why none of them qualifies as an effective thesis statement. How could each be improved?

▶ 1. In this essay, I will examine the environmental effects of residential and commercial development on the coastal regions of the United States.

▶ 2. Residential and commercial development in the coastal regions of the United States

▶ 3. How to avoid coastal overdevelopment

▶ 4. Coastal Development: Pro and Con

▶ 5. Residential and commercial development of America's coastal regions benefits some people, but it has a number of disadvantages.

6. The environmentalists' position on coastal development

7. More and more coastal regions in the United States are being overdeveloped.

8. Residential and commercial development guidelines need to be developed for coastal regions of the United States.

9. Coastal development is causing beach erosion.

10. At one time I enjoyed walking on the beach, but commercial and residential development ruined the experience for me.

Exercise 3.2

Review all the notes you have accumulated so far, and use them to help you develop a thesis for an essay on the topic you chose in Exercise 2.1.

3d Constructing an Informal Outline

Once you have decided on a thesis statement, you may want to construct an informal outline. An **outline** is a blueprint for an essay, a plan that gives you more detailed, specific information about structuring your essay than a thesis statement does. Of course, you don't always need to prepare an outline; a short essay on a topic with which you are very familiar may require nothing more than a thesis statement and a list of three or four main points. Often, however, an **informal outline,** one that arranges your essay's main points and major supporting ideas in an orderly way, can be a useful guide as you write. Kimberly's informal outline appears below.

Informal Outline

College Students and Computer Literacy

<u>Thesis statement:</u> I was at a real disadvantage when I entered college because I lacked important computer skills.

Students are expected to be familiar with computers

- Basic word-processing programs
- Internet
- Email

Many students have very little or no experience with computers

- No access at home
- No access at school

Consequences of computer illiteracy

- Difficulty with everyday tasks
- Embarrassment
- Missed opportunities

Possible solutions to problem

- Classes
- ??????

Personal experience

- Few computer skills
- Classes in computer lab

> ### Checklist: Constructing an Informal Outline
>
> ☐ Copy down the most important ideas from your notes.
> ☐ Arrange the notes into categories and subcategories in the order in which you plan to discuss them.
> ☐ Expand the outline with additional material from your notes, adding any new ideas that come to mind.

NOTE: Sometimes—particularly when you are writing a long or complex essay—you will need to construct a _formal outline_, which indicates both the exact order and importance of all the ideas you will explore.

See 4c4

Exercise 3.3

Find an editorial in the newspaper or on the Internet. Then, prepare an informal outline that includes all the writer's main points and major supporting ideas. (Use Kimberly's outline on page 32 as a guide.)

Exercise 3.4

Prepare an informal outline for the paper you have been developing in Chapters 2 and 3.

Chapter 4 | Drafting and Revising

4a Writing a Rough Draft

(1) Understanding Drafting

A rough draft is far from perfect; in fact, it usually includes false starts, irrelevant information, and unrelated details. At this stage, though, the absence of focus and order is not a problem. You write your rough draft simply to get your ideas down so that you can react to them. You should expect to add or delete words, to reword sentences, to rethink ideas, and to reorder paragraphs. You should also expect to discover some new ideas—or even to take an unexpected detour.

When you write your rough draft, concentrate on the body of your essay, and don't waste time mapping out an introduction and conclusion. (These paragraphs are likely to change substantially in subsequent drafts.) For now, focus on drafting the support paragraphs of your essay.

Using her informal outline to guide her, Kimberly wrote the rough draft that appears below. Notice that she made boldfaced and bracketed notes to remind herself to add or check information later.

Rough Draft

College Students and Computer Literacy

Today, most colleges expect their entering students to be familiar with computers. From registering for courses to contacting professors, students are required to use computers on a daily basis. I was at a real disadvantage when I entered college because I lacked important computer skills. [Add more here]

Computers have become increasingly important on college campuses. When I arrived at school, I was asked to use <u>Microsoft Word</u> to type my papers. I was also encouraged to use the Internet for research. [Do I document this?] In fact, many professors posted their syllabi on Web pages. I also quickly learned the importance of email. Although I'd been exposed to email in high school, I'd never had to learn how to use an email program like <u>Eudora</u> or download it to my computer. I had to call the help desk and it was really embarrassing. All of my other friends seemed to have few problems doing this.

If you don't have high computer literacy skills, there are many consequences. Students have a lot of difficulty completing everyday tasks. It may take them a long time to email a professor or register for a course simply because they are unfamiliar with the software being used. Students who feel uncomfortable using computers also feel embarrassed. They may not want to admit that they don't understand how to use particular software programs. If they don't seek help, they miss out on a lot of opportunities. Computers are so important in school that students who

don't understand them may avoid taking exciting classes
that require a working knowledge of specific computer
programs.

The reality is that a lot of students don't have a lot
of experience with computers. Students who do understand
computers are usually math and science people. If you're
interested in English, you probably aren't familiar with
computers. Even if they are familiar with computers, she
may have never used the Internet. In small towns, students
probably don't have access to a computer at home. Many high
schools also have trouble providing their students with
computer access, which is a big problem for many students.
[Need more/better support here]

Our school does provide students with several
opportunities to improve their computer skills, but most
students don't know about them. The library offers several
classes that teach students how to access useful
information online. The computer lab also holds classes on
how to use software programs like Microsoft Word and
Microsoft Publisher. Students can even learn how to design
their own Web pages. Unfortunately, these classes are not
well advertised. Course listings appear on the Information
Technology Web site, but for those students who avoid using
the Internet, finding out when and where to take classes is
difficult. Ironically, students who need these classes will
probably not be using the Internet a lot to get information
about the university. [Check on all of this to make sure]

When I arrived at college, I had very few computer
skills. Our high school had a couple of computers, but we
didn't have Internet access. My first required class was a
writing course and was held in a computer lab. I was forced
to learn how to use computers and the Internet to write my
papers. After a few weeks of pretending to know what I was

doing, I decided to try to find some help. I was too
embarrassed to ask my professor where to go for help, so it
took me a few days to find out when and where the classes
were. I ended up going to the library and asking the
librarian. She was really helpful and I enrolled in a
couple of them. After a course on <u>Microsoft Word</u> and the
Internet, I felt much more comfortable using computers.

It is important to remember that some students arrive
at college with few computer skills and that they are at a
significant disadvantage. [Add more!]

(2) Developing Drafting Strategies

Taking a systematic approach to writing your first draft will greatly
simplify the revision process.

Checklist: Drafting Strategies

The following suggestions should help you revise
effectively:

- [ ] **Prepare your work area.** Once you begin to write,
  you should not have to stop because you need better lighting,
  important notes, or anything else.
- [ ] **Fight writer's block.** An inability to start (or continue) writing, writer's block is usually caused by fear that you will not
  write well or that you have nothing to say. If you really don't
  feel ready to write, take a short break. If you decide that you
  really don't have enough ideas to get you started, use one of
  the strategies for <u>finding something to say</u>.

See 2d

- [ ] **Get your ideas down on paper as quickly as you can.** Don't
  worry about sentence structure, about spelling and punctuation, or about finding exactly the right word—just write. Writing quickly helps you uncover new ideas and new connections
  between ideas. You may find that following an <u>informal out-
  line</u> enables you to move smoothly from one point to the next,
  but if you find this structure too confining, go ahead and write
  without consulting your outline.

See 3d

- [ ] **Write notes to yourself.** As you type your drafts, get into the
  habit of including bracketed, boldfaced notes to yourself.
  These comments, suggestions, and questions can help you
  later, when you revise.

☐ **Take regular breaks as you write.** Try writing one section of your essay at a time. When you have completed a section—for example, one paragraph—take a break. Your mind will continue to focus on your assignment while you do other things. When you return to your essay, writing will be easier.

☐ **Leave yourself enough time to revise.** All writing benefits from revision, so be sure you have time to reconsider your work and to write as many drafts as you need.

☐ **Save your drafts.** Using the Save option in your word processor's file menu saves only your most recent draft. If you prefer to save every draft you write (so you can return to an earlier draft to locate a different version of a sentence or to reconsider a section you have deleted), use the Save As option instead.

☐ **Label your files.** To help you keep track of which version of your paper is which, label every file in your folder by content and date (for example, `first draft, 10/20`).

Exercise 4.1

Write a rough draft of the essay you began planning in Chapter 2.

4b Moving from Rough Draft to Final Draft

As you revise successive drafts of your essay, you should shift your focus from larger elements, such as overall structure and content, to increasingly smaller elements, such as sentence structure and word choice.

(1) Revising Your Rough Draft

After you finish your rough draft, set it aside for a day or two if you can. When you return to it, focus on only a few areas at a time. As you review this first draft, evaluate the thesis-and-support structure of your essay and your paper's general organization. Once you feel satisfied that your thesis statement says what you want it to say and that your essay's content supports this thesis and is logically arranged, you can turn your attention to other matters. For example, you can make sure that you have included all the **transitional words and phrases** that readers will need to follow your discussion.

See 5b2

As you reread this draft, you may want to consult the questions in the "Revising the Whole Essay" checklist on pages 50–51. If you have the benefit of a peer-review session or a conference with your instructor, consider your readers' comments carefully, focusing for now on their suggestions about content, organization, and thesis and support.

(2) Writing and Revising Additional Drafts

After you have read over your rough draft several times, making notes about plans for revision, you are ready to write a second draft.

Because it can be more difficult to see errors on the computer screen than on hard copy, you should print out every draft, making revisions by hand on printed drafts and then returning to the computer to type these changes into the document.

As you type your draft, be sure to triple-space. This will make any errors or inconsistencies more obvious and at the same time give you plenty of room to write questions, add new material, or try out new versions of sentences.

You will also find it helpful to develop a system of symbols, each designating a different type of revision. For instance, you can circle individual words or box longer groups of words (or even entire paragraphs) that you want to relocate. You can use an arrow to indicate the new location, or you can use matching numbers or letters to indicate how you want to rearrange ideas. When you want to add words, use a caret like ${}_\wedge^{this}$. (An excerpt from Kimberly's draft, with handwritten revisions, appears below.)

Draft (Excerpt)

There are many reasons why a student entering college might have low computer literacy skills. Students who do understand computers are usually math and science people. If you're interested in English, you probably aren't familiar with computers. Even if they are familiar with computers, she may have never used the Internet.

Draft with Handwritten Revisions (Excerpt)

Despite the necessity of a strong working knowledge of computers and the Internet, many students arrive at college with very little to no experience of either.

$_\wedge$There are many reasons why a student entering college might have low computer literacy skills. Students *might not, for example, have had access to a computer in their home.*

$_\wedge$~~who do understand computers are usually math and science people. If you're interested in English, you probably aren't familiar with computers.~~ Even if they are familiar with computers, $_\wedge$~~she~~ *they* may have never used the Internet.

As you assess your rough draft, as well as any drafts that follow, you will narrow your focus to your essay's individual paragraphs, sentences, and words; if you like, you can use the "Revising Paragraphs," "Revising Sentences," and "Revising Words" checklists on pages 51–52 to guide your revision.

http://kirsznermandell.wadsworth.com

Computer Tip: Revising

If you revise directly on the computer, be very careful not to delete material that you may need later; instead, move this material to the end of your document so that you can assess its usefulness later on and retrieve it if necessary. Or, use the Save As feature to save each new version of your essay under a different file name that includes the date of the draft each time you revise.

4c Using Specific Revision Strategies

Revision is a process you engage in from the moment you begin to discover ideas for your essay. As you work, you are constantly rethinking your ideas and reconsidering their relevance, their relative importance, the logical and sequential relationships between them, and the patterns in which you arrange them. Five strategies in particular can help you revise at any stage of the writing process.

(1) Using Word-Processing Tools

Your word-processing program includes a variety of tools designed to make the revision process easier. For example, *Microsoft Word*'s **Track Changes** feature allows you to make changes to a draft and to see the original version of the draft and the changes simultaneously. Changes appear in color as underlined text, and writers have the option of viewing the changes on the screen or in print. This feature also allows you to accept or reject all changes or just specific changes.

Another useful revision tool is the **Compare Drafts** feature. Whereas Track Changes allows you to keep track of changes to a single document, Compare Drafts allows you to analyze the changes in two completely separate versions of a document, usually an original and its most recent update. Changes appear in color as highlighted text.

Kimberly used Track Changes as she revised her rough draft. Her draft, along with her changes, appears below.

Draft (with Track Changes)

```
               College Students and Computer Literacy

       Today, most colleges expect their entering students to

be familiar with computers. From registering for courses to

contacting professors, students are required to use

computers on a daily basis. I was at a real disadvantage
```

when I entered college because I lacked important computer skills.

Computers have become increasingly important ~~on college campuses~~ in today's society. Consequently, many scholars and public officials are concerned that those without access to computers will be at a disadvantage. Henry Louis Gates Jr., for example, argues in "One Internet, Two Nations" that the content on the Internet, which is primarily aimed at whites, threatens to leave African Americans behind. Similarly, college students who arrive with low computer literacy skills are at a disadvantage.

When I arrived at school, I was asked to use computers in several ways. First, I was required to use Microsoft Word when typing~~to type~~ my papers. I was also encouraged to use the Internet for research. In fact, many professors posted their syllabi on Web pages. I also quickly learned the importance of email. Although I'd been exposed to email in high school, I'd never had to learn how to use an email program like Eudora or download it to my computer. I had to call the help desk and it was really embarrassing. All of my other friends seemed to have few problems doing this.

If you don't have high computer literacy skills, there are many consequences. Students who aren't familiar with the Internet or email may have a lot of difficulty completing everyday tasks. For example, i~~I~~t may take them a long time to email a professor or register for a course simply because they are unfamiliar with the software being used. Students who feel uncomfortable using computers also feel embarrassed. They may not want to admit that they don't understand how to use particular software programs. If they don't seek help, they miss out on a lot of opportunities. Computers are so important in school that students who don't understand them

may avoid taking exciting classes that require a working
knowledge of specific computer programs.

    There are many reasons why a student entering college
might have low computer literacy skills. ~~The reality is
that a lot of students don't have a lot of experience with
computers.~~ Students who do understand computers are usually
math and science people. If you're interested in English,
you probably aren't familiar with computers. Even if they
are familiar with computers, she may have never used the
Internet. In small towns, students probably don't have
access to a computer at home. Many high schools also have
trouble providing their students with computer access,
which is a big problem for many students.

    There are many steps a student can take to improve his
or her computer skills. ~~Our school does provide students
with several opportunities to improve their computer
skills, but most students don't know about them.~~ The
library offers several classes that teach students how to
access useful information online. The computer lab also
holds classes on how to use software programs like
Microsoft Word and Microsoft Publisher. Students can even
learn how to design their own Web pages. Unfortunately,
these classes are not well advertised. Course listings
appear on the Information Technology Web site, but for
those students who avoid using the Internet, finding out
when and where to take classes is difficult. Ironically,
students who need these classes will probably not be using
the Internet a lot to get information about the university.

    When I arrived at college, I had very few computer
skills. Our high school had a couple of computers, but we
didn't have Internet access. My first required class was a
writing course and was held in a computer lab. I was forced

to learn how to use computers and the Internet to write my papers. After a few weeks of pretending to know what I was doing, I decided to try to find some help. I was too embarrassed to ask my professor where to go for help, so it took me a few days to find out when and where the classes were. I ended up going to the library and asking the librarian. She was really helpful and I enrolled in a course~~couple of them~~ about~~After a course on~~ Microsoft Word and a course that taught students the basics of email and the Internet. After taking these two classes, I felt much more comfortable using computers.

It is important to remember that some students arrive at college with few computer skills and that they are at a significant disadvantage.

(2) Participating in Peer Review

Peer review—a collaborative revision strategy that enables you to get feedback from your classmates—is another useful activity. With peer review, instead of trying to imagine an audience for your paper, you address a real audience, exchanging drafts with classmates and commenting on their drafts. Such collaborative work can be formal or informal, conducted in person or electronically. For example, you and a classmate may email drafts back and forth, perhaps using *Word*'s Comment feature (see below), or your instructor may conduct the class as a workshop, assigning students to work in groups to critique other students' essays.

http://kirsznermandell.wadsworth.com

Computer Tip: Peer Review

Certain features in word-processing programs are particularly useful for peer review. For example, the Comment tool allows several readers to insert comments at any point, or to highlight a particular portion of the text they would like to comment on and then insert annotations. To write comments, a reviewer clicks the Insert menu and selects Comment.

A particular advantage of this function for peer-review groups is that a single paper can receive comments from multiple readers.

Comments are identified by the initials of the reviewer and by a color assigned to the reviewer, so the paper's author can go to the View menu, select Comments, and then select the reviewer's comments he or she wants to view (or select All Reviewers to see all comments at once).

An excerpt from Kimberly's second draft with peer reviewers' comments appears below.

Second Draft with Peer Reviewers' Comments (Excerpt)

When I arrived at school, I was asked to use

> **Comment:** That's for sure ☺!

computers |in several ways|. First, I was required

to use <u>Microsoft Word</u> when typing my papers. I was also

encouraged to use the Internet for research. In fact,

many professors posted their syllabi on Web pages.

> **Comment:** Talking w/profs. is another imp. use of email.

I also quickly learned |the importance of email.|

Although I'd been exposed to email in high

> **Comment:** Yes! I emailed Prof. Wilson when I couldn't make office hrs.

school, I'd never had to learn how to use an

email program like <u>Eudora</u> or download it to my

computer. I had to call the help desk and it was

really embarrassing. All of my other friends seemed

to have few problems doing this.

> **Comment:** There's a lot more to talk about here. What about listservs? <u>PowerPoint</u>?

Checklist: Questions for Peer Review

The following questions can help guide you through the peer-review process.

- ☐ What is the essay about? Does the topic fulfill the requirements of the assignment?
- ☐ What is the essay's main idea? Is the thesis clearly worded? If not, how can the wording be improved?
- ☐ Is the essay arranged logically? Do the body paragraphs appear in an appropriate order?

(continued)

Questions for peer review (continued)

☐ What ideas support the thesis? Does each body paragraph develop one of these ideas?

☐ Is any necessary information missing? Identify any areas that seem to need further development. Is any information irrelevant? If so, suggest possible deletions.

☐ Can you think of any ideas or examples from your own reading, experience, or observations that would strengthen the writer's essay?

☐ Can you follow the writer's ideas? If not, would clearer connections between sentences or paragraphs be helpful? Where are such connections needed?

☐ Is the introductory paragraph interesting to you? Would another opening strategy be more effective?

☐ Does the conclusion leave you with a sense of closure? Would another concluding strategy be more effective?

☐ Is anything unclear or confusing?

☐ What is the essay's greatest strength?

☐ What is the essay's greatest weakness?

(3) Using Instructors' Comments

Instructors' comments—in correction symbols, in marginal comments, or in conferences—can also help you revise. (Some instructors may prefer to record their comments electronically, perhaps using the Comment tool described in **4c2**.)

Correction Symbols Your instructor may indicate concerns about style, grammar, mechanics, or punctuation by using the correction symbols listed on the inside back cover of this book. Instead of correcting a problem, the instructor will often identify it and supply the number of the section in this handbook that deals with the error. After reading the appropriate pages, you should be able to make the necessary corrections on your own. For example, the symbol and number beside the following sentence referred a student to **19e2**, the section in the handbook that discusses sexist usage.

Draft with Instructor's Comment: Equal access to jobs

Sxt—see 19e2

is a desirable goal for all mankind.

After reading section 19e2, the student made the following change.

Revised: Equal access to jobs is a desirable goal for all people.

Marginal Comments Instructors frequently make marginal comments on your essays to suggest changes in content or structure. Such comments may ask you to add supporting information or to arrange paragraphs differently within the essay, or they may recommend stylistic changes, such as more varied sentences. Marginal comments may also question your logic, suggest a more explicit thesis statement, ask for clearer transitions, or propose a new direction for a discussion. In some cases, you can consider these comments to be suggestions rather than corrections. You may decide to incorporate these ideas into a revised draft of your essay, or you may not. In all instances, however, you should take your instructor's comments seriously.

Second Draft with Instructor's Comments (Excerpt)

When I arrived at school, I was asked to use computers in several ways. First, I was required to use <u>Microsoft Word</u> when typing my papers. I was also encouraged to use the Internet for research. In fact, many professors posted their syllabi on Web pages. I also quickly learned the importance of email. Although I'd been exposed to email in high school, |I'd|never had to learn how to use an email program like <u>Eudora</u> or download it to my computer. I had to call the help desk and it was really |embarrassing|. All of my other friends seemed to have few problems doing this.

> **Comment:** In your final draft, edit out all contractions. (Contractions are too informal for most college writing.) See 32b1.

> **Comment:** Consider making this point less personal. Use this paragraph to talk about all of the reasons a student might use a computer in college. Remember, you are moving from general to specific. See 5b1.

Conferences Many instructors require or encourage one-on-one conferences, and you should certainly schedule a conference if you can. During a conference, you can respond to your instructor's questions and ask for clarification of marginal comments. If a certain section of your paper presents a problem, use your conference time to focus on it, perhaps asking for help in sharpening your thesis or choosing more accurate words.

Conferences can also take place online, in virtual chat rooms or in synchronous online communication sessions in which you and your instructor are online at the same time and engage in real-time dialogue about your paper. You can also discuss your writing online by posting your questions about your work-in-progress to a discussion board for both instructor and peer review.

Perhaps the most common way to discuss a paper online is through email. If you send emails to your instructor or to members of your peer-review group, include a specific subject line that clearly identifies the message as coming from a student writer (for example, "question about assignment" or "comments on your paper"). This is especially important if your email address does not include your name. And when you attach a document to an email and send it to your instructor for comments, mention the attachment in your subject line (for example, "first draft—see attachment")—and be sure your name appears on the attachment itself, not just on the email.

An excerpt from Kimberly's second draft, along with her instructor's comments, appears below. (Note that her instructor used *Microsoft Word*'s Comment tool to insert comments.)

(4) Constructing a Formal Outline

Outlining can be helpful early in the revision process, when you are reworking the larger structural elements of your essay, or later on, when you are checking the logic of a completed draft. For example, a formal outline reveals at once whether points are irrelevant or poorly placed—or, worse, missing. It also reveals the hierarchy of your ideas—which points are dominant and which are subordinate.

A **formal outline** uses a system of letters and numbers to indicate the order of your ideas and the relationship of main ideas to supporting details. A formal outline is more polished and much more detailed than an informal outline. It is more strictly parallel and more precise, pays more attention to form, and presents points in the exact order in which you plan to present them in your draft.

A formal outline may be a **topic outline,** in which each entry is a single word or a short phrase, or a **sentence outline,** in which each entry is a complete sentence. A sentence outline is a more fully developed guide for your paper; you have a head start on your paper when you are able to use the sentences of your outline in your draft. Because it is so polished and complete, however, a sentence outline is more difficult and time consuming to construct, especially at an early stage of the writing process. An example of Kimberly's sentence outline appears on pages 47–50.

Close-up: The Conventions of Outlining

Formal outlines conform to specific conventions of structure, content, and style. If you follow the conventions of outlining carefully, your formal outline can help you make sure that your paper presents all relevant ideas in an effective order, with appropriate emphasis.

Structure
- Outline format should be followed strictly.

  I. First major point of your paper
  - A. First subpoint
  - B. Next subpoint
    1. First supporting example
    2. Next supporting example
       a. First specific detail
       b. Next specific detail

  II. Second major point

- Headings should not overlap.
- No heading should have a single subheading. (A category cannot be subdivided into one part.)
- Each entry should be preceded by an appropriate letter or number, followed by a period.
- The first word of each entry should be capitalized.

Content
- The outline should include the paper's thesis statement.
- The outline should cover only the body of the essay, not the introductory or concluding paragraphs.
- Headings should be concise and specific.
- Headings should be descriptive, clearly related to the topic to which they refer.

Style
- Headings of the same rank should be grammatically parallel.
- A **sentence outline** should use complete sentences, with all sentences in the same tense.
- In a sentence outline, each entry should end with a period.
- A **topic outline** should use words or short phrases, with all headings of the same rank using the same parts of speech.
- In a topic outline, entries should not end with periods.

Sentence Outline

         College Students and Computer Literacy

    Thesis statement: Students who enter college with weak
computer skills are at a significant disadvantage.

    I. Computers are increasingly important in today's

       society.

       A. According to Gates, many are concerned about

          the division between those who have access to

          the Internet and those who do not.

B. This "digital divide" exists among college
   students.

II. College students are expected to be familiar with
    computers.

   A. Students are expected to be familiar with basic
      computer programs.

      1. Students are expected to use <u>Microsoft Word</u>
         to type their papers.

      2. Instructors ask their students to use
         <u>PowerPoint</u> for their presentations.

   B. Students are expected to be familiar with the
      Internet.

      1. Students register for classes on the
         Internet.

      2. Announcements for campuswide events are
         posted on the Internet.

      3. Professors post their syllabi on Web pages.

      4. Students are expected to use the Internet to
         conduct research.

   C. Students are expected to be familiar with
      email.

      1. Discussion questions are posted on
         listservs.

      2. Students need to communicate with one
         another via email.

      3. Students need to communicate with their
         professors via email.

III. The reality is that many students arrive at
     college with very little experience with
     computers or the Internet.

   A. They might not have access at home.

      1. Many families are not able to afford a
         computer.

2. Computers might not be seen as a necessity.

B. College students may have had limited access to computers in elementary or high school.

1. K–12 schools are getting more computers.

2. However, these computers are often obsolete or not connected to the Internet.

IV. There are many consequences for students with low computer skills.

A. Students may have difficulty with everyday tasks.

1. Registering for classes is difficult.

2. Contacting professors and other students is difficult.

B. Students feel embarrassed.

1. Students do not want to ask for help.

2. Students do not improve their skills.

C. Students miss out on opportunities.

1. They miss out on the benefits of using the Internet to do research.

2. They miss out on the benefits of sophisticated software programs.

V. Our school has an outreach program.

A. Many classes are available.

1. Students can learn how to use basic computer programs.

2. Students can learn how to use email.

3. Students can learn to use the Internet for library research.

B. Publicity for the outreach program is poor.

1. The administration needs to advertise these programs during freshman orientation.

2. The administration needs to understand the embarrassment that some students might feel.

VI. I have personal experience with this problem.

   A. I came to school with few computer skills.

   B. I took a writing class in a computer lab.

   C. I took classes on <u>Word</u>, email, and the
      Internet.

   D. I now realize that more efforts should be made
      at the high school level.

      1. My high school is now making such efforts.

      2. My high school now requires computer
         literacy classes for both students and
         teachers.

VII. The future is hopeful.

   A. High schools are making changes.

   B. College students will be better prepared.

(5) Using Checklists

A revision checklist—one that your instructor prepares or one that you develop yourself—enables you to examine your writing systematically by helping you to focus on revising one element at a time. Depending on the problems you have and the amount of time you have to deal with them, you can use all the questions on a checklist or only some of them.

The four revision checklists that follow are keyed to sections of this text. Moving from global to specific concerns, they parallel the actual revision process. As your understanding of the writing process increases and you become better able to assess the strengths and weaknesses of your writing, you may want to add items to (or delete items from) the checklists. You can also use your instructors' comments to tailor these checklists to your own needs.

Checklist: Revising the Whole Essay

☐ Have you maintained an appropriate distance from your readers? (**See 1b.**)

☐ Are thesis and support logically related, with each body paragraph supporting your thesis statement? (**See 3a.**)

☐ Is your thesis statement clearly and specifically worded? (**See 3b1.**)

☐ Have you discussed everything promised in your thesis statement? (**See 3b1.**)

☐ Have you presented your ideas in a logical sequence? Can you think of a different arrangement that might be more appropriate for your purpose? (**See 3c.**)

☐ Do clear transitions between paragraphs allow your readers to follow your essay's structure? (**See 5b6.**)

☐ Are the patterns of paragraph development you use in your essay consistent with your assignment and purpose? (**See 5d.**)

Checklist: Revising Paragraphs

☐ Does each body paragraph have one main idea? (**See 5a.**)

☐ Are topic sentences clearly worded and logically related to your thesis? (**See 5a1.**)

☐ Are your body paragraphs developed enough to support your points? (**See 5c.**)

☐ Does your introductory paragraph arouse reader interest and prepare readers for what is to come? (**See 5e2.**)

☐ Does each body paragraph have a clear organizing principle? (**See 5b1.**)

☐ Are the relationships between sentences within paragraphs clear? (**See 5b2–5.**)

☐ Are your paragraphs arranged according to familiar patterns of development? (**See 5d.**)

☐ Does your concluding paragraph sum up your main points? (**See 5e3.**)

☐ Have you provided transitional paragraphs where necessary? (**See 5e1.**)

Checklist: Revising Sentences

☐ Have you strengthened your sentences with repetition, balance, and parallelism? (**See 16c–d, 18a.**)

☐ Have you avoided overloading your sentences with too many clauses? (**See 17c.**)

☐ Have you used correct sentence structure? (**See Chs. 24 and 25.**)

☐ Have you placed modifiers clearly and logically? (**See Ch. 27.**)

☐ Have you avoided potentially confusing shifts in tense, voice, mood, person, or number? (**See 28a1–4.**)

☐ Are your sentences constructed logically? (**See 28b–d.**)

☐ Have you used emphatic word order? (**See 16a.**)

(continued)

Revising sentences (continued)

☐ Have you used sentence structure to signal the relative importance of clauses in a sentence and their logical relationship to one another? (**See 16b.**)

☐ Have you avoided wordiness and eliminated unnecessary repetition? (**See 17a–b.**)

☐ Have you varied your sentence structure? (**See Ch. 15.**)

☐ Have you combined sentences where ideas are closely related? (**See 15a.**)

Checklist: Revising Words

☐ Is your level of diction appropriate for your audience and your purpose? (**See 19a–b.**)

☐ Have you selected words that accurately reflect your intentions? (**See 19b1.**)

☐ Have you chosen words that are specific, concrete, and unambiguous? (**See 19b3–4.**)

☐ Have you enriched your writing with figurative language? (**See 19c.**)

☐ Have you eliminated jargon, neologisms, pretentious diction, clichés, and offensive language from your writing? (**See 19d–e.**)

Exercise 4.2

Revise your rough draft, using one or more of the strategies for revision discussed in 4c. At this point, focus on your paper's thesis and support and on content and arrangement of ideas. Try not to worry now about stylistic issues, such as sentence variety and word choice.

Exercise 4.3

Review the second draft of your paper, this time focusing on paragraphing, topic sentences, and transitions and on the way you structure your sentences and select your words. If possible, ask a friend to read your draft and to respond to the peer-review questions in 4c2. Then, revise your draft, incorporating any suggestions you find helpful.

Exercise 4.4

Using the revision checklists in 4c5 as a guide, create a customized checklist—one that reflects the specific concerns that you need to consider when you revise an essay. Then, use this checklist to help you in your revision.

4d Editing and Proofreading

Once you have revised your drafts to your satisfaction, two final tasks remain: editing and proofreading.

Editing When you edit, you concentrate on grammar and spelling, punctuation and mechanics. Although you have dealt with these issues as you revised previous drafts of your paper, editing is now your primary focus. As you edit, read each sentence carefully. As you proceed, consult the items on the Editing and Proofreading Checklist below. Keep your preliminary notes and drafts and your reference books (such as this handbook and a current dictionary) nearby as you work.

Proofreading After you have completed your editing, print out a final draft and proofread, rereading every word carefully to make sure neither you nor your computer missed any errors. Finally, make sure the final typed copy of your paper conforms to your instructor's format requirements.

http://kirsznermandell.wadsworth.com

Computer Tip: Editing and Proofreading

- As you edit and proofread, try looking at only a small portion of text at a time. Reduce the size of your window so that you can see only one or two lines of text at a time. If you use this technique, you can dramatically reduce the number of surface-level errors in your paper.
- Use the Search or Find command to look for usage errors you commonly make—for instance, confusing *it's* with *its*, *lay* with *lie*, *effect* with *affect*, *their* with *there*, or *too* with *to*. You can also uncover <u>sexist language</u> by searching for words like *he*, *his*, *him*, or *man*.

See 19e2

- Finally, keep in mind that neatness does not equal correctness. The clean text that your computer produces can mask flaws that might otherwise be apparent; for this reason, it is up to you to make sure spelling errors and typos do not slip by.

Checklist: Editing and Proofreading

Grammar

☐ Have you used the appropriate case for each pronoun? (**See 21a–b.**)

☐ Are pronoun references clear and unambiguous? (**See 21c.**)

☐ Are verb forms correct? (**See 22a.**)

(continued)

Editing and proofreading (continued)

☐ Are tense, mood, and voice of verbs logical and appropriate? (**See 22b–d.**)
☐ Do subjects and verbs agree? (**See 26a.**)
☐ Do pronouns and antecedents agree? (**See 26b.**)
☐ Are adjectives and adverbs used correctly? (**See Ch. 23.**)

Punctuation

☐ Is end punctuation used correctly? (**See Ch. 29.**)
☐ Are commas used correctly? (**See Ch. 30.**)
☐ Are semicolons used correctly? (**See Ch. 31.**)
☐ Are apostrophes used correctly? (**See Ch. 32.**)
☐ Are quotation marks used where they are required? (**See Ch. 33.**)
☐ Are quotation marks used correctly with other punctuation marks? (**See 33e.**)
☐ Are other punctuation marks—colons, dashes, parentheses, brackets, slashes, and ellipses—used correctly? (**See Ch. 34.**)

Mechanics

☐ Is capitalization consistent with standard English usage? (**See Ch. 36.**)
☐ Are italics used correctly? (**See Ch. 37.**)
☐ Are hyphens used where required and placed correctly within and between words? (**See Ch. 38.**)
☐ Are abbreviations used where convention calls for their use? (**See Ch. 39.**)
☐ Are numerals and spelled-out numbers used appropriately? (**See Ch. 40.**)

Spelling

☐ Are all words spelled correctly? (**See Ch. 35.**)

http://kirsznermandell.wadsworth.com

Computer Tip: Using Spell Checkers and Grammar Checkers

Although spell checkers and grammar checkers can make the process of editing and proofreading your papers easier, they have limitations. For this reason, neither a spell checker nor a grammar checker is a substitute for careful editing and proofreading.

• **Spell Checkers** A spell checker simply identifies strings of letters it does not recognize; it does *not* distinguish between homophones or spot every typographical error. For example, it does not recognize *there* in "They forgot <u>there</u> books" as incorrect, nor does it identify a typo that produces a correctly spelled word, such as *word* for *work* or *thing* for *think*. Moreover, a spell checker may not recognize every technical term, proper noun, or foreign word you may use.

- **Grammar Checkers** Grammar checkers scan documents for certain features (the number of words in a sentence, for example); however, they are not able to read a document to see if it makes sense. For this reason, grammar checkers are not always accurate. For example, they may identify a long sentence as a run-on when it is in fact grammatically correct, and they generally advise against using passive voice—even in contexts where it is appropriate. Moreover, grammar checkers do not always supply answers; often, they ask questions—for example, whether *which* should be *that* or whether *which* should be preceded by a comma—that you must answer. In short, grammar checkers can guide your editing, but you must be the one who decides when a sentence is (or is not) correct.

Close-up: Choosing a Title

When you are ready to decide on a title for your essay, keep these criteria in mind.

- A title should be descriptive, giving an accurate sense of your essay's focus. Whenever possible, use one or more of the key words and phrases that are central to your paper.
- A title can echo the wording of your assignment, reminding you (and your instructor) that you have not lost sight of it.
- Ideally, a title should arouse interest, perhaps by using a provocative question or a quotation or by taking a controversial position.

Assignment: Write about a problem faced on college campuses today.

Topic: Free speech on campus

Possible titles:

`Free Speech: A Problem for Today's Colleges` (echoes wording of assignment and includes key words of essay)

`How Free Should Free Speech on Campus Be?` (provocative question)

`The Right to "Shout 'Fire' in a Crowded Theater"` (quotation)

`Hate Speech: A Dangerous Abuse of Free Speech on Campus` (controversial position)

Exercise 4.5

Using the checklist on pages 53–54 as a guide, edit your essay. Then proofread it carefully, give it an appropriate title, and print out your final draft.

4e Preparing a Final Draft

The annotated essay that follows is the final draft of Kimberly's essay, which you first saw on pages 34–36. It incorporates the suggestions that her peer reviewers and her instructor made on her second draft (pages 43 and 45–46).

Romney 1

Kimberly Romney

Professor Wilson

English 101

10 October 2003

College Students and Computer Literacy

Today, most colleges expect their entering   Introduction

students to be familiar with computers. From

registering for courses to contacting professors,

students are required to use computers on a daily

basis. For this reason, those students who enter   Thesis
statement
college with weak computer literacy skills are at a

significant disadvantage.

Computers are increasingly important in today's   Importance
of computers
society. As Henry Louis Gates Jr. writes in his   in society

article "One Internet, Two Nations," many people are

concerned that there is a division between those who

have access to the Internet and those who do not. He

writes, "Today we stand at the brink of becoming two

societies, one largely white and plugged in and the

other black and unplugged" (500). This gap is often

referred to as the "digital divide." The gap between

those who are technologically literate and those who

are not extends beyond race and ethnicity to include

the elderly, the disabled, and those who live in

rural areas. This division is particularly apparent

among college students.

As students enter higher education, they are   Importance
of computers
expected to be familiar with a variety of software   in college

programs as well as with the Internet. Most

professors, for example, require their students to use <u>Microsoft Word</u> to write their papers. Further, instructors often ask their students to use <u>PowerPoint</u> to present their papers or research projects.

Importance of the Internet

Students are also expected to be familiar with the Internet. For example, registration for classes is often conducted online. Professors and administrators use the Internet to post information about campuswide events, and many professors create their own Web pages where they post their syllabi and class assignments. Finally, most professors ask their students to use the Internet when conducting research.

A good understanding of how email works is also necessary for a student to be successful in college. Discussion questions for class are often posted on listservs. If a student wants to communicate with

Importance of email

someone in the class, email is one of the most efficient ways to do so. Communicating with the professor is also easier if one uses email. For example, if a student cannot attend office hours, he or she can still ask the professor a question.

Despite the importance of a strong working knowledge of computers and the Internet, many students

Reason for students' poor skills: lack of access at home

arrive at college with very little experience with either. There are several reasons why students might have poor computer skills. They might not, for example, have had access to a computer at

Romney 3

home. Many families cannot afford computers, and others simply do not see a computer as a necessity.

In many cases, students may not have been taught computer skills in elementary or high school. A recent study of efforts to bridge the "digital divide" in elementary and high schools reported that although many schools are improving their access to computers, the computers they have may be obsolete models or not connected to the Internet (Swain 328). According to the report, "even though 98% of all schools have computers, as of fall 2000, only 77% of instructional rooms have Internet access" (Swain 328).

Reason for students' poor skills: lack of access at school

For those students who arrive at college with weak computer skills, there are many consequences. They may have difficulty completing everyday tasks in a timely manner. Registering for classes on the Internet and contacting professors or other students via email become time-consuming (rather than timesaving) tasks. Students may also be embarrassed by their weak computer skills. As a result, they often do not ask for help. Without help, they have difficulty improving their skills. As a result, they do not benefit from the opportunities offered by the Internet (such as faster and more thorough research) or by sophisticated software programs (such as professional-looking papers and presentations).

Problems caused by weak computer skills

Our college does have an outreach program aimed at students with sub-par computer skills. Once a week, the computer lab offers classes on software

Possible solution to problems: classes

Romney 4

programs such as <u>Microsoft Word</u>, <u>PowerPoint</u>, and <u>Dreamweaver</u>. There is also a class about email that not only gives students basic information (such as how to send and open attachments), but also tells them how to use programs (such as <u>Outlook Express</u>) to track their daily schedules and appointments. The library also offers several classes, both broad research classes and more discipline-specific ones, about how to use the Internet for research.

Limitations of classes

While the college's outreach program provides students with many opportunities to improve their skills, the publicity for this program is very poor. Students are not given information about these classes at orientation, and they are not well advertised in the student newspaper, or even at the computer lab and library. The administration is also not very sensitive to the embarrassment that many students might feel about having poor computer skills. Many students might avoid asking a librarian or computer lab proctor for information about these programs, and this is a problem that a good advertising campaign would remedy.

Personal experience: problems in college

As a student from a small town where computer classes were not a part of the high school curriculum, I have personal experience with this problem. I came to college with few computer skills. Although I had a basic working knowledge of <u>Microsoft Word</u> and had used the Internet and email a few times, I was not very comfortable using computers. One of my first classes here was a writing class that was held

Romney 5

in a computer lab. I was confronted with my problem
every Monday, Wednesday, and Friday, and because
I was embarrassed about my poor computer skills,
I did not want to ask the professor for help. Trying
to find help on my own was difficult. It took me two
weeks to figure out when and where classes on
Microsoft Word and the Internet were held. However,
after taking these classes, my skills were greatly
improved.

Through my experience at school, I have come to
realize that more efforts need to be made to educate
students about technology at the high school level.
In my hometown, the school district instituted a
computer literacy class for all high school freshmen
the year after I graduated.

According to my high school English teacher, Vicky
Wellborn, students really enjoy this class: they go to
the new computer lab during breaks or after school, and
the lab is frequently full. Even better, the district
now requires teachers to take a computer literacy class
so that they are better prepared to answer students'
questions (Wellborn).

Despite my own frustrating experiences, I
believe the future is hopeful. As high schools
continue to make efforts to incorporate technology
into the classroom, students entering college will be
better prepared for the technological challenges they
will face. And as they become more competent computer
users, they will narrow the "digital divide."

Personal
experience:
changes in
high school

Conclusion

Romney 6

Works Cited

Gates, Henry Louis Jr. "One Internet, Two Nations."

  The Blair Reader. 4th ed. Ed. Laurie G. Kirszner

  and Stephen R. Mandell. Upper Saddle River:

  Prentice, 2002. 499-501.

Swain, Colleen, and Tamara Pearson. "Educators and

  Technology Standards: Influencing the Digital

  Divide." Journal of Research on Technology in

  Education 34.3 (2002): 326-35. Expanded Academic

  ASAP. Gale Group Databases. U of Texas Lib.

  System, TX. 15 Sept. 2003 <http://

  www.galegroup.com>.

Wellborn, Vicky. "Re: Computer Literacy." Email to

  the author. 23 Sept. 2003.

Chapter 5	Writing Paragraphs

A **paragraph** is a group of related sentences. It may be complete in itself or part of a longer piece of writing.

5a Writing Unified Paragraphs

A paragraph is **unified** when it develops a single main idea. The **topic sentence** states the main idea of the paragraph, and the other sentences in the paragraph support that idea.

(1) Using Topic Sentences

A topic sentence usually comes at the beginning of a paragraph. Occasionally, a topic sentence may occur at the end of a paragraph, particularly if a writer wants to present an unexpected conclusion.

Topic Sentence at the Beginning A topic sentence at the beginning of a paragraph tells readers what to expect and helps them to understand your paragraph's main idea immediately.

> I was a listening child, careful to hear the very different sounds of Spanish and English. Wide-eyed with hearing, I'd listen to sounds more than words. First, there were English (*gringo*) sounds. So many words were still unknown that when the butcher or the lady at the drugstore said something to me, exotic polysyllabic sounds would bloom in the midst of their sentences. Often the speech of people in public seemed to me very loud, booming with confidence. The man behind the counter would literally ask, "What can I do for you?" But by being so firm and so clear, the sound of his voice said that he was a *gringo;* he belonged in public society. (Richard Rodriguez, *Aria: A Memoir of a Bilingual Childhood*)

Topic Sentence at the End If you are presenting an unusual or hard-to-accept idea, you may decide to place the topic sentence at the end of a paragraph. If you present a logical chain of reasoning and then state your conclusion in the topic sentence, you are more likely to convince readers that your conclusion is reasonable.

> These sprays, dusts and aerosols are now applied almost universally to farms, gardens, forests, and homes—nonselective chemicals that have the power to kill every insect, the "good" and the "bad," to still the song of birds and the leaping of fish in the streams, to coat the leaves with a deadly film, and to linger on in soil—all this though the intended target may be only a few weeds or insects. Can anyone believe it is possible to lay down such a barrage of poisons on the surface without making it unfit for life? They should not be called "insecticides," but "biocides." (Rachel Carson, "The Obligation to Endure," *Silent Spring*)

(2) Testing for Unity

Each sentence in a paragraph should support the main idea that is stated in the topic sentence. The following paragraph is not unified because it includes sentences that do not support the main idea.

Paragraph Lacking Unity

> One of the first problems I had as a college student was learning to use a computer. All students were required to buy a computer before school started. Throughout the first semester, we took a special course to teach us to use a computer. My laptop has a large memory and can do word processing and spreadsheets. It has a large screen and a DVD drive. My parents were happy that I had a computer, but they

```
were concerned about the price. Tuition was high, and
when they added in the price of the computer, it was
almost out of reach. To offset expenses, I got a part-
time job in the school library. I am determined to
overcome "computer anxiety" and to master my computer
by the end of the semester.
```
(student writer)

When he revised, the writer deleted the sentences about his parents' financial situation and the computer's characteristics and added details related to the main idea (expressed in his topic sentence).

Revised Paragraph

```
    One of the first problems I had as a college student
was learning to use a computer. All first-year
students were required to buy a computer before school
started. Throughout the first semester, we took a
special course to teach us to use the computer. In
theory this system sounded fine, but in my case it was
a disaster. In the first place, I had never owned a
computer before. The closest I had ever come to a
computer was the computer lab in high school. In the
second place, I could not type well. And to make
matters worse, many of the people in my computer
orientation course already knew everything there was
to know about operating a computer. By the end of the
first week, I was convinced that I would never be able
to keep up with them.
```

Exercise 5.1

The following paragraph is unified by one main idea, but that idea is not explicitly stated. Identify the main idea, write a topic sentence that expresses it, and decide where in the paragraph to place it.

"Lite" can mean that a product has fewer calories, or less fat, or less sodium, or it can simply mean that the product has a "light" color, texture, or taste. It may also mean none of these. Food can be advertised as 86 percent fat free when it is actually 50 percent fat because the term "fat free" is based on weight, and fat is extremely light. Another misleading term is "no cholesterol," which is found on some products that never had any cholesterol in the first place. Peanut butter, for example, contains no cholesterol—a fact that manufacturers have recently made an issue—but it is very high in fat and so would not be a very good food for most dieters. Sodium labeling presents still another problem. The terms "sodium free," "very low sodium," "low sodium," "reduced sodium," and "no salt added" have very specific meanings, frequently not explained on the packages on which they appear.

5b Writing Coherent Paragraphs

A paragraph is **coherent** when all its sentences are logically related to one another. You can achieve coherence by arranging details according to an organizing principle, by using transitional words and phrases, by using pronouns, by using parallel structure, and by repeating key words and phrases.

(1) Arranging Details

Even if its sentences are all about the same subject, a paragraph lacks coherence if the sentences are not arranged according to a general organizing principle—that is, if they are not arranged *spatially, chronologically,* or *logically.*

Spatial order establishes the perspective from which readers will view details. For example, an object or scene can be viewed from top to bottom or from near to far. Spatial order is central to <u>descriptive paragraphs</u>. Notice how the following descriptive paragraph begins on top of a hill, moves down to a valley, follows a river through the valley into the distance, and then moves to a point behind the speaker.

See
5d2

> East of us rose another hill like ours. Between the hills, far below, was the highway which threaded south into the valley. This was the Yakima valley; I had never seen it before. It is justly famous for its beauty, like every planted valley. It extended south into the horizon, a distant dream of a valley, a Shangri-la. All its hundreds of low, golden slopes bore orchards. Among the orchards were towns, and roads, and plowed and fallow fields. Through the valley wandered a thin, shining river; from the river extended fine, frozen irrigation ditches. Distance blurred and blued the sight, so that the whole valley looked like a thickness or sediment at the bottom of the sky. Directly behind us was more sky, and empty lowlands blued by distance, and Mount Adams. Mount Adams was an enormous, snow-covered volcanic cone rising flat, like so much scenery. (Annie Dillard, "Total Eclipse")

Chronological order presents events in sequence, using transitional words and phrases that establish the time order of events—*at first, yesterday, later, in 1930,* and so on. Chronological order is central to <u>narrative paragraphs</u> and <u>process paragraphs</u>. The following narrative paragraph gains coherence from the orderly sequence of events.

See
5d1, 4

> They married in February, 1921, and began farming. Their first baby, a daughter, was born in January, 1922, when my mother was 26 years old. The second baby, a son, was born in March, 1923. They were renting

farms; my father, besides working his own fields, also was a hired man for two other farmers. They had no capital initially, and had to gain it slowly, working from dawn until midnight every day. My town-bred mother learned to set hens and raise chickens, feed pigs, milk cows, plant and harvest a garden, and can every fruit and vegetable she could scrounge. She carried water nearly a quarter of a mile from the well to fill her wash boilers in order to do her laundry on a scrub board. She learned to shuck grain, feed threshers, shuck and husk corn, feed corn pickers. In September, 1925, the third baby came, and in June, 1927, the fourth child—both daughters. In 1930, my parents had enough money to buy their own farm, and that March they moved all their livestock and belongings themselves, 55 miles over rutted, muddy roads. (Donna Smith-Yackel, "My Mother Never Worked")

Logical order presents details or ideas in terms of their logical relationship to one another. For example, the ideas in a paragraph may move from *general to specific,* as in the conventional topic-sentence-at-the-beginning paragraph, or the ideas may progress from *specific to general,* as they do when the topic sentence appears at the end of the paragraph. A writer may also choose to begin with the *least important* idea and move to the *most important.* Logical order is central to <u>exemplification paragraphs</u> and <u>comparison-and-contrast paragraphs</u>. The following paragraph moves from a general statement about the need to address the problem of the injury rate in boxing to specific solutions.

See 5d3, 6

```
    Several things could be done to reduce the high
injury rate in boxing. First, all boxers should wear
protective equipment—head gear and kidney protectors,
for example. This equipment is required in amateur
boxing and should be required in professional boxing.
Second, the object of boxing should be to score
points, not to knock out opponents. An increased
glove weight would make knockouts almost impossible.
And finally, all fights should be limited to ten
rounds. Studies show that most serious injuries
occur in boxing between the eleventh and twelfth
rounds—when the boxers are tired and vulnerable.
By limiting the number of rounds a boxer could
fight, officials could substantially reduce the
number of serious injuries. (student writer)
```

(2) Using Transitional Words and Phrases

Transitional words and phrases clarify the relationships between sentences by identifying spatial, chronological, and logical connections. The following paragraph, which has no transitional words and phrases, illustrates just how important these elements are.

Paragraph without Transitional Words and Phrases

Napoleon certainly made a change for the worse by leaving his small kingdom of Elba. He went back to Paris, and he abdicated for a second time. He fled to Rochefort in hope of escaping to America. He gave himself up to the English captain of the ship *Bellerophon*. He suggested that the Prince Regent grant him asylum, and he was refused. All he saw of England was the Devon coast and Plymouth Sound as he passed on to the remote island of St. Helena. He died on May 5, 1821, at the age of fifty-two.

In the preceding narrative paragraph, the topic sentence clearly states the main idea of the paragraph, and the rest of the sentences support this idea. However, the paragraph is not only choppy, but also difficult to understand. Because of the absence of transitional words and phrases, readers cannot tell exactly how one event relates to another in time. Notice how much easier it is to read this passage once transitional words and phrases (such as *after, finally, once again,* and *in the end*) have been added.

Paragraph with Transitional Words and Phrases

Napoleon certainly made a change for the worse by leaving his small kingdom of Elba. After Waterloo, he went back to Paris, and he abdicated for a second time. A hundred days after his return from Elba, he fled to Rochefort in hope of escaping to America. Finally, he gave himself up to the English captain of the ship *Bellerophon*. Once again, he suggested that the Prince Regent grant him asylum, and once again, he was refused. In the end, all he saw of England was the Devon coast and Plymouth Sound as he passed on to the remote island of St. Helena. After six years of exile, he died on May 5, 1821, at the age of fifty-two. (Norman Mackenzie, *The Escape from Elba*)

Frequently Used Transitional Words and Phrases

To Signal Sequence or Addition

again	in addition
also	moreover
besides	one . . . another
first . . . second . . . third	too
furthermore	

To Signal Time

afterward	earlier
as soon as	finally
at first	in the meantime
at the same time	later
before	meanwhile

(continued)

Frequently used transitional words and phrases (continued)

To Signal Time

next	subsequently
now	then
soon	until

To Signal Comparison

also	likewise
by the same token	similarly
in comparison	

To Signal Contrast

although	nevertheless
but	nonetheless
despite	on the contrary
even though	on the one hand . . . on the
however	other hand
in contrast	still
instead	whereas
meanwhile	yet

To Introduce Examples

for example	specifically
for instance	thus
namely	

To Signal Narrowing of Focus

after all	in particular
indeed	specifically
in fact	that is
in other words	

To Introduce Conclusions or Summaries

as a result	in summary
consequently	therefore
in conclusion	thus
in other words	to conclude

To Signal Concession

admittedly	naturally
certainly	of course
granted	

To Introduce Causes or Effects

accordingly	since
as a result	so
because	then
consequently	therefore
hence	

(3) Using Pronouns

By referring to nouns or other pronouns, pronouns establish connections between sentences. Clear, well-placed pronoun references
can eliminate unnecessary repetition and make a paragraph's ideas
easier to follow.

(4) Using Parallel Structure

Parallelism—the use of matching words, phrases, clauses, or sentence structures to express similar ideas—can increase coherence in a
paragraph. Note in the following paragraph how parallel constructions beginning with "He was . . ." link Thomas Jefferson's accomplishments.

> Thomas Jefferson was born in 1743 and died at
> Monticello, Virginia, on July 4, 1826. During his
> eighty-four years, he accomplished a number of things.
> Although best known for his draft of the Declaration
> of Independence, Jefferson was a man of many talents
> who had a wide intellectual range. He was a patriot
> who was one of the revolutionary founders of the
> United States. He was a reformer who, when he was
> governor of Virginia, drafted the Statute for
> Religious Freedom. He was an innovator who drafted an
> ordinance for governing the West and devised the first
> decimal monetary system. He was a president who
> abolished internal taxes, reduced the national debt,
> and made the Louisiana Purchase. And, finally, he was
> an architect who designed Monticello and the
> University of Virginia. (student writer)

(5) Repeating Key Words and Phrases

Repeating **key words and phrases**—those essential to meaning—
throughout a paragraph connects the sentences to one another and
to the paragraph's main idea. The following paragraph repeats the
key word *mercury* to help readers focus on the subject. (Notice that
to avoid monotony the writer sometimes refers indirectly to the subject of the paragraph with phrases such as *similarly affected* and *this
problem*.)

> Mercury poisoning is a problem that has long
> been recognized. "Mad as a hatter" refers to the
> condition prevalent among nineteenth-century workers
> who were exposed to mercury during the manufacturing
> of felt hats. Workers in many other industries, such
> as mining, chemicals, and dentistry, were similarly
> affected. In the 1950s and 1960s, there were cases of
> mercury poisoning in Minamata, Japan. Research showed
> that there were high levels of mercury pollution in

> streams and lakes surrounding the village. In the
> United States, this problem came to light in 1969,
> when a New Mexico family got sick from eating food
> tainted with <u>mercury</u>. Since then, pesticides
> containing <u>mercury</u> have been withdrawn from the
> market, and chemical wastes can no longer be dumped
> into the ocean. (student writer)

(6) Achieving Coherence between Paragraphs

See
5e1

The same methods you use to establish coherence within paragraphs
may also be used to link paragraphs in an essay. (You can also use a
<u>transitional paragraph</u> as a bridge between two paragraphs.) The
following group of related paragraphs shows how some of the strategies discussed in 5b1–5 work together to create coherence.

> <u>A language may borrow a word directly or indirectly.</u> A direct bor-
> rowing means that the borrowed item is a native word in the language
> it is borrowed from. *Festa* was borrowed directly from French and can
> be traced back to Latin *festa*. On the other hand, the word *algebra* was
> borrowed from Spanish, which in turn borrowed it from Arabic. Thus
> *algebra* was indirectly borrowed from Arabic, with Spanish as an inter-
> mediary.
>   <u>Some languages are heavy borrowers.</u> Albanian has borrowed so heav-
> ily that few native words are retained. On the other hand, most Native
> American languages have borrowed little from their neighbors.
>   <u>English has borrowed extensively.</u> Of the 20,000 or so words in com-
> mon use, about three-fifths are borrowed. Of the 500 most frequently
> used words, however, only two-sevenths are borrowed, and because these
> "common" words are used over and over again in sentences, the actual
> frequency of appearance of native words is about 80 percent. Morphemes
> such as *and, be, have, it, of, the, to, will, you, on, that,* and *is* are all native to
> English. (Victoria Fromkin and Robert Rodman, *An Introduction to Lan-
> guage*)

These paragraphs are arranged according to a logical organizing
principle, moving from the general concept of borrowing words to a
specific discussion of English. In addition, each topic sentence repeats
a variation of the word group *A language may borrow.* Throughout the
three paragraphs, some form of this word group (as well as *word* and
the names of various languages) appears in almost every sentence.

Exercise 5.2

A. Read the following paragraph, and determine how the author
achieves coherence. Underline parallel elements, pronouns, repeated
words, and transitional words and phrases that link sentences.

Some years ago the old elevated railway in Philadelphia was torn down and replaced by the subway system. This ancient El with its barnlike stations containing nut-vending machines and scattered food scraps had, for generations, been the favorite feeding ground of flocks of pigeons, generally one flock to a station along the route of the El. Hundreds of pigeons were dependent upon the system. They flapped in and out of its stanchions and steel work or gathered in watchful little audiences about the feet of anyone who rattled the peanut-vending machines. They even watched people who jingled change in their hands, and prospected for food under the feet of the crowds who gathered between trains. Probably very few among the waiting people who tossed a crumb to an eager pigeon realized that this El was like a food-bearing river, and that the life which haunted its banks was dependent upon the running of the trains with their human freight. (Loren Eiseley, *The Night Country*)

B. Revise the following paragraph to make it more coherent.

```
The theory of continental drift was first put
forward by Alfred Wegener in 1912. The continents
fit together like a gigantic jigsaw puzzle. The
opposing Atlantic coasts, especially South America
and Africa, seem to have been attached. He believed
that at one time, probably 225 million years ago,
there was one supercontinent. This continent broke
into parts that drifted into their present
positions. The theory stirred controversy during
the 1920s and eventually was ridiculed by the
scientific community. In 1954, the theory was
revived. The theory of continental drift is accepted
as a reasonable geological explanation of the
continental system. (student writer)
```

5c Writing Well-Developed Paragraphs

A paragraph is **well developed** when it includes all the supporting information—examples, statistics, expert opinion, and so on—that readers need to understand and accept its main idea.

Keep in mind that length alone does not determine whether a paragraph is well developed. To determine the amount and kind of support you need, consider your audience, your purpose, and your paragraph's main idea.

(1) Testing for Adequate Development

At first glance, the following paragraph may seem adequately developed.

Underdeveloped Paragraph

> From Thanksgiving until Christmas, children and
> their parents are bombarded by ads for violent
> toys and games. Toy manufacturers persist in
> thinking that only toys that appeal to children's
> aggressiveness will sell. Despite claims that they
> (unlike action toys) have educational value, video
> games have escalated the level of violence. The real
> question is why parents continue to buy these
> violent toys and games for their children. (student
> writer)

Although it may seem to be adequately developed, this paragraph does not contain enough support to convince readers that children and parents are "bombarded by ads for violent toys." The first sentence of this paragraph is the topic sentence. The rest of the sentences qualify this topic sentence, but the paragraph contains no specific examples. What kinds of toys appeal to a child's aggressive tendencies? What particular video games does the writer object to?

(2) Revising Underdeveloped Paragraphs

You can strengthen underdeveloped paragraphs like the preceding one by adding specific examples that illustrate the points made in the paragraph.

Revised Paragraph (Examples Added)

> From Thanksgiving until Christmas, children and
> their parents are bombarded by ads for violent
> toys and games. Toy manufacturers persist in
> thinking that only toys that appeal to children's
> aggressiveness will sell. <u>One television
> commercial praises the merits of a commando team
> that attacks and captures a miniature enemy base.</u>
>
> Examples <u>Toy soldiers wear realistic uniforms and carry
> automatic rifles, pistols, knives, grenades, and
> ammunition. Another commercial shows laughing
> children shooting one another with plastic rocket
> launchers and tanklike vehicles</u>. Despite claims
> that they (unlike action toys) have educational
> value, video games have escalated the level
>
> Examples of violence. <u>The most popular video games
> involve children in strikingly realistic combat
> simulations. One game lets children search out
> and destroy enemy fighters on the ground and in
> the air. Other best-selling games graphically
> simulate hand-to-hand combat on city streets and
> feature dismembered bodies and the sound of</u>

breaking bones. The real question is why parents
continue to buy these violent toys and games for
their children.

Exercise 5.3

Write a paragraph for two of the following topic sentences. Make sure
you include all the examples and other support necessary to develop
the paragraphs adequately. Assume that you are writing your paragraphs for the students in your composition class.

1. First-year students can take specific steps to make sure that they
   are successful in college.
2. Setting up a first apartment can be quite a challenge.
3. Whenever I get depressed, I think of _____, and I feel better.
4. The person I admire most is _____.
5. If I won the lottery, I would do three things.

5d Patterns of Paragraph Development

Patterns of paragraph development—*narration, exemplification,* and
so on—reflect the way a writer arranges material to express ideas
most effectively.

(1) Narration

A **narrative** paragraph tells a story by presenting events in chronological (time) order. Most narratives move in a logical, orderly sequence from beginning to end, from first event to last (although
some narrative paragraphs may start at the end and then move back
to the beginning or may contain flashbacks). Clear transitional
words and phrases (*later, after that*) and time markers (*in 1990, two
years earlier, the next day*) establish the chronological sequence and
the relationship of each event to the others.

> My academic career almost ended as soon as it
> began when, three weeks after I arrived at
> college, I decided to pledge a fraternity. By
> midterms, I was wearing a pledge cap and saying
> "Yes, sir" to every fraternity brother I met.
> When classes were over, I ran errands for the
> fraternity members, and after dinner I socialized
> and worked on projects with the other people in
> my pledge class. In between these activities, I
> tried to study. Somehow I managed to write
> papers, take tests, and attend lectures. By the
> end of the semester, though, my grades had
> slipped, and I was exhausted. It was then that I

Topic sentence establishes subject of narrative

Sequence of events

began to ask myself some important questions. I
realized that I wanted to be popular, but not at
the expense of my grades and my future career. At
the beginning of my second semester, I dropped out
of the fraternity and got a job in the biology
lab. Looking back, I realize that it was then that
I actually began to grow up. (student writer)

(2) Description

A **descriptive** paragraph communicates how something looks, sounds, smells, tastes, or feels. The most natural arrangement of details in a description reflects the way you actually look at a person, scene, or object: near to far, top to bottom, side to side, or front to back. This arrangement of details is made clear by transitions that identify precise spatial relationships: *next to, near, beside, under, above,* and so on.

Topic
sentence
implied

Details that
convey
dominant
impression

When you are inside the jungle, away from the river, the trees vault out of sight. It is hard to remember to look up the long trunks and see the fans, strips, fronds, and sprays of glossy leaves. Inside the jungle you are more likely to notice the snarl of climbers and creepers round the trees' boles, the flowering bromeliads and epiphytes in every bough's crook, and the fantastic silk-cotton tree trunks thirty or forty feet across, trunks buttressed in flanges of wood whose curves can make three high walls of a room—a shady, loamy-aired room where you would gladly live, or die. Butterflies, iridescent blue, striped, or clear-winged, thread the jungle paths at eye level. And at your feet is a swath of ants bearing triangular bits of green leaf. The ants with their leaves look like a wide fleet of sailing dinghies—but they don't quit. In either direction they wobble over the jungle floor as far as the eye can see. I followed them off the path as far as I dared, and never saw an end to ants or to those luffing chips of green they bore. (Annie Dillard, "In the Jungle")

(3) Exemplification

An **exemplification** paragraph supports a topic sentence with a series of specific examples (or, sometimes, with a single extended example). These examples can be drawn from personal observation or experience or from research.

Topic
sentence

Series of
examples

Illiterates cannot travel freely. When they attempt to do so, they encounter risks that few of us can dream of. They cannot read traffic signs and, while they often learn to recognize and to decipher symbols, they cannot manage street names which they haven't seen before. The same is true for bus and subway stops. While ingenuity can sometimes help a man or woman to discern directions from familiar landmarks, buildings, cemeteries, churches, and the like, most illiterates are virtually immobilized. They seldom wander past the streets and neighborhoods they know. Geographical paralysis becomes a bitter metaphor for their entire existence. They are im-mobilized in almost every sense we can imagine. They can't move up. They can't move out. They cannot see beyond. Illiterates may take an oral test for drivers' permits in most sections of America. It is a questionable concession. Where will they go? How will they get there? How will they get home? Could it be that some of us might like it better if they stayed where they belong? (Jonathan Kozol, *Il-literate America*)

(4) Process

Process paragraphs describe how something works, presenting a se-ries of steps in strict chronological order. The topic sentence identi-fies the process, and the rest of the paragraph presents the steps involved. Transitional words such as *first, then, next, after this,* and *fi-nally* link steps in the process.

Some process paragraphs give **instructions,** providing all the spe-cific information that enables readers to perform a procedure them-selves. Instructions use commands and the present tense. Other process paragraphs simply explain the process to readers, with no ex-pectation that they will actually perform it. These process paragraphs may use first or third person and past tense (for a process that has been completed) or present tense (for a process that occurs regularly).

Members of the court have disclosed, however, the general way the conference is conducted. It begins at ten A.M. and usually runs on until late afternoon. At the start each justice, when he enters the room, shakes hands with all others there (thirty-six handshakes altogether). The custom, dating back generations, is evidently designed to begin the meeting at a friendly level, no matter how heated the intellectual differences may be. The conference takes up, first, the applications for review—a few appeals, many more petitions for certiorari. Those on the Appellate Docket, the regular paid cases, are considered first, then the pauper's applications on the Miscellaneous Docket. (If any of these are granted, they are then transferred to the Appellate Docket.) After this the justices consider, and vote on, all the cases argued during the preceding Monday through Thursday. These are tentative votes, which may be and quite often are changed as the opinion is written and the problem thought through more deeply. There may be further discussion at later conferences before the opinion is handed down. (Anthony Lewis, *Gideon's Trumpet*)

Topic sentence identifies process

Steps in process

Close-up: Instructions

When a process paragraph presents instructions to enable readers to actually perform the process, it is writ-ten in the present tense and in the imperative mood—"*Remove* the cover . . . and *check* the valve."

(5) Cause and Effect

A **cause-and-effect** paragraph explores causes or predicts or describes results; sometimes a single cause-and-effect paragraph does both. To establish clear causal relationships, transitional words and phrases such as *one cause, another cause, a more important result, because,* and *as a result* are essential.

Some paragraphs examine causes.

<table>
<tr>
<td>Topic
sentence
establishes
major
cause

Cause
explored
in detail</td>
<td>The main reason that a young baby sucks his thumb seems to be that he hasn't had enough sucking at the breast or bottle to satisfy his sucking needs. Dr. David Levy pointed out that babies who are fed every 3 hours don't suck their thumbs as much as babies fed every 4 hours, and that babies who have cut down on nursing time from 20 minutes to 10 minutes . . . are more likely to suck their thumbs than babies who still have to work for 20 minutes. Dr. Levy fed a litter of puppies with a medicine dropper so that they had no chance to suck during their feedings. They acted just the same as babies who don't get enough chance to suck at feeding time. They sucked their own and each other's paws and skin so hard that the fur came off. (Benjamin Spock, *Baby and Child Care*)</td>
</tr>
</table>

Other paragraphs focus on effects.

<table>
<tr>
<td>Topic
sentence
establishes
major
effect

Discussion
of other
effects</td>
<td>On December 8, 1941, the day after the Japanese attack on Pearl Harbor in Hawaii, my grandfather barricaded himself with his family—my grandmother, my teenage mother, her two sisters and two brothers—inside of his home in La'ie, a sugar plantation village on Oahu's North Shore. This was my maternal grandfather, a man most villagers called by his last name, Kubota. It could mean either "Wayside Field" or else "Broken Dreams," depending on which ideograms he used. Kubota ran La'ie's general store, and the previous night, after a long day of bad news on the radio, some locals had come by, pounded on the front door, and made threats. One was said to have brandished a machete. They were angry and shocked, as the whole nation was in the aftermath of the surprise attack. Kubota was one of the few Japanese Americans in the village and president of the local Japanese language school. He had become a target for their rage and suspicion. A wise man, he locked all his doors and windows and did not open his store the next day, but stayed closed and waited for news from some official. (Garrett Hongo, "Kubota")</td>
</tr>
</table>

(6) Comparison and Contrast

Comparison-and-contrast paragraphs examine the similarities and differences between two subjects. **Comparison** focuses on similarities; **contrast** emphasizes differences.

Comparison-and-contrast paragraphs can be organized in one of two ways. **Point-by-point** comparisons discuss two subjects together, alternating points about one subject with comparable points about the other.

> There are two Americas. One is the America of Lincoln and Adlai Stevenson; the other is the America of Teddy Roosevelt and the modern superpatriots. One is generous and humane, the other narrowly egotistical; one is self-critical, the other self-righteous; one is sensible, the other romantic; one is good-humored, the other solemn; one is inquiring, the other pontificating; one is moderate, the other filled with passionate intensity; one is judicious and the other arrogant in the use of great power. (J. William Fulbright, *The Arrogance of Power*)

Topic sentence establishes comparison

Alternating points about the two subjects

Subject-by-subject comparisons treat one subject completely and then move on to the other subject. In the following paragraph, notice how the writer shifts from one subject to the other with the transitional word *however.*

> First, it is important to note that men and women regard conversation quite differently. For women it is a passion, a sport, an activity even more important to life than eating because it doesn't involve weight gain. The first sign of closeness among women is when they find themselves engaging in endless, secretless rounds of conversation with one another. And as soon as a woman begins to relax and feel comfortable in a relationship with a man, she tries to have that type of conversation with him as well. However, the first sign that a man is feeling close to a woman is when he admits that he'd rather she please quiet down so he can hear the TV. A man who feels truly intimate with a woman often reserves for her and her alone the precious gift of one-word answers. Everyone knows that the surest way to spot a successful long-term relationship is to look around a restaurant for the table where no one is talking. Ah . . . now that's real love. (Merrill Markoe, "Men, Women, and Conversation")

Topic sentence establishes comparison

First subject discussed

Second subject introduced

(7) Division and Classification

A **division-and-classification** paragraph **divides** (breaks a subject into its component parts) and **classifies** (groups individual terms into categories). Division and classification are closely related processes. For example, when you *divide* the English language into three historical categories (Old English, Middle English, and Modern English), you can then *classify* examples of specific linguistic characteristics by assigning them to the appropriate historical period. Transitional words and phrases help to distinguish categories from one another: *one kind, another group, a related category, the most important component.*

Division paragraphs take a single item and break it into its components.

Topic
sentence
establishes
categories

Categories
discussed

The blood can be divided into four distinct
components: plasma, red cells, white cells, and
platelets. Plasma is 90 percent water and holds
a great number of substances in suspension. It
contains proteins, sugars, fat, and inorganic
salts. Plasma also contains urea and other by-
products from the breaking down of proteins,
hormones, enzymes, and dissolved gases. In
addition, plasma contains the red blood cells
that give it color, the white cells, and the
platelets. The red cells are most numerous; they
get oxygen from the lungs and release it in the
tissues. The less numerous white cells are part
of the body's defense against invading organisms.
The platelets, which occur in almost the same
number as white cells, are responsible for
clotting. (student writer)

Classification paragraphs take many separate items and group them into categories according to qualities or characteristics they share.

Topic
sentence
establishes
categories

Categories
discussed

Charles Babbage, an English mathematician, reflecting in 1830 on what he saw as the decline of science at the time, distinguished among three major kinds of scientific fraud. He called the first "forging," by which he meant complete fabrication—the recording of observations that were never made. The second category he called "trimming"; this consists of manipulating the data to make them look better, or, as Babbage wrote, "in clipping off little bits here and there from those observations which differ most in excess from the mean and in sticking them on to those which are too small." His third category was data selection, which he called "cooking"—the choosing of those data that fitted the researcher's hypothesis and the discarding of those that did not. To this day, the serious discussion of scientific fraud has not improved on Babbage's typology. (Morton Hunt, *New York Times Magazine*)

(8) Definition

A **formal definition** includes the term defined, the class to which it belongs, and the details that distinguish it from other members of its class.

(term)   (class to which it belongs)   (distinguishing details)
Carbon is a nonmetallic element sometimes occurring as diamond.

Definition paragraphs develop the formal definition with other patterns—for instance, defining *happiness* by telling a story (narration) or defining a diesel engine by telling how it works (process).

The following definition paragraph is developed by means of exemplification: it begins with a straightforward definition of *gadget* and then presents an example.

A gadget is nearly always novel in design or concept and it often has no proper name. For example, the semaphore which signals the arrival of the mail in our rural mailbox certainly has no proper name. It is a contrivance consisting of a piece of shingle. Call it what you like, it saves us frequent frustrating trips to the mailbox in winter when you have to dress up and wade through snow to get there. That's a gadget! (*Smithsonian*)

Topic sentence gives general definition

Definition expanded with examples

Exercise 5.4

A. Read each of the following paragraphs, and then answer these questions: In general terms, how could each paragraph be developed further? What pattern of development might be used in each case?

B. Choose one paragraph, and rewrite it to develop it further.

▸ 1. Many new words and expressions have entered the English language in the last ten years or so. Some of them come from the world of computers. Others come from popular music. Still others have politics as their source. There are even some expressions that have their origins in films or television shows.

2. Making a good spaghetti sauce is not a particularly challenging task. First, assemble the basic ingredients: garlic, onion, mushrooms, green pepper, and ground beef. Sauté these ingredients in a large saucepan. Then, add canned tomatoes, tomato paste, and water, and stir. At this point, you are ready to add the spices: oregano, parsley, basil, and salt and pepper. Don't forget a bay leaf! Simmer for about two hours, and serve over spaghetti.

3. High school and college are not at all alike. Courses are a lot easier in high school, and the course load is lighter. In college, teachers expect more from students; they expect higher quality work, and they assign more of it. Assignments tend to be more difficult and more comprehensive, and deadlines are usually shorter. Finally, college students tend to be more focused on a particular course of study—even a particular career—than high school students are.

5e Writing Special Kinds of Paragraphs

So far, this chapter has focused on **body paragraphs,** the paragraphs that carry the weight of your essay's discussion. Other kinds of paragraphs—*transitional paragraphs, introductory paragraphs,* and *concluding paragraphs*—have special functions in an essay.

(1) Transitional Paragraphs

A **transitional paragraph** connects one section of the essay to another. At their simplest, transitional paragraphs can be single sentences that move readers from one point to the next.

What is true for ants is also true for people.

This idea works better in theory than in practice.

Here are several examples.

More often, writers use transitional paragraphs to present concise summaries of what they have already said before they move on to a new point. The following transitional paragraph uses a series of questions to sum up some of the ideas the writer has been discussing. In the next part of his essay, he goes on to answer these questions.

> Can we bleed off the mass of humanity to other worlds? Right now the number of human beings on Earth is increasing by 80 million per year, and each year that number goes up by 1 and a fraction percent. Can we really suppose that we can send 80 million people per year to the Moon, Mars, and elsewhere, and engineer those worlds to support those people? And even so, nearly remain in the same place ourselves? (Isaac Asimov, "The Case against Man")

(2) Introductory Paragraphs

An **introductory paragraph** prepares readers for the essay to follow. It typically introduces the subject, narrows it, and then states the essay's thesis.

> ```
> Christine was just a girl in one of my classes.
> I never knew much about her except that she was
> strange. She didn't talk much. Her hair was dyed
> black and purple, and she wore heavy black boots and
> a black turtleneck sweater, even in the summer. She
> was attractive—in spite of the ring she wore through
> her left eyebrow—but she never seemed to care what
> the rest of us thought about her. Like the rest of
> my classmates, I didn't really want to get close to
> her. It was only when we were assigned to do our
> chemistry project together that I began to
> understand why Christine dressed the way she did.
> ```
> (student writer)

To arouse their audience's interest, writers may vary this direct approach by using one of the following introductory strategies.

Strategies for Effective Introductions

Quotation or Series of Quotations

When Mary Cassatt's father was told of her decision to become a painter, he said: "I would rather see you dead." When Edgar Degas saw a show of Cassatt's etchings, his response was: "I am not willing to admit that a woman can draw that well." When she returned to Philadelphia after twenty-eight years abroad, having achieved renown as an Impressionist painter and the esteem of Degas, Huysmans, Pissarro, and Berthe Morisot, the *Philadelphia Ledger* reported: "Mary Cassatt, sister of Mr. Cassatt, president of the Pennsylvania Railroad, returned from Europe yesterday. She has been studying painting in France and owns the smallest Pekingese dog in the world." (Mary Gordon, "Mary Cassatt")

Question or Series of Questions

Of all the disputes agitating the American campus, the one that seems to me especially significant is that over "the canon." What should be taught in the humanities and social sciences, especially in introductory courses? What is the place of the classics? How shall we respond to those professors who attack "Eurocentrism" and advocate "multiculturalism"? This is not the sort of tedious quarrel that now and then flutters through the academy; it involves matters of public urgency. I propose to see this dispute, at first, through a narrow, even sectarian lens, with the hope that you will come to accept my reasons for doing so. (Irving Howe, "The Value of the Canon")

Definition

Moles are collections of cells that can appear on any part of the body. With occasional exceptions, moles are absent at birth. They first appear in the early years of life, between ages two and six. Frequently, moles appear at puberty. New moles, however, can continue to appear throughout life. During pregnancy, new moles may appear and old ones darken. There are three major designations of moles, each with its own unique distinguishing characteristics. (student writer)

Unusual Comparison

Once a long time ago, people had special little boxes called refrigerators in which milk, meat, and eggs could be kept cool. The grandchildren of these simple devices are large enough to store whole cows, and they reach temperatures comparable to those at the South Pole. Their operating costs increase each

(continued)

Strategies for effective introductions (continued)

year, and they are so complicated that few home handymen attempt to repair them on their own. Why has this change in size and complexity occurred in America? It has not taken place in many areas of the technologically advanced world (the average West German refrigerator is about a yard high and less than a yard wide, yet refrigeration technology in Germany is quite advanced). Do we really need (or even want) all that space and cold? (Appletree Rodden, "Why Smaller Refrigerators Can Preserve the Human Race")

Controversial Statement

Something had to replace the threat of communism, and at last a workable substitute is at hand. "Multiculturalism," as the new menace is known, has been denounced in the media recently as the new McCarthyism, the new fundamentalism, even the new totalitarianism—take your choice. According to its critics, who include a flock of tenured conservative scholars, multiculturalism aims to toss out what it sees as the Eurocentric bias in education and replace Plato with Ntozake Shange and traditional math with the Yoruba number system. And that's just the beginning. The Jacobins of the multiculturalist movement, who are described derisively as P.C., or politically correct, are said to have launched a campus reign of terror against those who slip and innocently say "freshman" instead of "freshperson," "Indian" instead of "Native American" or, may the Goddess forgive them, "disabled" instead of "differently abled." (Barbara Ehrenreich, "Teach Diversity—with a Smile")

Close-up: Introductory Paragraphs

An introductory paragraph should make your readers want to read further. For this reason, you should try to avoid opening statements that simply announce your subject ("In my paper, I will talk about Lady Macbeth") or that undercut your credibility ("I don't know much about alternative energy sources, but I would like to present my opinion about the subject").

Checklist: Revising Introductions

☐ Does your introduction include your essay's thesis statement?
☐ Does it lead naturally into the body of your essay?
☐ Does it arouse your readers' interest?
☐ Does it avoid statements that simply announce your subject or that undercut your credibility?

(3) Concluding Paragraphs

A **concluding paragraph** typically begins with specifics—reviewing the essay's main points, for example—and then moves to more general statements. Whenever possible, it should end with a sentence that readers will remember, one that encourages them to think about the implications of what you have written.

> As an Arab-American, I feel I have the best of two worlds. I'm proud to be part of the melting pot, proud to contribute to the tremendous diversity of cultures, customs and traditions that makes this country unique. But Arab-bashing—public acceptance of hatred and bigotry—is something no American can be proud of. (Ellen Mansoor Collier, "I Am Not a Terrorist")

Writers may also use one of the following concluding strategies.

Strategies for Effective Conclusions

Prediction

Looking ahead, [we see that] prospects may not be quite as dismal as they seem. As a matter of fact, we are not doing so badly. It is something of a miracle that creatures who evolved as nomads in an intimate, small-band, wide-open-spaces context manage to get along at all as villagers or surrounded by strangers in cubicle apartments. Considering that our genius as a species is adaptability, we may yet learn to live closer and closer to one another, if not in utter peace, then far more peacefully than we do today. (John Pheiffer, "Seeking Peace, Making War")

Warning

The Internet is the twenty-first century's talking drum, the very kind of grassroots communication tool that has been such a powerful source of education and culture for our people since slavery. But this talking drum we have not yet learned to play. Unless we master the new information technology to build and deepen the forms of social connection that a tragic history has eroded, African-Americans will face a form of cybersegregation in the next century as devastating to our aspirations as Jim Crow segregation was to those of our ancestors. But this time, the fault will be our own. (Henry Louis Gates Jr., "One Internet, Two Nations")

Contradiction or Paradox

A piece of writing is never finished. It is delivered to a deadline, torn out of the typewriter on demand, sent off with a sense of accomplishment and shame and pride and frustration. If only there were a couple more days, time for just another run at it, perhaps then. . . . (Donald Murray, "The Maker's Eye: Revising Your Own Manuscripts")

(continued)

Strategies for effective conclusions (continued)

Recommendation for Action

Computers have revolutionized learning in ways that we have barely begun to appreciate. We have experienced enough, however, to recognize the need to change our thinking about our purposes, methods, and outcome of higher education. Rather than resisting or postponing change, we need to anticipate and learn from it. We must harness the technology and use it to educate our students more effectively than we have been doing. Otherwise, we will surrender our authority to those who can. (Peshe Kuriloff, "If John Dewey Were Alive Today, He'd Be a Webhead")

Quotation

When we let freedom ring, when we let it ring from every village and every hamlet, from every state and every city, we will be able to speed up that day when all of God's children, black men and white men, Jews and Gentiles, Protestants and Catholics, will be able to join hands and sing in the words of the old Negro spiritual, "Free at last! Free at last! Thank God almighty, we are free at last!" (Martin Luther King Jr., "I Have a Dream")

Close-up: Concluding Paragraphs

Because a good conclusion provides closure to an essay, it should not introduce new points or go off in new directions. Because a dull conclusion can weaken an otherwise strong essay, you should try to make your conclusion as interesting as you can. Your conclusion is your essay's last word, so don't waste time repeating your introduction in different words or apologizing or undercutting your credibility ("I may not be an expert" or "At least, this is my opinion").

Checklist: Revising Conclusions

☐ Does your conclusion remind readers of the primary focus of your essay?
☐ Does it review your essay's main points?
☐ Does it end memorably?
☐ Does it do more than repeat the introduction?
☐ Does it avoid apologies?

As you read and write essays, you should carefully consider the strengths and weaknesses of the ideas they present. This is especially true in argumentative essays—those that take a stand on a debatable topic. Although some writers try their best to be fair, others are less scrupulous. They attempt to manipulate readers by using emotionally charged language, by unfairly emphasizing certain facts over others, and by intentionally using flawed logic. For this reason, it is particularly important that you apply **critical thinking** strategies when you read, learning to distinguish fact from opinion, evaluate supporting evidence, detect bias, evaluate visuals, and understand the basic principles of inductive and deductive reasoning.

See
Ch. 7

6a Distinguishing Fact from Opinion

A **fact** is a verifiable statement that something is true or that something occurred. An **opinion** is a personal judgment or belief that can never be substantiated beyond any doubt and is, therefore, debatable.

Fact: Measles is a potentially deadly disease.

Opinion: All children should be vaccinated against measles.

An opinion may be *supported* or *unsupported.*

Unsupported Opinion: All children in Pennsylvania should be vaccinated against measles.

Supported Opinion: Despite the fact that an effective measles vaccine is widely available, several unvaccinated Pennsylvania children have died of measles each year since 1992. States that have instituted vaccination programs have had no deaths in the same time period. For this reason, all children in Pennsylvania should be vaccinated against measles.

As the examples above show, supported opinion is more convincing than unsupported opinion.

Opinions can be supported with examples, statistics, or expert opinion.

Examples
The American Civil Liberties Union is an organization that has been unfairly characterized as left wing. It is true that it has opposed prayer in the public schools, defended conscientious objectors, and challenged police methods of conducting questioning

and searches of suspects. However, it has also backed the antiabortion group Operation Rescue in a police brutality suit and presented a legal brief in support of a Republican politician accused of violating an ethics law.

Statistics

A recent National Institute of Mental Health study concludes that mentally ill people account for more than 30 percent of the homeless population (Young 27). Because so many homeless people have psychiatric disabilities, the federal government should seriously consider expanding the state mental hospital system.

Expert Opinion

Clearly no young soldier ever really escapes the emotional consequences of war. As William Manchester, noted historian and World War II combat veteran, observes in his essay "Okinawa: The Bloodiest Battle of All," "the invisible wounds remain" (72).

NOTE: Remember that support can only make a statement more convincing; it cannot turn an opinion into a fact.

Exercise 6.1

Some of the following statements are facts; others are opinions. Identify each fact with the letter *F* and each opinion with the letter *O*. Then consider what kind of information, if any, could support each opinion.

- ► 1. The incidence of violent crime fell in the first six months of this year.
- ► 2. New gun laws and more police officers led to a decrease in crime early in the year.
- ► 3. The television rating system uses a system similar to the familiar movie rating codes to let parents know how appropriate a certain show might be for their children.
- ► 4. The new television rating system would be better if it gave specifics about the violence, sexual content, and language in rated television programs.
- ► 5. Affirmative action laws and policies have helped women and minority group members advance in the workplace.
  6. Affirmative action policies have outlived their usefulness.
  7. Women who work are better off today than they were twenty years ago.
  8. The wage gap between men and women in similar jobs is smaller now than it was twenty years ago.
  9. The Charles River and Boston Harbor currently test much lower for common pollutants than they did ten years ago.

10. We do not need to worry about environmental legislation anymore because we have made great advances in cleaning up our environment.

6b Evaluating Supporting Evidence

The examples, statistics, or expert opinions that you use to support your statements are called **evidence**. The more reliable the sup-porting evidence, the more willing readers will be to accept a statement. All evidence, however—no matter what kind—must be *accurate, sufficient, representative,* and *relevant.*

See 7b1

Evidence is likely to be **accurate** if it comes from a trustworthy source. Such a source quotes *exactly* and does not present remarks out of context. It also presents examples, statistics, and expert testimony fairly, drawing them from other reliable sources.

Evidence is likely to be **sufficient** if a writer presents an adequate amount. It is not enough, for instance, for a writer to cite just one example in an attempt to demonstrate that most poor women do not receive adequate prenatal care. Similarly, the opinions of a single expert, no matter how reputable, are not enough to support this position.

Evidence is likely to be **representative** if it reflects a fair range of sources and viewpoints. Writers should not just choose evidence that supports their thesis and ignore evidence that does not. In other words, they should not permit their biases to govern their choice of evidence. For example, a writer who is making the point that Asian immigrants have had great success in achieving professional status in the United States must draw from a range of Asian immigrant groups—Vietnamese, Chinese, Japanese, Indian, and Korean, for example—not just one.

Finally, evidence is likely to be **relevant** if it applies to the case being discussed. For example, a writer cannot support the position that the United States should send medical aid to developing nations by citing examples that apply only to our own nation's health-care system.

Exercise 6.2

Read the following student paragraph, and evaluate its supporting evidence.

The United States is becoming more and more violent every day. I was talking to my friend Gayle, and she mentioned that a guy her roommate knows was attacked at dusk and had his skull crushed by the barrel of a gun. Later she heard that he was in the hospital with a blood clot in his brain. Two friends

of mine were walking home from a party when they
were attacked by armed men right outside the A-Plus
Mini Market. These two examples make it very clear
to me how violent our nation is becoming. My English
professor, who is in his fifties, remembers a few
similar violent incidents occurring when he was
growing up, and he was even mugged in London last
year. He believes that if more London police carried
guns, the city would be safer. Two of the twenty-five
people in our class have been the victims of violent
crime, and I feel lucky that I am not one of them.

6c Detecting Bias

A **bias** is a tendency to base conclusions on preconceived ideas rather than on evidence. As a critical reader, you should be aware that bias may sometimes lead writers to see what they want to see and therefore to select only that evidence that is consistent with their own positions.

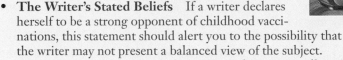

Close-up: Detecting Bias

When you read, look for the following kinds of bias:

- **The Writer's Stated Beliefs**   If a writer declares herself to be a strong opponent of childhood vaccinations, this statement should alert you to the possibility that the writer may not present a balanced view of the subject.
- **Sexist or Racist Statements**   A writer who assumes all engineers are male or all nurses are female reflects a clear bias. A researcher who assumes certain racial or ethnic groups are intellectually superior to others is also likely to present a biased view.
- **Slanted Language**   Some writers use **slanted language**—language that contains value judgments—to influence readers' reactions. For example, a newspaper article that states "The politician gave an impassioned speech" gives one impression; the statement "The politician delivered a diatribe" gives another.
- **Tone**   The tone of a piece of writing indicates a writer's attitude toward readers or toward his or her subject. An angry or sarcastic tone might indicate that the writer is not presenting his or her case fairly.
- **Choice of Evidence**   Frequently, the examples or statistics cited in a piece of writing reveal the writer's bias. For example, a writer may include only examples that support a point and leave out examples that may contradict it.

- **The Writer's Choice of Experts**   A writer should cite experts who represent a fair range of opinion. If, for instance, a writer assessing the president's policy on stem-cell research includes only statements by experts who vehemently oppose this procedure, he or she is presenting a biased case.

Exercise 6.3

Read the following essay about home schooling, a movement supported by parents who have abandoned traditional schools in favor of teaching their children at home. After evaluating the quality of the writer's supporting evidence, identify her biases, and decide if these biases undercut her argument in any way.

Questioning the Motives of Home-Schooling Parents

America's most famous home-schooling parents at the moment are Andrea Yates and JoAnn McGuckin. Yates allegedly drowned her five children in a Houston suburb. McGuckin was arrested and charged with child neglect in Idaho. Her six kids barricaded themselves in the family's hovel when child-care workers came to remove them.

The intention here is not to smear the parents who instruct 1.5 million mostly normal children at home. But a social phenomenon that isolates children from the outside world deserves closer inspection.

The home-schooling movement runs an active propaganda machine. It portrays its followers in the most flattering terms—as bulwarks against the moral decay found in public, and presumably private, schools. Although now associated with conservative groups, modern home-schooling got its start among left-wing dropouts in the '60s.

Home-schooled students do tend to score above average on standardized tests. The most likely reason, however, is that most of the parents are themselves upper income and well educated. Students from those backgrounds also do well in traditional schools.

Advocates of home-schooling have become a vocal lobbying force in Washington, D.C. Children taught at home may be socially isolated, but the parents have loads of interaction. Membership in the anti-public-education brigade provides much comradeship.

The mouthpiece for the movement, the Home School Legal Defense Association (*www.hslda.org*), posts articles on its Web site with headlines like, "The Clinging Tentacles of Public Education." Trashing the motivations of professional teachers provides much sport.

Perhaps the time has come to question the motives of some home-schooling parents. Are the parents protecting their children from a cesspool of bad values in the outside world? Or are the parents just people who can't get along with others? Are they "taking charge" of their children's education? Or are they taking their children captive?

Yates and McGuckin are, of course, extreme cases and probably demented. But a movement that insists on parents' rights to do as they wish with their children gives cover for the unstable, for narcissists and for child-abusers.

In West Akron, Ohio, reporters would interview Thomas Lavery on how he successfully schooled his five children in their home. The kids all had top grades and fine manners. They recalled how their father loved to strut before the media.

Eventually, however, the police came for Lavery and charged him with nine counts of child endangerment. According to his children, Lavery smashed a daughter over the head with a soda can after she did poorly in a basketball game. Any child who wet a bed would spend the night alone, locked in the garage.

A child who spilled milk had to drop on his or her knees and lick it up from the floor. And in an especially creepy attempt to establish himself as master, Lavery would order his children to damn the name of God.

The best way to maintain the sanctity of a family madhouse is to keep the inmates inside. Allowing children to move about in the world could jeopardize the deal.

In some cases, it might also prevent tragedy. Suppose one of Andrea Yates' children had gone to a school and told a teacher of the mother's spiraling mental state. The teacher could have called a child-welfare officer and five little lives might have been saved.

Putting the horror stories aside, there's something sad about home-schooled children. During the New Hampshire presidential primary race, I attended an event directed at high-school and college students. The students were a lively bunch, circulating around the giant room, debating and arguing. Except for my table.

About four young people and a middle-aged woman were just sitting there. The teenagers were clearly intelligent and well behaved. I tried to chat, but they seemed wary of talking with strangers. The woman proudly informed me that they were her children and home-schooled.

The Home School Legal Defense Association condemns government interference in any parent's vision of how a child might be educated. The group's chairman, Michael Farris, says things like, "We just want to say to the government: We are doing a good job, so leave us alone."

Could that be where JoAnn McGuckin found her twisted sense of grievance? "Those are my kids," she said as Idaho removed her children from their filthy home. "The state needs to mind its own business." (Froma Harrop, *Seattle Times*)

6d Understanding Inductive Reasoning

Argumentative essays rely primarily on **logic**. Logical reasoning enables you to construct arguments that reach conclusions in a persuasive and systematic way. Before you can evaluate or write arguments, you need to understand the basic principles of inductive and <u>deduc-</u> <u>tive</u> reasoning.

See
6e

(1) Moving from Specific to General

Inductive reasoning moves from specific facts, observations, or experiences to a general conclusion. Writers use inductive reasoning when they address a skeptical audience that requires a lot of evidence before it will accept a conclusion. You can see how inductive reasoning operates by studying the following list of specific statements that focus on the relationship between SAT scores and admissions at one liberal arts college.

- The SAT is an admission requirement for all applicants.
- High school grades and rank in class are also examined.
- Nonacademic factors, such as sports, activities, and interests, are taken into account as well.
- Special attention is given to the applications of athletes, minorities, and children of alumni.
- Fewer than 52 percent of applicants for a recent class with SAT verbal scores between 600 and 700 were accepted.
- Fewer than 39 percent of applicants with similar math scores were accepted.
- Approximately 18 percent of applications with SAT verbal scores between 450 and 520 and about 19 percent of applicants with similar SAT math scores were admitted.

After reading the statements above, you can use inductive reasoning to reach the general conclusion that although important, SAT scores are not the one single factor that determines whether or not a student is admitted.

(2) Making Inferences

No matter how much evidence is presented, an inductive conclusion is never certain, only probable. You arrive at an inductive conclusion by making an **inference,** a statement about the unknown based on the known. In order to bridge the gap that exists between your specific observations and your general conclusion, you have to make an **inductive leap.** If you have presented enough specific evidence, this gap will be relatively small and your readers will readily accept your conclusion. If the gap is too big, your readers will accuse you of making a <u>hasty generalization</u> and will not accept your conclusion. Even with the most effective support, absolute certainty is not possible with inductive reasoning. The best you can do is present a convincing case to readers.

See
6f

6e   Understanding Deductive Reasoning

(1) Moving from General to Specific

Deductive reasoning moves from a generalization believed to be true or self-evident to a more specific conclusion. Writers use deductive reasoning when they address an audience that is more likely to be influenced by logic than by evidence. The process of deduction has traditionally been illustrated with a **syllogism,** a three-part set of statements or propositions that includes a **major premise,** a **minor premise,** and a **conclusion.**

> **Major Premise:** All books from that store are new.
>
> **Minor Premise:** These books are from that store.
>
> **Conclusion:** Therefore, these books are new.

The major premise of a syllogism makes a general statement that the writer believes to be true. The minor premise presents a specific example of the belief that is stated in the major premise. If the reasoning is sound, the conclusion should follow from the two premises. (Note that these two premises contain all the information expressed in the conclusion; that is, the conclusion introduces no terms that have not already appeared in the major and minor premises.) The advantage of a deductive argument is that if readers accept the premises, they usually grant the conclusion.

See Ch. 7

When you write an <u>argumentative essay</u>, you can use a syllogism during the planning stage (to test the validity of your points), or you can use it as a revision strategy (to test your logic). In either case, the syllogism enables you to express your deductive argument in its most basic form and to see whether it makes sense.

(2) Constructing Valid Syllogisms

A syllogism is **valid** (or logical) when its conclusion follows from its premises. A syllogism is **true** when it makes accurate claims—that is, when the information it contains is consistent with the facts. To be **sound,** a syllogism must be both valid and true. However, a syllogism may be valid without being true or true without being valid. The following syllogism, for example, is valid but not true.

Syllogism That Is Valid but Not True

> **Major Premise:** All politicians are male.
>
> **Minor Premise:** Barbara Boxer is a politician.
>
> **Conclusion:** Therefore, Barbara Boxer is male.

As odd as it may seem, this syllogism is valid. In the major premise, the phrase *all politicians* establishes that the entire class *politicians* is male. After Barbara Boxer is identified as a politician, the conclusion that she is male automatically follows—but, of course, she is not. Because the major premise of this syllogism is not true, no conclusion based on it can be true. Even though the logic of the syllogism is correct, its conclusion is not.

(3) Recognizing Enthymemes

An enthymeme is a syllogism in which one of the premises—often the major premise—is unstated. Enthymemes often occur as sentences containing words that signal conclusions—*therefore, consequently, for this reason, for, so, since,* or *because.*

Melissa is on the Dean's List; therefore, she is a good student.

The preceding sentence contains the minor premise and the conclusion of a syllogism. The reader must fill in the missing major premise in order to complete the syllogism and see whether or not the reasoning is logical.

Major Premise: All those on the Dean's List are good students.

Minor Premise: Melissa is on the Dean's List.

Conclusion: Therefore, Melissa is a good student.

Political pronouncements frequently take the form of enthymemes: "Because tax cuts help the economy, we should support the president's tax proposals." In such cases, writers leave one or more premises unstated. By keeping their basic assumptions ambiguous or simply assuming that the assumptions are so self-evident that they need not be stated, these writers attempt to influence their audience. Bumper stickers often take this process to extremes, stating just a conclusion ("Eating meat is murder"), leaving readers to supply both the major and minor premises. Careful readers, however, are not so easily fooled. They supply the missing premise (or premises), and then determine if the resulting syllogism is sound.

Review: Inductive and Deductive Reasoning

Inductive	Deductive
1. Begins with specific observations.	1. Begins with a general statement or proposition.
2. Moves from the specific to the general.	2. Moves from the general to the specific.
3. Conclusion is probable, never certain.	3. Conclusion can be logical or illogical.

(continued)

Review: Inductive and deductive reasoning (continued)

4. Progresses by means of inference.

5. Draws a conclusion about the unknown based on what is known.

4. Progresses by means of the syllogism.

5. Draws a conclusion about the known based on what is known.

6f Recognizing Logical Fallacies

Fallacies are flawed arguments. A writer who inadvertently uses logical fallacies is not thinking clearly or logically; a writer who intentionally uses them is trying to deceive readers. Learn to recognize fallacies—to challenge them when you read and to avoid them when you write.

Close-up: Logical Fallacies

- **Hasty Generalization**   Drawing a conclusion based on too little evidence

  The person I voted for is not doing a good job in Congress. Therefore, voting is a waste of time. (One disappointing experience does not warrant the statement that you will never vote again.)

- **Sweeping Generalization**   Making a generalization that cannot be supported no matter how much evidence is supplied

  Everyone should exercise. (Some people, for example those with severe heart conditions, might not benefit from exercise.)

- **Equivocation**   Shifting the meaning of a key word or phrase during an argument

  It is not in the public interest for the public to lose interest in politics. (Although clever, the shift in the meaning of the term *public interest* clouds the issue.)

- **Non Sequitur (Does Not Follow)**   Arriving at a conclusion that does not logically follow from what comes before

  Kim Williams is a good lawyer, so she will make a good senator. (Kim Williams may be a good lawyer, but it does not necessarily follow that she will make a good senator.)

- **Either/Or Fallacy**   Treating a complex issue as if it has only two sides

  Either we institute universal health care, or the health of all Americans will decline. (Good health does not necessarily depend on universal health care.)

- **Post Hoc** Establishing an unjustified link between cause and effect

  The United States sold wheat to Russia. This must be what caused the price of wheat to rise. (Other factors, unrelated to the sale, could have caused the price to rise.)

- **Begging the Question** (circular reasoning) Stating a debatable premise as if it were true

  Stem-cell research should be banned because nothing good can come from something so inherently evil. (Where is the evidence that stem-cell research is "inherently evil"?)

- **False Analogy** Assuming that because things are similar in some ways, they are similar in other ways

  When forced to live in crowded conditions, people act like rats. They turn on each other and act violently. (Both people and rats might dislike living in crowded conditions, but unlike rats, most people do not necessarily resort to violence in this situation.)

- **Red Herring** Changing the subject to distract readers from the issue

  Our company may charge high prices, but we give a lot to charity each year. (What does charging high prices have to do with giving to charity?)

- **Argument to Ignorance** Saying that something is true because it cannot be proved false, or vice versa

  How can you tell me to send my child to a school where there is a child who has AIDS? After all, doctors can't say for sure that my child won't catch AIDS, can they? (Just because a doctor cannot prove the speaker's claim to be false, it does not follow that the claim is true.)

- **Bandwagon** Trying to establish that something is true because everyone believes it is true

  Everyone knows that eating candy makes a child hyperactive. (Where is the evidence to support this claim?)

- **Argument to the Person** (*Ad Hominem*) Attacking the person and not the issue

  Of course the congressman supports drilling for oil in the Arctic wildlife preserve. He worked for an oil company before he was elected to Congress. (By attacking his opponent, the speaker attempts to avoid the issue.)

- **Argument to the People** Appealing to people's prejudices

  Because foreigners are attempting to overrun our shores, we should cut back on immigration. (By exploiting prejudice, the speaker attempts to avoid the issue.)

ESL Tip

In many cultures, people present arguments in order to persuade others to believe something. However, the rules for constructing such arguments are different in different cultures. In US academic settings, writers are discouraged from using the types of arguments outlined in this section because they are not considered fair.

Exercise 6.4

Identify the logical fallacies in the following statements. In each case, name the fallacy, and then rewrite the statement to correct the problem.

▸ 1. Membership in the Coalition against Pornography has more than quadrupled since the 1990s. Convenience stores in many parts of the country have limited their selection of pornography and, in many cases, taken pornography off the shelves. In 1995, the defense appropriations bill included a ban on the sale of pornography on military installations. The American public clearly believes that pornography has a harmful effect on its audience.

▸ 2. With people like Larry Flynt and Hugh Hefner arguing that pornography is harmless, you know that pornography is causing its readers to live immoral lifestyles.

▸ 3. The Republican Party and conservative thinkers are all for the free market when the issue is environmental degradation, but they will be the first ones to call for a limit to what can be shown on movies, television, and the Internet.

▸ 4. Television is out of control. There is more foul language, sex, and sexual innuendo on television than there has ever been before. The effects of this obscene and pornographic material have been clearly documented in studies that proved that serial killers and other criminals were much more likely to be regular consumers of pornographic materials.

▸ 5. We know that television causes children to be more violent. So what can we use to control television? The V-chip, television ratings, and more governmental control of television content will help us reduce violence.

6. Study after study has been completed, and none of the researchers has presented incontrovertible evidence that rap music causes an increase in violent behavior among its listeners.

7. A boy in Idaho set fire to his family's home after watching a television stunt show. From this incident, we can see that television has a negative influence on children's behavior.

8. We want our children to grow up in safe neighborhoods. We would like to see less violence in the schools and on the playgrounds. We would like to be less fearful when we have to go out at night. If we stop polluting our culture with violent images from television and popular music, we can reclaim our communities and our children.

9. Ted Bundy and Richard Ramirez, two of the most violent serial killers ever caught, both used pornography regularly. Pornography caused them to kill women.

10. Some people believe that violence on television affects children and want the government to find ways to limit violence. Others believe that children are unaffected by the violence they see on television. I do not think violence on television causes children to become violent.

Checklist: Thinking Critically

☐ Are the writer's points supported primarily by fact or by opinion? Does the writer present opinion as fact?

☐ Does the writer offer supporting evidence for his or her statements?

☐ What kind of evidence is provided? How convincing is it?

☐ Is the evidence accurate? sufficient? representative? relevant?

☐ Does the writer display any bias? If so, is the bias revealed through language, tone, or choice of evidence?

☐ Does the writer omit pertinent examples?

☐ Does the writer present a balanced picture of the issue?

☐ Are any alternative viewpoints overlooked?

☐ Are any visuals misleading?

☐ Are any charts or graphs misleading?

☐ Does the writer use valid reasoning?

☐ Does the writer use logical fallacies?

☐ Does the writer oversimplify complex ideas?

☐ Does the writer make reasonable inferences?

☐ Does the writer represent the ideas of others accurately? fairly?

Chapter 7 | Writing Argumentative Essays

For most people, the true test of their critical thinking skills comes when they write an argumentative essay, one that takes a stand on an issue and uses logic and evidence to convince readers. When you

See
Chs.
2–4
write an argument, you follow the same process you use when you write any essay. However, because the purpose of an argument is to change the way readers think or to move them to action, you need to use some additional strategies to present your ideas to your audience.

7a Planning an Argumentative Essay

(1) Choosing a Debatable Topic

Because an argumentative essay attempts to change the way people think, it must focus on a **debatable topic,** one about which reasonable people may disagree. Factual statements—verifiable assertions about which reasonable people do *not* disagree—are, therefore, not suitable as topics for argument.

> **Fact:** First-year students are not required to purchase a meal plan from the university.
>
> **Debatable Topic:** First-year students *should be* required to purchase a meal plan from the university.

In addition to being debatable, your topic should be one that you know something about. The more information you can provide, the more likely you are to influence your audience. General knowledge is seldom convincing by itself, however, so you will probably have to do some research.

See
Pt. 7

Your topic should also be narrow enough so that you can write about it within your page limit. After all, in your argumentative essay, you will have to develop your own ideas and present convincing support while also pointing out the strengths and weaknesses of opposing arguments. If your topic is too broad, you will not be able to treat it in enough detail.

Finally, your topic should be interesting. Keep in mind that some topics—such as "The Need for Gun Control" or "The Fairness of the Death Penalty"—have been discussed and written about so often that you will probably not be able to say anything very interesting about them. Instead of relying on an overused topic, choose one that enables you to contribute something to the debate.

(2) Developing an Argumentative Thesis

After you have chosen a topic, your next step is to state your position in an **argumentative thesis,** one that takes a strong stand. Properly worded, this thesis statement lays the foundation for the rest of your argument.

See
3b

One way to make sure that your thesis statement actually does take a stand is to formulate an **antithesis,** a statement that takes an arguable position that is the opposite of yours. If you can create an antithesis, your thesis statement takes a stand. If you cannot, your statement needs further revision to make it argumentative.

> **Thesis Statement:** Term limits would improve government by bringing people with fresh ideas into office every few years.
>
> **Antithesis:** Term limits would harm government because elected officials would always be inexperienced.

(3) Defining Your Terms

You should always define the key terms you use in your argument; after all, the soundness of an entire argument may hinge on the definition of a word that may mean one thing to one person and another thing to someone else. For example, in the United States, *democratic* elections involve the selection of government officials by popular vote; in other countries, the same term may be used to describe elections in which only one candidate is running or in which all candidates represent the same party. For this reason, if your argument hinges on a key term like *democratic*, you should make sure that your readers know exactly what you mean.

> ### Close-up: Defining Your Terms
>
> Be careful to use precise terms in your thesis statement. Avoid vague and judgmental words, such as *wrong, bad, good, right,* and *immoral.*
>
> **Vague:** Censorship of the Internet would be wrong.
>
> **Clearer:** Censorship of the Internet would unfairly limit free speech.

(4) Considering Your Audience

As you plan your essay, keep a specific <u>audience</u> in mind. Are your readers unbiased observers or people deeply concerned about the issue you plan to discuss? Can they be cast in a specific role— concerned parents, victims of discrimination, irate consumers—or are they so diverse that they cannot be categorized? If you cannot be certain who your readers are, direct your arguments to a general audience.

See 1b

    Always assume a skeptical audience. Even if your readers are sympathetic to your position, you cannot assume that they will accept your ideas without question. Even so, the strategies you use to convince your readers will vary according to your relationship with them. Somewhat sympathetic readers may need to see only that your argument is logical and that your evidence is solid. More skeptical readers may need a good deal of reassurance that you understand their concerns and that you concede some of their points. However, you may never be able to convince hostile readers that your conclusion is valid. The best you can hope for is that these readers will acknowledge the strengths of your argument even if they reject your conclusion.

(5) Refuting Opposing Arguments

As you develop your argument, you should also **refute**—that is, disprove—opposing arguments by showing that they are untrue, unfair, illogical, unimportant, or irrelevant. In the following paragraph, a student refutes the argument that Sea World should keep whales in captivity.

> Of course, some will say that Sea World wants to capture only a few whales, as George Will points out in his commentary in <u>Newsweek</u>. Unfortunately, Will downplays the fact that Sea World wants to capture a hundred whales, not just "a few." And, after releasing ninety of these whales, Sea World intends to keep ten for "further work." At hearings in Seattle last week, several noted marine biologists went on record as condemning Sea World's research program.

When an opponent's position is so strong that it cannot be refuted, concede the point, and then identify its limitations. Martin Luther King Jr. uses this tactic in his "Letter from Birmingham Jail."

Concedes point

You express a great deal of anxiety over our willingness to break laws. This is certainly a legitimate concern. Since we so diligently urge people to obey the Supreme Court's decision of 1954 outlawing segregation in the public schools, at first glance it may seem rather paradoxical for us consciously to break laws. One may well ask: "How can you advocate breaking some laws and obeying others?" The answer lies in the fact that there are two types of laws: just and unjust. I would be the first to advocate obeying just laws. Conversely, one has a moral responsibility to disobey unjust laws. I would agree with St. Augustine that "an unjust law is no law at all."

Discusses its limitations

NOTE: When you acknowledge an opposing view, be careful not to distort or oversimplify it. This tactic, known as creating a **straw man,** can seriously undermine your credibility.

7b Using Evidence Effectively

(1) Supporting Your Argument

See 6b

Most arguments are built on **assertions**—statements that you make about your topic—backed by <u>evidence</u>—supporting information, in the form of examples, statistics, or expert opinion. If, for instance, you asserted that law-enforcement officials are winning the war against violent crime, you could then support this assertion by referring to a government report stating that violent crime—especially murder—has dramatically decreased during the past decade. This report would be one piece of persuasive evidence. (Keep in mind that all information—words and ideas—that you get from a source requires documentation.)

See
Chs.
46–47

Only assertions that are *self-evident* ("All human beings are mortal"), *true by definition* (2 + 2 = 4), or *factual* ("The Atlantic Ocean separates England and the United States") need no proof. All other kinds of assertions require support.

NOTE: Remember that you can never prove a thesis conclusively—if you did, there would be no argument. The best you can do is to provide enough evidence to establish a high probability that your thesis is reasonable or valid.

(2) Establishing Credibility

Clear reasoning, compelling evidence, and strong refutations go a long way toward making an argument solid. But these elements in themselves are not sufficient to create a convincing argument. In order to convince readers, you have to satisfy them that you are someone they should listen to—in other words, that you have **credibility.**

Establishing Common Ground When you write an argument, it is tempting to go on the attack, emphasizing the differences between your position and those of your opponents. Writers of effective arguments, however, know they can gain a greater advantage by establishing common ground between their opponents and themselves.

One way to establish common ground is to use the techniques of **Rogerian argument,** based on the work of the psychologist Carl Rogers. According to Rogers, you should think of the members of your audience as colleagues with whom you must collaborate to find solutions to problems. Instead of verbally assaulting them, you should emphasize points of agreement. In this way, rather than taking a confrontational stance, you establish common ground and work toward a resolution of the problem you are discussing.

Demonstrating Knowledge Including relevant personal experiences in your argumentative essay can show readers that you know a lot about your subject; demonstrating this kind of knowledge gives you authority. For example, describing what you observed at a National Rifle Association convention can give you authority in an essay arguing for (or against) gun control.

You can also demonstrate knowledge by showing you have done research into a subject. By referring to important sources of information and by providing accurate **documentation** for your information, you show readers that you have done the necessary background reading.

Maintaining a Reasonable Tone   Your tone is almost as important as the information you convey. Talk *to* your readers, not *at* them. If you lecture your readers or appear to talk down to them, you will alienate them. Remember that readers are more likely to respond to a writer who is conciliatory than to one who is strident or insulting. For this reason, you should use moderate language, qualify your statements, and avoid words and phrases such as *never, all,* and *in every case,* which can make your claims seem exaggerated and unrealistic.

Presenting Yourself as Someone Worth Listening To   Present your argument in positive terms, and don't apologize for your views. For example, do not rely on phrases—such as "In my opinion" and "It seems to me"—that undercut your credibility. Be consistent, and be careful not to contradict yourself. Finally, limit your use of the first person ("I"), and avoid slang and colloquialisms.

(3) Being Fair

Argument promotes one point of view, so it is seldom objective. However, college writing requires that you stay within the bounds of fairness and avoid **bias**. To be sure that the support for your argument is not misleading or distorted, you should take the following steps.

Avoid Distorting Evidence.   Distortion is misrepresentation. Writers sometimes intentionally misrepresent their opponents' views by exaggerating them and then attacking this extreme position, but you should avoid this unfair tactic in your college writing.

Avoid Quoting Out of Context.   Be careful not to take someone's words out of their original setting and use them in another. When you select certain statements and ignore others, you can change the meaning of what someone has said or suggested.

Avoid Slanting.   It is not fair to select only information that supports your case and ignore information that does not. Inflammatory language, another form of slanting that creates bias in your writing, should also be avoided.

Avoid Using Unfair Appeals.   Traditionally, writers of arguments try to influence readers by appealing to their sense of reason or to their emotions. Problems arise when these appeals are used unfairly. For example, writers can use **fallacies** to fool readers into thinking that a conclusion is logical when it is not. Writers can also employ inappropriate emotional appeals—to prejudice or fear, for example—to influence readers. These unfair appeals are inappropriate in college writing.

7c Organizing an Argumentative Essay

In its simplest form, an argument consists of a thesis statement and supporting evidence. However, argumentative essays frequently use inductive and deductive reasoning as well as additional strategies to win audience approval and overcome potential opposition.

See
6d–e

Close-up: Elements of an Argumentative Essay

Introduction

The introduction of your argumentative essay orients your readers to your subject. Here you can show how your subject concerns your audience, establish common ground with your readers, and perhaps explain how your subject has been misunderstood.

See
5e2

Background

In this section, you can briefly present a narrative of past events, an overview of others' opinions on the issue, definitions of key terms, or a review of basic facts.

Thesis Statement

Your thesis statement can appear anywhere in your argumentative essay. Most often, you present your thesis in your introduction. However, if you are presenting a highly controversial argument—one to which you believe your readers might react negatively—you may postpone stating your thesis until later in your essay.

See
3b–c

Arguments in Support of Your Thesis

Here you present your assertions and the evidence to support them. Most often, you begin with your weakest argument and work up to your strongest. If all your arguments are equally strong, you might begin with those with which your readers are already familiar and therefore likely to accept.

Refutation of Opposing Arguments

In an argumentative essay, you should summarize and refute the major arguments against your thesis. If the opposing arguments are relatively weak, refute them after you have made your case. However, if the opposing arguments are strong, concede their strengths and then discuss their limitations before you present your own arguments.

(continued)

Elements of an argumentative essay (continued)

See
5e3

Conclusion

Often, the conclusion restates the major arguments in support of your thesis. Your conclusion can also summarize key points, restate your thesis, remind readers of the weaknesses of opposing arguments, or underscore the logic of your position. Many writers like to end their arguments with a strong last line, such as a quotation or a statement that sums up the argument.

7d Writing and Revising an Argumentative Essay

The following student essay includes many of the elements discussed in this chapter. The student, Samantha Masterton, was asked to write an argumentative essay on a topic of her choice, drawing her supporting evidence from her own knowledge and experience as well as from other sources.

Masterton 1

Samantha Masterton

Professor Egler

English 102

4 April 2003

The Returning Student: Older Is Definitely Better

After graduating from high school, young people
must decide what they want to do with the rest of
their lives. Many graduates (often without much
thought) decide to continue their education
uninterrupted, and they go on to college. This group
of teenagers makes up what many see as typical first-
year college students. Recently, however, this
stereotype has been challenged by an influx of older
students, including myself, into American colleges
and universities. Not only do these students make a
valuable contribution to the schools they attend, but
they also offer an alternative to young people who go
to college simply because they do not know what else
to do. A few years off between high school and
college can give many—perhaps most—students the
life experience they need to appreciate the value of
higher education and gain more from it.

The college experience of an eighteen-year-old
is quite different from that of an older
"nontraditional" student. On the one hand, the
typical high school graduate is often concerned with
things other than cracking books—for example, going
to parties, dating, and testing personal limits. On
the other hand, older students—those who are twenty-

Introduction

Thesis
statement

Background

Masterton 2

five years of age or older—take seriously the idea of returning to college. Although many high school students do not think twice about whether or not to attend college, older students have much more to consider when they think about returning to college. For example, they must decide how much time they can spend getting their degree and consider the impact attending college will have on their family and their finances.

Background (continued)

In the United States, the demographics of college students is changing. According to a 2002 US Department of Education report titled <u>Nontraditional Undergraduates</u>, the percentage of students who could be classified as "nontraditional" has increased over the last decade. Thus, in spite of the challenges that older students face when they return to school, more and more are choosing to make the effort.

Argument in support of thesis

Most older students return to school with well-defined goals. The US Department of Education's <u>Nontraditional Undergraduates</u> report shows that more than one-third of nontraditional students decided to attend college because it was required by their job, and 87 percent enrolled in order to gain skills (10). Getting a college degree is often a requirement for professional advancement, and older students are therefore more likely to take college seriously. In general, older students enroll in college with a definite course of study in mind. For older students, college is an extension of work rather than a place

Masterton 3

to discover what they want to be when they graduate. A 2001 study by psychologists Eric R. Landrum, Je Taime Hood, and Jerry M. McAdams concluded, "Nontraditional students seemed to be more appreciative of their opportunities, as indicated by their higher enjoyment of school and appreciation of professors' efforts in the classroom" (744). Clearly defining their goals enables older students to take advantage of the opportunities presented by professors as well as to make use of career offices and other services colleges provide.

The experience adult students have gained in the workplace also gives them advantages in the classroom. Generally, young people just out of high school have not been challenged by real-world situations that include meeting deadlines and setting priorities. Although success in college depends on the ability to set realistic goals and organize time and materials, college itself does little to help students develop these skills. On the contrary, the workplace—where reward and punishment are usually immediate and tangible—is the best place to learn such lessons. Working teaches the basics that are necessary for success: the value of punctuality and attendance, the importance of respect for superiors and colleagues, and the need for establishing priorities and meeting deadlines.

Older students understand the actual benefits of doing well in school and successfully completing a

Argument in support of thesis

Masterton 4

degree program. Often, they are juggling demands of

home and work to attend classes, and the difficulties

Argument in support of thesis

of balancing school, family, and work compel older

students to be disciplined and focused. This pays

off; older students tend to devote more hours per

week to studying and tend to have a higher GPA than

younger students do (Landrum, Hood, and McAdams

742-43).

My experience as an older student has convinced

me that many students would benefit from delaying

entry into college. Given their greater maturity and

experience, older students bring more into the

classroom than younger students do. Eighteen-year-olds

Personal experience used as evidence in support of thesis

have been driving for only a year or two, they have

just earned the right to vote, and they usually have

not lived on their own. They cannot be expected to

have formulated definite goals or developed firm ideas

about themselves or about the world in which they

live. In contrast, older students have generally had a

variety of real-life experiences. Most have worked for

several years, many have started families. Their years

in the "real world" have helped them become more

focused and more responsible than they were when they

graduated from high school. As a result, they are

better prepared for college than they would have been

when they were young. Thus, they not only bring more

into the classroom, but they also take more out of it.

Of course, postponing college for a few years is

not for everyone. Certainly some teenagers have a

Masterton 5

definite sense of purpose and maturity well beyond
their years, and these individuals would benefit from
an early college experience, so that they can get a
head start on their careers. Charles Woodward, a law
librarian, went to college directly after high
school, and for him the experience was positive. "I
was serious about learning, and I loved my subject,"
he said. "I felt fortunate that I knew what I wanted
from college and from life." Many younger students,
however, are not like Woodward; they graduate from
high school without any clear sense of purpose. For
this reason, it makes sense for them to postpone
college until they are mature enough to benefit from
the experience.

Refutation of opposing argument

　　Granted, some older students have difficulties
when they return to college. Because these students
have been out of school so long, they may have
difficulty studying and adapting to the routines
of academic life. As I have seen, though, these
problems disappear soon after an initial period of
adjustment. Older students quickly get into the swing
of things and adapt to college; they even participate
in campus life. It is true that many older students
find it difficult to balance the needs of their
family with college and to cope with the financial
burden that tuition and books bring to their family
budget. However, this challenge is becoming easier
with the growing number of online courses and the
availability of distance education, as well as the

Refutation of opposing argument

Masterton 6

introduction of governmental programs, such as
educational tax credits and grants, to ease the
financial burden of returning to school (Agbo
164-65).

All things considered, higher education is
often wasted on the young, who are either too
immature or too unfocused to take advantage of it.
Taking a few years off between high school and
college would give these students the breathing room
they need to make the most of a college education.
Conclusion   The increasing number of older students returning to
college seems to indicate that many students are
taking this path. According to a US Department of
Education report, Digest of Education Statistics,
2001, 40 percent of students enrolled in American
colleges in 2000 were twenty-five years of age or
older. Older students such as these have taken time
off to serve in the military, to gain valuable work
experience, or to raise a family. Many have
traveled, have engaged in informal study, and have
taken the time to mature. By the time they get to
college, they have defined their goals and made a
commitment to achieve them.

Masterton 7

Works Cited

Works-cited
list begins
new page

Agbo, S. "The United States: Heterogeneity of the
    Student Body and the Meaning of 'Nontraditional'
    in U.S. Higher Education." Higher Education and
    Lifelong Learners: International Perspectives on
    Change. Eds. Hans G. Schuetze and Maria Slowey.
    London: Routledge, 2000. 149-69.

Landrum, R. Eric, Je Taime Hood, and Jerry M.
    McAdams. "Satisfaction with College by
    Traditional and Nontraditional College
    Students." Psychological Reports 89 (2001):
    740-46.

United States. Dept. of Educ. Office of Educ.
    Research and Improvement. Natl. Center for Educ.
    Statistics. Digest of Education Statistics,
    2001. Washington: US Dept. of Educ., 2001. 27
    Feb. 2003 <http://nccs.ed.gov/pubs2002/
    digest2001/tables/dt174.asp>.

---. ---. Nontraditional Undergraduates. Washington:
    US Dept. of Educ., 2002. 27 Feb. 2003
    <http://nces.ed.gov/pubs2002/2002012.pdf>.

Woodward, Charles B. Personal interview. 21 Mar.
    2003.

Two sets of
unspaced
hyphens
indicate that
both
"United
States" and
"Dept. of
Educ." are
repeated
from previ-
ous entry

Checklist: Writing Argumentative Essays

☐ Is your topic debatable?
☐ Does your essay have an argumentative thesis?
☐ Have you adequately defined the terms you use in your argument?
☐ Have you considered the opinions, attitudes, and values of your audience?
☐ Have you summarized and refuted opposing arguments?
☐ Have you supported your assertions with evidence?
☐ Have you used visuals that strengthen your argument?
☐ Have you established your credibility?
☐ Have you documented all information that is not your own?
☐ Have you been fair?
☐ Have you constructed your arguments logically?
☐ Have you avoided logical fallacies?
☐ Have you provided your readers with enough background information?
☐ Have you presented your points clearly and organized them logically?
☐ Have you written an interesting introduction and a strong conclusion?

Close-up: Using Transitions in Argumentative Essays

Argumentative essays should include transitional words and phrases to indicate which paragraphs are arguments in support of the thesis, which are refutations of arguments that oppose the thesis, and which are conclusions.

Arguments in Support of Thesis

accordingly	given
because	generally
for example	in general
for instance	since

Refutations

although	in all fairness
admittedly	naturally
certainly	nonetheless
despite,	of course
granted	

Conclusions

all things considered	in summary
as a result	therefore
in conclusion	thus

PART 2

Developing Strategies for Academic Success

Central to developing effective reading skills is learning the techniques of **active reading.** Being an active reader means being actively involved in the text: reading with pen in hand, physically marking the text in order to identify parallels, question ambiguities, distinguish important points from not-so-important ones, and connect causes with effects and generalizations with specific examples. The understanding you gain from active reading prepares you to think (and write) critically about a text.

ESL Tip

When you read a text for the first time, don't worry about understanding every word. Instead, just try to get a general idea of what the text is about and how it is organized. Later on, you can use a dictionary to look up any unfamiliar words.

8a Previewing a Text

Before you actually begin reading a text, you should **preview** it—that is, skim it to get a sense of the author's subject and emphasis.

When you preview a *book*, start by looking at its table of contents, especially at the sections that pertain to your topic. Then, turn to its index. A quick glance at the index will reveal the amount of coverage the book gives to subjects that may be important to you. As you leaf through the chapters, look at pictures, graphs, or tables, and read the captions that appear with them.

When you preview a *periodical article*, scan the introductory and concluding paragraphs for summaries of the author's main points. (Journal articles in the sciences and social sciences often begin with summaries called **abstracts.**) Thesis statements, topic sentences, repeated key terms, transitional words and phrases, and transitional paragraphs can also help you to identify the points a writer is making. In addition, look for the visual cues—such as <u>headings and lists</u>—that writers use to emphasize ideas.

See
11b–c

8b Highlighting a Text

When you have finished previewing a work, you should **highlight** it—that is, use a system of graphic symbols and underlining—to identify the writer's key points and their relationships to one another. (If you are working with library material, photocopy the pages you need before you highlight them.) Be sure to use symbols that you will understand when you reread your material later on.

Checklist: Using Highlighting Symbols
☐ Underline to indicate information you should read again.
☐ Box or circle key words or important phrases.
☐ Put question marks next to confusing passages, unclear points, or words you need to look up.
☐ Draw lines or arrows to show connections between ideas.
☐ Number points that appear in sequence.
☐ Draw a vertical line in the margin to set off an important section of text.
☐ Star especially important ideas.

8c Annotating a Text

After you have read through a text once, read it again—this time, more critically. At this stage, you should **annotate** the pages, recording your responses to what you read. This process of recording notes in the margins or between the lines will help you understand the writer's ideas and your own reactions to those ideas.

Some of your annotations may be relatively straightforward. For example, you may define new words, identify unfamiliar references, or jot down brief summaries. Other annotations may be more personal: you may identify a parallel between your own experience and one described in the reading selection, or you may record your opinion of the writer's position.

The following passage illustrates a student's highlighting and annotations on an article about the decline of American public schools.

One of the most compelling arguments about the <u>Vietnam War</u> is that it lasted as long as it did because of its "classist" nature. The central thesis is that because neither the decision makers in the government *nor anyone they knew* had children fighting and dying in Vietnam, they had no personal incentive to bring the war to a halt. The government's generous college-deferment system, steeped as it was in class distinctions, allowed the white middle class to avoid the tragic consequences of the war. <u>And the people who did the fighting and dying in place of the college-deferred were those whose voices were least heard in Washington: the poor and the disenfranchised.</u>

I bring this up because <u>I believe that the decline of the public schools is rooted in the same cause.</u> Just as with the Vietnam War, as soon as the middle class no longer had a stake in the

Is this comparison valid? (seems forced)

public schools, the surest pressure on school systems to provide a decent education instantly disappeared. Once the middle class was gone, no mayor was going to get booted out of office because the schools were bad. No incompetent teacher had to worry about angry parents calling for his or her head *bias* "downtown." No third-rate educationalist at the local teachers college had to fear having his or her methods criticized by anyone that mattered.

Who are these people? Does he really represent them?

The analogy to the Vietnam War can be extended even to the extent of the denial. It amuses me sometimes to hear people like myself decry the state of the public schools. We bemoan the lack of money, the decaying facilities, the absurd credentialism, the high foolishness of the school boards. We applaud the burgeoning reform movement. And everything we say is deeply, undeniably true. We can see every problem with the schools

Is this "one small example" enough to support his claim?

clearly except one: the fact that our decision to abandon the schools has helped create all the other problems. One small example: In the early 1980s, Massachusetts passed one of those tax cap measures, called Proposition 2 1/2, which has turned out to be a force for genuine evil in the public schools. Would Proposition 2 1/2 have passed had the middle class still had a stake in the schools? I wonder. I also wonder whether 20 years from now, in the next round of breast-beating memoirs, the exodus of

bias

the white middle class from the public schools will finally be seen

Oversimpli-fication–Do all parents have the same motives?

for what it was. Individually, every parent's rationale made impeccable sense—"I can't deprive my children of a decent education"—but collectively, it was a deeply destructive act.

The main reason the white middle class fled, of course, is race, or more precisely, the complicated admixture of race and class

Is this a valid assumption?

and good intentions gone awry. The fundamental good intention—which even today strikes one as both moral and

Why does he assume intent was "good" + "moral"? Is he right?

right—was to integrate the public classroom, and in so doing, to equalize the resources available to all school children. In Boston, this was done through enforced busing. In Washington, it was done through a series of judicial edicts that attempted to spread the good teachers and resources throughout the system. In other big city districts, judges weren't involved; school committees, seeing the handwriting on the wall, tried to do it themselves.

However moral the intent, the result almost always was the same. The white middle class left. The historic parental vigilance I mentioned earlier had had a lot to do with creating the two-tiered system—one in which schools attended by the kids of the white middle class had better teachers, better equipment, better everything than those attended by the kids of the poor. This did not happen because the white middle-class parents were racists, necessarily; it happened because they knew how to manipulate the system and were willing to do so on behalf of their kids. Their neighborhood schools became little havens of decent education, and they didn't much care what happened in the other public schools.

Interesting point—but is it true?

In retrospect, this behavior, though perfectly understandable, was tragically short-sighted. When the judicial fiats made those safe havens untenable, the white middle class quickly discovered what the poor had always known: There weren't enough good teachers, decent equipment, and so forth to go around. For that matter, there weren't even enough good students to go around; along with everything else, middle-class parents had to start worrying about whether their kids were going to be mugged in school.

Slanted language (over-emotional) Generalization

Slanted language (over-emotional)

Faced with the grim fact that their children's education was quickly deteriorating, middle-class parents essentially had two choices: They could stay and pour the energy that had once gone into improving the neighborhood school into improving the entire school system—a frightening task, to be sure. Or they could leave. Invariably, they chose the latter.

Either/or fallacy? Were there other choices?

Oversimplification? No exceptions?

And it wasn't just the white middle class that fled. The black middle class, and even the black poor who were especially ambitious for their children, were getting out as fast as they could too, though not to the suburbs. They headed mainly for the parochial schools, which subsequently became integration's great success story, even as the public schools became integration's great failure. (Joseph Nocera, "The Case Against Joe Nocera: How People Like Me Helped Ruin the Public Schools")

Exercise 8.1

Find an article that interests you in a newspaper or magazine (or on-line). Read it carefully, highlighting it as you read. When you have finished, annotate the article.

Checklist: Reading Texts

As you read a text, consider the following questions:

☐ Does the writer provide any information about his or her background? If so, how does this information affect your reading of the text?

(continued)

Reading texts (continued)

☐ Are there parallels between the writer's experiences and your own?

See Ch. 1

☐ What is the writer's **purpose**? How can you tell?

☐ What **audience** is the text aimed at? How can you tell?

☐ What is the text's most important idea? What support does the writer provide for that idea?

☐ What information can you learn from the text's introduction and conclusion?

See 3a

☐ What information can you learn from the **thesis statement** and topic sentences?

☐ What key words are repeated? What does this repetition tell you about the writer's purpose and emphasis?

☐ How would you characterize the writer's tone?

☐ Where do you agree with the writer? Where do you disagree?

☐ What, if anything, is not clear to you?

Chapter 9 | Writing Essay Exams

To write an essay examination, or even a paragraph-length answer, you must do more than memorize facts; you must see the relationships among them. In other words, you must **think critically** about your subject.

See Ch. 6

9a Planning an Essay Exam Answer

Because you are under time pressure during an exam, you may be tempted to skip the planning and revision stages of the writing process. But if you write in a frenzy and hand in your exam without a second glance, you are likely to produce a disorganized or even incoherent answer. With careful planning and editing, you can write an answer that demonstrates your understanding of the material.

(1) Review Your Material

Be sure you know beforehand the scope and format of the exam. How much of your text and class notes will be covered—the entire semester's work or only the material presented since the last test? Will you have to answer every question, or will you be able to choose among alternatives? Will the exam be composed entirely of fill-in, multiple-choice, or true/false questions, or will it call for sentence-, paragraph-, or essay-length answers? Will the exam test your ability to recall specific facts, or will it require you to demonstrate your understanding of the course material by drawing conclusions?

All exams challenge you to recall and express in writing what you already know—what you have read, what you have heard in class, what you have reviewed in your notes. Before you take any exam, then, you must study: reread your text and class notes, highlight key points, and perhaps outline particularly important sections of your notes.

Different kinds of exams, however, require different strategies. When you prepare for a short-answer exam, you may memorize facts without analyzing their relationship to one another or their relationship to a body of knowledge as a whole: the definition of *pointillism*, the date of Queen Victoria's death, or the formula for a quadratic equation, for example. When you prepare for an essay exam, however, you must do more than remember bits of information; you must also make connections among ideas.

When you are sure you know what to expect, see if you can anticipate the essay questions your instructor might ask. Try out likely questions on classmates, and see whether you can do some collaborative brainstorming to outline answers to possible questions. If you have time, you might even practice answering one or two in writing.

(2) Consider Your Audience and Purpose

The <u>audience</u> for an exam is the instructor who prepared it. As you read the questions, think about what your instructor has emphasized in class. Keep in mind that your <u>purpose</u> is to demonstrate that you understand the material, not to make clever remarks or introduce irrelevant information. Also, try to use the vocabulary of the particular academic discipline and to follow any discipline-specific stylistic conventions your instructor has discussed.

See
Ch. 1

(3) Read through the Entire Exam

Before you begin to write, read the questions carefully to determine your priorities and your strategy. First, be sure that your copy of the test is complete and that you understand exactly what each question requires. If you need clarification, ask your instructor or proctor for help. Then, plan carefully, deciding how much time you should devote to answering each question. Often, the point value of each question or the number of questions on the exam indicates how much time you should spend on each answer. If an essay question is worth fifty out of one hundred points, for example, you will probably have to spend at least half (and perhaps more) of your time planning, writing, and proofreading your answer.

Next, decide where to start. Responding first to questions whose answers you are sure of is usually a good strategy. This tactic ensures that you will not become bogged down in a question that baffles you, left with too little time to write a strong answer to a question that you understand well. Moreover, starting with the questions that you are sure of can help build your confidence.

(4) Read Each Question Carefully

To write an effective answer, you need to understand the question. As you read any essay question, you may find it helpful to underline key words and important terms.

Sociology: <u>Distinguish</u> among <u>Social Darwinism</u>, <u>instinct theory</u>, and <u>sociobiology</u>, giving <u>examples</u> of each.

Music: <u>Explain how</u> Milton <u>Babbitt</u> used the <u>computer</u> to expand <u>Schoenberg's twelve-tone</u> method.

Philosophy: <u>Define existentialism</u> and <u>identify three</u> influential existentialist <u>works</u>, explaining <u>why</u> they are important.

Look carefully at the wording of each question. If the question calls for a comparison and contrast of two styles of management, a description or analysis of one style, no matter how comprehensive, will not be acceptable. If the question asks for causes and effects, a discussion of causes alone will not do.

> ### Close-up: Key Words in Exam Questions
>
> Pay careful attention to the words used in exam questions.
>
> | | | |
> |---|---|---|
> | • explain | • clarify | • classify |
> | • compare | • relate | • identify |
> | • contrast | • justify | • illustrate |
> | • trace | • analyze | • define |
> | • evaluate | • interpret | • support |
> | • discuss | • describe | • summarize |

---

(5) Brainstorm to Find Ideas

See
2d

Once you think you understand the question, you need to <u>find something to say</u>. Begin by **brainstorming,** quickly listing all the relevant ideas you can remember. Then, identify the most important points on your list, and delete the others. A quick review of the exam question and your supporting ideas should lead you toward a workable thesis for your essay answer.

9b Shaping an Essay Exam Answer

Like an essay, an effective exam answer has a thesis-and-support structure.

(1) Stating a Thesis

Often, you can rephrase the exam question as a **thesis statement.** For example, the American history exam question "Give a detailed summary of the effects of the Great Depression on the United States, briefly discussing the major causes of the economic collapse" suggests the following thesis statement.

> **Effective Thesis Statement:** The Great Depression, caused by the American government's economic policies, had major political, economic, and social effects on the United States.

(2) Making an Informal Outline

Because time is limited, you should plan your answer before you write it. Therefore, once you have decided on a suitable thesis, you should make an informal outline that lists your major points. Once you have completed your outline, check it against the exam question to make certain it covers everything the question calls for—and *only* what the question calls for.

9c Writing and Revising an Essay Exam Answer

Referring to your outline, you can now begin to draft your answer. Don't bother crafting an elaborate or unusual **introduction;** your time is precious, and so is your reader's. A simple statement of your thesis that summarizes your answer is your best introductory strategy: this approach is efficient, and it reminds you to address the question directly.

To develop the **body** of the essay, follow your outline point by point, using clear topic sentences and transitions to indicate your progression and to help your instructor see that you are answering the question in full. Such signals, along with parallel sentence structure and repeated key words, make your answer easy to follow.

The most effective **conclusion** for an essay examination is a clear, simple restatement of the thesis or a summary of the essay's main points.

Although essay answers should be complete and detailed, they should not contain irrelevant material. Every unnecessary fact or opinion increases your chance of error, so don't repeat yourself or volunteer unrequested information, and don't express your own feelings or opinions unless such information is specifically asked for.

In addition, be sure to support all your general statements with specific examples.

Finally, be sure to leave enough time to revise what you have written. If you suddenly remember something you want to add, you can insert a few additional words with a caret ($_\wedge$). Neatly insert a longer addition at the end of your answer, box it, and label it so your instructor will know where it belongs.

ESL Tip

Because of time pressure, it is difficult to write in-class essay exam answers that are as polished as your out-of-class writing. You should do your best to convey your ideas as clearly as you can, but keep in mind that instructors are usually more concerned with the accuracy of the content of your answers than with your writing style. Therefore, instead of wasting time searching for the "perfect" words or phrases, use words and grammatical constructions that are familiar to you. You can use any remaining time to check your grammar and mechanics.

In the essay answer that appears below, notice how the student restates the question in her thesis statement and keeps the question in focus by repeating key words like *cause, effect, result, response,* and *impact.*

Effective Essay Exam Answer

Question: Give a detailed summary of the effects of the Great Depression on the United States, briefly discussing the major causes of the economic collapse.

Introduction—
thesis
statement
rephrases
exam question

The Great Depression, caused by the American government's economic policies, had major political, economic, and social effects on the United States.

Policies
leading to
Depression
(¶ 2 summa-
rizes causes)

The Depression was precipitated by the stock market crash of October 1929, but its actual causes were more subtle: they lay in the US government's economic policies. First, personal income was not well distributed. Although production rose during the 1920s, the farmers and other workers got too little of the profits; instead, a disproportionate amount of income went to the richest 5 percent of the population. The tax policies at this time made inequalities in income even worse. A good deal of income also went into development of new manufacturing plants. This expansion stimulated the economy but encouraged the production of more goods than consumers could purchase. Finally, during the economic boom of the 1920s, the government did not attempt to limit speculation or impose regulations on the securities market; it also did little to help build up farmers' buying power. Even after the crash began, the government made mistakes: instead of trying to address the country's deflationary economy, the government focused on keeping the budget balanced and making sure the United States adhered to the gold standard.

The Depression, devastating to millions of individuals, had a tremendous impact on the nation as a whole. Its political, economic, and social consequences were great.

Between October 1929 and Roosevelt's inauguration on March 4, 1932, the economic situation grew worse. Businesses were going bankrupt, banks were failing, and stock prices were falling. Farm prices fell drastically, and hungry farmers were forced to burn their corn to heat their homes. There was massive unemployment, with millions of workers jobless and humiliated, losing skills and self-respect. President Hoover's Reconstruction Finance Corporation made loans available to banks, railroads, and businesses, but Hoover thought state and local funds (not the federal government) should finance public works programs and relief. Confidence in the president declined as the country's economic situation worsened.

One result of the Depression was the election of Franklin Delano Roosevelt. By the time of his inauguration, most American banks had closed, thirteen

Transition from causes to effects

Early effects (¶s 4–8 summarize important results in chronological order)

Additional effects: Roosevelt's emergency measures

million workers were unemployed, and millions of
farmers were threatened by foreclosure. Roosevelt's
response was immediate: two days after he took office,
he closed all the remaining banks and took steps to
support the stronger ones with loans and to prevent the
weaker ones from reopening. During the first hundred
days of his administration, he kept Congress in special
session. Under his leadership, Congress enacted
emergency measures designed to provide "Relief,
Recovery, and Reform."

Additional
effects:
Roosevelt's
reform
measures
In response to the problems caused by the
Depression, Roosevelt set up agencies to reform some of
the conditions that had helped to cause the Depression
in the first place. The Tennessee Valley Authority,
created in May 1933, was one of these. Its purposes
were to control floods by building new dams and
improving old ones and to provide cheap, plentiful
electricity. The TVA improved the standard of living of
area farmers and drove down the price of power all over
the country. The Agricultural Adjustment
Administration, created the same month as the TVA,
provided for taxes on basic commodities, with the tax
revenues used to subsidize farmers to produce less.
This reform measure caused prices to rise.

Additional
effects: NIRA,
other laws,
and so on
Another response to the problems of the Depression
was the National Industrial Recovery Act. This act
established the National Recovery Administration, an
agency that set minimum wages and maximum hours for
workers and set limits on production and prices. Other
laws passed by Congress between 1935 and 1940
strengthened federal regulation of power, interstate
commerce, and air traffic. Roosevelt also changed the
federal tax structure to redistribute American income.

One of the most important results of the Depression was the Social Security Act of 1935, which established unemployment insurance and provided financial aid for the blind and disabled and for dependent children and their mothers. The Works Progress Administration (WPA) gave jobs to over two million workers, who built public buildings, roads, streets, bridges, and sewers. The WPA also employed artists, musicians, actors, and writers. The Public Works Administration (PWA) cleared slums and created public housing. In the National Labor Relations Act (1935), workers received a guarantee of government protection for their unions against unfair labor practices by management.

Additional effects: Social Security, WPA, and so on

As a result of the economic collapse known as the Great Depression, Americans saw their government take responsibility for providing immediate relief, for helping the economy recover, and for taking steps to ensure that the situation would not be repeated. The economic, political, and social impact of the laws passed during the 1930s is still with us, helping to keep our government and our economy stable.

Conclusion— restatement of thesis

Notice that in her answer the student does not include any irrelevant material: she does not, for example, describe the conditions of people's lives in detail, blame anyone in particular, discuss the president's friends and enemies, or consider parallel events in other countries. She covers only what the question asks for. Notice, too, how topic sentences ("One result of the Depression . . ."; "In response to the problems caused by the Depression . . ."; "One of the most important results of the Depression . . .") keep the primary purpose of the discussion in focus and guide her instructor through the essay.

Work is often a part of the college experience, with many students having part-time jobs, internships, work-study positions, or cooperative education experiences. The skills that you develop in these activities frequently are transferable to the employment that you will have after you graduate. For this reason, it is important that you learn how to write for the workplace.

10a Writing Letters of Application

Letters of application should be short and focused. When you apply for employment, your primary objective is to obtain an interview. The **letter of application** summarizes your qualifications for a specific position.

Begin your letter of application by identifying the job you are applying for and stating where you heard about it—in a newspaper, in a professional journal, on a Web site, or from your school's job placement service, for example. Be sure to include the date of the advertisement and the exact title of the position. End your introduction with a statement that expresses your ability to do the job.

In the body of your letter, provide the information that will convince your reader of your qualifications—for example, relevant courses you have taken and pertinent job experience. Be sure to address any specific points mentioned in the advertisement. Above all, emphasize your strengths, and explain how they relate to the specific job for which you are applying.

Conclude by saying that you have enclosed your résumé and stating that you are available for an interview, noting any dates on which you will not be available. (Be sure to include your phone number and your email address.)

NOTE: After you have been interviewed, you should send a letter to the person (or persons) who interviewed you. First, thank your interviewer for taking the time to see you. Then, briefly summarize your qualifications and your interest in the position. Because so few applicants write follow-up letters, such letters can have a very positive effect on those who receive them.

Sample Letter of Application

Heading	246 Hillside Drive Urbana, IL 61801 Kr237@metropolis.105.com
	October 20, 2003
Inside address	Mr. Maurice Snyder, Personnel Director Guilford, Fox, and Morris 22 Hamilton Street Urbana, IL 61822
Salutation	Dear Mr. Snyder:

My college advisor, Dr. Raymond Walsh, has told me that you are interested in hiring a part-time accounting assistant. I believe that my academic background and my work experience qualify me for this position.

Body

I am presently a junior accounting major at the University of Illinois. During the past year, I have taken courses in taxation, trusts, and business law. I am also proficient in <u>Lotus</u> and <u>ClarisWorks</u>. Last spring, I gained practical accounting experience by working in our department's tax clinic.

Double- ⟶
space

After I graduate, I hope to get a master's degree in taxation and then return to the Urbana area. I believe that my experience in taxation as well as my familiarity with the local business community would enable me to

Single- ⟶
space

contribute to your firm.

I have enclosed a résumé for your examination. I will be available for an interview any time after midterm examinations, which end October 25. I look forward to hearing from you.

Complimentary
close   Sincerely yours,

Written
signature   *Sandra Kraft*
Typed
signature   Sandra Kraft
               Enc.: Résumé

Exercise 10.1

Look through the employment advertisements in your local newspaper or in the files of your college placement service. Choose one job, and write a letter of application in which you summarize your achievements and discuss your qualifications for the position.

10b Designing Print Résumés

A résumé lists relevant information about your education, your job experience, your goals, and your personal interests.

There is no single correct format for a résumé. You will probably want to arrange your résumé in **chronological order** (see page 129), listing your education and work experience in sequence (beginning with the most recent), but you may also use **emphatic order** beginning with the material that will be of most interest to an employer (for example, important skills). Whatever a résumé's arrangement, it should be brief—one page is usually sufficient for an undergraduate—easy to read, clear and emphatic, logically organized, and free of errors.

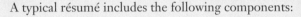

Close-up: Components of a Résumé

A typical résumé includes the following components:

- The **heading** includes your name, school address, home address, telephone number, and email address.
- A statement of your **career objective** (optional), placed at the top of the page, identifies your professional goals.
- The **education section** includes the schools you have attended, starting with the most recent one and moving back in time. (After graduation from college, do not list your high school unless you have a compelling reason to do so—for instance, if it is nationally recognized for its academic standards or it has an active alumni network in your field.)
- The **summary of work experience** generally starts with your most recent job and moves backward in time.
- The **background** or **interests section** lists your most important (or most relevant) special interest and community activities.
- The **honors section** lists academic achievements and awards.
- The **references section** lists the full names and addresses of at least three references. If your résumé is already one full page long, a line saying that your references will be sent upon request is sufficient.

Sample Résumé: Chronological Order

KAREN L. OLSON

SCHOOL
3812 Hamilton St. Apt. 18
Philadelphia, PA 19104
215-382-0831
olsont@dunm.ocs.drexel.edu

HOME
110 Ascot Ct.
Harmony, PA 16037
412-452-2944

EDUCATION

DREXEL UNIVERSITY, Philadelphia, PA 19104
Bachelor of Science in Graphic Design
Anticipated Graduation: June 2004
Cumulative Grade Point Average: 3.2 on a 4.0 scale

COMPUTER SKILLS AND COURSEWORK

HARDWARE
Familiar with both Macintosh and PC systems
SOFTWARE
Adobe *Illustrator*, *Photoshop*, and *Type Align*; *QuarkXPress*; *CorelDRAW*; *Micrografx Designer*
COURSES
Corporate Identity, Environmental Graphics, Typography, Photography, Painting and Printmaking, Sculpture, Computer Imaging, Art History

EMPLOYMENT EXPERIENCE

THE TRIANGLE, Drexel University, Philadelphia, PA 19104
January 2001–present
Graphics Editor. Design all display advertisements submitted to Drexel's student newspaper.

UNISYS CORPORATION, Blue Bell, PA 19124
June–September 2001, Cooperative Education
Graphic Designer. Designed interior pages as well as covers for target marketing brochures. Created various logos and spot art designed for use on interoffice memos and departmental publications.

CHARMING SHOPPES, INC, Bensalem, PA 19020
June-December 2000, Cooperative Education
Graphic Designer/Fashion Illustrator. Created graphics for future placement on garments. Did some textile designing. Drew flat illustrations of garments to scale in computer. Prepared presentation boards.

DESIGN AND IMAGING STUDIO, Drexel University, Philadelphia, PA 19104
October 1999–June 2001
Monitor. Supervised computer activity in studio. Answered telephone. Assisted other graphic design students in using computer programs.

ACTIVITIES AND AWARDS

The Triangle, Graphics Editor: 2000–present
Kappa Omicron Nu Honor Society, vice president: 1999–present
Dean's List: spring 1998, fall and winter 1999
Graphics Group, vice president: 1999–present

REFERENCES AND PORTFOLIO

Available upon request.

Close-up: Résumé Style

Use strong action verbs to describe your duties, responsibilities, and accomplishments.

accomplished	achieved	supervised
communicated	collaborated	instructed
completed	implemented	proposed
performed	organized	trained

NOTE: Use past tense for past positions and present tense for current positions.

10c Designing Electronic Résumés

Presently, the majority of résumés are still submitted on paper, but electronic résumés—scannable and Web-based—are gaining in popularity, and many experts believe the paper résumé will soon be a thing of the past.

(1) Scannable Résumés

Many employers request scannable résumés that they can download into a database for future reference. If you have to prepare such a résumé, keep in mind that scanners will not pick up columns, bullets, or italics and that shaded or colored paper will make your résumé difficult to scan.

Whereas in a print résumé you use specific action verbs (*edited company newsletter*) to describe your accomplishments, in a scannable résumé you also use key nouns (*editor*) that can be entered into a company database. These words will help employers find your résumé when they carry out a keyword search for applicants with certain skills. To facilitate a keyword search, applicants often include a Keyword section on their résumé. For example, if you wanted to emphasize your computer skills, you would include keywords such as *WordPerfect*, *FileMaker Pro*, and *PowerPoint*.

(2) Web-Based Résumés

See
Ch. 12

It is becoming common to have a version of your résumé posted on a personal Web site. Usually, a Web-based résumé is an alternative to a print résumé that you have mailed or a scannable version that you have submitted to a database or as an email attachment. Figure 10.1 shows a Web-based version of a student's résumé. The student has also included on her Web site a PDF (portable document format) version of her résumé that is available for downloading and printing (see Figure 10.2).

Figure 10.1 Sample student Web-based résumé.

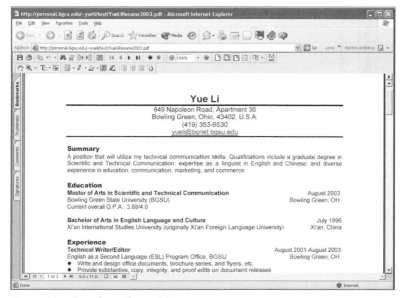

Figure 10.2 Sample student PDF résumé.

See
1a

Exercise 10.2

Prepare two versions of your résumé—one print and the other scannable—that you could include with the letter of application you wrote for Exercise 1. How are these two résumés alike? How are they different?

10d Writing Memos

Memos communicate information within an organization. A memo can be short or long, depending on its <u>purpose</u>.

Begin your memo with a purpose statement that presents your reason for writing it. Follow this statement with a background section that gives readers the information they will need to understand the current situation. Then, in the body of your memo, present your support, the detailed information that supports the main point of your memo. If your memo is short, use bulleted or numbered lists to emphasize information. If it is long—more than two or three paragraphs—use headings to designate the various sections of the memo (*Summary, Background, Benefits,* and so on). End your memo with a statement of your conclusions and recommendations.

Sample Memo

TO: Ina Ellen, Senior Counselor   Opening
FROM: Kim Williams, Student Tutor Supervisor   component
SUBJECT: Construction of a Tutoring Center
DATE: November 10, 2003

Purpose
This memo proposes the establishment of a tutoring center in   statement
the Office of Student Affairs.

BACKGROUND
Under the present system, tutors must work with students at a
number of facilities scattered across the university campus. As
a result, tutors waste a lot of time running from one facility to another and are often late for appointments.

NEW FACILITY   Body
I propose that we establish a tutoring facility adjacent to the Office of Student Affairs. The two empty classrooms next to the
office, presently used for storage of office furniture, would be
ideal for this use. We could furnish these offices with the desks
and file cabinets already stored in these rooms.

BENEFITS
The benefits of this facility would be the centralizing of the tutoring services and the proximity of the facility to the Office of
Student Affairs. The tutoring facility could also use the secretar-
ial services of the Office of Student Affairs.

Conclusion
RECOMMENDATIONS
To implement this project we would need to do the following:
   1. Clean up and paint rooms 331 and 333
   2. Use folding partitions to divide each room into five
      single-desk offices
   3. Use stored office equipment to furnish the center

I am certain these changes would do much to improve the tutoring service. I look forward to discussing this matter with you
in more detail.

10e Writing Emails

In many workplaces, virtually all internal (and some external) communications are transmitted as email. Although personal email tends to be quite informal, business email should observe the conventions of standard written communication.

Checklist: Writing Emails

The following guidelines can help you communicate effectively in an electronic environment:

☐ Write in complete sentences. Avoid the slang, imprecise diction, and abbreviations that are commonplace in personal email.
☐ Use an appropriate tone. Address readers with respect, just as you would in a standard business letter.
☐ Include a subject line that clearly identifies your content. If your subject line is vague, your email may be deleted without being read.
☐ Make your message as short as possible. Because most emails are read on the screen, long discussions are difficult to follow.
☐ Use short paragraphs, and leave an extra space between paragraphs.
☐ Use lists and internal headings to make your message easier to read and understand. (Keep in mind, however, that your recipient may not be able to view certain formatting elements, such as boldface, italics, and indentation.)
☐ Take the time to edit your email, and delete excess words and phrases.
☐ Proofread carefully before sending your email. Look for errors in grammar, spelling, and punctuation.
☐ Make sure that your list of recipients is accurate and that you do not send your email to unintended recipients.
☐ Do not send your email until you are absolutely certain your message says exactly what you want it to say.
☐ Do not forward an email unless you have the permission of the sender.
☐ Watch what you write. Always remember that email written at work is the property of the employer, who has the legal right to access it, even without your permission.

Chapter 11 | Designing Effective Documents

The term **document design** denotes the principles that help you determine how to design a piece of written work—a research paper, report, or Web page, for example—so that it communicates your ideas clearly and effectively. Although formatting conventions—for example, how tables and charts are constructed and how information is arranged on a title page—may differ from discipline to discipline, all well-designed documents share the same general characteristics: an effective format, clear headings, useful lists, and helpful visuals.

11a Creating an Effective Visual Format

An effective document contains visual cues that help readers find, read, and interpret information on a page. For example, wide margins can give a page a balanced, uncluttered appearance; white space can break up a long discussion; and distinctive type size and typeface can make a word or phrase stand out on a page.

(1) Margins

Margins frame a page and keep it from looking overcrowded. Because long lines of text can overwhelm readers and make a document difficult to read, a page should have margins of at least one inch all around. If the material you are writing about is highly technical or unusually difficult, use wider margins (one and a half inches).

Except for documents such as flyers and brochures, where you might want to isolate blocks of text for emphasis, you should **justify** (uniformly align, except for paragraph indentations) the left-hand margin. You can either leave a ragged edge on the right, or you can justify your text so all the words are aligned evenly along the right margin. (A ragged edge is often preferable because it varies the visual landscape of your text, making it easier to read.)

(2) White Space

White space is the area of a page that is intentionally left blank. Used effectively, white space can isolate material and thereby focus a reader's attention on it. You can use white space around a block of text—a paragraph or a section, for example—or around visuals such as charts, graphs, and photographs. White space can eliminate clutter, break a discussion into manageable components, and help readers process information more easily.

(3) Color

While white space is important in breaking up material on the page, **color** (when used in moderation) can help to emphasize and clarify information while making it visually appealing. In addition to using color to emphasize information, you can use it to distinguish certain types of information—for example, titles can be one color and subheadings can be another, complementary color. You can also use color to differentiate the segments of a chart or the bars on a graph. Remember, however, that too many colors can confuse readers and detract from your visual emphasis. Many software applications, including *Microsoft Word* and *PowerPoint*, contain design templates that make it easy for you to choose a color scheme or to create your own.

(4) Typeface and Type Size

Your computer gives you a wide variety of typefaces and type sizes (measured in **points**) from which to choose. **Typefaces** are distinctively designed sets of letters, numbers, and punctuation marks. The typeface you choose should be suitable for your purpose and audience. In your academic writing, avoid fancy or elaborate typefaces— *Script* or **old English**, for example—that call attention to themselves and distract readers. Instead, select a typeface that is simple and direct—Courier, Times New Roman, or Arial, for example. In nonacademic documents—such as Web pages and flyers—decorative typefaces may be used to emphasize a point or attract a reader's attention.

You also have a wide variety of **type sizes** available to you. For most of your academic papers, you will use a 10- or 12-point type (headings will sometimes be larger). Documents such as advertisements, brochures, and Web pages, however, may use a variety of type sizes. (Keep in mind that point size alone is not a reliable guide for size. For instance, 12-point type in **Chicago** is much larger than 12-point type in Courier or Arial Condensed Light.)

(5) Line Spacing

Line spacing refers to the amount of space between the lines of a document. If the lines are too far apart, the text will seem to lack cohesion; if the lines are too close together, the text will appear crowded and be difficult to read. The type of writing you do may determine line spacing: the paragraphs of business letters, memos, and some reports are usually single-spaced and separated by a double space, but the paragraphs of academic papers are usually double-spaced.

11b Using Headings

Used effectively, headings act as signals that help readers process information, and they also break up a text, making it inviting and easy to read. Different academic disciplines have different requirements concerning headings. For this reason, you should consult the appropriate style manual before inserting headings in a paper.

Headings perform three functions in a document:

- *Headings tell readers that a new idea is being introduced.* In this way, headings tell readers what to expect in a section before they actually read it.
- *Headings emphasize key ideas.* By isolating an idea from the text around it, headings help readers identify important information.
- *Headings indicate how information is organized in a text.* Headings use various typefaces and type sizes (as well as indentation) to indicate the relative importance of ideas. For example, the most important information in a text will be set off as first-level headings and have the same typeface and type size. The next most important information will be set off as second-level headings, also with the same typeface and type size.

(1) Number of Headings

The number of headings you use depends on the document. A long, complicated document will need more headings than a shorter, less complicated one. Keep in mind that too few headings may not be of much use, but too many headings will make your document look like an outline.

(2) Phrasing

Headings should be brief, informative, and to the point. They can be single words—*Summary* or *Introduction*, for example—or they can be phrases (always stated in <u>parallel</u> terms): *Traditional Family Patterns, Alternate Family Patterns, Modern Family Patterns.* Finally, headings can be questions (*How Do You Choose a Major?*) or statements (*Choose Your Major Carefully*).

See 18a

(3) Indentation

Indenting is one way of distinguishing one level of heading from another. The more important a heading is, the closer it is to the left-hand margin: first-level headings are justified left, second-level headings are indented five spaces, and third-level headings are indented another two or three spaces. Headings and subheadings may also be *centered*, placed *flush left*, or *run into the text*.

(4) Typographical Emphasis

You can emphasize important words in headings by using **boldface,** *italics*, or ALL CAPITAL LETTERS. Used in moderation, these distinctive typefaces make a text easier to read. Used excessively, however, they slow readers down.

(5) Consistency

Headings at the same level should have the same format—the same typeface, type size, spacing, and color. In addition, if one first-level heading is boldfaced and centered, all other first-level headings must be boldfaced and centered. Using consistent patterns reinforces the connection between content and ideas and makes a document easier to understand.

NOTE: Never separate a heading from the text that goes with it: if a heading is at the bottom of one page and the text that goes with it is on the next page, move the heading onto the next page so readers can see the heading and the text together.

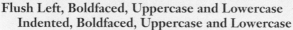

Close-up: Sample Heading Formats

Flush Left, Boldfaced, Uppercase and Lowercase
   Indented, Boldfaced, Uppercase and Lowercase
      Indented, italicized, lowercase; run into the text at the beginning of a paragraph; ends with a period.

Or

Centered, Boldfaced, Uppercase and Lowercase
<u>Flush Left, Underlined, Uppercase and Lowercase</u>
   <u>Indented, underlined, lowercase; run into the text at the beginning of a paragraph; ends with a period.</u>

Or

ALL CAPITAL LETTERS, CENTERED

11c Constructing Lists

By breaking long discussions into a series of key ideas, a list makes information easier to understand. By isolating individual pieces of information this way and by providing visual cues (such as bullets or numbers), a list directs readers to important information on a page.

Checklist: Constructing Effective Lists

When constructing lists, you should follow these guidelines.

☐ **Indent each item.** Each item on a list should be indented so that it stands out from the text around it.

☐ **Set off items with numbers or bullets.** Use **bullets** when items are not organized according to any particular sequence or priority (the members of a club, for example). Use **numbers** when you want to indicate that items are organized according to a sequence (the steps in a process, for example) or priority (the things a company should do to decrease spending, for example).

☐ **Introduce a list with a complete sentence.** Do not simply drop a list into a document; introduce it with a complete sentence (followed by a colon) that tells readers what the list contains and why you are including it in your discussion.

☐ **Use parallel structure.** Lists are easiest to read when all items are parallel and about the same length.

A number of factors can cause high unemployment:

• a decrease in consumer spending
• a decrease in factory orders
• a decrease in factory output

☐ **Punctuate correctly.** If the items on a list are fragments (as in the previous example), begin each item with a lowercase letter, and do not end it with a period. However, if the items on a list are complete sentences (as in the example below), begin each item with a capital letter and end it with a period.

Here are the three steps we must take to reduce our spending:

1. We must cut our workforce by 10 percent.
2. We must use less-expensive vendors.
3. We must decrease overtime payments.

☐ **Don't overuse lists.** Too many lists will undercut a document's effectiveness by making it seem cluttered. In addition, a document that contains one list after another will give readers the impression that you are simply listing points instead of discussing them.

Figure 11.1 on page 140 shows a page from a student's report that incorporates some of the effective design elements discussed in 11a–c. Notice that the use of different typefaces and type sizes contributes to the document's overall readability.

Different heading formats distinguish levels of importance

Single-spaced paragraphs separated by double space

White space breaks up text

Box isolates quotation

Horizontal rules divide sections

Justified margins contribute to a clean look

Numbered list identifies three subsections of report

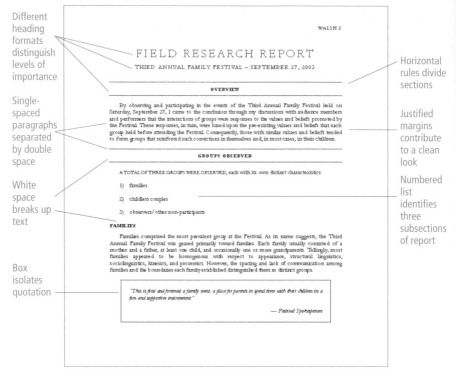

Figure 11.1 A well-designed page from a student's report.

11d Using Visuals

Visuals, such as tables, graphs, diagrams, and photographs, can help you convey complex ideas that are difficult to communicate with words and can also help you attract readers' attention.

You can create your own tables and graphs by using applications in software packages like *Excel, Lotus,* or *Word.* In addition, many stand-alone graphics software packages enable you to create complex charts, tables, and graphs that contain three-dimensional effects. You can also photocopy or scan diagrams and photographs from a print source or download them from the Internet or from CD-ROMs or DVDs. Remember, however, that if you use a visual from a source, you must use appropriate documentation.

(1) Tables

Tables present data in a condensed, visual format—arranged in rows and columns. Tables may contain numerical data, text, or a combination of the two. When you plan your table, make sure you include only the data that you will need; discard information that is too detailed or difficult to understand. Keep in mind that tables can distract readers, so include only those necessary to support your discussion. (The table in Figure 11.2 reports the student writer's original research and therefore needs no documentation.)

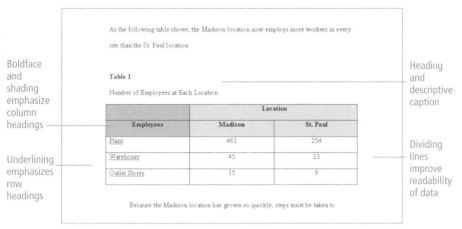

Boldface and shading emphasize column headings

Underlining emphasizes row headings

Heading and descriptive caption

Dividing lines improve readability of data

As the following table shows, the Madison location now employs more workers in every site than the St. Paul location

Table 1

Number of Employees at Each Location

Employees	Location	
	Madison	St. Paul
Plant	461	254
Warehouse	45	23
Outlet Stores	15	9

Because the Madison location has grown so quickly, steps must be taken to

Figure 11.2 Sample table from a student paper.

(2) Graphs

Like tables, graphs present data in visual form. Whereas tables may present specific numerical data, graphs convey the general pattern or trend that the data suggest. Because graphs tend to be more general (and therefore less accurate) than tables, they are frequently accompanied by tables. Figure 11.3 on page 142 is an example of a bar graph showing data from a source.

(3) Diagrams

A diagram calls readers' attention to specific details of a mechanism or object. Diagrams are often used in scientific and technical writing to clarify concepts that are difficult to explain in words. Figure 11.4 on page 142, which illustrates the sections of an orchestra, serves a similar purpose in a music education paper.

(4) Photographs

Photographs enable you to show exactly what something or someone looks like—an animal in its natural habitat, a work of fine art, or

the demographics of college students is changing. According to a 2002 US Department of

Education report entitled Nontraditional Undergraduates, the percentage of students who

could be classified as "nontraditional" has increased over the last decade (see fig. 1).

Data

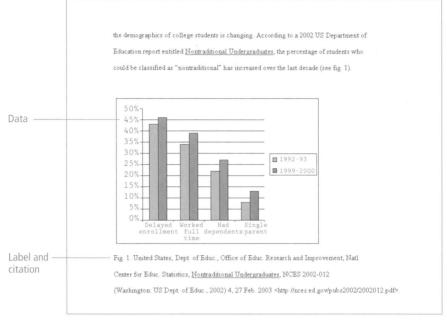

Label and
citation

Fig. 1. United States, Dept. of Educ., Office of Educ. Research and Improvement, Natl.

Center for Educ. Statistics, Nontraditional Undergraduates, NCES 2002-012

(Washington: US Dept. of Educ., 2002) 4, 27 Feb. 2003 <http://nces.ed.gov/pubs2002/2002012.pdf>.

Figure 11.3 Sample graph from a student paper.

The sections of an orchestra are arranged precisely to allow for a powerful and cohesive

performance. Fig. 1 illustrates the placement of individual sections of an orchestra.

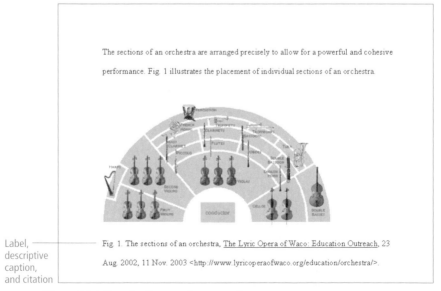

Label,
descriptive
caption,
and citation

Fig. 1. The sections of an orchestra, The Lyric Opera of Waco: Education Outreach, 23

Aug. 2002, 11 Nov. 2003 <http://www.lyricoperaofwaco.org/education/orchestra/>.

Figure 11.4 Sample diagram from a student paper.

an actor in costume, for example. Although computer technology that enables you to paste photographs directly into a text is widely available, you should use it with restraint. Not every photograph will support or enhance your written text; in fact, an irrelevant photograph will distract readers. The photograph of a wooded trail in Figure 11.5 illustrates the student writer's description.

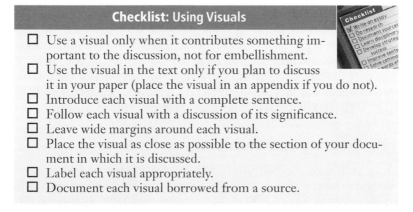

Photo sized and placed appropriately within text with consistent white space above and below

travelers are well advised to be prepared, to always carry water and dress for the conditions. Loose fitting, lightweight wicking material covering all exposed skin is necessary in summer, and layers of warm clothing are needed for cold weather outings. Hats and sunscreen are always a good idea no matter what the temperature, although most of the trails are quite shady with huge oak trees. Figure 1 shows how nice and shady the trail can be.

Reference to photo provides context

Figure 1   Greenbelt Trail in springtime (author photo)

Label and descriptive caption

Figure 11.5 Sample photograph from a student paper.

Checklist: Using Visuals

☐ Use a visual only when it contributes something important to the discussion, not for embellishment.
☐ Use the visual in the text only if you plan to discuss it in your paper (place the visual in an appendix if you do not).
☐ Introduce each visual with a complete sentence.
☐ Follow each visual with a discussion of its significance.
☐ Leave wide margins around each visual.
☐ Place the visual as close as possible to the section of your document in which it is discussed.
☐ Label each visual appropriately.
☐ Document each visual borrowed from a source.

Chapter 12 Designing Web Sites

At some point in your college career, you may be asked to create a Web page or even a full Web site—for example, as a course assignment or as a way of marketing your job skills. Like other documents, Web pages follow the conventions of <u>document design</u>. Because so much of the content is meant to be read directly online, your choices of text, color, and navigation strategy are especially important.

See Ch. 11

Close-up: Components of a Web Page

A **personal home page** usually contains information about how to contact the author, along with a brief biography. A home page can also be the first page of a **Web site**, a group of related Web pages about a personal, professional, or academic topic. In this case, the home page contains **links**—highlighted words, images, or URLs—that allow users to move from one page to another or to another Web site.

12a Planning Your Web Site

See Ch. 1

When you plan your Web site, you should consider your <u>purpose</u>, <u>audience</u>, and tone, just as you would when planning a print document. In addition, of course, you should consider what content to include. Finally, just as an essay or research paper may have a set page limit, your own Web site may have size and file-type limitations.

Before you create your Web site, you should consider how your Web pages will relate to one another. Beginning with the home page, users will navigate from one part of your Web site to another. For this reason, your home page should provide an overview of your site and give users a clear sense of the material the site contains.

You should start planning your Web site by considering how its pages will be organized. One way to do this is to list the information on your Web site under headings or categories, just as you would if you were making an <u>informal outline</u>. Later on, you can use this list to create a **site map** (see Figure 12.1), a feature that helps users of large Web sites locate and link to relevant content.

See 3d

12b Creating Your Web Site

Once you have planned your Web site, you will need to select a method for creating the site itself. Essentially, there are three ways to create pages within your Web site: you can use Web authoring software packages; you can use Web tools within your word-processing

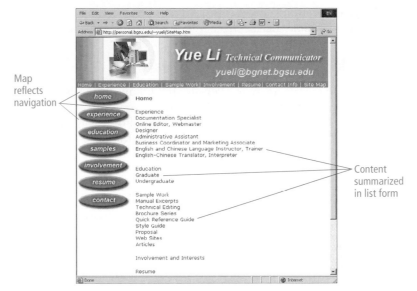

Map reflects navigation

Content summarized in list form

Figure 12.1 Sample site map for a student's Web portfolio.

program; or you can create a page from scratch by using **HTML** (hypertext markup language), the programming language used to convert standard documents into World Wide Web hypertext documents.

- **Web Authoring Packages** Many Web authoring packages—for example, *Macromedia Dreamweaver* and *Microsoft FrontPage*—will automatically translate your pages into HTML. The advantage of an authoring package is that you do not have to have a working knowledge of HTML in order to develop your site. Some of these packages even make certain interactive functions—such as navigation bars, forms, or media effects—easier to implement.
- **Web Tools within Your Word-Processing Program** Most word processors have an option under the File menu or the Save menu that automatically saves word-processed documents as HTML documents suitable for Web delivery. Although this option is appropriate for a single document, such as your résumé, it does not have the features you will need to create an entire Web site. For example, you cannot insert navigation buttons or include columns and tables that will transfer to the Web.
- **Text Editors that Allow Coding "By Hand"** If you have advanced knowledge of HTML, this is a good option. Text editors, including *Simple Text* for the Mac and *Notepad* for the PC, enable you to control all elements of your Web site design. The major

drawback of using a text editor is that HTML coding can be confusing, and some special effects require complicated codes.

12c Selecting and Inserting Visuals

You can find visuals for your Web site by looking for other sites on the Web that make visuals available for others to use. You can usually find them with your search engine—*Google*, for example, has an image directory at http://images.google.com that you can search. You can also create and upload visuals yourself by using either a digital camera or a scanner. Once a visual has been created and saved electronically, you can use a graphics package such as *Adobe Photoshop* to adjust the visual's size, contrast, or color scheme; to crop the image; or to add text. Other visual options include creating your own banners and backgrounds with special colors and textures.

Once you have edited a visual, you must save it in one of two standard formats for the Web: JPG (for photographic images containing a wide range of colors) or GIF (for graphic files with fewer colors, line art, and text).

12d Planning Navigation

Web sites use a number of design features to make navigation easier. As you create the pages of your Web site, you should consider the following options for helping readers navigate your site.

- **Splash Pages**   Many Web designers include a splash page on their Web sites. A splash page is usually more visual than textual, usually containing only limited background information and navigation features, such as links to the site's content. Its purpose is to create interest and draw users into the site. (A more detailed overview of the site appears on another page that serves as the true home page.)
- **Navigation Text, Buttons, and Bars**   Navigation text, buttons, bars, or other graphic icons, such as arrows or pictures, enable readers to move from one page of a Web site to another (see Figure 12.2).
- **Anchors**   Anchors (or **relative links**) enable readers to jump from one part of a Web page to another (see Figure 12.2).
- **Horizontal Rules**   Horizontal rules divide sections and parts of a page (see Figure 12.2). You can use colored or patterned rules that coordinate with the color scheme of the Web site.
- **Chunking or Clustering**   Chunking or clustering means placing related items of text close to one another (see Figure 12.2). This technique cuts down on scrolling and helps users read con-

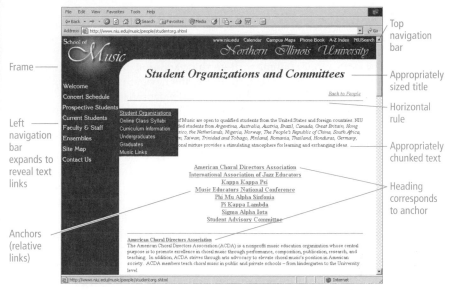

Figure 12.2 Sample Web page with navigation links, anchors, and frames.

tent easily on the screen. By surrounding clusters of information with white space, you can create separate "screens" of content.

- **Frames**   Like tables, frames organize text and graphics. Unlike tables, however, frames enable you to divide a single Web page into multiple windows (see Figure 12.2).

- **Text Formatting Features**   Like printed texts, Web texts follow the principles of <u>document design</u>, using design elements such as single-spaced text, headings, subheadings, and bulleted lists, as well as boldface and italics to emphasize points. (Underlining is usually not used in Web texts because readers might mistake underlined text for a hyperlink.)

See Ch. 11

Checklist: Designing Effective Web Pages

- ☐ Use the same type size and typeface for equivalent information. Keep headings and body text consistent throughout your site.
- ☐ Select images that reinforce your theme or argument. Do not let style substitute for content.
- ☐ Use text, buttons, and bars to facilitate navigation.
- ☐ Use special multimedia effects in moderation. Animation, video, and audio are distracting if they are not consistent with your site's purpose.

(continued)

Designing effective Web pages (continued)

☐ Indicate what players, plug-ins, and other extensions are required for accessing multimedia files. Give readers the option of viewing your content without these additional elements.

☐ Avoid pages so full of text, graphics, and navigation aids that they make reading difficult and increase loading time.

☐ For best visibility, use text and background colors that contrast well. Use textured or patterned backgrounds only if they do not obscure text.

☐ Provide your email address so you can receive feedback from users.

12e Linking Your Content

Hyperlinks are obviously a very important part of Web design. When you provide a link, you are directing people to a particular Web site. For this reason, you should make sure that the site you link to is up and running and that the information appearing there is both accurate and reliable.

It is important to select a visible color for your text-based links to indicate that they are in fact links and not just highlighted text. You will need three colors to indicate the status of a link: one for the link before it is clicked; one for the active link (or the change in color as the link itself is being clicked); and one for the visited link (the color after the link has been successfully accessed).

Finally, make certain that you have the exact URL for the sites to which you are linking. The Web relies on exact URLs to deliver information; if even one letter or directory slash is incorrect, the page will not load.

Close-up: Web Sites and Copyright

As a rule, assume that any material on a Web site is copyrighted unless the author makes an explicit statement to the contrary. This means you must obtain written permission if you are going to reproduce this material on your Web site. The only exception to this rule is the **fair use doctrine,** which allows the use of copyrighted material for the purpose of commentary, parody, or research and education.

NOTE: The material you quote in a research paper for one of your classes falls under the fair use doctrine and does not require permission.

12f Editing and Proofreading Your Web Site

Before you post your Web site, you should proofread and edit it just as you would any other document. (Even if you run a spell check and a grammar check, you must still proofread carefully.)

Checklist: Style Conventions of Writing for the Web

☐ Avoid long, wordy sentences. Using active verbs will help keep your sentences short and concise.

☐ Avoid long paragraphs. Chunk content into small sections that are easy to read and access online.

☐ Speak directly to your audience, using the first person (*I*) and the second person (*you*) to establish a connection with readers.

☐ Avoid technical terminology that only a certain segment of your audience will understand.

☐ Choose your external links wisely. Do not provide so many that your audience is drawn away from your site.

☐ Use headings and bulleted lists to organize information visually and textually.

☐ Provide a title in the browser window for each page within your site to help users keep track of where they are.

☐ Proofread carefully offline before loading your content online.

PART 3

Sentence Style

A **sentence** is an independent grammatical unit that includes a subject and a predicate and expresses a complete thought.

The quick brown fox jumped over the lazy dog.

It has come from outer space.

See
13b1
A **simple subject** is a noun or noun substitute (*fox*, *it*) that tells who or what the sentence is about. A **simple predicate** is a verb or verb phrase (*jumped*, *has come*) that tells or asks something about the subject. The **complete subject** of a sentence includes the simple subject plus all its modifiers (*the quick brown fox*). The **complete predicate** includes the verb or verb phrase as well as all the words associated with it—such as modifiers, objects, and complements (*jumped over the lazy dog*, *has come from outer space*).

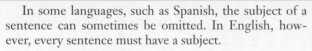

ESL Tip

In some languages, such as Spanish, the subject of a sentence can sometimes be omitted. In English, however, every sentence must have a subject.

13a Constructing Simple Sentences

A **simple sentence** consists of at least one subject and one predicate. Simple sentences conform to one of five basic patterns.

(1) Subject + Intransitive Verb (s + v)

See
20c1
The most basic simple sentence consists of just a subject and a verb or **verb phrase** (the main verb plus all its auxiliary verbs).

         s   v

The price of gold rose.

     s   v

Stock prices may fall.

Here the verbs *rose* and *may fall* are **intransitive**—that is, they do not need an object to complete their meaning.

(2) Subject + Transitive Verb + Direct Object (s + v + do)

Another kind of simple sentence consists of the subject, a verb, and a direct object.

     s   v   do
Van Gogh created *The Starry Night.*

     s   v   do
Caroline saved Jake.

Here the verbs *created* and *saved* are **transitive**—each requires an object to complete its meaning in the sentence. In each sentence, the **direct object** indicates where the verb's action is directed and who or what is affected by it.

ESL Tip

To determine whether a verb is intransitive or transitive, consult a dictionary. Remember, though, that some verbs, such as *write*, can be intransitive or transitive.

She wrote all night. (intransitive)
She wrote a paper about her experiences studying in Spain. (transitive)

(3) Subject + Transitive Verb + Direct Object + Object Complement (s + v + do + oc)

Some simple sentences include an **object complement,** a word or phrase that renames or describes the direct object.

     s   v   do   oc
The class elected Bridget treasurer. (Object complement *treasurer* renames direct object *Bridget.*)

   s   v   do   oc
I found the exam easy. (Object complement *easy* describes direct object *exam.*)

(4) Subject + Linking Verb + Subject Complement (s + v + sc)

Another kind of simple sentence consists of a subject, a linking verb (a verb that connects a subject to its complement), and the **subject complement** (the word or phrase that describes or renames the subject).

See 20c1

     s   v   sc
The injection was painless.

    s   v   sc
Tony Blair became prime minister.

Note that the linking verb is like an equal sign, equating the subject with its complement (*Tony Blair = prime minister*).

(5) Subject + Transitive Verb + Indirect Object + Direct Object (s + v + io + do)

Some simple sentences include an **indirect object,** which indicates to whom or for whom the verb's action was done.

        s   v   io   do
Cyrano wrote Roxanne a poem. (Cyrano wrote a poem for Roxanne.)

        s   v   io   do
The officer handed Frank a ticket. (The officer handed a ticket to Frank.)

Exercise 13.1

In each of the following sentences, underline the subject once and the predicate twice. Then, label direct objects, indirect objects, subject complements, and object complements.

                           sc
Example: Isaac Asimov was a science fiction writer.

▸ 1. Isaac Asimov first saw science fiction stories in his parents' Brooklyn store.
▸ 2. He practiced writing by telling his schoolmates stories.
▸ 3. Asimov published his first story in *Astounding Science Fiction*.
▸ 4. The magazine's editor, John W. Campbell, encouraged Asimov to continue writing.
▸ 5. The young writer researched scientific principles to make his stories more accurate.
   6. Asimov's "Foundation" series of novels is a "future history."
   7. The World Science Fiction Convention gave the series a Hugo Award.
   8. Sometimes Asimov used "Paul French" as a pseudonym.
   9. *Biochemistry and Human Metabolism* was Asimov's first nonfiction book.
  10. Asimov coined the term *robotics*.

13b Identifying Phrases and Clauses

Individual words may be combined into *phrases* and *clauses*.

(1) Identifying Phrases

A **phrase** is a group of related words that lacks a subject or predicate or both and functions as a single part of speech. It cannot stand alone as a sentence.

- A **verb phrase** consists of a main verb and all its auxiliary verbs.

Time <u>is flying</u>.

- A **noun phrase** includes a noun or pronoun plus all related modifiers.

I'll climb <u>the highest mountain</u>.

- A **prepositional phrase** consists of a preposition, its object, and any modifiers of that object.

They discussed the ethical implications <u>of the animal studies</u>.

He was last seen heading <u>into the orange sunset</u>.

- A **verbal phrase** consists of a **verbal** (participle, gerund, or infinitive) and its related objects, modifiers, or complements. A verbal phrase may be a **participial phrase,** a **gerund phrase,** or an **infinitive phrase.**

<u>Encouraged by the voter turnout</u>, the candidate predicted a victory. (participial phrase)

<u>Taking it easy</u> always makes sense. (gerund phrase)

The jury recessed <u>to evaluate the evidence</u>. (infinitive phrase)

- An **absolute phrase** usually consists of a noun and a participle, accompanied by modifiers. It modifies an entire independent clause rather than a particular word or phrase.

<u>Their toes tapping</u>, they watched the auditions.

(2) Identifying Clauses

A **clause** is a group of related words that includes a subject and a predicate. An **independent** (main) **clause** can stand alone as a sentence, but a **dependent** (subordinate) **clause** cannot. It must always be combined with an independent clause to form a <u>complex sentence</u>. See 14b

[Lucretia Mott was an abolitionist.] [She was also a pioneer for women's rights.] (two independent clauses)

[Lucretia Mott was an abolitionist] [who was also a pioneer for women's rights.] (independent clause, dependent clause)

[Although Lucretia Mott is widely known for her support of women's rights,] [she was also a prominent abolitionist.] (dependent clause, independent clause)

Dependent clauses may be *adjective, adverb,* or *noun* clauses.

- **Adjective clauses,** sometimes called **relative clauses,** modify nouns or pronouns and always follow the nouns or pronouns they modify. They are introduced by relative pronouns—*that, what, whatever, which, who, whose, whom, whoever,* or *whomever*—or by the adverbs *where* or *when.*

The television series *M*A*S*H*, which depicted life in an army hospital in Korea during the Korean War, ran for eleven years. (Adjective clause modifies the noun *M*A*S*H*.)

William Styron's novel *Sophie's Choice* is set in Brooklyn, where the narrator lives in a house painted pink. (Adjective clause modifies the noun *Brooklyn*.)

NOTE: Some adjective clauses, called **elliptical clauses,** are grammatically incomplete but nevertheless can be easily understood from the context of the sentence. Typically, a part of the subject or predicate (or the entire subject or predicate) is missing.

Although [they were] full, they could not resist dessert.

- **Adverb clauses** modify single words (verbs, adjectives, or adverbs), entire phrases, or independent clauses. They are always introduced by subordinating conjunctions. Adverb clauses provide information to answer the questions *how? where? when? why?* and *to what extent?*

Exhausted after the match was over, Kim decided to take a long nap. (Adverb clause modifies *exhausted*, telling *when* Kim was exhausted.)

Mark will go wherever there's a party. (Adverb clause modifies *will go*, telling *where* Mark will go.)

Because 75 percent of its exports are fish products, Iceland's economy is heavily dependent on the fishing industry. (Adverb clause modifies independent clause, telling *why* the fishing industry is so important.)

- **Noun clauses** function as subjects, objects, or complements. A noun clause may be introduced by a relative pronoun or by *whether, when, where, why,* or *how.*

What you see is what you get. (Noun clauses serve as subject and subject complement.)

They finally decided which candidate was most qualified. (Noun clause serves as direct object of verb *decided*.)

Which of the following groups of words are independent clauses? Which are dependent clauses? Which are phrases? Label each word group *IC*, *DC*, or *P*.

Example: Coming through the rye. (P)

▸ 1. Beauty is truth.   6. Whenever you're near.
▸ 2. When knights were bold.   7. The clock struck ten.
▸ 3. In a galaxy far away.   8. The red planet.
▸ 4. He saw stars.   9. Slowly I turned.
▸ 5. I hear a symphony.   10. For the longest time.

Chapter 14 | Building Compound and Complex Sentences

Writing that includes <u>varied sentences</u> is more interesting than writing that does not. One way to vary your sentences is to use compound and complex sentences along with simple sentences.

14a Building Compound Sentences

A **compound sentence** consists of two or more independent clauses joined with *coordinating conjunctions, transitional words or phrases, correlative conjunctions, semicolons,* or *colons.*

(1) Using Coordinating Conjunctions

You can join two **independent clauses** with a **coordinating conjunction**—*and, or, nor, but, for, so,* or *yet*—preceded by a comma.

> She carried a thin, small cane made from an umbrella, <u>and</u> with this she kept tapping the frozen earth in front of her. (Eudora Welty, "A Worn Path")

> In the fall the war was always there, <u>but</u> we did not go to it any more. (Ernest Hemingway, "In Another Country")

(2) Using Transitional Words and Phrases

You can join two independent clauses with a **transitional word or phrase,** preceded by a semicolon (and followed by a comma).

Aerobic exercise can help lower blood pressure; <u>however</u>, those with high blood pressure should still limit salt intake.

The saxophone does not belong to the brass family; <u>in fact</u>, it is a member of the woodwind family.

See 5b2 **NOTE:** Commonly used <u>transitional words and phrases</u> include **conjunctive adverbs** like *however, therefore, nevertheless, consequently, finally, still,* and *thus* and expressions like *for example, in fact, on the other hand,* and *for instance.*

(3) Using Correlative Conjunctions

See 20g You can use <u>correlative conjunctions</u> to join two independent clauses into a compound sentence.

<u>Either</u> he left his coat in his locker, <u>or</u> he left it on the bus.

(4) Using Semicolons

See 31a A <u>semicolon</u> can join two closely related independent clauses into a compound sentence.

Alaska is the largest state; Rhode Island is the smallest.

Theodore Roosevelt was president after the Spanish-American War; Andrew Johnson was president after the Civil War.

(5) Using Colons

See 34a A <u>colon</u> can join two independent clauses.

He got his orders: he was to leave for France on Sunday.

They thought they knew the outcome: Truman would lose to Dewey.

Close-up: Using Compound Sentences

Joining independent clauses into compound sentences helps to show readers the relationships between the clauses. Compound sentences can indicate the following relationships:

- Addition (*and, in addition, not only . . . but also*)
- Contrast (*but, however*)
- Causal relationships (*so, therefore, consequently*)
- Alternatives (*or, either . . . or*)

Exercise 14.1

Add appropriate coordinating conjunctions, conjunctive adverbs, or correlative conjunctions (as indicated) to combine each pair of sentences into one well-constructed compound sentence that retains the meaning of the original pair. Be sure to use correct punctuation.

Example: The American population is aging, *so people* ~~People~~ seem to be increasingly concerned about what they eat. (coordinating conjunction)

▸ 1. The average American consumes 128 pounds of sugar each year. Most of us eat much more sugar than any other food additive, including salt. (conjunctive adverb)

▸ 2. Many of us are determined to reduce our sugar intake. We have consciously eliminated sweets from our diets. (conjunctive adverb)

▸ 3. Unfortunately, sugar is not found only in sweets. It is also found in many processed foods. (correlative conjunction)

▸ 4. Processed foods like puddings and cake contain sugar. Foods like ketchup and spaghetti sauce do too. (coordinating conjunction)

▸ 5. We are trying to cut down on sugar. We find limiting sugar intake extremely difficult. (coordinating conjunction)

6. Processors may use sugar in foods for taste. They may also use it to help prevent foods from spoiling and to improve the texture and appearance of food. (correlative conjunction)

7. Sugar comes in many different forms. It is easy to overlook on a package label. (coordinating conjunction)

8. Sugar may be called sucrose or fructose. It may also be called corn syrup, corn sugar, brown sugar, honey, or molasses. (coordinating conjunction)

9. No sugar is more nourishing than the others. It really does not matter which is consumed. (conjunctive adverb)

10. Sugars contain empty calories. Whenever possible, they should be avoided. (conjunctive adverb)

(Adapted from Jane Brody's Nutrition Book)

14b Building Complex Sentences

A **complex sentence** consists of one **independent clause** and at least one **dependent clause.**

A dependent clause cannot stand alone; it must be combined with an independent clause to form a sentence. In a complex sentence, a **subordinating conjunction** or **relative pronoun** links the independent and dependent clauses and indicates the relationship between them.

dependent clause   independent clause
[After the town was evacuated,] [the hurricane began.]

independent clause   dependent clause
[Officials watched the storm,] [which threatened to destroy the town.]

NOTE: Sometimes a dependent clause may be embedded within an independent clause.

dependent clause
Town officials, [who were very concerned], watched the storm.

Frequently Used Subordinating Conjunctions

after	in order that	unless
although	now that	until
as	once	when
as if	rather than	whenever
as though	since	where
because	so that	whereas
before	that	wherever
even though	though	while
if		

Relative Pronouns

that	whatever	who (whose, whom)
what	which	whoever (whomever)

Close-up: Using Complex Sentences

When you join clauses to create complex sentences, you help readers to see the relationships between your ideas. Complex sentences can indicate the following relationships:

• Time relationships (*before, after, until, when, since*)
• Contrast (*however, although*)
• Causal relationships (*therefore, because, so that*)
• Conditional relationships (*if, unless*)
• Location (*where, wherever*)
• Identity (*who, which, that*)

Exercise 14.2

Use a subordinating conjunction or relative pronoun to combine each of the following pairs of sentences into one well-constructed complex sentence. Be sure to choose a connecting word that indicates the relationship between the two sentences. You may have to change or re-order words.

Example: ~~Some~~ *Because some* colles are tightening admissions requirements~~.~~ *, their* ~~Their~~ pool of students is growing smaller.

▸ 1. Many high school graduates are currently out of work. They need new skills for new careers.

▸ 2. Talented high school students are usually encouraged to go to college. Some high school graduates are now starting to see that a college education may not guarantee them a job.

▸ 3. A college education can cost a student more than $100,000. Vocational education is becoming increasingly important.

▸ 4. Vocational students complete their work in less than four years. They can enter the job market more quickly.

▸ 5. Nurses' aides, paralegals, travel agents, and computer technicians do not need college degrees. They have little trouble finding work.

6. Some four-year colleges are experiencing growth. Public community colleges and private trade schools are growing much more rapidly.

7. The best vocational schools are responsive to the needs of local businesses. They train students for jobs that actually exist.

8. For instance, a school in Detroit might offer advanced automotive design. A school in New York City might focus on fashion design.

9. Other schools offer courses in horticulture, respiratory therapy, and computer programming. They are able to place their graduates easily.

10. Laid-off workers, housewives returning to school, recent high school graduates, and even college graduates are reexamining vocational education. They all hope to find rewarding careers.

Close-up: Compound-Complex Sentences

Another way to vary your sentences is to create an occasional compound-complex sentence. A **compound-complex sentence** consists of two or more independent clauses and at least one dependent clause.

dependent clause
[When small foreign imports began dominating the US
independent clause
automobile industry,] [consumers were very responsive,] but
independent clause
[American auto workers were dismayed.]

Chapter 15 | Writing Varied Sentences

Using varied sentences can help make your writing livelier and more interesting and can also ensure that you emphasize the most important ideas in your sentences.

15a Combining Choppy Simple Sentences

Strings of short simple sentences can be tedious—and sometimes hard to follow, as this paragraph illustrates.

> John Peter Zenger was a newspaper editor. He waged and won an important battle for freedom of the press in America. He criticized the policies of the British governor. He was charged with criminal libel as a result. Zenger's lawyers were disbarred. Andrew Hamilton defended him. Hamilton convinced the jury that Zenger's criticisms were true. Therefore, the statements were not libelous.

You can revise choppy sentences like these by using *coordination*, *subordination*, or *embedding* to combine them with adjacent sentences.

(1) Using Coordination

Coordination pairs similar elements—words, phrases, or clauses—giving equal weight to each. The following revision links two of the choppy simple sentences in the paragraph above with *and* to create a compound sentence.

See 14a

> John Peter Zenger was a newspaper editor. He waged and won an important battle for freedom of the press in America. <u>He criticized the policies of the British governor, and as a result, he was charged with criminal libel</u>. Zenger's lawyers were disbarred. Andrew Hamilton defended him. Hamilton convinced the jury that Zenger's criticisms were true. Therefore, the statements were not libelous.

ESL Tip

Some ESL students rely on simple sentences and coordination in their writing because they are afraid of making sentence structure errors. The result is a monotonous style. To add variety, try using **subordination** and **embedding** (explained in **15a2** and **15a3**) in your sentences.

---

(2) Using Subordination

Subordination places the more important idea in the independent clause and the less important idea in the dependent clause. The following revision of the preceding paragraph uses subordination to change two simple sentences into dependent clauses, creating two <u>complex sentences</u>.

> See
> 14b

John Peter Zenger was a newspaper editor who waged and won an important battle for freedom of the press in America. He criticized the policies of the British governor, and as a result, he was charged with criminal libel. When Zenger's lawyers were disbarred, Andrew Hamilton defended him. Hamilton convinced the jury that Zenger's criticisms were true. Therefore, the statements were not libelous.

(3) Using Embedding

Embedding is the working of additional words and phrases into a sentence. In the following revision, the sentence *Hamilton convinced the jury . . .* has been reworded to create a phrase (*convincing the jury*) that is embedded into another sentence, where it now modifies the independent clause *Andrew Hamilton defended him.*

John Peter Zenger was a newspaper editor who waged and won an important battle for freedom of the press in America. He criticized the policies of the British governor, and as a result, he was charged with criminal libel. When Zenger's lawyers were disbarred, Andrew Hamilton defended him, convincing the jury that Zenger's criticisms were true. Therefore, the statements were not libelous.

This final revision of the original paragraph's choppy sentences is interesting and readable because it is now composed of varied and logically linked sentences. The final short simple sentence has been retained for emphasis.

Exercise 15.1

Using coordination, subordination, and embedding, revise this string of choppy simple sentences into a more varied and interesting paragraph.

> ►The first modern miniature golf course was built in New York in 1925. ►It was an indoor course with 18 holes. ►Entrepreneurs Drake Delanoy and John Ledbetter built 150 more indoor and outdoor courses. ►Garnet Carter made miniature golf a worldwide fad. ►Carter built an elaborate miniature golf course. ►He later joined with Delanoy and Ledbetter. ►Together they built more miniature golf courses.

They abbreviated playing distances. They highlighted the game's hazards at the expense of skill. This made the game much more popular. By 1930, there were 25,000 miniature golf courses in the United States. Courses grew more elaborate. Hazards grew more bizarre. The craze spread to London and Hong Kong. The expansion of miniature golf grew out of control. Then, interest in the game declined. By 1931, most miniature golf courses were out of business. The game was revived in the early 1950s. Today, there are between eight and ten thousand miniature golf courses. The architecture of miniature golf remains an enduring form of American folk art. (Adapted from *Games*)

15b Breaking Up Strings of Compound Sentences

When you write, try to avoid creating an unbroken series of compound sentences. A string of compound sentences can be extremely monotonous; moreover, if you connect clauses only with coordinating conjunctions, you may find it difficult to indicate exactly how ideas are related and which is most important.

All Compound Sentences: A volcano that is erupting is considered *active*, but one that may erupt is designated *dormant*, and one that has not erupted for a long time is called *extinct*. Most active volcanoes are located in "The Ring of Fire," a belt that circles the Pacific Ocean, and they can be extremely destructive. Italy's Vesuvius erupted in AD 79, and it destroyed the town of Pompeii. In 1883, Krakatoa, located between the Indonesian islands of Java and Sumatra, erupted, and it caused a tidal wave, and more than 36,000 people were killed. Martinique's Mont Pelée erupted in 1902, and its hot gas and ash killed 30,000 people, and this completely wiped out the town of St. Pierre.

Varied Sentences: A volcano that is erupting is considered *active*. (**simple sentence**) One that may erupt is designated *dormant*, and one that has not erupted for a long time is called *extinct*. (**compound sentence**) Most active volcanoes are located in "The Ring of Fire," a belt that circles the Pacific Ocean. (**simple sentence with modifier**) Active volcanoes can be extremely destructive. (**simple sentence**) Erupting in AD 79, Italy's Vesuvius destroyed the town of Pompeii. (**simple sentence with modifier**) When Krakatoa, located between the Indonesian islands of Java and Sumatra, erupted in 1883, it caused a tidal wave that killed 36,000 people. (**complex sentence with modifier**) The eruption of Martinique's Mont Pelée in 1902 produced hot gas and ash that killed 30,000 people, completely wiping out the town of St. Pierre. (**complex sentence with modifier**)

Exercise 15.2

Revise the compound sentences in this passage so the sentence structure is varied. Be sure that the writer's emphasis and the relationships between ideas are clear.

▶Dr. Alice I. Baumgartner and her colleagues at the Institute for Equality in Education at the University of Colorado surveyed two thousand Colorado schoolchildren, and they found some startling results. ▶They asked, "If you woke up tomorrow and discovered that you were a (boy) (girl), how would your life be different?" and the answers were sad and shocking. The researchers assumed they would find that boys and girls would see advantages in being either male or female, but instead they found that both boys and girls had a fundamental contempt for females. Many elementary schoolboys titled their answers "The Disaster" or "Doomsday," and they described the terrible lives they would lead as girls, but the girls seemed to feel they would be better off as boys, and they expressed feelings that they would be able to do more and have easier lives. (Adapted from *Redbook*)

15c Varying Sentence Openings

Rather than begin every sentence with the subject (*I* or *It*, for example), add interest and variety by beginning with a modifying word, phrase, or clause.

(1) Beginning with an Adjective, an Adverb, or a Dependent Clause

Proud and relieved, they watched their daughter receive her diploma. (adjectives)

Hungrily, he devoured his lunch. (adverb)

After Woodrow Wilson was incapacitated by a stroke, his wife unofficially performed many presidential duties. (dependent clause)

(2) Beginning with a Prepositional Phrase, a Participial Phrase, or an Absolute Phrase

For better or worse, credit cards are now readily available to college students. (prepositional phrase)

Located on the west coast of Great Britain, Wales is part of the United Kingdom. (participial phrase)

His interests widening, Picasso designed ballet sets and illustrated books. (absolute phrase)

(3) Beginning with a Coordinating Conjunction or a Transitional Word or Phrase

The Big Bang may be the beginning of the universe, or it may be a discontinuity in which information about the earlier history of the universe was destroyed. <u>But</u> it is certainly the earliest event about which we have any record. (coordinating conjunction) (Carl Sagan, *The Dragons of Eden*)

Pantomime was first performed in ancient Rome. <u>However</u>, it remains a popular dramatic form today. (transitional word)

NOTE: If you begin a sentence with a coordinating conjunction, make sure that it is a complete sentence and not a <u>fragment</u>.

Exercise 15.3

Each of these sentences begins with the subject. Revise each so that it has a different opening; then, identify your opening strategy.

Example: ˄*In The Names,* N. Scott Momaday, the prominent Native American writer, tells the story of his first fourteen years ˄*in The Names.* (prepositional phrase)

▸ 1. Momaday was taken as a very young child to Devil's Tower, the geological formation in Wyoming that is called Tsoai (Bear Tree) in Kiowa, and there he was given the name Tsoai-talee (Bear Tree Boy).

▸ 2. The Kiowa myth of the origin of Tsoai is about a boy who playfully chases his seven sisters up a tree, which rises into the air as the boy is transformed into a bear.

3. The boy-bear becomes increasingly ferocious and claws the bark of the tree, which becomes a great rock with a flat top and deeply scored sides.

4. The sisters climb higher and higher to escape their brother's wrath, and eventually they become the seven stars of the Big Dipper.

5. This story, from which Momaday received one of his names, appears in his works *The Way to Rainy Mountain*, *House Made of Dawn*, and *The Ancient Child*.

Chapter 16   Writing Emphatic Sentences

In speaking, we emphasize certain ideas and deemphasize others with intonation and gesture; in writing, we convey **emphasis**—the relative importance of ideas—through the selection and arrangement of words.

16a Conveying Emphasis through Word Order

Because readers tend to focus on the beginning and end of a sentence, you should place information there.

(1) Beginning with Important Ideas

Placing key ideas at the beginning of a sentence stresses their importance. The unedited version of the following sentence places emphasis on the study, not on those who conducted it or on those who participated in it. Editing shifts this focus and puts the emphasis on the researcher, not on the study.

~~In a landmark study of alcoholism~~, Dr. George Vaillant of
    , in a landmark study of alcoholism,
Harvard followed two hundred Harvard graduates and four hundred inner-city, working-class men from the Boston area.

Situations that demand a straightforward presentation—laboratory reports, memos, technical papers, business correspondence, and the like—call for sentences that present vital information first and qualifiers later.

Treating cancer with interferon has been the subject of a good deal of research. (emphasizes the treatment, not the research)

Dividends will be paid if the stockholders agree. (emphasizes the dividends, not the stockholders)

Close-up: Writing Emphatic Sentences

Placing an empty phrase like *there is* or *there are* at the beginning of a sentence generally weakens the sentence.

MIT places
~~There is~~ heavy emphasis ~~placed~~ on the development of computational skills~~, at MIT~~/

---

(2) Ending with Important Ideas

Placing key elements at the end of a sentence is another way to convey their importance.

Using a Colon or a Dash   A colon or a dash can emphasize an important word or phrase by isolating it at the end of a sentence.

Beth had always dreamed of owning one special car: a 1953 Corvette.

The elderly need a good deal of special attention—and they deserve that attention.

Close-up: Placing Transitional Expressions

When placed at the end of a sentence, conjunctive adverbs and other transitional expressions lose their power to indicate the relationship between ideas. Placed earlier in the sentence, <u>transitional words and phrases</u> can link ideas and add emphasis.

> *however,*
> Smokers do have rights;ₐthey should not try to impose their habit on others/ ~~however.~~

See
5b2

Using Climactic Word Order **Climactic word order,** the arrangement of a series of items from the least to the most important, places emphasis on the most important idea at the end of the sentence.

Binge drinking can lead to unwanted pregnancies, car accidents, and even death. (*Death* is the most serious consequence.)

Exercise 16.1

Underline the most important idea in each sentence of the following paragraph. Then, identify the strategy that the writer uses to emphasize those ideas. Are the key ideas placed at the beginning or the end of a sentence? Does the writer use climactic order?

►Listening to diatribes by angry callers or ranting about today's news, the talk radio host spreads ideas over the air waves. ►Every day at the same time, the political talk show host discusses national events and policies, the failures of the opposing view, and the foibles of the individuals who espouse those opposing views. ►Listening for hours a day, some callers become recognizable contributors to many different talk radio programs. ►Other listeners are less devoted, tuning in only when they are in the car and never calling to voice their opinions. Political radio hosts usually structure their programs around a specific agenda, espousing the party line and ridiculing the opponent's position. With a style of presentation aimed both at entertainment and information, the host's ideas become caricatures of party positions. Sometimes, in order to keep the information lively and interesting, a host may either state the issues too simply or deliberately mislead the audience. A host can excuse these errors by insisting that the show is harmless: it's for entertainment, not information. Many are concerned about how the political process is affected by this misinformation.

(3) Experimenting with Word Order

ESL
48d

In English sentences, the most common <u>word order</u> is subject-verb-object (or subject-verb-complement). By occasionally departing from this expected word order, you can call attention to the word, phrase, or clause that you have relocated.

> More modest and less inventive than Turner's paintings are John Constable's landscapes.

Here the writer calls attention to the modifying phrase *more modest and less inventive than Turner's paintings* by inverting word order, placing the complement and the verb before the subject.

Exercise 16.2

Revise the following sentences to make them more emphatic. For each, decide which ideas should be highlighted, and place these key ideas at sentence beginnings or endings. Use climactic order or depart from conventional word order where appropriate.

▶ 1. Police want to upgrade their firepower because criminals are better armed than ever before.
▶ 2. A few years ago, felons used so-called Saturday night specials, small-caliber six-shot revolvers.
3. Now, semiautomatic pistols capable of firing fifteen to twenty rounds, along with paramilitary weapons like the AK-47, have replaced these weapons.
4. Police are adopting such weapons as new fast-firing shotguns and 9mm automatic pistols in order to gain an equal footing with their adversaries.
5. Faster reloading and a hair trigger are among the numerous advantages that automatic pistols, the weapons of choice among law-enforcement officers, have over the traditional .38-caliber police revolver.

16b Conveying Emphasis through Sentence Structure

As you write, try to construct sentences that emphasize more important ideas and deemphasize less important ones.

(1) Using Cumulative Sentences

A **cumulative sentence** begins with an independent clause, followed by additional words, phrases, or clauses that expand or develop it.

> She holds me in strong arms, arms that have chopped cotton, dismembered trees, scattered corn for chickens, cradled infants,

shaken the daylights out of half-grown upstart teenagers.
(Rebecca Hill, *Blue Rise*)

Because a cumulative sentence presents its main idea first, it tends to
be clear and straightforward. (Most English sentences are cumulative.)

(2) Using Periodic Sentences

A **periodic sentence** moves from supporting details, expressed in
modifying phrases and dependent clauses, to the key idea, which is
placed in the independent clause at the end of the sentence.

Unlike World Wars I and II, which ended decisively with the un-
conditional surrender of the United States's enemies, the war in
Vietnam did not end when American troops withdrew.

NOTE: In some periodic sentences, the modifying phrase or dependent
clause comes between subject and predicate: Columbus, after several
discouraging and unsuccessful voyages, finally reached America.

Exercise 16.3

A. Bracket the independent clause(s) in each sentence, and underline
each modifying phrase and dependent clause. Label each sentence
cumulative or periodic.
B. Relocate the supporting details to make cumulative sentences
periodic and periodic sentences cumulative, adding words or
rephrasing to make your meaning clear.
C. Be prepared to explain how your revision changes the emphasis of
the original sentence.

Example: Feeling isolated, sad, and frightened, [the small child sat
alone in the train depot.] (periodic)

Revised: The small child sat alone in the train depot, feeling isolated, sad, and frightened. (cumulative)

▸ 1. However different in their educational opportunities, both Jefferson and Lincoln as young men became known to their contemporaries as "hard students." (Douglas L. Wilson, "What Jefferson
and Lincoln Read," *Atlantic Monthly*)
2. The road came into being slowly, league by league, river
crossing by river crossing. (Stephen Harrigan, "Highway 1,"
Texas Monthly)
3. Without willing it, I had gone from being ignorant of being
ignorant to being aware of being aware. (Maya Angelou, *I Know
Why the Caged Bird Sings*)

16c Conveying Emphasis through Parallelism and Balance

By reinforcing the similarity between grammatical elements, <u>parallelism</u> can help you emphasize information.

> We seek an individual <u>who is</u> a self-starter, <u>who owns</u> a late-model automobile, and <u>who is</u> willing to work evenings. (classified advertisement)

> <u>Do not pass</u> Go; <u>do not collect</u> $200. (instructions)

> The Faust legend is central <u>in</u> Benét's *The Devil and Daniel Webster*, <u>in</u> Goethe's *Faust*, and <u>in</u> Marlowe's *Dr. Faustus*. (examination answer)

A **balanced sentence** is neatly divided between two parallel structures—for example, two independent clauses in a compound sentence. The symmetrical structure of a balanced sentence adds emphasis by highlighting similarities or differences between the ideas in the two clauses.

> In the 1950s, the electronic miracle was the television; in the 1980s, the electronic miracle was the computer.

> Alive, the elephant was worth at least a hundred pounds; dead, he would only be worth the value of his tusks, five pounds, possibly. (George Orwell, "Shooting an Elephant")

16d Conveying Emphasis through Repetition

<u>Unnecessary repetition</u> makes sentences dull and monotonous as well as wordy.

> He had a good pitching arm and <u>also</u> could field well and was <u>also</u> a fast runner.

Effective repetition, however, can emphasize key words or ideas.

> They decided to begin again: <u>to begin</u> hoping, <u>to begin</u> trying to change, <u>to begin</u> working toward a goal.

> During those years when I was just learning to speak, my mother and father addressed me only <u>in Spanish; in Spanish</u> I learned to reply. (Richard Rodriguez, *Aria: A Memoir of a Bilingual Childhood*)

Exercise 16.4

Revise the sentences in this paragraph, using parallelism and balance to highlight corresponding elements and using repetition of key words and phrases to add emphasis. You may combine sentences and add, delete, or reorder words.

►Many readers distrust newspapers. ►They also distrust what they read in magazines. ►They do not trust what they hear on the radio and what television shows them, either. ►Of these media, newspapers have been the most responsive to audience criticism. ►Some newspapers even have ombudsmen. ►They are supposed to listen to readers' complaints. ►They are also charged with acting on these grievances. One complaint that many people have is that newspapers are inaccurate. Newspapers' disregard for people's privacy is another of many readers' criticisms. Reporters are seen as arrogant, and readers feel that journalists can be unfair. They feel that reporters tend to glorify criminals, and they believe there is a tendency to place too much emphasis on bizarre or offbeat stories. Finally, readers complain about poor writing and editing. Polls show that despite its efforts to respond to reader criticism, the press continues to face hostility. (Adapted from *Newsweek*)

16e Conveying Emphasis through Active Voice

See
22d

The active voice is generally more emphatic than the passive voice.

Passive: The prediction that oil prices will rise is being made by economists.

Active: Economists now predict that oil prices will rise.

Notice that the passive voice focuses your readers' attention on the action or on its receiver rather than on who is performing it. The receiver of the action is the subject of a passive sentence, so the actor fades into the background (*by economists*) or is omitted entirely (*the prediction is now being made*). The active voice, however, places emphasis where it belongs: on the actor or actors (*Economists*).

http://kirsznermandell.wadsworth.com

Computer Tip: Eliminating Passive Constructions

Your word processor's grammar checker will highlight passive voice constructions in your writing and offer revision suggestions.

Sometimes, of course, you *want* to stress the action rather than the actor. If so, it makes sense to use the passive voice.

Passive: The West was explored by Lewis and Clark. (stresses the exploration of the West, not who explored it)

Active: Lewis and Clark explored the West. (stresses the contribution of the explorers)

NOTE: Passive voice is also used when the identity of the person performing the action is irrelevant or unknown (*The course was canceled*). For this reason, the passive voice is frequently used in scientific and technical writing: *The beaker was filled with a saline solution.*

Exercise 16.5

Revise this paragraph to eliminate awkward or excessive use of passive constructions.

▸Jack Dempsey, the heavyweight champion between 1919 and 1926, had an interesting but uneven career. ▸He was considered one of the greatest boxers of all time. ▸Dempsey began fighting as "Kid Blackie," but his career didn't take off until 1919, when Jack "Doc" Kearns became his manager. ▸Dempsey won the championship when Jess Willard was defeated by him in Toledo, Ohio, in 1919. ▸Dempsey immediately became a popular sports figure; President Franklin D. Roosevelt was one of his biggest fans. Influential friends were made by Jack Dempsey. Boxing lessons were given by him to the actor Rudolph Valentino. He made friends with Douglas Fairbanks Sr., Damon Runyon, and J. Paul Getty. Hollywood serials were made by Dempsey, but the title was lost by him to Gene Tunney, and Dempsey failed to regain it the following year. After his boxing career declined, a restaurant was opened by Dempsey, and many major sporting events were attended by him. This exposure kept him in the public eye until he lost his restaurant. Jack Dempsey died in 1983.

Chapter 17   Writing Concise Sentences

A sentence is not concise simply because it is short; it is concise when it contains only the words necessary to make its point.

17a Eliminating Wordiness

Whenever possible, delete nonessential words—*deadwood, utility words,* and *circumlocution*—from your writing.

(1) Eliminating Deadwood

The term **deadwood** refers to unnecessary phrases that take up space and add nothing to meaning. By eliminating deadwood, you make your sentences more concise and easier to read.

Many
~~There were many~~ factors ~~that~~ influenced his decision to become a priest.

The two plots are ~~both~~ similar in ~~the way~~ that they trace the characters' increasing rage.

This
~~In this~~ article ~~it~~ discusses lead poisoning.

is
The only truly tragic character in *Hamlet* ~~would have to be~~ Ophelia.

Deadwood also includes unnecessary statements of opinion, such as *I believe, I feel,* and *it seems to me.*

(2) Eliminating Utility Words

Utility words function as filler and contribute nothing to the meaning of a sentence. Utility words include nouns with imprecise meanings (*factor, situation, type, aspect,* and so on); adjectives so general that they are almost meaningless (*good, bad, important*); and common adverbs denoting degree (*basically, actually, quite, very, definitely*). Often, you can just delete the utility word; if you cannot, replace it with a more precise word.

Registration
~~The registration situation~~ was disorganized.

an
The scholarship ~~basically~~ offered Fran ~~a good~~ opportunity to study Spanish in Spain.

It was ~~actually~~ a worthwhile book, but I didn't ~~completely~~ finish it.

(3) Avoiding Circumlocution

Circumlocution is taking a roundabout way to say something (using ten words when five will do). Instead of complicated constructions, use concise, specific words and phrases that come right to the point.

The   *probably*
~~It is not unlikely that the~~ trend will continue.

The curriculum was ~~of a~~ unique ~~nature~~.

while
Joe was in the army ~~during the same time that~~ I was in college.

Close-up: Revising Wordy Phrases	

A wordy phrase can almost always be replaced by a more concise, more direct term.

Wordy	**Concise**
at the present time	now
at this point in time	now
for the purpose of	for
due to the fact that	because
on account of the fact that	because
until such time as	until
in the event that	if
by means of	by
in the vicinity of	near
have the ability to	be able to

Exercise 17.1

Revise the following paragraph to eliminate deadwood, utility words, and circumlocution. Whenever possible, delete wordy phrases or replace them with more concise expressions.

▶For all intents and purposes, the shopping mall is no longer an important factor in the American cultural scene. ▶In the '80s, shopping malls became gathering places where teenagers met, walkers came to get in a few miles, and shoppers who were looking for a wide selection and were not concerned about value went to shop. ▶There are several factors that have worked to undermine the mall's popularity. ▶First, due to the fact that today's shoppers are more likely to be interested in value, many of them have headed to the discount stores. ▶Today's shopper is now more likely to shop in discount stores or bulk-buying warehouse stores than in the small, expensive specialty shops in the large shopping malls. Add to this a resurgence of the values of community, and we can see how malls would have to be less attractive than shopping at local stores. Many malls actually have up to 20 percent empty storefronts, and some have had to close down altogether. Others have met the challenge by expanding their roles from shopping centers into community centers. They have added playgrounds for the children and more amusements and restaurants for the adults. They have also appealed to the growing sense of value shopping by giving gift certificates and discounts to shoppers who spend money in their stores. In the '90s, it seemed as if the huge shopping malls that had become familiar cultural icons were dying out, replaced by catalog and Internet shopping. Now, however, it looks as if some of those icons just might make it and survive by reinventing themselves as more than just places to shop.

17b Eliminating Unnecessary Repetition

See
16d

Although <u>repetition</u> can make your writing more emphatic, unnecessary repetition and **redundant** word groups (repeated words or phrases that say the same thing, such as *free gift* and *unanticipated surprise*) can clog your sentences and obscure your meaning.

You can correct unnecessary repetition by using any of the following strategies.

(1) Deleting Redundancy

People's clothing ~~attire~~ can reveal a good deal about their personalities.

http://kirsznermandell.wadsworth.com

Computer Tip: Deleting Redundancy

Your word processor's grammar checker will often highlight redundant expressions and offer suggestions for revision.

(2) Creating an Appositive

Red Barber ~~was~~ a sportscaster./ ~~He~~ was known for his colorful expressions.

(3) Creating a Compound

John F. Kennedy was the youngest man ever elected president./
and
~~He was~~ the first Catholic to hold this office.

(4) Creating a Complex Sentence

, which
Americans value freedom of speech./ ~~Freedom of speech~~ is guaranteed by the First Amendment.

Exercise 17.2

Eliminate any unnecessary repetition of words or ideas in this paragraph. Also revise to eliminate deadwood, utility words, or circumlocution.

> ►For a wide variety of different reasons, more and more people today are choosing a vegetarian diet. ►There are three kinds of vegetarians: strict vegetarians eat no animal foods at all; lactovegetarians eat dairy products, but they do not eat meat, fish, poultry, or eggs; and ovolactovegetarians eat eggs and dairy products, but they do not eat meat, fish, or poultry. ►Famous vegetarians include such well-known people as George Bernard Shaw, Leonardo da Vinci, Ralph Waldo

Emerson, Henry David Thoreau, and Mahatma Gandhi. ▸Like these well-known vegetarians, the vegetarians of today have good reasons for becoming vegetarians. For instance, some religions recommend a vegetarian diet. Some of these religions are Buddhism, Brahmanism, and Hinduism. Other people turn to vegetarianism for reasons of health or for reasons of hygiene. These people believe that meat is a source of potentially harmful chemicals, and they believe meat contains infectious organisms. Some people feel meat may cause digestive problems and may lead to other difficulties as well. Other vegetarians adhere to a vegetarian diet because they feel it is ecologically wasteful to kill animals after we feed plants to them. These vegetarians believe we should eat the plants. Finally, there are facts and evidence to suggest that a vegetarian diet may possibly help people live longer lives. A vegetarian diet may do this by reducing the incidence of heart disease and lessening the incidence of some cancers. (Adapted from *Jane Brody's Nutrition Book*)

17c Tightening Rambling Sentences

The combination of nonessential words, unnecessary repetition, and complicated syntax creates **rambling sentences.** Revising rambling sentences frequently requires extensive editing.

(1) Eliminating Excessive Coordination

When you string a series of clauses together with coordinating conjunctions, you create a rambling, unfocused compound sentence that presents your ideas as if they all have equal weight. To revise such sentences, identify the main idea or ideas, and then subordinate the supporting details.

See
14a

Wordy: Puerto Rico is a large island in the Caribbean, and it is very mountainous, and it has steep slopes, and they fall to gentle plains along the coast.

Concise: A large island in the Caribbean, Puerto Rico is very mountainous, with steep slopes falling to gentle plains along the coast. (Puerto Rico's mountainous terrain is the sentence's main idea.)

(2) Eliminating Adjective Clauses

A series of adjective clauses is also likely to produce a rambling sentence. To revise, substitute more concise modifying words or phrases for the adjective clauses.

See
13b2

Wordy: *Moby-Dick*, which is a novel about a white whale, was written by Herman Melville, who was friendly with Nathaniel Hawthorne, who urged him to revise the first draft.

    Concise: *Moby-Dick*, a novel about a white whale, was written
by Herman Melville, who revised the first draft at the urging of
his friend Nathaniel Hawthorne.

(3) Eliminating Passive Constructions

ESL
48a6

Excessive use of the passive voice can create rambling sentences.
Correct this problem by changing passive to active voice.

    ~~Water rights are being fought for in court by~~ Indian tribes like
are fighting in court for water rights.
the Papago in Arizona and the Pyramid Lake Paiute in Nevada⌄

(4) Eliminating Wordy Prepositional Phrases

When you revise, substitute adjectives or adverbs for wordy prepositional phrases.

             dangerous   *exciting*
The trip was ⌄~~one of danger~~ but also⌄~~one of excitement.~~

          confidently   *authoritatively*
He spoke⌄~~in a confident manner~~ and⌄~~with a lot of authority.~~

(5) Eliminating Wordy Noun Constructions

Substitute strong verbs for wordy noun phrases.

          decided
We have⌄~~made the decision~~ to postpone the meeting until ~~the~~
                           appear
~~appearance of~~ all the board members⌄.

                               accumulates
Sometimes ~~there is an accumulation of~~ water⌄on the roof.

Exercise 17.3

Revise the rambling sentences in these paragraphs by eliminating excessive coordination; unnecessary use of the passive voice; and overuse of
adjective clauses, prepositional phrases, and noun constructions. As you
revise, make your sentences more concise by deleting nonessential words
and unnecessary repetition.

    ▸Some colleges that have been in support of fraternities for a number
of years are at this time in the process of conducting a reevaluation of the
position of those fraternities on campus. ▸In opposition to the fraternities are a fair number of students, faculty members, and administrators
who claim fraternities are inherently sexist, which they say makes it impossible for the groups to exist in a coeducational institution, which is

supposed to offer equal opportunities for members of both sexes. ►More and more members of the college community also see fraternities as elitist as well as sexist and favor their abolition. ►In addition, many point out that fraternities are associated with dangerous practices, such as hazing and alcohol abuse.

However, some students, faculty, and administrators remain wholeheartedly in support of traditional fraternities, which they believe are responsible for helping students make the acquaintance of people and learn the leadership skills that they believe will be of assistance to them in their future lives as adults. Supporters of fraternities believe that students should retain the right to make their own social decisions and that joining a fraternity is one of those decisions, and they also believe fraternities are responsible for providing valuable services. Some of these are tutoring, raising money for charity, and running campus escort services. Therefore, these individuals are not of the opinion that the abolition of traditional fraternities makes sense.

Chapter 18 · Using Parallelism

Parallelism—the use of matching words, phrases, clauses, or sentence structures to express equivalent ideas—adds unity, balance, and force to your writing. Effective parallelism makes sentences easy to follow and emphasizes relationships among equivalent ideas, but faulty parallelism can create awkward sentences that obscure your meaning and confuse readers.

See
18b

18a Using Parallelism Effectively

Parallelism highlights the correspondence between *items in a series*, *paired items*, and elements in *lists and outlines*.

(1) With Items in a Series

Coordinate elements—words, phrases, or clauses—in a series should be presented in parallel form. (For information on punctuating elements in a series, **see 30b** and **31c**.)

Eat, drink, and be merry.

I came; I saw; I conquered.

Baby food consumption, toy production, and school construction are likely to decline as the US population grows older.

Three factors influenced his decision to seek new employment: <u>his desire to relocate</u>, <u>his need for greater responsibility</u>, and <u>his dissatisfaction with his current job</u>.

(2) With Paired Items

Because parallelism emphasizes their equivalence, paired ideas (words, phrases, or clauses) should be presented in parallel form.

The thank-you note was <u>short</u> but <u>sweet</u>.

<u>Roosevelt represented the United States</u>, and <u>Churchill represented Great Britain</u>.

The research focused on <u>muscle tissue</u> and <u>nerve cells</u>.

<u>Ask not what your country can do for you</u>; <u>ask what you can do for your country</u>. (John F. Kennedy, inaugural address)

Paired items linked by **correlative conjunctions** (such as *not only/ but also, both/and, either/or, neither/nor,* and *whether/or*) should be presented in parallel form.

The design team paid close attention not only <u>to color</u> but also <u>to texture</u>.

Either <u>repeat physics</u> or <u>take calculus</u>.

Parallelism also highlights the contrast between paired elements linked by *than* or *as*.

Richard Wright and James Baldwin chose <u>to live in Paris</u> rather than <u>to remain in the United States</u>.

Success is as much <u>a matter of hard work</u> as <u>a matter of luck</u>.

(3) In Lists and Outlines

Elements in a list should be presented in parallel form.

The Irish potato famine had four major causes:
1. The establishment of the landlord-tenant system
2. The failure of the potato crop
3. The reluctance of England to offer adequate financial assistance
4. The passage of the Corn Laws

See
4c4

Elements in a <u>formal outline</u> also should be parallel.

Exercise 18.1

Identify the parallel elements in these sentences by bracketing parallel phrases and clauses.

Example: Manek spent six years in America [going to school] and [working for a computer company].

▸ 1. After he completed his engineering degree, Manek returned to India to visit his large extended family and to find a wife.
▸ 2. Unfamiliar with marriage practices in India and accustomed to American notions of marriage for love, Manek's American friends frowned on his plans.
   3. Not only Manek but also his parents wanted an arranged marriage.
   4. He didn't believe that either you married for love or you had a loveless marriage.
   5. His parents' marriage, an arranged one, continues happily; his aunt's marriage, also arranged, has lasted thirty years.

18b Revising Faulty Parallelism

Faulty parallelism occurs when equivalent ideas in a sentence are not presented in parallel form.

Faulty Parallelism: Many people in developing countries suffer because the countries lack <u>sufficient housing to accommodate them</u>, <u>sufficient food to feed them</u>, and <u>their health-care facilities are inadequate</u>.

Because the three reasons in the preceding sentence are presented in a series, readers expect them to be presented in parallel form. The first two elements satisfy this expectation: *sufficient housing to accommodate them . . . ; sufficient food to feed them. . . .* The third item in the series, however, breaks this pattern: *their health-care facilities are inadequate.*

Revised: Many people in developing countries suffer because the countries lack <u>sufficient housing to accommodate them</u>, <u>sufficient food to feed them</u> and <u>sufficient health-care facilities to serve them</u>.

You can revise faulty parallelism by using parallel elements, by repeating key words, and by repeating relative pronouns.

(1) Using Parallel Elements

Revise faulty parallelism by matching nouns with nouns, verbs with verbs, and phrases and clauses with similarly constructed phrases and clauses.

Faulty Parallelism	Revised
Popular exercises for men and women include spinning, weight lifters, and jogging.	Popular exercises for men and women include <u>spinning</u>, weight <u>lifting</u>, and <u>jogging</u>.
Some of the side effects are skin irritation and eye irritation, and mucous membrane irritation may also develop.	Some of the side effects that may develop are <u>skin</u>, <u>eye</u>, and <u>mucous membrane</u> irritation.
I look forward to hearing from you and to have an opportunity to tell you more about myself.	I look forward to <u>hearing from you</u> and to <u>having an opportunity</u> to tell you more about myself.

(2) Repeating Key Words

Although the use of similar grammatical structures may sometimes be enough to convey parallelism, sentences are often clearer and more emphatic if certain key words (articles, prepositions, and the *to* in infinitives, for example) are repeated in each element of a pair or series.

Faulty Parallelism	Revised
Computerization has helped industry by not allowing labor costs to skyrocket, increasing the speed of production, and improving efficiency. (Does *not* apply to all three phrases, or only the first?)	Computerization has helped industry <u>by not allowing labor costs to skyrocket</u>, <u>by increasing the speed of production</u>, and <u>by improving efficiency</u>. (Preposition *by* is repeated to clarify the boundaries of the three parallel phrases.)

(3) Repeating Relative Pronouns

Like <u>correlative conjunctions</u>, the relative pronoun constructions *who . . . and who, whom . . . and whom,* and *which . . . and which* are always paired and always introduce parallel clauses. When you revise, make sure a relative pronoun introduces each clause.

Faulty: *The Thing,* directed by Howard Hawks, and which was released in 1951, featured James Arness as the monster.

Revised: *The Thing,* <u>which</u> was directed by Howard Hawks <u>and</u> <u>which</u> was released in 1951, featured James Arness as the monster.

http://kirsznermandell.wadsworth.com

Computer Tip: Revising Faulty Parallelism

Grammar checkers are not very useful for identifying faulty parallelism. Although your grammar checker may highlight some nonparallel constructions, it may identify some parallelism problems as wordiness.

Exercise 18.2

Identify and correct faulty parallelism in these sentences. Then, underline the parallel elements—words, phrases, and clauses—in your corrected sentences. If a sentence is already correct, mark it with a *C*, and underline the parallel elements.

Example: Alfred Hitchcock's films include *North by Northwest*, *Vertigo*, *Psycho*, ~~and he also directed~~ *Notorious,* and *Saboteur.*

▶ 1. The world is divided between those with galoshes on and those who discover continents.

▶ 2. World leaders, members of Congress, and the American Catholic bishops all pressed the president to limit the arms race.

3. A national task force on education recommended improving public education by making the school day longer, higher teachers' salaries, and integrating more technology into the curriculum.

4. The fast food industry has expanded to include many kinds of restaurants: those that serve pizza, fried chicken chains, some offering Mexican-style menus, and hamburger franchises.

5. The consumption of Scotch in the United States is declining because of high prices, tastes are changing, and increased health awareness has led many whiskey drinkers to switch to wine or beer.

Chapter 19	Choosing Words

19a   Choosing an Appropriate Level of Diction

Diction, which comes from the Latin word for *say,* refers to the choice and use of words. Different audiences and situations call for different levels of diction.

(1) Formal Diction

Formal diction is grammatically correct and uses words familiar to an educated audience. A writer who uses formal diction often maintains emotional distance from the audience by using the impersonal *one* rather than the more personal *I* and *you*. In addition, the tone of the writing—as determined by word choice, sentence structure, and choice of subject—is dignified and objective.

> We learn to perceive in the sense that we learn to respond to things in particular ways because of the contingencies of which they are a part. We may perceive the sun, for example, simply because it is an extremely powerful stimulus, but it has been a permanent part of the environment of the species throughout its evolution, and more specific behavior with respect to it could have been selected by contingencies of survival (as it has been in many other species). (B. F. Skinner, *Beyond Freedom and Dignity*)

ESL Tip

Some of the expressions you learn from other students or from television are not appropriate for use in college writing. When you hear new expressions, pay attention to the contexts in which they are used.

(2) Informal Diction

Informal diction is the language that people use in conversation and in personal letters and informal emails. You should use informal diction in your college writing only to reproduce speech or dialect or to give a paper a conversational tone.

Colloquial Diction   **Colloquial diction** is the language of everyday speech. Contractions—*isn't, I'm*—are typical colloquialisms, as are **clipped forms**—*phone* for *telephone, TV* for *television, dorm* for *dormitory*. Other colloquialisms include placeholders like *kind of* and utility words like *nice* for *acceptable, funny* for *odd,* and *great* for almost anything. Colloquial English also includes expressions like *get across* for *communicate, come up with* for *find,* and *check out* for *investigate*.

Slang   **Slang,** language that calls attention to itself, is used to establish or reinforce identity within a group—urban teenagers, rock musicians, or computer users, for example. One characteristic of slang vocabulary is that it is usually relatively short-lived, coming into existence and fading out much more quickly than other words do. Because slang terms can emerge and disappear so quickly, no dictionary

—even a dictionary of slang—can list all or even most of the slang terms currently in use. Some slang words, however, eventually lose their slang status and become accepted as part of the language.

Regionalisms Regionalisms are words, expressions, and idiomatic forms that are used in particular geographical areas but may not be understood by a general audience. In eastern Tennessee, for example, a paper bag is a *poke*, and empty soda bottles are *dope bottles*. And New Yorkers stand *on line* for a movie, whereas people in most other parts of the country stand *in line*.

Nonstandard Diction **Nonstandard diction** refers to words and expressions not generally considered a part of standard English—words like *ain't, nohow, anywheres, nowheres, hisself,* and *theirselves.*

No absolute rules distinguish standard from nonstandard usage. In fact, some linguists reject the idea of nonstandard usage altogether, arguing that this designation relegates both the language and those who use it to second-class status.

NOTE: Keep in mind that colloquial expressions, slang, regionalisms, and nonstandard usages are almost always inappropriate in your college writing.

(3) College Writing

The level of diction appropriate for college writing depends on your assignment and your audience. A personal-experience essay calls for a somewhat informal style, but a research paper, an exam, or a report requires a more formal vocabulary and a more objective tone. In general, most college writing falls somewhere between formal and informal English, using a conversational tone but maintaining grammatical correctness and using a specialized vocabulary when the situation requires it. (This is the level of diction that is used in this book.)

Exercise 19.1

After reading the following paragraph, underline the words and phrases that identify it as formal diction. Then, rewrite the paragraph, using the level of diction that you would use in your college writing. Consult a dictionary if necessary.

In looking at many small points of difference between species, which, as far as our ignorance permits us to judge, seem quite unimportant, we must not forget that climate, food, etc., have no doubt produced some direct effect. It is also necessary to bear in mind that owing to the law of correlation, when one part varies and the variations are accumulated through natural selection, other modifications, often of the most unexpected nature, will ensue. (Charles Darwin, *The Origin of Species*)

19b Choosing the Right Word

Choosing the right word to use in a particular context is very important. If you use the wrong word—or even *almost* the right one—you run the risk of misrepresenting your ideas.

(1) Denotation and Connotation

A word's **denotation** is its basic dictionary meaning, what it stands for without any emotional associations. A word's **connotations** are the emotional, social, and political associations it has in addition to its denotative meaning.

Word	Denotation	Connotation
politician	someone who holds a political office	opportunist; wheeler-dealer

Selecting a word with the appropriate connotation can be challenging. For example, the word *skinny* has negative connotations, whereas *thin* is neutral, and *slender* is positive. And words and expressions like *mentally ill, insane, neurotic, crazy, psychopathic,* and *emotionally disturbed,* although similar in meaning, have different emotional, social, and political connotations that affect the way people respond. If you use terms without considering their connotations, you run the risk of undercutting your credibility, to say nothing of confusing and possibly angering your readers.

ESL Tip

Dictionary entries sometimes give a word's connotations as well as its denotations. You can also figure out a word's connotations from the context in which the word appears.

Exercise 19.2

The following words have negative connotations. For each, list one word with a similar meaning whose connotation is neutral and another whose connotation is favorable.

Example: *Negative*   skinny
              Neutral   thin
              Favorable   slender

▸ 1. deceive	6. blunder
▸ 2. antiquated	7. weird
▸ 3. pushy	8. politician
▸ 4. pathetic	9. shack
▸ 5. cheap	10. stench

(2) Euphemisms

A **euphemism** is a polite term used in place of a blunt or harsh term that describes a subject that many people consider offensive or unpleasant. College writing is no place for euphemisms. Say what you mean—*pregnant,* not *expecting; died,* not *passed away;* and *strike,* not *work stoppage.*

(3) Specific and General Words

Specific words refer to particular persons, items, or events; **general** words denote entire classes or groups. *Queen Elizabeth II,* for example, is more specific than *monarch; jeans* is more specific than *clothing;* and *SUV* is more specific than *vehicle.* You can use general words to describe entire classes of items, but you must use specific words to clarify such generalizations.

(4) Abstract and Concrete Words

Abstract words—*beauty, truth, justice,* and so on—refer to ideas, qualities, or conditions that cannot be perceived by the senses. **Concrete** words name things that readers can see, hear, taste, smell, or touch. As with general and specific words, whether a word is abstract or concrete is relative. The more concrete your words and phrases, the more vivid the image you evoke in the reader.

Close-up: Using Specific Words

Take particular care to avoid general words such as *nice, great,* and *terrific* that say nothing and could be used in almost any sentence. These <u>utility words</u> convey only enthusiasm, not precise meanings. Replace them with more specific words.

See
17a2

Exercise 19.3

Revise the following paragraph from a job application letter by substituting specific, concrete language for general or abstract words and phrases.

►I have had several part-time jobs lately. ►Some of them would qualify me for the position you advertised. ►In my most recent job, I sold products in a store. My supervisor said I was a good worker who had a number of valuable qualities. I am used to dealing with different types of people in different settings. I feel that my qualifications would make me a good candidate for your job opening.

19c Using Figures of Speech

Writers often use **figures of speech** (such as *similes* and *metaphors*) to go beyond the literal meanings of words. By doing so, they add interest and variety to their writing.

Close-up: Commonly Used Figures of Speech

A **simile** is a comparison between two essentially unlike things on the basis of a shared quality. A simile is introduced by *like* or *as*.

Like travelers with exotic destinations on their minds, the graduates were remarkably forgetful. (Maya Angelou, *I Know Why the Caged Bird Sings*)

A **metaphor** also compares two essentially dissimilar things, but instead of saying that one thing is *like* another, it *equates* them.

Perhaps it is easy for those who have never felt the stings and darts of segregation to say, "Wait." (Martin Luther King Jr., "Letter from Birmingham Jail")

An **analogy** explains an unfamiliar item or concept by comparing it to a more familiar one.

According to Robert Frost, writing free verse is like playing tennis without a net.

Personification gives an idea or inanimate object human attributes, feelings, or powers.

Truth strikes us from behind, and in the dark, as well as from before in broad daylight. (Henry David Thoreau, *Journals*)

A **hyperbole** (or overstatement) is an intentional exaggeration for emphasis. For example, Jonathan Swift uses hyperbole in his essay "A Modest Proposal" when he suggests that eating Irish babies would help the English solve their food shortage.

Understatement intentionally downplays the seriousness of a situation or sentiment by saying less than is really meant.

According to Mao Tse-tung, a revolution is not a tea party.

19d Avoiding Inappropriate Language

(1) Jargon

Jargon, the specialized or technical vocabulary of a trade, a profession, or an academic discipline, is useful for communicating in the field for which it was developed. Outside that field, however, it is often imprecise and confusing. For example, business executives may want departments to *interface* effectively, and sociologists may identify the need for *perspectivistic thinking* to achieve organizational goals. If they are addressing other professionals in their respective fields, these terms can facilitate communication. If, however, they are addressing a general audience, these terms are confusing and should be avoided.

(2) Neologisms

Neologisms are newly coined words that are not part of standard English. New situations call for new words, and frequently such words become a part of the language—*email, carjack,* and *outsource,* for example. Others, however, are never fully accepted. For example, questionable neologisms are created when the suffix *-wise* is added to existing words—creating nonstandard words like *weatherwise, sportswise, timewise,* and *productwise.*

If you are not sure whether to use a word, look it up in a current college **dictionary**. If the word is not there, you probably should not use it.

 See 35a

(3) Pretentious Diction

Good writing is clear and direct, not pompous or flowery. Revise to eliminate **pretentious diction,** inappropriately elevated and wordy language.

          asleep   *thought*   *hiking*
As I fell ~~into slumber~~, I ~~cogitated~~ about my day ~~ambling~~ through ~~the splendor of~~ the Appalachian Mountains.

Close-up: Using Pretentious Diction

Frequently, pretentious diction is formal diction used in a relatively informal situation. In such a context, it is always out of place. For every pretentious word, there is usually a clear and direct alternative.

Pretentious	Clear	Pretentious	Clear
ascertain	discover	reside	live
commence	start	terminate	end
implement	carry out	utilize	use
minuscule	small	individual	person

(4) Clichés

Figures of speech, such as metaphors and similes, stimulate thought by calling up vivid images in a reader's mind. When overused, however, figures of speech lose their power and become clichés—pat, meaningless phrases.

off the beaten path	happy as a clam
sit on the fence	a shot in the arm
free as a bird	smooth sailing
spread like wildfire	fit like a glove
Herculean efforts	fighting like cats and dogs

Writers sometimes resort to clichés when they run out of ideas. If readers sense that you are filling your writing with empty, tired phrases, they will lose interest and disregard your ideas. To keep their attention, you should take the time to think of original expressions that will give your writing the impact and appeal your ideas deserve.

Exercise 19.4

Go through a newspaper or magazine, and list the examples of jargon, neologisms, pretentious diction, or clichés that you find. Then, substitute more appropriate words for the ones you identified. Be prepared to discuss your interpretation of each word and of the word you chose to put in its place.

19e Avoiding Offensive Language

Because the language we use not only expresses our ideas but also shapes our thinking, you should avoid using words that insult or degrade others.

(1) Stereotypes

Racial and Ethnic When referring to any racial, ethnic, or religious group, use words with neutral connotations or words that the group uses in *formal* speech or writing to refer to itself—for example, *African American, Native American, Asian,* or *Latino/Latina*.

Age Avoid potentially offensive labels relating to age. Many older people like to call themselves *senior citizens* or *seniors*, and these terms are commonly used by the media and the government.

Class Do not demean certain jobs because they are low paying or praise others because they have impressive titles. Similarly, do not use words—*hick, cracker, redneck,* or *white trash*, for example—that denigrate people based on their social class.

Sexual Orientation Use neutral terms (such as *gay* and *lesbian*). Do not mention a person's sexual orientation unless it is relevant to your discussion.

(2) Sexist Language

Sexist language entails much more than the use of derogatory words, such as *hunk*, *chick*, and *bimbo*. Assuming that some professions are exclusive to one gender—for instance, that *nurse* denotes only women and that *doctor* denotes only men—is also sexist. So is the use of outdated job titles, such as *postman* for *letter carrier, fireman* for *firefighter,* and *stewardess* for *flight attendant.*

Sexist language also occurs when a writer fails to apply the same terminology to both men and women. For example, refer to two scientists with PhDs not as Dr. Sagan and Mrs. Yallow, but as Dr. Sagan and Dr. Yallow. Refer to two writers as James and Wharton, or Henry James and Edith Wharton, not James and Mrs. Wharton.

In your writing, always use *women*—not *girls, gals,* or *ladies*—when referring to adult females. Use *Ms.* as the form of address when a woman's marital status is unknown or irrelevant. (If the woman you are addressing refers to herself as *Mrs.* or *Miss,* however, use the form of address she prefers.) Finally, avoid using the generic *he* or *him* when your subject could be either male or female. Use the third-person plural (*they*) or the phrase *he or she* (not *he/she*).

Sexist: Before boarding, each passenger should make certain that <u>he</u> has <u>his</u> ticket.

Revised: Before boarding, <u>passengers</u> should make certain that they have <u>their</u> tickets.

Revised: Before boarding, each <u>passenger</u> should make certain that <u>he or she</u> has a ticket.

NOTE: Remember not to overuse *his or her* or *he or she* constructions, which can make your writing repetitious and wordy.

Close-up: Eliminating Sexist Language

For every sexist usage, there is usually a nonsexist alternative.

Sexist Usage	Possible Revisions
Mankind	People, human beings
Man's accomplishments	Human accomplishments
Man-made	Synthetic

(continued)

Eliminating sexist language (continued)

Sexist Usage	Possible Revisions
Female engineer/lawyer/ accountant, and so on; male model	Engineer/lawyer/accountant, and so on; model
Policeman/woman Salesman/woman/girl Businessman/woman	Police officer Salesperson, representative Businessperson, executive
<u>Everyone</u> should complete <u>his</u> application by Tuesday.	<u>Everyone</u> should complete <u>his or her</u> application by Tuesday. <u>All students</u> should complete <u>their</u> applications by Tuesday.

NOTE: When trying to avoid sexist use of *he* and *him* in your writing, be careful not to use the plural pronoun *they* or *their* to refer to a singular antecedent.

> *Drivers*
> ~~Any driver~~ caught speeding should have their driving privileges
> suspended.

Exercise 19.5

Suggest at least one alternative form for each of the following words or phrases. In each case, comment on the advantages and disadvantages of the alternative you recommend. If you feel that a particular term is not sexist, explain why.

- forefathers
- man-eating shark
- manpower
- workman's compensation
- men at work
- waitress
- first baseman
- congressman
- manhunt
  longshoreman
  committeeman
  (to) man the battle stations

Girl Friday
point man
draftsman
man overboard
fisherman
foreman
manned space program
gentleman's agreement
no man's land
spinster
old maid
old wives' tale

Exercise 19.6

Each of the following pairs of terms includes a feminine form that was at one time in wide use; most are still used to some extent. Which do you think are likely to remain in our language for some time, and which do you think will disappear? Explain your reasoning.

heir/heiress
benefactor/benefactress
murderer/murderess
actor/actress
hero/heroine
host/hostess
aviator/aviatrix
executor/executrix

author/authoress
poet/poetess
tailor/seamstress
comedian/comedienne
villain/villainess
prince/princess
widow/widower

PART 4

> **Grammar Checker**
>
> Subject-Verb Agreement:
>
> All of these little details makes the hard to understand.

Understanding Grammar

Chapter 20 | Parts of Speech

The eight basic **parts of speech**—the building blocks for all English sentences—are *nouns, pronouns, verbs, adjectives, adverbs, prepositions, conjunctions,* and *interjections.* How a word is classified depends on its function in a sentence.

20a Nouns

Nouns name people, animals, places, things, ideas, actions, or qualities.

A **common noun** names any one of a class of people, places, or things: *artist, judge, building, event, city.*

A **proper noun,** always capitalized, designates a particular person, place, or thing: *Mary Cassatt, World Trade Center, Crimean War.*

A **count noun** names something that can be counted: five *dogs,* two dozen *grapes.*

A **noncount noun** names a quantity that is not countable: *time, dust, work, gold.* Noncount nouns generally have only a singular form.

A **collective noun** designates a group thought of as a unit: *committee, class, navy, band, family.* Collective nouns are generally singular unless the members of the group are referred to as individuals.

An **abstract noun** designates an intangible idea or quality: *love, hate, justice, anger, fear, prejudice.*

20b Pronouns

Pronouns are words used in place of nouns. The word for which a pronoun stands is called its **antecedent.**

If you use a <u>quotation</u> in your paper, you must document <u>it</u>. (Pronoun *it* refers to antecedent *quotation.*)

A **personal pronoun** stands for a person or thing. Personal pronouns include *I, me, we, us, my, mine, our, ours, you, your, yours, he, she, it, its, him, his, her, hers, they, them, their,* and *theirs.*

The firm made Debbie an offer, and <u>she</u> couldn't refuse <u>it</u>.

An <u>indefinite pronoun</u> does not refer to any particular person or thing, so it does not require an antecedent. Indefinite pronouns include *another, any, each, few, many, some, nothing, one, anyone, everyone, everybody, everything, someone, something, either,* and *neither.*

<u>Many</u> are called, but <u>few</u> are chosen.

196

A **reflexive pronoun** ends with *-self* and refers to a recipient of an action that is the same as the initiator of the action. The reflexive pronouns are *myself, yourself, himself, herself, itself, oneself, themselves, ourselves,* and *yourselves.*

They found <u>themselves</u> in downtown Pittsburgh.

An **intensive pronoun** emphasizes a noun or pronoun that directly precedes it. (Intensive pronouns have the same form as reflexive pronouns.)

Darrow <u>himself</u> was sure his client was innocent.

A **relative pronoun** introduces an adjective clause or a noun clause in a sentence. Relative pronouns include *which, who, whom, that, what, whose, whatever, whoever, whomever,* and *whichever.*

Gandhi was the charismatic man <u>who</u> helped lead India to independence. (introduces adjective clause)

<u>Whatever</u> happens will be a surprise. (introduces noun clause)

An **interrogative pronoun** introduces a question. Interrogative pronouns include *who, which, what, whom, whose, whoever, whatever,* and *whichever.*

<u>Who</u> was that masked man?

A **demonstrative pronoun** points to a particular thing or group of things. *This, that, these,* and *those* are demonstrative pronouns.

<u>This</u> is one of Shakespeare's early plays.

A **reciprocal pronoun** denotes a mutual relationship. The reciprocal pronouns are *each other* and *one another. Each other* indicates a relationship between two individuals; *one another* denotes a relationship among more than two.

Romeo and Juliet declared their love for <u>each other</u>.

Concertgoers jostled <u>one another</u> in the ticket line.

NOTE: Although different types of pronouns may have the same form, they are distinguished from one another by their function in a sentence.

20c Verbs

(1) Recognizing Verbs

A <u>verb</u> may express an action or a state of being.

ESL
48a

He <u>ran</u> for the train. (physical action)

He <u>worried</u> about being late. (emotional action)

Elizabeth II <u>became</u> queen after the death of her father, George VI. (state of being)

Verbs can be classified into two groups: *main verbs* and *auxiliary verbs*.

Main Verbs **Main verbs** carry most of the meaning in a sentence. Some main verbs are **action verbs.**

Emily Dickinson <u>wrote</u> poetry.

Other main verbs function as linking verbs. A **linking verb** does not show any physical or emotional action. Its function is to link the sentence's subject to a **subject complement,** a word or phrase that renames or describes the subject.

Carbon disulfide <u>smells</u> bad.

Frequently Used Linking Verbs				
appear	believe	look	seem	taste
be	feel	prove	smell	turn
become	grow	remain	sound	

Auxiliary Verbs **Auxiliary verbs** (also called **helping verbs**), such as *be* and *have*, combine with main verbs to form **verb phrases.** Auxiliary verbs indicate tense, voice, or mood.

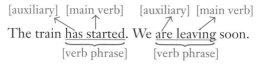

The train <u>has started</u>. We <u>are leaving</u> soon.

[verb phrase]   [verb phrase]

Certain auxiliary verbs, known as **modal auxiliaries,** indicate necessity, possibility, willingness, obligation, or ability.

In the future, farmers <u>might</u> cultivate seaweed as a food crop.

Coal mining <u>would</u> be safer if dust were controlled in the mines.

Modal Auxiliaries			
can	might	ought [to]	will
could	must	shall	would
may	need [to]	should	

(2) Recognizing Verbals

Verbals, such as *known* or *swimming* or *to go*, are verb forms that act as adjectives, adverbs, or nouns. A verbal can never serve as a sentence's main verb unless it is used with one or more auxiliary verbs (*has known, should be swimming*). Verbals include *participles, infinitives,* and *gerunds*.

Participles Virtually every verb has a **present participle,** which ends in *-ing* (*loving, learning, going, writing*), and a **past participle,** which usually ends in *-d* or *-ed* (*agreed, learned*). Some verbs have <u>irregular</u> past participles (*gone, begun, written*). Participles may function in a sentence as adjectives or as nouns.

Twenty brands of <u>running</u> shoes were displayed at the exhibition. (Present participle *running* serves as adjective modifying noun *shoes*.)

The <u>crowded</u> bus went past those waiting at the corner. (Past participle *crowded* serves as adjective modifying noun *bus*.)

The <u>wounded</u> were given emergency first aid. (Past participle *wounded* serves as a noun, the sentence's subject.)

NOTE: Participles also combine with helping verbs to form the <u>perfect tense</u> and the <u>progressive tense</u>.

Infinitives An **infinitive**—the *to* form of the verb—may function as an adjective, an adverb, or a noun.

Ann Arbor was clearly the place <u>to be</u>. (Infinitive serves as adjective modifying noun *place*.)

They say that breaking up is hard <u>to do</u>. (Infinitive serves as adverb modifying adjective *hard*.)

Carla went outside <u>to think</u>. (Infinitive serves as adverb modifying verb *went*.)

<u>To win</u> was everything. (Infinitive serves as noun, the sentence's subject.)

Gerunds **Gerunds** (which, like present participles, end in *-ing*) always function as nouns.

<u>Seeing</u> is <u>believing</u>. (Gerund *seeing* serves as sentence's subject; gerund *believing* serves as subject complement.)

He worried about <u>interrupting</u>. (Gerund *interrupting* is object of preposition *about*.)

Andrew loves <u>skiing</u>. (Gerund *skiing* is direct object of verb *loves*.)

NOTE: When the *-ing* form of a verb is used as a noun, it is a *gerund;* when it is used as an adjective, it is a *present participle.*

20d Adjectives

Adjectives describe, limit, qualify, or in some other way modify nouns or pronouns.

(1) Descriptive Adjectives

Descriptive adjectives name a quality of the noun or pronoun they modify.

> After the game, they were <u>exhausted</u>.
>
> They ordered a <u>chocolate</u> soda and a <u>butterscotch</u> sundae.

Some descriptive adjectives are formed from common nouns or from verbs (*friend/friendly, agree/agreeable*). Others, called **proper adjectives,** are formed from proper nouns.

> A <u>Shakespearean</u> sonnet consists of an octave and a sestet.

Two or more words may be joined (hyphenated before a noun, without a hyphen after a noun) to form a <u>compound adjective</u>: *His parents are very <u>well-read</u> people; most people are not so <u>well read</u>.*

See
38b1

(2) Determiners

When articles, pronouns, numbers, and the like function as adjectives, limiting or qualifying nouns or pronouns, they are referred to as <u>determiners</u>.

ESL
48b
2–3

Articles (*a, an, the*)

> <u>The</u> boy found <u>a</u> four-leaf clover.

Possessive nouns

> <u>Lesley's</u> mother lives in New Jersey.

Possessive pronouns (the personal pronouns *my, your, his, her, its, our, their*)

> <u>Their</u> lives depended on <u>my</u> skill.

Demonstrative pronouns (*this, these, that, those*)

> <u>This</u> song reminds me of <u>that</u> song we heard yesterday.

Interrogative pronouns (*what, which, whose*)

<u>Whose</u> book is this?

Indefinite pronouns (*another, each, both, many, any, some,* and so on)

<u>Both</u> candidates agreed to return <u>another</u> day.

Relative pronouns (*what, whatever, which, whichever, whose, whoever*)

I forgot <u>whatever</u> reasons I had for leaving.

Numbers (*one, two, first, second,* and so on)

The <u>first</u> time I played baseball, I got only <u>one</u> hit.

20e Adverbs

ESL
48d5

<u>Adverbs</u> describe the action of verbs or modify adjectives, other adverbs, or complete phrases, clauses, or sentences. They answer the questions "How?" "Why?" "Where?" "When?" "Under what conditions?" and "To what extent?"

He walked <u>rather hesitantly</u> toward the front of the room. (walked *how?*)

Let's meet <u>tomorrow</u> for coffee. (meet *when?*)

Adverbs that modify other adverbs or adjectives limit or qualify the words they modify.

He pitched an <u>almost</u> perfect game.

Interrogative adverbs—*how, when, why,* and *where*—introduce questions.

<u>Why</u> did the compound darken?

Conjunctive adverbs act as **transitional words**, joining and relating independent clauses. Conjunctive adverbs may appear in various positions in a sentence.

See
5b2

Jason forgot to register for chemistry. <u>However</u>, he managed to sign up during the drop/add period.

Jason forgot to register for chemistry; <u>however</u>, he managed to sign up during the drop/add period.

Jason forgot to register for chemistry. He managed, <u>however</u>, to sign up during the drop/add period.

Jason forgot to register for chemistry. He managed to sign up during the drop/add period, <u>however</u>.

Frequently Used Conjunctive Adverbs

accordingly	furthermore	meanwhile	similarly
also	hence	moreover	still
anyway	however	nevertheless	then
besides	incidentally	next	thereafter
certainly	indeed	nonetheless	therefore
consequently	instead	now	thus
finally	likewise	otherwise	undoubtedly

20f Prepositions

ESL 48c

A <u>preposition</u> introduces a noun or pronoun (or a phrase or clause functioning in the sentence as a noun), linking it to other words in the sentence. The word or word group the preposition introduces is called its **object.**

prep   obj   prep   obj

They received a postcard <u>from</u> Bobby telling <u>about</u> his trip.

Frequently Used Prepositions

about	beneath	inside	since
above	beside	into	through
across	between	like	throughout
after	beyond	near	to
against	by	of	toward
along	concerning	off	under
among	despite	on	underneath
around	down	onto	until
as	during	out	up
at	except	outside	upon
before	for	over	with
behind	from	past	within
below	in	regarding	without

20g Conjunctions

Conjunctions connect words, phrases, clauses, or sentences.

    Coordinating conjunctions (*and, or, but, nor, for, so, yet*) connect words, phrases, or clauses of equal weight.

The choice was simple: chicken <u>or</u> fish. (*Or* links two nouns.)

The United States is a government "of the people, by the people, <u>and</u> for the people." (*And* links three prepositional phrases.) Thoreau wrote *Walden* in 1854, <u>and</u> he died in 1862. (*And* links two independent clauses.)

Correlative conjunctions, always used in pairs, also link grammatically equivalent items.

<u>Both</u> Hancock <u>and</u> Jefferson signed the Declaration of Independence. (Correlative conjunctions link two nouns.) <u>Either</u> I will renew my lease, <u>or</u> I will move. (Correlative conjunctions link two independent clauses.)

Correlative Conjunctions

both . . . and	neither . . . nor
either . . . or	not only . . . but also
just as . . . so	whether . . . or

Subordinating conjunctions include *since, because, although, if, after, when, while, before, unless,* and so on. A subordinating conjunction introduces a dependent (subordinate) clause, connecting it to an independent (main) clause to form a **complex sentence**.

<u>Although</u> drug use is a serious concern for parents, many parents are afraid to discuss it with their children.

It is best to diagram your garden <u>before</u> you start to plant it.

NOTE: A subordinating conjunction indicates the relationship between clauses.

See
14b

20h Interjections

Interjections are exclamations used to express emotion: *Oh! Ouch! Wow! Alas! Hey!* These words are grammatically independent; that is, they do not have a grammatical function in a sentence.

An interjection may be set off in a sentence by commas.

The message, <u>alas</u>, arrived too late.

For greater emphasis, an interjection can be punctuated as an independent unit, set off with an exclamation point.

<u>Alas</u>! The message arrived too late.

NOTE: Other kinds of words may also be used in isolation. These include *yes, no, hello, good-bye, please,* and *thank you.* All such words, including interjections, are collectively referred to as **isolates.**

Chapter 21 Using Nouns and Pronouns

21a Understanding Case

Case is the form a noun or pronoun takes to indicate its function in a sentence. Nouns change form only in the possessive case: the *cat's* eyes, *Molly's* book. Pronouns, however, have three cases: *subjective, objective,* and *possessive.*

Pronoun Case Forms

Subjective
I	he, she	it	we	you	they	who
						whoever

Objective
me	him, her	it	us	you	them	whom
						whomever

Possessive
my	his, her	its	our	your	their	whose
mine	hers		ours	yours	theirs	

(1) Subjective Case

A pronoun takes the **subjective case** in the following situations.

Subject of a Verb: I bought a new mountain bike.

Subject Complement: It was he who volunteered to drive.

(2) Objective Case

A pronoun takes the **objective case** in the following situations.

Direct Object: Our supervisor asked Adam and me to work on the project.

Indirect Object: The plumber's bill gave him quite a shock.

Object of a Preposition: Between us, we own ten shares of stock.

Close-up: Pronoun Case in Compound Constructions

I is not necessarily more appropriate than *me*. In compound constructions like the following, *me* is correct.

Just between you and <u>me</u> [not *I*], I think we're going to have a quiz. (*Me* is the object of the preposition *between*.)

(3) Possessive Case

A pronoun takes the **possessive case** when it indicates ownership (*our* car, *your* book). The possessive case is also used before a <u>gerund</u>.

See 20c2

Napoleon gave <u>his</u> approval to <u>their</u> ruling Naples. (*His* indicates ownership; *ruling* is a gerund.)

Exercise 21.1

Underline the correct form of the pronoun within the parentheses. Be prepared to explain why you chose each form.

Example: Toni Morrison, Alice Walker, and (<u>she</u>, her) are perhaps the most widely recognized African-American women writing today.

▸ 1. Both Walt Whitman and (he, him) wrote a great deal of poetry about nature.
▸ 2. Our instructor gave Matthew and (me, I) an excellent idea for our project.
   3. The sales clerk objected to (me, my) returning the sweater.
   4. I understand (you, your) being unavailable to work tonight.
   5. The waiter asked Michael and (me, I) to move to another table.

21b Determining Pronoun Case in Special Situations

(1) Comparisons with *Than* or *As*

When a comparison ends with a pronoun, the pronoun's function in the sentence determines your choice of pronoun case. If the pronoun functions as a subject, use the subjective case; if it functions as an object, use the objective case. You can determine the function of the pronoun by completing the comparison.

Darcy likes John more than <u>I</u>. (*I* is the subject: more than I like John)

Darcy likes John more than <u>me</u>. (*Me* is the object: more than she likes me.)

(2) *Who* and *Whom*

The case of the pronouns *who* and *whom* depends on their function *within their own clause*. When a pronoun serves as the subject of its clause, use *who* or *whoever*; when it functions as an object, use *whom* or *whomever*.

The Salvation Army gives food and shelter to <u>whoever</u> is in need. (*Whoever* is the subject of the dependent clause *whoever is in need.*)

I wonder <u>whom</u> jazz musician Miles Davis influenced. (*Whom* is the object of *influenced* in the dependent clause *whom jazz musician Miles Davis influenced.*)

Close-up: Pronoun Case in Questions

To determine whether to use subjective case (*who*) or objective case (*whom*) in a question, use a personal pronoun to answer the question. If the personal pronoun is the subject, use *who*; if the personal pronoun is the object, use *whom*.

<u>Who</u> wrote *The Age of Innocence?* <u>She</u> wrote it. (subject)

<u>Whom</u> do you support for mayor? I support <u>her</u>. (object)

---

(3) Appositives

ESL
48e4

An <u>appositive</u> is a noun or noun phrase that identifies or renames an adjacent noun or pronoun. The case of a pronoun in an appositive depends on the function of the word the appositive identifies or renames.

We heard two Motown recording artists, Smokey Robinson and <u>him</u>. (*Artists* is the object of the verb *heard,* so the pronoun in the appositive *Smokey Robinson and him* takes the objective case.)

Two Motown recording artists, Smokey Robinson and <u>he</u>, recorded for Motown Records. (*Artists* is the subject of the sentence, so the pronoun in the appositive *Smokey Robinson and he* takes the subjective case.)

(4) *We* and *Us* before a Noun

When a first-person plural pronoun directly precedes a noun, the case of the pronoun depends on the way the noun functions in the sentence.

<u>We</u> women must stick together. (*Women* is the subject of the sentence, so the pronoun *we* must be in the subjective case.)

Teachers make learning easy for us students. (*Students* is the object of the preposition *for*, so the pronoun *us* must be in the objective case.)

Exercise 21.2

Using the word in parentheses, combine each pair of sentences into a single sentence. You may change word order and add or delete words.

Example: After he left the band The Police, bass player Sting continued as a solo artist. He once taught middle-school English. (who)

Revised: After he left the band The Police, bass player Sting, who once taught middle-school English, continued as a solo artist.

▸ 1. Herb Ritts has photographed world leaders, leading artistic figures in dance and drama, and a vanishing African tribe. He got his start by taking photographs of Hollywood stars. (who)
▸ 2. Tim Green has written several novels about a fictional football team. He played for the Atlanta Hawks and has a degree in law. (who)
3. Some say Carl Sagan did more to further science education in America than any other person. He wrote many books on science and narrated many popular television shows. (who)
4. Jodie Foster has won two Academy Awards for her acting. She was a child star. (who)
5. Sylvia Plath met the poet Ted Hughes at Cambridge University in England. She later married him. (whom)

21c Revising Pronoun Reference Errors

An **antecedent** is the word or word group to which a pronoun refers. The connection between a pronoun and its antecedent should always be clear. If the **pronoun reference** is not clear, you will need to revise the sentence.

ESL
48e1

(1) Ambiguous Antecedent

Sometimes it is not clear to which antecedent a pronoun—for example, *this, that, which,* or *it*—refers. In such cases, eliminate the ambiguity by substituting a noun for the pronoun.

The accountant took out his calculator and completed the tax
                    the calculator
return. Then, he put ɪt into his briefcase. (The pronoun *it* can refer either to *calculator* or to *tax return*.)

(2) Remote Antecedent

If a pronoun is far from its antecedent, readers will have difficulty making a connection between them. To eliminate this problem, replace the pronoun with a noun.

> During the mid-1800s, many Czechs began to immigrate to America. By 1860, about 23,000 Czechs had left their country;
> *America's*
> by 1900, 13,000 Czech immigrants were coming to ~~its~~ shores each year.

(3) Nonexistent Antecedent

Sometimes a pronoun—for example, *this*—refers to an antecedent that does not exist. In such cases, add the missing antecedent.

> Some one-celled organisms contain chlorophyll yet are
> *paradox*
> considered animals. This illustrates the difficulty of classifying single-celled organisms. (Exactly what does *this* refer to?)

NOTE: Expressions such as "*It* says in the paper" and "*They* said on the news," which refer to unidentified antecedents, are not acceptable in college writing. Substitute the appropriate noun for the unclear pronoun: "The *article* in the paper says . . ." and "In his commentary, *Ted Koppel* observes. . . ."

(4) *Who, Which,* and *That*

In general, *who* refers to people or to animals that have names. *Which* and *that* refer to things or to unnamed animals. When referring to an antecedent, be sure to choose the appropriate pronoun (*who, which,* or *that*).

> David Henry Hwang, <u>who</u> wrote the Tony Award-winning play *M. Butterfly*, also wrote *Family Devotions* and *FOB*.

> The spotted owl, <u>which</u> lives in old growth forests, is in danger of extinction.

> Houses <u>that</u> are built today are usually more energy efficient than those built twenty years ago.

Never use *that* to refer to a person.

> *who*
> The man ~~that~~ holds the world record for eating hot dogs is my neighbor.

NOTE: Make certain that you use *which* in nonrestrictive clauses, which are always set off with commas. In most cases, use *that* in restrictive clauses, which are not set off with commas. *Who* may be used in both restrictive clauses and nonrestrictive clauses.

See
30d1

Exercise 21.3

Analyze the pronoun reference errors in each of the following sentences. After doing so, revise each sentence by substituting an appropriate noun or noun phrase for the underlined pronoun.

Example: Jefferson asked Lewis to head the expedition, and Lewis
selected <ins>him</ins> as his associate. (*Him* refers to a nonexistent antecedent.)

Clark

▸ 1. The purpose of the expedition was to search out a land route to the Pacific and to gather information about the West. The Louisiana Purchase increased the need for <u>it</u>.
▸ 2. The expedition was going to be difficult. <u>They</u> trained the men in Illinois, the starting point.
  3. Clark and most of the men who descended the Yellowstone River camped on the bank. <u>It</u> was beautiful and wild.
  4. Both Jefferson and Lewis had faith that <u>he</u> would be successful in this transcontinental journey.
  5. The expedition was efficient, and only one man was lost. <u>This</u> was extraordinary.

Chapter 22	Using Verbs

22a Understanding Verb Forms

Every verb has four **principal parts:** a **base form** (the form of the verb used with *I, we, you,* and *they* in the present tense), a **present participle** (the *-ing* form of the verb), a **past tense form,** and a **past participle.**

NOTE: The verb *be* is so irregular that it is the one exception to this definition; its base form is *be*.

(1) Regular Verbs

A **regular verb** forms both its past tense and its past participle by adding *-d* or *-ed* to the base form of the verb.

Principal Parts of Regular Verbs

Base Form	Past Tense Form	Past Participle
smile	smiled	smiled
talk	talked	talked
jump	jumped	jumped

(2) Irregular Verbs

Irregular verbs do not follow the pattern discussed above. The chart that follows lists the principal parts of the most frequently used irregular verbs.

Frequently Used Irregular Verbs

Base Form	Past Tense Form	Past Participle
arise	arose	arisen
awake	awoke, awaked	awoke, awaked
be	was/were	been
beat	beat	beaten
begin	began	begun
bend	bent	bent
bet	bet, betted	bet
bite	bit	bitten
blow	blew	blown
break	broke	broken
bring	brought	brought
build	built	built
burst	burst	burst
buy	bought	bought
catch	caught	caught
choose	chose	chosen
cling	clung	clung
come	came	come
cost	cost	cost
deal	dealt	dealt
dig	dug	dug
dive	dived, dove	dived
do	did	done
drag	dragged	dragged
draw	drew	drawn
drink	drank	drunk
drive	drove	driven
eat	ate	eaten
fall	fell	fallen

Base Form	Past Tense Form	Past Participle
fight	fought	fought
find	found	found
fly	flew	flown
forget	forgot	forgotten, forgot
freeze	froze	frozen
get	got	gotten
give	gave	given
go	went	gone
grow	grew	grown
hang (execute)	hanged	hanged
hang (suspend)	hung	hung
have	had	had
hear	heard	heard
keep	kept	kept
know	knew	known
lay	laid	laid
lead	led	led
lend	lent	lent
let	let	let
lie (recline)	lay	lain
lie (tell an untruth)	lied	lied
make	made	made
prove	proved	proved, proven
read	read	read
ride	rode	ridden
ring	rang	rung
rise	rose	risen
run	ran	run
say	said	said
see	saw	seen
set (place)	set	set
shake	shook	shaken
shrink	shrank, shrunk,	shrunk, shrunken
sing	sang	sung
sink	sank	sunk
sit	sat	sat
sneak	sneaked	sneaked
speak	spoke	spoken
speed	sped, speeded	sped, speeded
spin	spun	spun
spring	sprang	sprung
stand	stood	stood
steal	stole	stolen
strike	struck	struck, stricken

(continued)

Frequently used irregular verbs (continued)

Base Form	Past Tense Form	Past Participle
swear	swore	sworn
swim	swam	swum
swing	swung	swung
take	took	taken
teach	taught	taught
throw	threw	thrown
wake	woke, waked	waked, woken
wear	wore	worn
wring	wrung	wrung
write	wrote	written

http://kirsznermandell.wadsworth.com

Computer Tip: Using Correct Verb Forms

Your word processor's grammar checker will high-light incorrect verb forms in your writing and offer revision suggestions.

Close-up: *Lie/Lay* and *Sit/Set*

Lie means "to recline" and does not take an object ("He likes to *lie* on the floor"); *lay* means "to place" or "to put" and does take an object ("He wants to *lay* a rug on the floor").

Base Form	Past Tense Form	Past Participle
lie	lay	lain
lay	laid	laid

Sit means "to assume a seated position" and does not take an object ("She wants to *sit* on the table"); *set* means "to place" or "to put" and usually takes an object ("She wants to *set* a vase on the table").

Base Form	Past Tense Form	Past Participle
sit	sat	sat
set	set	set

Exercise 22.1

Complete the sentences in the following paragraph with an appropriate form of the verbs in parentheses.

Example: An air of mystery surrounds many of those who have
_____*sung*_____ (sing) and played the blues.

▸The legendary bluesman Robert Johnson supposedly _____ (sell) his soul to the devil in order to become a guitar virtuoso. ▸Myth has it that the young Johnson could barely chord his instrument and annoyed other musicians by trying to sit in at clubs, where he _____ (sneak) onto the bandstand to play every chance he got. He disappeared for a short time, the story goes, and when he returned he was a phenomenal guitarist, having _____ (swear) a Faustian oath to Satan. Johnson's song "Crossroads Blues"—rearranged and recorded by the sixties band Cream as simply "Crossroads"—supposedly recounts this exchange, telling how Johnson _____ (deal) with the devil. Some of his other songs, such as "Hellhound on My Trail," are allegedly about the torment he suffered as he _____ (fight) for his soul.

Exercise 22.2

Complete the following sentences with appropriate forms of the verbs in parentheses.

Example: Mary Cassatt _____*laid*_____ down her paintbrush. (lie, lay)

▸ 1. Impressionist artists of the nineteenth century preferred everyday subjects and used to _____ fruit on a table to paint. (sit, set)
▸ 2. They were known for their technique of _____ dabs of paint quickly on canvas, giving an "impression" of a scene, not extensive detail. (lying, laying)
  3. Claude Monet's *Women in the Garden* featured one woman in the foreground who _____ on the grass in a garden. (sat, set)
  4. In Pierre Auguste Renoir's *Nymphs*, two nude figures talk while _____ on flowers in a garden. (lying, laying)
  5. Paul Cézanne liked to _____ in front of his subject as he painted and often completed paintings out of doors rather than in a studio. (sit, set)

22b Understanding Tense

ESL
48a2

<u>Tense</u> is the form a verb takes to indicate when an action occurred or when a condition existed.

English Verb Tenses

Simple Tenses
Present (I *finish*, she or he *finishes*)
Past (I *finished*)
Future (I *will finish*)

(continued)

English verb tenses (continued)

Perfect Tenses
Present perfect (I *have finished*, she or he *has finished*)
Past perfect (I *had finished*)
Future perfect (I *will have finished*)

Progressive Tenses
Present progressive (I *am finishing*, she or he *is finishing*)
Past progressive (I *was finishing*)
Future progressive (I *will be finishing*)
Present perfect progressive (I *have been finishing*)
Past perfect progressive (I *had been finishing*)
Future perfect progressive (I *will have been finishing*)

(1) Using the Simple Tenses

The **simple tenses** include *present, past,* and *future.*

The **present tense** usually indicates an action that is taking place at the time it is expressed in speech or writing. It can also indicate an action that occurs regularly.

I <u>see</u> your point. (an action taking place when it is expressed)

We <u>wear</u> wool in the winter. (an action that occurs regularly)

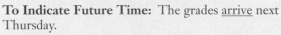

Close-up: Special Uses of the Present Tense

The present tense has four special uses.

To Indicate Future Time: The grades <u>arrive</u> next Thursday.
To State a Generally Held Belief: Studying <u>pays</u> off.
To State a Scientific Truth: An object at rest <u>tends</u> to stay at rest.
To Discuss a Literary Work: *Family Installments* <u>tells</u> the story of a Puerto Rican family.

The **past tense** indicates that an action has already taken place.

John Glenn <u>orbited</u> the earth three times on February 20, 1962. (an action completed in the past)

As a young man, Mark Twain <u>traveled</u> through the Southwest. (an action that occurred once or many times in the past but did not extend into the present)

The **future tense** indicates that an action will or is likely to take place.

Halley's Comet <u>will reappear</u> in 2061. (a future action that will definitely occur)

The land boom in Nevada <u>will</u> probably <u>continue</u>. (a future action that is likely to occur)

(2) Using the Perfect Tenses

The **perfect tenses** designate actions that were or will be completed before other actions or conditions. The perfect tenses are formed with the appropriate tense form of the auxiliary verb *have* plus the past participle.

The **present perfect** tense can indicate two types of continuing action beginning in the past.

Dr. Kim <u>has finished</u> studying the effects of BHA on rats. (an action that began in the past and is finished at the present time)

My mother <u>has invested</u> her money wisely. (an action that began in the past and extends into the present)

The **past perfect** tense indicates an action occurring before a certain time in the past.

By 1946, engineers <u>had built</u> the first electronic digital computer.

The **future perfect** tense indicates that an action will be finished by a certain future time.

By Tuesday, the transit authority <u>will have run</u> out of money.

Close-up: *Could Have, Should Have,* and *Would Have*

Do not use the preposition *of* after *would, should, could,* and *might*. Use the auxiliary verb *have* after these words.

have
I should ~~of~~ left for class earlier.

---

(3) Using the Progressive Tenses

The **progressive tenses** express continuing action. They are formed with the appropriate tense of the verb *be* plus the present participle.

The **present progressive** tense indicates that something is happening at the time it is expressed in speech or writing.

The volcano <u>is erupting</u>, and lava <u>is flowing</u> toward the town.

The **past progressive** tense indicates two kinds of past action.

Roderick Usher's actions <u>were becoming</u> increasingly bizarre. (a continuing action in the past)

The French revolutionary Marat was stabbed to death while he <u>was bathing</u>. (an action occurring at the same time in the past as another action)

The **future progressive** tense indicates a continuing action in the future.

The treasury secretary <u>will be monitoring</u> the money supply regularly.

The **present perfect progressive** tense indicates action continuing from the past into the present and possibly into the future.

Rescuers <u>have been working</u> around the clock.

The **past perfect progressive** tense indicates that a past action went on until another one occurred.

Before President Kennedy was assassinated, he <u>had been working</u> on civil rights legislation.

The **future perfect progressive** tense indicates that an action will continue until a certain future time.

By eleven o'clock we <u>will have been driving</u> for seven hours.

(4) Using Verb Tenses in a Sentence

You use different tenses in a sentence to indicate that actions are taking place at different times. By choosing tenses that accurately express these times, you enable readers to follow the sequence of actions:

- *When a **verb** appears in a dependent clause, its tense depends on the tense of the main verb in the independent clause.* When the main verb in the independent clause is in the past tense, the verb in the dependent clause is usually in the past or past perfect tense. When the main verb in the independent clause is in the past perfect tense, the verb in the dependent clause is usually in the past tense. (When the main verb in the independent clause is in any tense except the past or past perfect, the verb in the dependent clause may be in any tense needed for meaning.)

Main Verb	Verb in Dependent Clause
George Hepplewhite <u>was</u> (past) an English cabinetmaker	who <u>designed</u> (past) distinctive chair backs.
The battle <u>had ended</u> (past perfect)	by the time reinforcements <u>arrived</u>. (past)

- *When an **infinitive** appears in a verbal phrase, the tense it expresses depends on the tense of the sentence's main verb.* The *present infinitive* (the *to* form of the verb) indicates an action happening at the same time as or later than the main verb. The *perfect infinitive* (*to have* plus the past participle) indicates action happening earlier than the main verb.

Main Verb	Infinitive
I <u>went</u>	<u>to see</u> the Rangers play last week. (The going and seeing occurred at the same time.)
I <u>want</u>	<u>to see</u> the Rangers play tomorrow. (Wanting occurs in the present, and seeing will occur in the future.)
I would <u>like</u>	<u>to have seen</u> the Rangers play. (Liking occurs in the present, and seeing would have occurred in the past.)

- *When a **participle** appears in a verbal phrase, its tense depends on the tense of the sentence's main verb.* The *present participle* indicates action happening at the same time as the action of the main verb. The *past participle* or the *present perfect participle* indicates action occurring before the action of the main verb.

Participle	Main Verb
<u>Addressing</u> the 1896 Democratic Convention,	William Jennings Bryan <u>delivered</u> his Cross of Gold speech. (The addressing and the delivery occurred at the same time.)
<u>Having written</u> her term paper,	Camille <u>studied</u> for her history final. (The writing occurred before the studying.)

Exercise 22.3

A verb is missing from each of the following sentences. Fill in the form of the verb indicated in parentheses.

Example: The Outer Banks <u>*stretch*</u> (stretch: present) along the North Carolina coast for more than 175 miles.

▶ 1. Many portions of the Outer Banks of North Carolina _____ (give: present) the visitor a sense of history and timelessness.

▶ 2. Many students of history _____ (read: present perfect) about the Outer Banks and its mysteries.

▶ 3. It was on Roanoke Island in the 1580s that English colonists _____ (establish: past) the first settlement in the New World.

▶ 4. That colony vanished soon after it was settled, _____ (become: present participle) known as the famous "lost colony."

➤ 5. By 1718, the pirate Blackbeard _____ (made: past perfect) the Outer Banks a hiding place for his treasures.

6. It was at Ocracoke, in fact, that Blackbeard _____ (meet: past) his death.

7. Even today, fortune hunters _____ (search: present progressive) the Outer Banks for Blackbeard's hidden treasures.

8. The Outer Banks are also famous for Kitty Hawk and Kill Devil Hills; even as technology has advanced into the space age, the number of tourists flocking to the site of the Wright brothers' epic flight _____. (grow: present perfect progressive)

9. Long before that famous flight occurred, however, the Outer Banks _____ (claim: past perfect) countless ships along its ever-shifting shores, resulting in its nickname—the "Graveyard of the Atlantic."

10. If the Outer Banks continue to be protected from the ravages of overdevelopment and commercialization, visitors _____ (enjoy: future progressive) the mysteries of this tiny finger of land for years to come.

22c Understanding Mood

Mood is the form a verb takes to indicate whether a writer is making a statement or asking a question (*indicative mood*), giving a command (*imperative mood*), or expressing a wish or a contrary-to-fact statement (*subjunctive mood*).

The **indicative** mood expresses an opinion, states a fact, or asks a question: Jackie Robinson <u>had</u> a great impact on professional baseball. The indicative is the mood used in most English sentences.

The **imperative** mood is used in commands and direct requests. Usually, the imperative includes only the base form of the verb without a subject: <u>Use</u> a dictionary.

The **subjunctive** mood was common in the past, but it now is used less and less often, and usually only in formal contexts.

(1) Forming the Subjunctive Mood

The **present subjunctive** uses the base form of the verb, regardless of the subject. The **past subjunctive** has the same form as the past tense of the verb. (The auxiliary verb *be*, however, takes the form *were* regardless of the number or person of the subject.)

Dr. Gorman suggested that I <u>study</u> the Cambrian Period. (present subjunctive)

I wish I <u>were</u> going to Europe. (past subjunctive)

(2) Using the Subjunctive Mood

The present subjunctive may be used in *that* clauses after words such as *ask, suggest, require, recommend,* and *demand.*

The report recommended that juveniles <u>be</u> given mandatory counseling.

Captain Ahab insisted that his crew <u>hunt</u> the white whale.

The past subjunctive may be used in **conditional statements** (statements beginning with *if* that are contrary to fact, including statements that express a wish).

If John <u>were</u> here, he could see Marsha. (John is not here.)

The father acted as if he <u>were</u> having the baby. (The father couldn't be having the baby.)

I wish I <u>were</u> more organized. (expresses a wish)

NOTE: In many situations, the subjunctive mood can sound stiff or formal. Alternative expressions can often eliminate the need for subjunctive constructions.

The group asked ~~that~~ the mayor _∧<u>ban</u> *to* smoking in public places.

Exercise 22.4

Complete the sentences in the following paragraph by inserting the appropriate form (indicative, imperative, or subjunctive) of the verb in parentheses. Be prepared to explain your choices.

Harry Houdini was a famous escape artist. ▸He _____ (perform) escapes from every type of bond imaginable: handcuffs, locks, straitjackets, ropes, sacks, and sealed chests underwater. ▸In Germany, workers _____ (challenge) Houdini to escape from a packing box. ▸If he _____ (be) to escape, they would admit that he _____ (be) the best escape artist in the world. Houdini accepted. Before getting into the box, he asked that the observers _____ (give) it a thorough examination. He then asked that a worker _____ (nail) him into the box. "_____ (place) a screen around the box," he ordered after he had been sealed inside. In a few minutes, Houdini _____ (step) from behind the screen. When the workers demanded that they _____ (see) the box, Houdini pulled down the screen. To their surprise, they saw the box with the lid still nailed tightly in place.

22d Understanding Voice

Voice is the form a verb takes to indicate whether its subject acts or is acted upon. When the subject of a verb does something—that is, acts—the verb is in the **active voice.** When the subject of a verb receives the action—that is, is acted upon—the verb is in the **passive voice.**

Active Voice: Hart Crane wrote *The Bridge.*

Passive Voice: *The Bridge* was written by Hart Crane.

Close-up: Voice

Because the active voice emphasizes the person or thing performing an action, it is usually briefer, clearer, and more emphatic than the passive voice. Some situations, however, require use of the passive voice. For example, you should use passive constructions when the actor is unknown or unimportant or when the recipient of an action should logically receive the emphasis.

DDT was found in soil samples. (Passive voice emphasizes the discovery of DDT; who found it is not important.)

Grits are eaten throughout the South. (Passive voice emphasizes the fact that grits are eaten, not who eats them.)

Still, whenever possible, you should use active constructions in your college writing.

---

(1) Changing Verbs from Passive to Active Voice

You can change a verb from passive to active voice by making the subject of the passive verb the object of the active verb. The person or thing performing the action then becomes the subject of the new sentence.

Passive: The novel *Frankenstein* was written by Mary Shelley.

Active: Mary Shelley wrote the novel *Frankenstein.*

If a passive verb has no object, you must supply one that will become the subject of the active verb.

Passive: Baby elephants are taught to avoid humans. (By whom are baby elephants taught?)

Active: Adult elephants teach baby elephants to avoid humans.

Exercise 22.5

Determine which sentences in the following paragraph should be in the active voice, and rewrite those sentences.

▸Rockets were invented by the Chinese about AD 1000. ▸Gunpowder was packed into bamboo tubes and ignited by means of a fuse. ▸These rockets were fired by soldiers at enemy armies and usually caused panic. ▸In thirteenth-century England, an improved form of gunpowder was introduced by Roger Bacon. ▸As a result, rockets were used in battles and were a common—although unreliable—weapon. In the early eighteenth century, a twenty-pound rocket that traveled almost two miles was constructed by William Congreve, an English artillery expert. By the late nineteenth century, thought was given to supersonic speeds by the physicist Ernst Mach, and the sonic boom was predicted by him. The first liquid-fuel rocket was launched by the American Robert Goddard in 1926. A pamphlet written by him anticipated almost all future rocket developments. As a result of his pioneering work, he is called the father of modern rocketry.

(2) Changing Verbs from Active to Passive Voice

You can change a verb from active to passive voice by making the object of the active verb the subject of the passive verb. The person or thing performing the action then becomes the object of the passive verb.

Active: Sir James Murray compiled *The Oxford English Dictionary.*

Passive: *The Oxford English Dictionary* was compiled by Sir James Murray.

Remember that an active verb must have an object or else it cannot be put into the passive voice. If an active verb has no object, supply one. This verb will become the subject of the passive sentence.

Active: Jacques Cousteau invented.
             Cousteau invented _____?_____.

Passive: _____?_____ was invented by Jacques Cousteau.
              The scuba was invented by Jacques Cousteau.

Exercise 22.6

Determine which sentences in the following paragraph should be in the passive voice, and rewrite those sentences.

▸The Regent Diamond is one of the world's most famous and coveted jewels. ▸A slave discovered the 410-carat diamond in 1701 in an Indian mine. ▸Over the years, people stole and sold the diamond several times. In 1717, the regent of France bought the diamond for an enormous sum, but during the French Revolution, it disappeared again. Someone later found it in a ditch in Paris. Eventually, Napoleon had the diamond set into his ceremonial sword. At last, when the French monarch fell, the government placed the Regent Diamond in the Louvre, where it remains today.

23a Understanding Adjectives and Adverbs

Adjectives modify nouns and pronouns. **Adverbs** modify verbs, adjectives, or other adverbs—or entire phrases, clauses, or sentences. Both adjectives and adverbs describe, limit, or qualify other words, phrases, or clauses.

The *function* of a word in a sentence, not its *form*, determines whether it is an adjective or an adverb. Although many adverbs (such as *immediately* and *hopelessly*) end in *-ly*, others (such as *almost* and *very*) do not. Moreover, some words that end in *-ly* (such as *lively*) are adjectives. Only by locating the modified word and determining what part of speech it is can you determine whether a modifier is an adjective or an adverb.

ESL Tip
For information on correct placement of adjectives and adverbs in a sentence, **see 48d5.** For information on correct order of adjectives in a series, **see 48d6.**

23b Using Adjectives

See
20c1

Be sure to use an **adjective**—not an adverb—as a subject complement. A **subject complement** is a word that follows a linking verb and modifies the sentence's subject, not its verb. A linking verb does not show physical or emotional action. *Seem, appear, believe, become, grow, turn, remain, prove, look, sound, smell, taste, feel,* and the forms of the verb *be* are or can be used as linking verbs.

> Michelle seemed <u>brave</u>. (*Seemed* shows no action, so it is a linking verb. Because *brave* is a subject complement that modifies the subject *Michelle*, it takes the adjective form.)
>
> Michelle smiled <u>bravely</u>. (*Smiled* shows action, so it is not a linking verb. *Bravely* modifies *smiled*, so it takes the adverb form.)

NOTE: Sometimes the same verb can function as either a linking verb or an action verb: He remained <u>stubborn</u>. (He was still stubborn.) He remained <u>stubbornly</u>. (He remained, in a stubborn manner.)

Also, be sure to use an adjective—not an adverb—as an **object complement,** a word that follows a sentence's direct object and modifies that object and not the verb. Objects are nouns or pronouns, so their modifiers must be adjectives.

Most people called him <u>timid</u>. (People consider him to be timid; here *timid* is an object complement that modifies *him*, the sentence's direct object, so the adjective form is correct.)

Most people called him <u>timidly</u>. (People were timid when they called him; here *timidly* modifies the verb *called*—not the object— so the adverb form is correct.)

23c Using Adverbs

Be sure to use an **adverb**—not an adjective—to modify verbs, adjectives, or other adverbs—or entire phrases, clauses, or sentences.

        very well
Most students did ~~great~~ on the midterm.

          conservatively
My parents dress a lot more ~~conservative~~ than my friends do.

Close-up: Using Adjectives and Adverbs

In informal speech, adjective forms such as *good, bad, sure, real, slow, quick,* and *loud* are often used to modify verbs, adjectives, and adverbs. Avoid these informal modifiers in college writing.

        really well
The program ran ~~real good~~ the first time we tried it, but the
               badly
new system performed ~~bad~~.

Exercise 23.1

Revise each of the incorrect sentences in the following paragraph so that only adjectives modify nouns and pronouns and only adverbs modify verbs, adjectives, or other adverbs.

▶A popular self-help trend in the United States today is subliminal tapes. ▶These tapes, with titles like *How to Attract Love, Freedom from Acne,* and *I Am a Genius,* are intended to address every problem known to modern society—and to solve these problems quick and easy. ▶The tapes are said to work because their "hidden messages" bypass conscious defense mechanisms. ▶The listener hears only music or relaxing sounds, like waves rolling slow and steady. At decibel levels perceived only subconsciously, positive words and phrases are embedded, usually by someone who speaks deep and rhythmic. The top-selling cassettes are those that help listeners lose weight or quit smoking. The popularity of such tapes is not hard to understand. They promise easy solutions to complex problems. But the main benefit of these tapes appears to be for the sellers, who are accumulating profits real fast.

Exercise 23.2

Being careful to use adjectives—not adverbs—as subject complements and object complements, write five sentences in imitation of each of the following sentences. Consult the list of linking verbs in 20c1, and use a different linking verb in each of your sentences.

▸ 1. Julie looked worried.
   2. Dan considers his collection valuable.

23d Using Comparative and Superlative Forms

Most adjectives and adverbs have **comparative** and **superlative** forms that can be used with nouns to indicate degree.

Comparative and Superlative Forms

Form	Function	Example
Positive	Describes a quality; does not indicate a comparison	big, lovely
Comparative	Indicates a comparison between *two* qualities (greater or lesser)	bigger, lovelier
Superlative	Indicates a comparison among *more than two* qualities (greatest or least)	biggest, loveliest

NOTE: Some adverbs, particularly those indicating time, place, and degree (*almost, very, here,* and *immediately*), do not have comparative or superlative forms.

(1) Comparative Forms

To form the comparative, all one-syllable adjectives and many two-syllable adjectives (particularly those that end in -*y*, -*ly*, -*le*, -*er*, and -*ow*) add -*er*: slow<u>er</u>, funn<u>ier</u>. (Note that a final *y* becomes *i* before -*er* is added.)

Other two-syllable adjectives and all long adjectives form the comparative with *more*: <u>more</u> famous, <u>more</u> incredible.

Adverbs ending in -*ly* also form the comparative with *more*: <u>more</u> slowly. Other adverbs use the -*er* ending to form the comparative: soon<u>er</u>.

All adjectives and adverbs indicate a lesser degree with *less*: <u>less</u> lovely, <u>less</u> slowly.

(2) Superlative Forms

Adjectives that form the comparative with *-er* add *-est* to form the superlative: nic<u>est</u>, funni<u>est</u>. Adjectives that indicate the comparative with *more* use *most* to indicate the superlative: <u>most</u> famous, <u>most</u> challenging.

The majority of adverbs use *most* to indicate the superlative: <u>most</u> quickly. Others use the *-est* ending: soon<u>est</u>.

All adjectives and adverbs use *least* to indicate the least degree: <u>least</u> interesting, <u>least</u> willingly.

Close-up: Using Comparatives and Superlatives

- Never use both *more* and *-er* to form the comparative or both *most* and *-est* to form the superlative.

  Nothing could have been ~~more~~ easier.

  Jack is the ~~most~~ meanest person in town.

- Never use the superlative when comparing only two things.

  taller
  Stacy is the ~~tallest~~ of the two sisters.

- Never use the comparative when comparing more than two things.

  earliest
  We chose the ~~earlier~~ of the four appointments.

---

(3) Irregular Comparatives and Superlatives

Some adjectives and adverbs have irregular comparative and superlative forms. Instead of adding a word or an ending to the positive form, they use different words to indicate the comparative and the superlative.

Irregular Comparatives and Superlatives

	Positive	Comparative	Superlative
Adjectives:	good	better	best
	bad	worse	worst
	a little	less	least
	many, some, much	more	most
Adverbs:	well	better	best
	badly	worse	worst

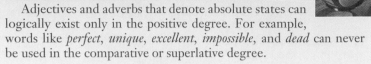

Close-up: Illogical Comparative and Superlative Forms

Adjectives and adverbs that denote absolute states can logically exist only in the positive degree. For example, words like *perfect*, *unique*, *excellent*, *impossible*, and *dead* can never be used in the comparative or superlative degree.

>   *an*
> I read ~~the most~~ excellent story.
>   ^

The vase in the museum's collection is ~~very~~ unique.

These words can, however, be modified by words that suggest approaching the absolute state—*nearly* or *almost*, for example.

> He revised until his draft was <u>almost perfect</u>.

Exercise 23.3

Supply the correct comparative and superlative forms for each of the following adjectives or adverbs. Then, use each form in a sentence.

Example: strange   stranger   strangest

> The story had a *strange* ending.
> The explanation sounded *stranger* each time I heard it.
> This is the *strangest* gadget I have ever seen.

▸ 1. difficult   ▸ 5. mysterious   9. often
▸ 2. eccentric   6. softly   10. tiny
▸ 3. confusing   7. embarrassing
▸ 4. bad   8. well

23e Avoiding Double Negatives

ESL
48a4

Be careful not to create a <u>double negative</u> by using a negative modifier (such as *never*, *no*, or *not*) with another negative word (such as *nearly*, *hardly*, *none*, or *nothing*).

Old dogs cannot learn ~~no~~ new tricks.

Remember that many contractions include the negative word *not*.

The instructor doesn't give ~~no~~ partial credit.

http://kirsznermandell.wadsworth.com

Computer Tip: Revising Double Negatives

Your word processor's grammar checker will highlight double negatives and offer suggestions for revision.

24a Recognizing Sentence Fragments

A **sentence fragment** is an incomplete sentence—a phrase or clause that is punctuated as if it were a complete sentence. A sentence may be incomplete for any of the following reasons.

- **It lacks a subject.**

  Many astrophysicists now believe that galaxies are distributed in clusters. <u>And even form supercluster complexes.</u>

- **It lacks a verb.**

  Every generation has its defining moments. <u>Usually the events with the most news coverage.</u>

- **It lacks both a subject and a verb.**

  Researchers are engaged in a variety of studies. <u>Suggesting a link between alcoholism and heredity.</u> (*Suggesting* is a **verbal,** which cannot serve as a sentence's main verb.)

- **It is a dependent clause.**

  Bishop Desmond Tutu was awarded the 1984 Nobel Peace Prize. <u>Because he fought to end apartheid.</u>

  The pH meter and the spectrophotometer are two scientific instruments. <u>That changed the chemistry laboratory dramatically.</u>

NOTE: A sentence cannot consist of a single clause that begins with a subordinating conjunction (such as *because*) or a relative pronoun (such as *that*); moreover, unless it is a question, a sentence cannot consist of a single clause beginning with *when, where, who, which, what, why,* or *how.*

Close-up: Revising Sentence Fragments

If you identify a fragment in your writing, use one of the following two strategies to revise it:

1. *Attach the fragment to an adjacent independent clause.*

   According to German legend, Lohengrin is the son of
   Parzival./ ~~And~~ ^{and} a knight of the Holy Grail.

   Pioneers traveled west./ ~~Because~~ ^{because} they hoped to find a better life.

(continued)

Revising sentence fragments (continued)

2. *Turn the fragment into a sentence.*

Lancaster County, Pennsylvania, is home to many
                      They are descended
Pennsylvania Dutch.~~Descended~~ from German immigrants.
(missing subject and verb added)

                         City
Property taxes rose sharply,~~Although city~~ services declined.
(subordinating conjunction *although* deleted)

http://kirsznermandell.wadsworth.com

Computer Tip: Identifying Fragments

Your grammar checker will identify many (although not all) sentence fragments. However, not every word group identified as a fragment will actually be a fragment. You, not your grammar checker, will have to make the final decision and correct any errors.

Exercise 24.1

Identify each of the following word groups as either a sentence fragment or a complete sentence. Be prepared to explain why each fragment is not a complete sentence. When you have finished, type each sentence into your word-processing program, and run the grammar checker to check your responses.

▸ 1. Consisting of shortness of breath, a high fever, and a racing pulse.

▸ 2. Held in contempt of court by the presiding judge.

▸ 3. Walking to the end of the road and back is good exercise.

▸ 4. On her own at last, after many years of struggle for independence.

▸ 5. Because he felt torn between two cultures.

6. With boundaries extending from the ocean to the bay.

7. Although language study can be challenging.

8. In addition, a new point guard will be a valuable addition to the team.

9. Defeated by his own greed but not in the least regretful.

10. Moreover, the continued presence of troops in Iraq.

Sections 24b–d identify the grammatical structures most likely to appear as fragments and illustrate the most effective ways of revising each kind.

24b Revising Dependent Clause Fragments

A **dependent clause** contains both a subject and a verb, but it cannot stand alone as a sentence. Because it needs an independent clause to complete its meaning, a **dependent clause** (also called a *subordinate clause*) must always be attached to at least one independent clause to form a complete sentence. You can recognize a dependent clause because it is always introduced by a **subordinating conjunction** (*although*, *because*, and so on) or a **relative pronoun** (*that*, *which*, *who*, and so on).

See 14b

In most cases, the best way to correct a dependent clause fragment is to join the dependent clause to a neighboring independent clause, creating a complex sentence.

because
The United States declared war/ ~~Because~~ the Japanese bombed Pearl Harbor. (Dependent clause has been attached to an independent clause, creating a complex sentence.)

, which
The battery is dead/ ~~Which~~ means the car won't start. (Dependent clause has been attached to an independent clause, creating a complex sentence.)

Another way to correct a dependent clause fragment is simply to delete the subordinating conjunction or relative pronoun, turning the fragment into a complete independent clause.

The
The United States declared war. ~~Because the~~ Japanese bombed Pearl Harbor. (Subordinating conjunction *because* has been deleted; the result is a new independent clause.)

This
The battery is dead. ~~Which~~ means the car won't start. (Relative pronoun *which* has been replaced by *this*; the result is a new independent clause.)

Exercise 24.2

Identify the sentence fragments in the following paragraph. Then, correct each fragment either by attaching the fragment to an independent clause or by deleting the subordinating conjunction or relative pronoun to create a sentence that can stand alone. (In some cases, you will have to replace a relative pronoun with another word that can serve as the subject.)

► The drive-in movie came into being just after World War II. ► When both movies and cars were central to the lives of many Americans. ► Drive-ins were especially popular with teenagers and young families during the 1950s. ▸When cars and gas were relatively inexpensive. ▸Theaters charged by the carload. ▸Which meant that a group of teenagers or a family with several children could spend an evening at the movies for a few dollars. ▸In 1958, when the fad peaked, there were over four thousand drive-ins in the United States. ▸While today there are fewer than three thousand. Many of these are in the Sunbelt, with most in California. Although many Sunbelt drive-ins continue to thrive because of the year-round warm weather. Many northern drive-ins are in financial trouble. Because land is so expensive. Some drive-in owners break even only by operating flea markets or swap meets in daylight hours. While others, unable to attract customers, are selling their theaters to land developers. Soon, drive-ins may be a part of our nostalgic past. Which will be a great loss for many who enjoy them.

24c   Revising Phrase Fragments

A **phrase** provides information—description, examples, and so on—about other words or word groups in a sentence. However, because it lacks a subject, a verb, or both, a phrase cannot stand alone. When a phrase is incorrectly punctuated as a sentence, a fragment is created.

Close-up: Fragments Introduced by Transitions

See
5b2

Many phrase fragments are word groups that are introduced by **transitional words and phrases**, such as *also, finally, in addition*, and *now*, but are missing subjects and verbs. To correct such a fragment, you need to add the missing subject and verb.

     It was also
~~Also~~ a step in the right direction.

       he found
Finally, a new home for the family.

         we need
In addition, three new keyboards for the computer lab.

     I will explain
Now, the first step.

See
20f

ESL
48c

(1) Prepositional Phrases

A **prepositional** phrase consists of a preposition, its object, and any modifiers of the object.

To correct a prepositional phrase fragment, attach it to the independent clause that contains the word or word group that it modifies.

                                    for
President Lyndon Johnson did not seek reelection. ~~For~~ a number of reasons. (Prepositional phrase has been attached to an independent clause, creating a complete sentence.)

He ran sixty yards for a touchdown*in*∕ In̂ the final minutes of the game. (Prepositional phrase has been attached to an independent clause, creating a complete sentence.)

Exercise 24.3

Read the following passage, and identify the prepositional phrase fragments. Then, correct each one by attaching it to the independent clause that contains the word or word group it modifies.

▶Most college athletes are caught in a conflict. ▶Between their athletic and academic careers. ▶Sometimes college athletes' responsibilities on the playing field make it hard for them to be good students. ▶Often, athletes must make a choice. ▶Between sports and a degree. ▶Some athletes would not be able to afford college. ▶Without athletic scholarships. ▶Ironically, however, their commitments (training, exercise, practice, and travel to out-of-town games, for example) deprive athletes. ▶Of valuable classroom time. ▶The role of college athletes is constantly being questioned. Critics suggest that athletes exist only to participate in and promote college athletics. Because of the importance of this role to academic institutions, scandals occasionally develop. With coaches and even faculty members arranging to inflate athletes' grades to help them remain eligible. For participation in sports. Some universities even lower admissions standards. To help remedy this and other inequities. The controversial Proposition 48, passed at the NCAA convention in 1982, established minimum College Board scores and grade standards for college students. But many people feel that the NCAA remains overly concerned. With profits rather than with education. As a result, college athletic competition is increasingly coming to resemble pro sports. From the coaches' pressure on the players to win to the network television exposure to the wagers on the games' outcomes.

(2) Verbal Phrases

A verbal phrase consists of a **verbal**—a present participle (*walking*), past participle (*walked*), infinitive (*to walk*), or gerund (*walking*)—plus related objects and modifiers (*walking along the lonely beach*). Because a verbal cannot serve as a sentence's main verb, a verbal phrase is not a complete sentence and should not be punctuated as one.

To correct a verbal phrase fragment, you can attach the verbal phrase to a related independent clause.

In 1948, India became an independent country*divided*∕ D̂ivided into the nations of India and Pakistan. (Verbal phrase has been attached to a related independent clause, creating a complete sentence.)

, reminding
A familiar trademark can increase a product's sales/ ~~Reminding~~
shoppers that the product has a long-standing reputation.
(Verbal phrase has been attached to a related independent clause,
creating a complete sentence.)

You can also change the verbal to a verb and add a subject.

It was divided
In 1948, India became an independent country. ~~Divided~~ into the
nations of India and Pakistan. (Verb *was divided* has replaced
verbal *divided*, and subject *it* has been added; the result is a complete sentence.)

It reminds
A familiar trademark can increase a product's sales. ~~Reminding~~
shoppers that the product has a long-standing reputation.
(Verb *reminds* has replaced verbal *reminding*, and subject *it* has
been added; the result is a complete sentence.)

Exercise 24.4

Identify the sentence fragments in the following paragraph and correct each one. Either attach the fragment to a related independent
clause, or add a subject and a verb to create a complete sentence.

▶Many food products have well-known trademarks. ▶Identified by
familiar faces on product labels. ▶Some of these symbols have remained
the same, while others have changed considerably. ▶Products like Sun-
Maid Raisins, Betty Crocker potato mixes, Quaker Oats, and Uncle
Ben's Rice use faces. ▶To create a sense of quality and tradition and to
encourage shopper recognition of the products. ▶Many of the portraits
have been updated several times. ▶To reflect changes in society. Betty
Crocker's portrait, for instance, has changed many times since its cre-
ation in 1936. Symbolizing women's changing roles. The original Chef
Boy-ar-dee has also changed. Turning from the young Italian chef Hec-
tor Boiardi into a white-haired senior citizen. Miss Sunbeam, trademark of Sunbeam Bread, has had her hairdo modified several times
since her first appearance in 1942; the Blue Bonnet girl, also created in
1942, now has a more modern look, and Aunt Jemima has also been
changed. Slimmed down a bit in 1965. Similarly, the Campbell's Soup
kids are less chubby now than in the 1920s when they first appeared.
Still, manufacturers are very careful about selecting a trademark or
modifying an existing one. Typically spending a good deal of time and
money on research before a change is made.

(3) Appositives

An **appositive**—a noun or noun phrase that identifies or renames an
adjacent noun or pronoun—cannot stand alone as a sentence.

To correct an appositive fragment, attach the appositive to the independent clause that contains the word or word group the appositive renames.

Brian was the star forward of the Blue Devils. ~~The~~ *, the* team with the
best record. (Appositive has been attached to an independent
clause, creating a complete sentence.)

Piero della Francesca was a leader of the Umbrian school of

painting. ~~A~~ *, a* school that remained close to the traditions of Gothic
art. (Appositive has been attached to an independent clause,
creating a complete sentence.)

Close-up: Lists

When an appositive fragment is in the form of a <u>list</u>,
add a colon to connect the list to the independent clause
that introduces it.

See
11c

Tourists often outnumber residents in four European cities. *:*
Venice, Florence, Canterbury, and Bath.

Close-up: Fragments That Introduce Examples

Sometimes an appositive consists of a word or phrase
like *that is, for example, for instance, namely,* or *such as,* followed by an example. To correct this kind of appositive
fragment, attach the appositive to the preceding independent
clause.

Fairy tales are full of damsels in distress. ~~Such~~ *, such* as Cinderella and
Rapunzel.

NOTE: Sometimes you can correct an appositive fragment by embedding the appositive within an independent clause.

(for example, Charles Dickens and Mark Twain)
Some popular novelists are highly respected in later generations.
~~For example, Charles Dickens and Mark Twain.~~

Exercise 24.5

Identify the fragments in this paragraph, and correct them by attaching each one to the independent clause containing the word or word
group the appositive modifies.

▶Until the early 1900s, communities in West Virginia, Tennessee,
and Kentucky were isolated by the mountains that surrounded them.

▸The great chain of the Appalachian Mountains. ▸Set apart from the emerging culture of a growing America and American language, these communities retained a language rich with the dialect of Elizabethan English and sprinkled with hints of a Scotch-Irish influence. ▸In the 1910s and '20s, the communities in these mountains began to long for a better future for their children. ▸The key to that future, as they saw it, was education. In some communities, that education took the form of Settlement Schools. Schools led by the new rash of idealistic young graduates of eastern women's colleges. These teachers taught the basic academic subjects. Such as reading, writing, and mathematics. They also schooled their students in the culture of the mountains. For example, the crafts, music, and folklore of the Appalachians. In addition, they taught them skills that would help them survive when the coal market began to decline. The Settlement Schools attracted artisans from around the world. Quilters, weavers, basketmakers, and carpenters. The schools also opened the mountains to the world, causing the Elizabethan dialect to fade.

24d Revising Compounds

The last part of a **compound predicate, compound object,** or **compound complement** cannot stand alone as a sentence. To correct this type of fragment, connect the detached part of the compound to the sentence to which it belongs.

People with dyslexia have trouble reading, <ins>and</ins> ~~And~~ may also find it difficult to write. (Detached part of the compound predicate has been connected to the sentence to which it belongs.)

They took only a compass and a canteen, <ins>and</ins> ~~And~~ some trail mix. (Detached part of the compound object has been connected to the sentence to which it belongs.)

When their supplies ran out they were surprised, <ins>and</ins> ~~And~~ hungry. (Detached part of the compound complement has been connected to the sentence to which it belongs.)

Exercise 24.6

Identify the sentence fragments in this passage, and correct them by attaching each detached compound to the rest of the sentence.

▸As more and more Americans discover the pleasures of the wilderness, our national parks are feeling the stress. ▸Wanting to get away for a weekend or a week, hikers and backpackers stream from the cities into nearby state and national parks. ▸They bring with them a hunger for wilderness. ▸But very little knowledge about how to behave ethically in the wild. ▸They also do not know how to keep themselves safe.

▸Some of them think of the national parks as inexpensive amusement parks. ▸Without proper camping supplies and lacking enough food and water for their trip, they are putting at risk their lives and the lives of those who will be called on to save them. ▸One family went for a hike up a desert canyon with an eight-month-old infant. ▸And their seventy-eight-year-old grandmother. Although the terrain was difficult, they were not wearing the proper shoes. Or good socks. They did not even carry a first aid kit. Or a map or compass. They were on an unmarked trail in a little-used section of Bureau of Land Management lands. And following vague directions from a friend. Soon, they were lost. They had not brought water or food. Or even rain gear or warm clothes. Luckily for them, they had brought a cell phone. By the time they called for help, however, it was getting dark and a storm was building. A rescue plane eventually located the family. And brought them to safety. Still, a little planning before they hiked in an inhospitable area, and a little awareness and preparedness for the terrain they were traveling in, would have saved this family much worry. And the taxpayers a lot of money.

24e Using Fragments Intentionally

In professional and academic writing, sentence fragments are generally not acceptable except in certain special situations.

Checklist: Using Fragments Intentionally

☐ In lists
☐ In captions that accompany visuals
☐ In topic outlines
☐ In quoted dialogue
☐ In *PowerPoint* presentations
☐ In titles and subtitles of papers and reports
☐ In personal email and other informal communication

Chapter 25   Revising Comma Splices and Fused Sentences

25a Recognizing Comma Splices and Fused Sentences

A **run-on sentence** is created when two <u>independent clauses</u> are joined without the necessary punctuation or connective word. A

See
13b2

run-on sentence is not just a long sentence—in fact, run-ons can be quite short—but a grammatically incorrect construction. *Comma splices* and *fused sentences* are two kinds of run-on sentences.

A **comma splice** is an error that occurs when two independent clauses are joined with just a comma. A **fused sentence** is an error that occurs when two independent clauses are joined with no punctuation.

Comma Splice: Charles Dickens created the character of Mr. Micawber, he also created Uriah Heep.

Fused Sentence: Charles Dickens created the character of Mr. Micawber he also created Uriah Heep.

Close-up: Revising Comma Splices and Fused Sentences

To revise a comma splice or fused sentence, use one of the following four strategies:

1. Add a period between the clauses, creating two separate sentences.
2. Add a semicolon between the clauses, creating a compound sentence.
3. Add an appropriate coordinating conjunction, creating a compound sentence.
4. Subordinate one clause to the other, creating a complex sentence.

http://kirsznermandell.wadsworth.com

Computer Tip: Identifying Comma Splices

Your word processor's grammar checker will highlight comma splices and prompt you to revise them. It may also offer suggestions for revision.

25b Revising with Periods

You can revise a comma splice or fused sentence by adding a period between the independent clauses, creating two separate sentences. This is a good strategy to use when the clauses are long or when they are not closely related.

In 1894, Frenchman Alfred Dreyfus was falsely convicted of
treason, his struggle for justice pitted the army against civil libertarians.

Close-up: Comma Splices and Fused Sentences

Using a comma to punctuate an interrupted quotation that consists of two complete sentences creates a comma splice. Instead, use a period.

"This is a good course," Eric said/, "In fact, I wish I'd taken it sooner."

25c Revising with Semicolons

You can revise a comma splice or fused sentence by adding a semicolon between two closely related clauses that convey parallel or contrasting information.

See 31a

> In pre–World War II western Europe, only a small elite had access to a university education/; this situation changed dramatically after the war.
> Chippendale chairs have straight legs/; however, Queen Anne chairs have curved legs.

NOTE: When you use a **transitional word or phrase** (such as *however, therefore,* or *for example*) to connect two independent clauses, the transitional element must be preceded by a semicolon and followed by a comma; if you link the two clauses with just a comma, you create a comma splice. If you omit punctuation entirely, you create a fused sentence.

See 5b2

25d Revising with Coordinating Conjunctions

You can use a coordinating conjunction (*and, or, but, nor, for, so, yet*) to join two closely related clauses of equal importance into one **compound sentence**. The coordinating conjunction you choose indicates the relationship between the clauses: addition (*and*), contrast (*but, yet*), causality (*for, so*), or a choice of alternatives (*or, nor*). Be sure to add a comma before the coordinating conjunction.

See 14a1

> Elias Howe invented the sewing machine, *and* Julia Ward Howe was a poet and social reformer.

25e Revising with Subordinating Conjunctions or Relative Pronouns

When the ideas in two independent clauses are not of equal importance, you can use a subordinating conjunction or relative pronoun

See
14b
to join the clauses into one <u>complex sentence</u>, placing the less important idea in the dependent clause. The subordinating conjunction or relative pronoun you choose establishes the specific relationship between the clauses.

because

Stravinsky's ballet *The Rite of Spring* shocked Parisians in 1913, its rhythms seemed erotic.

, who

Lady Mary Wortley Montagu had suffered from smallpox herself, ~~she~~ helped spread the practice of inoculation.

Close-up: Acceptable Comma Splices

In a few special cases, comma splices are acceptable. For instance, a comma is conventionally used in dialogue between a statement and a tag question, even though each is a separate independent clause.

This is Ron's house, isn't it?

I'm not late, am I?

In addition, commas may be used to connect two short, balanced independent clauses or two or more short parallel independent clauses, especially when one clause contradicts the other.

Commencement isn't the end, it's the beginning.

Exercise 25.1

Identify the comma splices and fused sentences in the following paragraph. Correct each in two of the four possible ways listed in the Close-up box on page 236. If a sentence is correct, leave it alone.

Example: The fans rose in their seats, the game was almost over.

Revised: The fans rose in their seats; the game was almost over.

The fans rose in their seats, for the game was almost over.

▸Entrepreneurship is the study of small businesses, college students are embracing it enthusiastically. ▸Many schools offer one or more courses in entrepreneurship these courses teach the theory and practice of starting a small business. ▸Students are signing up for courses, moreover, they are starting their own businesses. ▸One student started with a car-waxing business, now he sells condominiums. Other students are setting up catering services they supply everything from waiters to bartenders. One student has a thriving cake-decorating business, in fact, she employs fifteen students to deliver the cakes. All over the country, student businesses are selling everything from tennis balls to bagels, the student owners are making impressive profits. Formal courses at the graduate as well as undergraduate level are attracting more business students than ever, several schools (such as Baylor University, the University of Southern California, and Babson College) even offer degree programs in entrepreneurship. Many business school students are no longer planning to be corporate executives instead, they plan to become entrepreneurs.

Exercise 25.2

Combine each of the following sentence pairs into one sentence without creating comma splices or fused sentences. In each case, either connect the clauses into a compound sentence with a semicolon or with a comma and a coordinating conjunction, or subordinate one clause to the other to create a complex sentence. You may have to add, delete, reorder, or change words or punctuation.

► 1. Several recent studies indicate that many American high school students have little knowledge of history. This is affecting our future as a democratic nation and as individuals.

► 2. Surveys show that nearly one-third of American seventeen-year-olds cannot identify the countries the United States fought against in World War II. One-third think Columbus reached the New World after 1750.

► 3. Several reasons have been given for this decline in historical literacy. The main reason is the way history is taught.

► 4. This problem is bad news. The good news is that there is increasing agreement among educators about what is wrong with current methods of teaching history.

► 5. History can be exciting and engaging. Too often, it is presented in a boring manner.

6. Students are typically expected to memorize dates, facts, and names. History as adventure—as a "good story"—is frequently neglected.

7. One way to avoid this problem is to use good textbooks. Textbooks should be accurate, lively, and focused.

8. Another way to create student interest in historical events is to use primary sources instead of so-called comprehensive textbooks. Autobiographies, journals, and diaries can give students insight into larger issues.

9. Students can also be challenged to think about history by taking sides in a debate. They can learn more about connections among historical events by writing essays than by taking multiple-choice tests.

10. Finally, history teachers should be less concerned about specific historical details. They should be more concerned about conveying the wonder of history.

ESL
48a1
Agreement is the correspondence between words in number, gender, and person. Subjects and verbs <u>agree</u> in **number** (singular or plural) and **person** (first, second, or third); pronouns and their antecedents agree in number, person, and **gender** (masculine, feminine, or neuter).

26a Making Subjects and Verbs Agree

Singular subjects take singular verbs, and plural subjects take plural verbs.

> **Singular:** <u>Hydrogen peroxide</u> <u>is</u> an unstable compound.
>
> **Plural:** <u>Characters</u> <u>are</u> not well developed in O. Henry's short stories.

ESL
48a2

See
26a4
<u>Present tense</u> verbs, except *be* and *have*, add *-s* or *-es* when the subject is third-person singular. Third-person singular subjects include nouns; the personal pronouns *he*, *she*, *it*, and *one*; and many <u>indefinite pronouns</u>.

> The <u>president</u> <u>has</u> the power to veto congressional legislation.
>
> <u>She</u> frequently <u>cites</u> statistics to support her assertions.
>
> In every group, <u>somebody</u> <u>emerges</u> as a natural leader.

Present tense verbs do not add *-s* or *-es* when the subject is a plural noun, a first-person or second-person pronoun (*I*, *we*, *you*), or third-person plural pronoun (*they*).

> <u>Experts</u> <u>recommend</u> that dieters avoid salty processed meat.
>
> In our Bill of Rights, <u>we</u> <u>guarantee</u> all defendants the right to a speedy trial.
>
> At this stratum, <u>you</u> <u>see</u> rocks dating back fifteen million years.
>
> <u>They</u> <u>say</u> that some wealthy people default on their student loans.

In the following special situations, subject-verb agreement can cause problems for writers.

(1) When Words Come between Subject and Verb

If a modifying phrase comes between subject and verb, the verb should agree with the subject, not with a word in the modifying phrase.

The sound of the drumbeats builds in intensity in *The Emperor Jones.*

The games won by the intramural team are usually few and far between.

NOTE: When phrases introduced by *along with, as well as, in addition to, including,* and *together with* come between subject and verb, these phrases do *not* change the subject's number: Heavy rain, together with high winds, causes hazardous driving conditions.

(2) When Compound Subjects Are Joined by *And*

Compound subjects joined by *and* usually take plural verbs.

Air bags and antilock brakes are standard on all new models.

There are, however, two exceptions to this rule. First, compound subjects joined by *and* that stand for a single idea or person are treated as a unit and take singular verbs.

Rhythm and blues is a forerunner of rock and roll.

Second, when *each* or *every* precedes a compound subject joined by *and*, the subject takes a singular verb.

Every desk and file cabinet was searched before the letter was found.

(3) When Compound Subjects Are Joined by *Or*

Compound subjects joined by *or* or by *either . . . or* or *neither . . . nor* may take either singular or plural verbs.

If both subjects are singular, use a singular verb; if both subjects are plural, use a plural verb.

Either radiation or chemotherapy is combined with surgery for the most effective results. (Both *radiation* and *chemotherapy* are singular, so the verb is singular.)

Either radiation treatments or chemotherapy sessions are combined with surgery for the most effective results. (Both *treatments* and *sessions* are plural, so the verb is plural.)

If one subject is singular and the other is plural, the verb agrees with the subject that is nearer to it.

Either radiation treatments or chemotherapy is combined with surgery for the most effective results. (Singular verb agrees with *chemotherapy*.)

<u>Either chemotherapy or radiation treatments</u> <u>are</u> combined with surgery for the most effective results. (Plural verb agrees with *treatments*.)

(4) When Indefinite Pronouns Serve as Subjects

Most <u>indefinite pronouns</u>—*another, anyone, everyone, one, each, either, neither, anything, everything, something, nothing, nobody,* and *somebody*—are singular and take singular verbs.

<u>Anyone</u> <u>is</u> welcome to apply for this grant.

Some indefinite pronouns—*both, many, few, several, others*—are plural and take plural verbs.

<u>Several</u> of the articles <u>are</u> useful.

A few indefinite pronouns—*some, all, any, more, most,* and *none*—can be singular or plural, depending on the noun they refer to.

Of course, <u>some</u> of this trouble <u>is</u> to be expected. (*Some* refers to *trouble*.)

<u>Some</u> of the spectators <u>are</u> getting restless. (*Some* refers to *spectators*.)

http://kirsznermandell.wadsworth.com

Computer Tip: Subject-Verb Agreement

Your word processor's grammar checker will highlight and offer revision suggestions for many subject-verb agreement errors, including errors in sentences that have indefinite pronoun subjects.

(5) When Collective Nouns Serve as Subjects

A **collective noun** names a group of persons or things—for instance, *navy, union, association, band.* When a collective noun refers to a group as a unit (as it usually does), it takes a singular verb; when it refers to the individuals or items that make up the group, it takes a plural verb.

To many people, <u>the royal family</u> <u>symbolizes</u> Great Britain. (The family, as a unit, is the symbol.)

<u>The family</u> all <u>eat</u> at different times. (Each member eats separately.)

NOTE: If a plural verb sounds awkward with a collective noun, reword the sentence: <u>Family members</u> all <u>eat</u> at different times.

Phrases that name fixed amounts—*three-quarters, twenty dollars, the majority*—are treated like collective nouns. When the amount denotes a unit, it takes a singular verb; when it denotes part of the whole, it takes a plural verb.

Three-quarters of his usual salary is not enough to live on. (*Three-quarters* denotes a unit.)

Three-quarters of workshop participants improve dramatically. (*Three-quarters* denotes part of the group.)

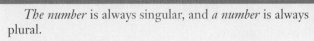

Close-up: Subject-Verb Agreement with Collective Nouns

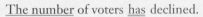

The number is always singular, and *a number* is always plural.

The number of voters has declined.

A number of students have missed the opportunity to preregister.

(6) When Singular Subjects Have Plural Forms

A singular subject takes a singular verb, even if the form of the subject is plural.

Politics makes strange bedfellows.

Statistics deals with the collection, classification, analysis, and interpretation of data.

When such a word has a plural meaning, however, use a plural verb.

Her politics are too radical for her parents. (*Politics* refers not to the science of political government but, rather, to political principles or opinions.)

The statistics prove him wrong. (*Statistics* denotes not a body of knowledge but the numerical facts or data themselves.)

NOTE: Some words retain their Latin plural forms, which do not look like English plural forms. Be particularly careful to use the correct verbs with such words: *criterion is, criteria are; medium is, media are; bacterium is, bacteria are; datum is, data are.*

(7) When Subject-Verb Order Is Inverted

Even when **word order** is inverted so that the verb comes before the subject (as it does in questions and in sentences beginning with *there is* or *there are*), the subject and verb must agree.

ESL
48d

I̲s̲ either answer correct?

There i̲s̲ a m̲o̲n̲u̲m̲e̲n̲t̲ to Emiliano Zapata in Mexico City.

There a̲r̲e̲ currently thirteen federal c̲i̲r̲c̲u̲i̲t̲ c̲o̲u̲r̲t̲s̲ of appeals.

(8) With Linking Verbs

A l̲i̲n̲k̲i̲n̲g̲ v̲e̲r̲b̲ should agree with its subject, not with the subject complement.

The p̲r̲o̲b̲l̲e̲m̲ w̲a̲s̲ termites.

Here, the verb *was* correctly agrees with the subject *problem*, not with the subject complement *termites*. If *termites* were the subject, the verb would be plural: T̲e̲r̲m̲i̲t̲e̲s̲ w̲e̲r̲e̲ the problem.

(9) With Relative Pronouns

When you use a r̲e̲l̲a̲t̲i̲v̲e̲ p̲r̲o̲n̲o̲u̲n̲ (*who, which, that*, and so on) to introduce a dependent clause, the verb in that clause should agree in number with the pronoun's **antecedent** (the word to which the pronoun refers).

The farmer is among the o̲n̲e̲s̲ who s̲u̲f̲f̲e̲r̲ during a grain embargo. (Verb *suffer* agrees with plural antecedent *ones*.)

The farmer is the only o̲n̲e̲ who s̲u̲f̲f̲e̲r̲s̲ during the grain embargo. (Verb *suffers* agrees with singular antecedent *one*.)

Exercise 26.1

Some of the following sentences are correct, but others contain common errors in subject-verb agreement. If a sentence is correct, mark it with a *C*; if it has an error, correct it.

▸ 1. *I Love Lucy* is one of those television shows that almost all Americans have seen at least once.
▸ 2. The committee presented its findings to the president.
▸ 3. Neither Western novels nor science fiction appeal to me.
▸ 4. Stage presence and musical ability makes a rock performer successful today.
▸ 5. *It's a Wonderful Life*, like many old Christmas movies, seems to be shown on television every year.
  6. Hearts are my grandmother's favorite card game.
  7. The best part of B. B. King's songs are the guitar solos.
  8. Time and tide waits for no man.
  9. Sports are my main pastime.
 10. *Vincent and Theo* is Robert Altman's movie about the French Impressionist painter Vincent van Gogh and his brother.

26b Making Pronouns and Antecedents Agree

See
20b

A pronoun must agree with its **antecedent**—the word or word group to which the pronoun refers. Singular pronouns—such as *he, him, she, her, it, me, myself,* and *oneself*—should refer to singular antecedents. Plural pronouns—such as *we, us, they, them,* and *their*—should refer to plural antecedents.

ESL
48e

In the following special situations, pronoun-antecedent agreement can cause problems for writers.

(1) With Compound Antecedents

In most cases, use a plural pronoun to refer to a **compound antecedent** (two or more antecedents connected by *and*).

> Mormonism and Christian Science were influenced in their beginnings by Shaker doctrines.

However, there are several exceptions to this general rule.

- If a compound antecedent denotes a single unit—one person, thing, or idea—use a singular pronoun to refer to the compound antecedent.

> In 1904, the husband and father brought his family from Germany to the United States.

- Use a singular pronoun when a compound antecedent is preceded by *each* or *every*.

> Every programming language and software package has its limitations.

- Use a singular pronoun to refer to two or more singular antecedents linked by *or* or *nor*.

> Neither Thoreau nor Whitman lived to see his work read widely.

- When one part of a compound antecedent is singular and one part is plural, the pronoun agrees in person and number with the closer antecedent.

> Neither the child nor her parents wore their seatbelts.

(2) With Collective Noun Antecedents

If the meaning of the collective noun antecedent is singular (as it will be in most cases), use a singular pronoun. If the meaning is plural, use a plural pronoun.

The nurses' <u>union</u> announced <u>its</u> plan to strike. (All the members acted as one.)

The <u>team</u> ran onto the court and took <u>their</u> positions. (Each member acted individually.)

<table>
<tr><td>See
26a4</td></tr>
<tr><td>ESL
48e3</td></tr>
</table>

(3) With Indefinite Pronoun Antecedents

Most <u>indefinite pronouns</u>—*each, either, neither, one, anyone,* and the like—are singular and take singular pronouns.

<u>Neither</u> of the men had <u>his</u> proposal ready by the deadline.

<u>Each</u> of these neighborhoods has <u>its</u> own traditions and values.

Close-up: Pronoun-Antecedent Agreement

In speech and in informal writing, many people use the plural pronouns *they* or *their* with singular indefinite pronouns that refer to people, such as *someone, everyone,* and *nobody.*

<u>Everyone</u> can present <u>their</u> own viewpoint.

In college writing, however, you should avoid using a plural pronoun to refer to a singular subject. Instead, you can use both the masculine and the feminine pronoun.

<u>Everyone</u> can present <u>his or her</u> own viewpoint.

Or, you can make the sentence's subject plural.

<u>All participants</u> can present <u>their</u> own viewpoints.

<table>
<tr><td>See
19e2</td></tr>
</table>

NOTE: The use of *his* to refer to a singular indefinite pronoun (<u>Every</u>-<u>one</u> can present *his* own viewpoint) is considered <u>sexist language</u>.

http://kirsznermandell.wadsworth.com

Computer Tip: Pronoun-Antecedent Agreement

Your word processor's grammar checker will highlight and offer revision suggestions for many pronoun-antecedent agreement errors.

Exercise 26.2

In the following sentences, find and correct any errors in subject-verb or pronoun-antecedent agreement.

► 1. The core of a computer is a collection of electronic circuits that are called the central processing unit.

► 2. Computers, because of advanced technology that allows the central processing unit to be placed on a chip, a thin square of semi-conducting material about one-quarter of an inch on each side, has been greatly reduced in size.

► 3. Computers can "talk" to each other over phone lines through a modem, an acronym for *modulator-demodulator*.

► 4. Pressing keys on keyboards resembling typewriter keyboards generate electronic signals that are input for the computer.

► 5. Computers have built-in memory storage, and equipment such as disks or tapes provide external memory.

6. RAM (random-access memory), the erasable and reusable computer memory, hold the computer program, the computations executed by the program, and the results.

7. After computer programs are "read" from a disk or tape, the computer uses the instructions as needed to execute the program.

8. ROM (read-only memory), the permanent memory that is "read" by the computer but cannot be changed, are used to store programs that are needed frequently.

9. A number of video games with impressive graphics, sound, and color is available for home computers.

10. Although some computer users write their own programs, most buy ready-made software programs such as the ones that allows a computer to be used as a word processor.

Chapter 27 | **Revising Faulty Modification**

27a Recognizing Faulty Modification

A **modifier** is a word, phrase, or clause that describes, limits, or qualifies another word in a sentence. A modifier should be placed close to the word it modifies.

Wendy watched the storm, <u>fierce and threatening</u>.

Faulty modification is the awkward or confusing placement of modifiers or the modification of nonexistent words.

Computer Tip: Revising Faulty Modification

See
27b4
Your grammar checker will identify some modification problems, including certain awkward split infinitives. However, the grammar checker will not offer revision suggestions.

27b Revising Misplaced Modifiers

A **misplaced modifier** is a word or word group whose placement suggests that it modifies one word or phrase when it is intended to modify another.

Confusing: Flying faster than a speeding bullet, the citizens of Metropolis saw Superman. (Were the citizens of Metropolis flying?)

Revised: The citizens of Metropolis saw Superman flying faster than a speeding bullet.

Confusing: With an IQ of just 52, the lawyer argued that his client should not get the death penalty. (Does the lawyer have an IQ of 52?)

Revised: The lawyer argued that his client, with an IQ of just 52, should not get the death penalty.

When you revise, check to make sure you have placed each modifying word, phrase, and clause in a position that clearly identifies the word it modifies and that does not awkwardly interrupt a sentence.

(1) Placing Modifying Words Precisely

Limiting modifiers—such as *almost, only, even, hardly, merely, nearly, exactly, scarcely, just,* and *simply*—should always immediately precede the words they modify. Different placements change the meaning of the sentence.

Nick *just* set up camp at the edge of the burned-out town.
(He set up camp just now.)

Just Nick set up camp at the edge of the burned-out town.
(He set up camp alone.)

Nick set up camp *just* at the edge of the burned-out town.
(His camp was precisely at the edge.)

When a limiting modifier is placed so that it is not clear whether it modifies a word before it or one after it, it is called a **squinting modifier.**

Squinting: The life that everyone thought would

fulfill her <u>totally</u> bored her. (Was she supposed to be totally fulfilled, or is she totally bored?)

To avoid ambiguity, place the modifier so the word it modifies is clear.

Revised: The life that everyone thought would <u>totally</u> fulfill her bored her. (Everyone expected her to be totally fulfilled.)

Revised: The life that everyone thought would fulfill her

bored her <u>totally</u>. (She was totally bored.)

Exercise 27.1

In the following sentence pairs, the modifier in each sentence points to a different word. Underline the modifier and draw an arrow to the word it modifies. Then, explain the meaning of each sentence.

Example: She <u>just</u> came in wearing a hat. (She just now entered.)

She came in wearing <u>just</u> a hat. (She wore only a hat.)

▸ 1. He wore his almost new jeans.
  He almost wore his new jeans.
▸ 2. He had only three dollars in his pocket.
  Only he had three dollars in his pocket.
  3. I don't even like freshwater fish.
  I don't like even freshwater fish.
  4. I go only to the beach on Saturdays.
  I go to the beach only on Saturdays.
  5. He simply hated driving.
  He hated simply driving.

(2) Relocating Misplaced Phrases

Placing a modifying phrase incorrectly can change the meaning of a sentence or create an unclear or confusing sentence.

Verbal Phrases The incorrect placement of a <u>verbal phrase</u> can make a sentence convey an entirely different meaning or make no

See
13b1

sense at all. To avoid ambiguity, place verbal phrases directly before or after the words they modify.

Confusing: Jane watched the boats <u>roller-skating along the shore</u>. (Were the boats roller-skating?)

Revised: <u>Roller-skating along the shore</u>, Jane watched the boats.

Prepositional Phrases Incorrect placement of a **prepositional phrase** modifier can create confusion or even unintended humor. To correct this problem, place prepositional phrase modifiers immediately after the words they modify.

Confusing: *Venus de Milo* is a statue created by a famous artist <u>with no arms</u>. (Did the artist have no arms?)

Revised: Created by a famous artist, *Venus de Milo* is a statue <u>with no arms</u>.

Exercise 27.2

Underline each verbal phrase or prepositional phrase in the following sentences and draw an arrow to the word it modifies.

Example: Calvin is the Democrat <u>running for town council</u>.

▸ 1. The bridge across the river swayed in the wind.
▸ 2. The spectators on the shore were involved in the action.
▸ 3. Mesmerized by the spectacle, they watched the drama unfold.
▸ 4. The spectators were afraid of a disaster.
▸ 5. Within the hour, the state police arrived to save the day.
  6. They closed off the area with roadblocks.
  7. Drivers approaching the bridge were asked to stop.
  8. Meanwhile, on the bridge, the scene was chaos.
  9. Motorists in their cars were paralyzed with fear.
 10. Struggling against the weather, the police managed to rescue everyone.

Exercise 27.3

Use the word or phrase that follows each sentence as a modifier in that sentence. Then, underline the modifier, and draw an arrow to indicate the word it modifies.

Example: He approached the lion. (timidly)

<u>Timidly</u>, he approached the lion.

▸ 1. The lion paced up and down in his cage, ignoring the crowd. (watching Jack)
▸ 2. Jack stared back at the lion. (nervous yet curious)
   3. The crowd around them grew. (anxious to see what would happen)
   4. Suddenly, Jack heard a growl from deep in the lion's throat. (terrifying)
   5. Jack ran from the zoo, leaving the lion behind. (scared to death)

(3) Revising Misplaced Dependent Clauses

A dependent clause that serves as a modifier must be clearly related to the word it modifies. An **adjective clause** usually appears immediately *after* the word it modifies.

During the Civil War, Lincoln was the president who governed the United States.

An **adverb clause** can appear in any of several positions, as long as its relationship to the word it modifies is clear.

When Lincoln was president, the Civil War raged.

The Civil War raged when Lincoln was president.

Exercise 27.4

Relocate each misplaced verbal phrase, prepositional phrase, or dependent clause so that it clearly points to the word it modifies.

with Bruce Dern
Example: *Silent Running* is a film about a scientist left alone in space with Bruce Dern.

▸ 1. She realized that she had married the wrong man after the wedding.
▸ 2. *The Prince and the Pauper* is a novel about an exchange of identities by Mark Twain.
   3. The energy was used up in the ten-kilometer race that he was saving for the marathon.
   4. He loaded the bottles and cans into his new car, which he planned to leave at the recycling center.
   5. The manager explained the sales figures to the board members using a graph.

(4) Revising Intrusive Modifiers

An **intrusive modifier** awkwardly interrupts a sentence, making it difficult to understand. Be on the lookout for intrusive modifiers in your writing, and revise them when you find them.

Interrupted Verb Phrases Revise when a long modifier comes between an auxiliary verb and a main verb.

Awkward: She <u>had</u>, without giving it a second thought or considering the consequences, <u>planned</u> to reenlist.

Revised: Without giving it a second thought or considering the consequences, she <u>had planned</u> to reenlist.

Split Infinitives Revise when a modifier awkwardly interrupts an **infinitive**—that is, when the modifier comes between (*splits*) the word *to* and the base form of the verb.

Awkward: She hoped <u>to</u> in a matter of months, if not days, <u>beat</u> her previous record.

Revised: She hoped <u>to beat</u> her previous record in a matter of months, if not days.

Interrupted Subjects and Verbs or Verbs and Objects or Complements Revise when a long **adverb phrase or clause** comes between a subject and a verb or between a verb and its object or complement.

Confusing: The <u>election</u>, because officials discovered that some people voted twice, <u>was</u> contested. (Adverb clause comes between subject and verb.)

Revised: Because officials discovered that some people voted twice, the <u>election was</u> contested. (Subject and verb are no longer separated.)

Confusing: A. A. Milne <u>wrote</u>, when his son Christopher Robin was a child, <u>*Winnie the Pooh*</u>. (Adverb clause comes between verb and object.)

Revised: When his son Christopher Robin was a child, A. A. Milne <u>wrote *Winnie the Pooh*</u>. (Verb and object are no longer separated.)

Exercise 27.5

Revise these sentences so that the modifying phrases or clauses do not interrupt the parts of a verb phrase or an infinitive or separate a subject from a verb or a verb from its object or complement.

Example: ˄ A play can sometimes be, ~~despite the playwright's best efforts,~~ mystifying to the audience.
Despite the playwright's best efforts, a

▸ 1. The people in the audience, when they saw the play was about to begin and realized the orchestra had finished tuning up and had begun the overture, finally quieted down.

> 2. They settled into their seats, expecting to very much enjoy the first act.
>
> 3. However, most people were, even after watching and listening for twenty minutes and paying close attention to the drama, completely baffled.
>
> 4. In fact, the play, because it had nameless characters, no scenery, and a rambling plot that did not seem to be heading anywhere, puzzled even the drama critics.
>
> 5. Finally, one of the three major characters explained, speaking directly to the audience, what the play was really about.

27c Revising Dangling Modifiers

A **dangling modifier** is a word or phrase that cannot logically modify any word in the sentence. The two options for correcting dangling modifiers are illustrated below.

(1) Creating a New Subject

One way to correct a dangling modifier is by supplying a subject that the modifier can logically describe.

Dangling: Using a pair of forceps, the skin of the rat's abdomen was lifted, and a small cut was made into the body with scissors. (Modifier cannot logically modify *skin*.)

Revised: Using a pair of forceps, the technician lifted the skin of the rat's abdomen and made a small cut into the body with scissors. (Subject of main clause has been changed from *the skin* to *the technician*.)

Close-up: Dangling Modifiers and the Passive Voice

Most sentences that include dangling modifiers are in the passive voice. Changing the <u>passive voice</u> to <u>active voice</u> corrects the dangling modifier by changing the subject of the sentence's main clause to a word that the dangling modifier can logically modify.

See
22d1

ESL

48a6

---

(2) Creating a Dependent Clause

Another way to correct a dangling modifier is by rewording the modifier to turn it into a dependent clause.

Dangling: To implement the new grading system, students were polled. (Modifier cannot logically modify *students*.)

Revised: Before the new grading system was implemented, students were polled. (Modifying phrase is now a dependent clause.)

Exercise 27.6

Eliminate the dangling modifier from each of the following sentences. Either supply a word the dangling modifier can logically modify, or change the dangling modifier into a dependent clause.

Example: Skiing down the mountain, my hat flew off.
(dangling modifier)

Revised: Skiing down the mountain, I lost my hat.
(new subject added)

As I skied down the mountain, my hat flew off.
(dependent clause)

▸ 1. Writing for eight hours every day, her lengthy books are published every year or so.
▸ 2. As an out-of-state student without a car, it was difficult to get to off-campus cultural events.
▸ 3. To build a campfire, kindling is necessary.
▸ 4. With every step upward, the trees became sparser.
▸ 5. Being an amateur tennis player, my backhand is weaker than my forehand.
  6. When exiting the train, the station will be on your right.
  7. Driving through the Mojave, the bleak landscape was oppressive.
  8. By requiring auto manufacturers to further improve emission-control devices, the air quality will get better.
  9. Using a piece of filter paper, the ball of sodium is dried as much as possible and placed in a test tube.
  10. Having missed work for seven days straight, my job was in jeopardy.

Chapter 28 | Revising Awkward or Confusing Sentences

The most common causes of awkward or confusing sentences are *unwarranted shifts*, *mixed constructions*, *faulty predication*, and *illogical comparisons*.

28a Revising Unwarranted Shifts

See 22b

ESL 48a2

(1) Shifts in Tense

Verb tense in a sentence (or in a related group of sentences) should only shift for a good reason—to indicate changes of time, for example.

The Wizard of Oz is a classic film that <u>was made</u> in 1939. (acceptable shift from present to past)

Unwarranted shifts in tense, like those in the following sentences, can be confusing.

I registered for the advanced philosophy seminar because I wanted a challenge. However, after the first week I <u>start</u> having $\overset{\text{started}}{\wedge}$ trouble understanding the reading. (unwarranted shift from past to present)

Jack Kerouac's novel *On the Road* follows a group of friends who <u>drove</u> across the United States. (unwarranted shift from $\overset{\text{drive}}{\wedge}$ present to past)

NOTE: The present tense is generally used in writing about literature.

(2) Shifts in Voice

Unwarranted shifts from active to passive <u>voice</u> (or from passive to active) can be confusing. In the following sentence, for instance, the shift from active (*wrote*) to passive (*was written*) makes it unclear who wrote *The Great Gatsby*.

> See 22d
>
> ESL
> 48a6

F. Scott Fitzgerald wrote *This Side of Paradise,* and later *The* $\overset{\text{wrote}}{\wedge}$ *Great Gatsby* <s>was written.</s>

(3) Shifts in Mood

Unnecessary shifts in **mood** also create awkward sentences. The following sentence shifts unnecessarily from the imperative to the indicative mood.

> See 22c

Next, heat the mixture in a test tube, and <s>you should make</s> sure $\overset{\text{be}}{\wedge}$ it does not boil.

(4) Shifts in Person and Number

<u>Person</u> indicates who is speaking (first person—*I, we*), who is spoken to (second person—*you*), and who is spoken about (third person—*he, she, it,* and *they*). Most unwarranted shifts in a sentence occur between second and third person.

> ESL
> 48a1

When <s>someone</s> looks for a car loan, you should compare the $\overset{\text{you}}{\wedge}$ interest rates of several banks. (shift from third to second person)

ESL
48a1

See
26b1

<u>Number</u> indicates one (singular—*novel, it*) or more than one (plural—*novels, they, them*). Singular pronouns should refer to singular <u>antecedents</u> and plural pronouns to plural antecedents.

he or she
If a person does not study regularly, ~~they~~ will have a difficult time passing a course.

(5) Shifts from Direct to Indirect Discourse

Direct discourse reports the exact words of a speaker or writer. It is always enclosed in quotation marks and is often accompanied by an identifying tag (*he says, she said*). **Indirect discourse** summarizes the words of a speaker or writer. No quotation marks are used, and the reported words are often introduced with the word *that* or, in the case of questions, with *who, what, why, whether, how,* or *if*.

> **Direct Discourse:** My instructor said, "I <u>want</u> your paper by this Friday."

> **Indirect Discourse:** My instructor said <u>that he wanted</u> my paper by this Friday.

Unwarranted shifts between indirect and direct discourse are often confusing.

> During the trial, John Brown repeatedly defended his actions and
> *he was*
> said that ~~I am~~ not guilty. (shift from indirect to direct discourse)
> *"Are you   ?"*
> My mother asked, ~~was I~~ ever going to get a job.
> (neither indirect nor direct discourse)

NOTE: For information on word order in direct and indirect quotations, **see 48d4.**

Exercise 28.1

Read the following sentences, and eliminate any shifts in tense, voice, mood, person, or number. Some sentences are correct, and some can be revised in more than one way.

you
Example: When ~~one~~ examines the history of the women's movement, you see that it had many different beginnings.

▸ 1. Some historians see World War II and women's work in the factories as the beginning of the push toward equal rights for women.
▸ 2. Women went to work in the fabric mills of Lowell, Massachusetts, in the late 1800s, and her efforts at reforming the workplace are seen by many as the beginning of the equal rights movement.

▸ 3. Farm girls from New Hampshire, Vermont, and western Massachusetts came to Lowell to make money, and they wanted to experience life in the city.

▸ 4. The factories promised the girls decent wages, and parents were promised that their daughters would live in a safe, wholesome environment.

▸ 5. Dormitories were built by the factory owners; they are supposed to ensure a safe environment for the girls.

6. First, visit the loom rooms at the Boot Mills Factory, and then you should tour a replica of a dormitory.

7. When one visits the working loom room at the factory, you are overcome with a sense of the risks and dangers the girls faced in the mills.

8. For a mill girl, moving to the city meant freedom and an escape from the drudgery of farm life; it also meant they had to face many new social situations for which they were not always prepared.

9. Harriet Robinson wrote *Loom and Spindle*, the story of her life as a mill girl, and then a book of poems was published.

10. When you look at the lives of the loom girls, one can see that their work laid part of the foundation for women's later demands for equal rights.

28b Revising Mixed Constructions

A **mixed construction** is created when a dependent clause, prepositional phrase, or independent clause is incorrectly used as the subject of a sentence.

Because she studies every day, ~~explains why~~ she gets good grades. (dependent clause incorrectly used as subject)

By calling for information ~~is the way to~~ *, you can* learn more about the benefits of ROTC. (prepositional phrase incorrectly used as subject)

Being
~~He was~~ late made him miss the first act of the play. (independent clause incorrectly used as subject)

Exercise 28.2

Revise the following mixed constructions so their parts fit together both grammatically and logically.

Example: *Investing*
~~By investing~~ in commodities made her rich.

▸ 1. In implementing the "motor voter" bill has made it easier for people to register to vote.

▸ 2. She sank the basket was the reason they won the game.

3. Just because situations change, does not change the characters' hopes and dreams.

4. By dropping the course would be his only chance to avoid a low GPA.

5. Even though she works for a tobacco company does not mean that she is against laws prohibiting smoking in restaurants.

28c Revising Faulty Predication

Faulty predication occurs when a sentence's predicate does not logically complete its subject.

(1) Incorrect Use of *Be*

See
20c1

Faulty predication is especially common in sentences that contain a <u>linking verb</u>—a form of the verb *be*, for example—and a subject complement.

Mounting costs and decreasing revenues ~~were~~ the downfall of the hospital. *[caused]*

This sentence incorrectly states that mounting costs and decreasing revenues *were* the downfall of the hospital when, in fact, they were the *reasons* for its downfall.

(2) *Is When* or *Is Where*

Another kind of faulty predication occurs when a sentence that presents a definition incorrectly includes a construction like *is where* or *is when*.

Taxidermy is ~~where you construct~~ a lifelike representation of an animal from its preserved skin. (In a definition, *is* must be preceded and followed by nouns or noun phrases.) *[the construction of]*

(3) *The Reason . . . Is Because*

A similar type of problem occurs when the phrase *the reason is* precedes *because*. In this situation, *because* (which means "for the reason that") is redundant and should be deleted.

The reason we drive is ~~because~~ we are afraid to fly. *[that]*

Computer Tip: Revising Faulty Predication

Your word processor's grammar checker will highlight certain instances of faulty predication and offer suggestions for revision. Your grammar checker will also highlight some other causes of awkward or confusing sentences, including shifts in voice, person, and number, and will frequently offer revision suggestions. However, the grammar checker will miss many unwarranted shifts, mixed constructions, and incomplete or illogical constructions.

Exercise 28.3

Revise the following sentences to eliminate faulty predication. Keep in mind that each sentence may be revised in more than one way.

Example: *Traffic*
       ~~The reason traffic~~ jams occur at 9 a.m. and 5 p.m. ~~is~~ because too many people work traditional rather than staggered hours.

▸ 1. Inflation is when the purchasing power of currency declines.
▸ 2. Hypertension is where the blood pressure is elevated.
  3. Television and the Internet were the decline in students' reading scores.
  4. Some people say the reason for the increasing violence in American cities is because guns are too easily available.
  5. The reason for all the congestion in American cities is because too many people live too close together.

28d Revising Incomplete or Illogical Comparisons

A comparison tells how two things are alike or unlike. When you make a comparison, be sure it is *complete* (that readers can tell which two items are being compared) and *logical* (that it equates two comparable items).

                       than Nina's
My chemistry course is harder. (What two things are being compared?)

                    dog's
A pig's intelligence is greater than a ~~dog~~. (illogically compares "a pig's intelligence" to "a dog")

Exercise 28.4

Revise the following sentences to correct any incomplete or illogical comparisons.

Example: Technology-based industries are concerned about

inflation as much as service industries*are.*

▸ 1. Opportunities in technical writing are more promising than business writing.
▸ 2. Technical writing is more challenging.
3. In some ways, technical writing requires more attention to detail and is, therefore, more difficult.
4. Business writers are concerned about clarity as much as technical writers.
5. Technology-based industries may one day create more writing opportunities than any other industry.

PART 5

Understanding Punctuation

29a Using Periods

(1) Ending a Sentence

Use a period to signal the end of a statement, a mild command or polite request, or an indirect question.

> Something is rotten in Denmark. (statement)
>
> Be sure to have the oil checked before you start out. (mild command)
>
> When the bell rings, please exit in an orderly fashion. (polite request)
>
> They wondered whether the water was safe to drink. (indirect question)

(2) Marking an Abbreviation

Use a period in most abbreviations.

> Mr. Spock   1600 Pennsylvania Ave.   9 p.m.
> Dr. Who   Aug.   etc.

If an abbreviation ends the sentence, do not add another period.

> He promised to be there at 6 a.m./

However, do add a question mark if the sentence is a question.

> Did he arrive at 6 p.m.?

If the abbreviation falls *within* a sentence, use normal punctuation after the period.

> He promised to be there at 6 p.m., but he forgot.

Close-up: Abbreviations without Periods

Abbreviations composed of all capital letters do not usually require periods unless they are the initials of people's names (E. B. White).

> MD   RN   BC

Familiar abbreviations of the names of corporations or government agencies and abbreviations of scientific and technical terms do not require periods.

IBM   EPA   DNA   CD-ROM

Acronyms—new words formed from the initial letters or first few letters of a series of words—do not include periods.

modem   op-ed   scuba   radar
OSHA   AIDS   NAFTA   CAT scan

Clipped forms (commonly accepted shortened forms of words, such as *flu, dorm, math,* and *fax*) do not include periods.

Postal abbreviations do not include periods.

NY   CA   MS   FL   TX

(3) Marking Divisions in Dramatic, Poetic, and Biblical References

Use periods to separate act, scene, and line numbers in plays; book and line numbers in long poems; and chapter and verse numbers in biblical references. (Do not space between the periods and the elements they separate.)

Dramatic Reference: *Hamlet* 2.2.1–5
Poetic Reference: *Paradise Lost* 7.163–67
Biblical Reference: Judges 4.14

NOTE: In MLA parenthetical references, titles of literary and biblical works are often abbreviated: Ham. 2.2.1-5; Judg. 4.14.

See
46a1

(4) Marking Divisions in Electronic Addresses

Periods, along with other punctuation marks (such as slashes and colons), are frequently used in electronic addresses (URLs).

http://kirsznermandell.wadsworth.com

NOTE: When you type a URL, do not end it with a period; do not add spaces after periods within the address.

Exercise 29.1

Correct these sentences by adding missing periods and deleting unnecessary ones. If a sentence is correct, mark it with a *C*.

Example: Their mission changed the war.

> 1. Julius Caesar was killed in 44 B.C.
> 2. Dr. McLaughlin worked hard to earn his Ph.D..
>   3. Carmen was supposed to be at A.F.L.-C.I.O. headquarters by
>   2 p.m.; however, she didn't get there until 10 p.m.
>   4. After she studied the fall lineup proposed by N.B.C., she decided
>   to work for C.B.S.
>   5. Representatives from the U.M.W. began collective bargaining
>   after an unsuccessful meeting with Mr. L Pritchard, the coal
>   company's representative.

29b Using Question Marks

(1) Marking the End of a Direct Question

Use a question mark to signal the end of a direct question.

Who was that masked man? (direct question)

"Is this a silver bullet?" they asked. (declarative sentence opening
with a direct question)

(2) Marking Questionable Dates or Numbers

Use a question mark in parentheses to indicate that a date or number
is uncertain.

Aristophanes, the Greek playwright, was born in 448 (?) BC and
died in 380 (?) BC.

(3) Editing Misused Question Marks

Do not use question marks in the following situations.

After an Indirect Question   Use a period, not a question mark, with
an **indirect question** (a question that is not quoted directly).

The personnel officer asked whether he knew how to type?

With Other Punctuation   Do not use question marks along with
other punctuation (except for closing quotation marks).

"Can it be true?," he asked.

With Another Question Mark   Do not use more than one question
mark to end a sentence.

You did what?? Are you crazy??

To Convey Sarcasm   Do not use question marks to convey sarcasm.
Instead, suggest your attitude through word choice.

                    not-so-very
I refused his generous (?) offer.

In an Exclamation Do not use a question mark after an exclamation that is phrased as a question.

Will you please stop that at once‽

Exercise 29.2

Correct the use of question marks and other punctuation in the following sentences.

Example: She asked whether Freud's theories were accepted during his lifetime‽

▶ 1. He wondered whether he should take a nine o'clock class?
▶ 2. The instructor asked, "Was the Spanish-American War a victory for America."
   3. Are they really going to China??!!
   4. He took a modest (?) portion of dessert—half a pie.
   5. "Is *data* the plural of *datum*?," he inquired.

29c Using Exclamation Points

Use an exclamation point to signal the end of an emotional or emphatic statement, an emphatic interjection, or a forceful command.

Remember the *Maine*!

No! Don't leave!

Finish this job at once!

NOTE: Except for recording dialogue, exclamation points are almost never appropriate in college writing. Even in informal writing, you should use exclamation points sparingly.

Chapter 30 Using Commas

30a Setting Off Independent Clauses

Use a comma when you form a compound sentence by linking two independent clauses with a **coordinating conjunction** (*and, but, or, nor, for, yet, so*) or a pair of <u>correlative conjunctions</u>.

See
20g

The House approved the bill, but the Senate rejected it.

<u>Either</u> the hard drive is full, <u>or</u> the modem is too slow.

NOTE: You may omit the comma if two clauses connected by a coordinating conjunction are very short.

> Seek and ye shall find.
>
> Love it or leave it.

Exercise 30.1

Combine each of the following sentence pairs into one compound sentence, adding commas where necessary.

Example: Emergency medicine became an approved medical
specialty in 1979̸ N̶o̶w̸ *, and now* pediatric emergency
medicine is becoming increasingly important. (and)

► 1. The Pope did not hesitate to visit Cuba. He did not hesitate to meet with President Fidel Castro. (nor)

► 2. Agents place brand-name products in prominent positions in films. The products will be seen and recognized by large audiences. (so)

3. Unisex insurance rates may have some drawbacks for women. These rates may be very beneficial. (or)

4. Cigarette advertising no longer appears on television. It does appear in print media. (but)

5. Dorothy Day founded the Catholic Worker movement in the 1930s. Her followers still dispense free food, medical care, and legal advice to the needy. (and)

30b Setting Off Items in a Series

(1) Coordinate Elements

Use commas between items in a series of three or more **coordinate elements** (words, phrases, or clauses joined by a coordinating conjunction).

> <u>Chipmunk</u>, <u>raccoon</u>, and <u>Mugwump</u> are Native American words.
>
> You may pay <u>by check</u>, <u>with a credit card</u>, or <u>in cash</u>.
>
> <u>Brazilians speak Portuguese</u>, <u>Colombians speak Spanish</u>, and <u>Haitians speak French and Creole</u>.

See 31c NOTE: If phrases or clauses in a <u>series</u> already contain commas, use semicolons to separate the items.

Do not use a comma to introduce or to close a series.

> Three important criteria are̸ fat content, salt content, and taste.
>
> Quebec, Ontario, and Alberta̸ are Canadian provinces.

NOTE: To avoid ambiguity, always use a comma before the *and* (or other coordinating conjunction) that separates the last two items in a series.

(2) Coordinate Adjectives

Use a comma between items in a series of two or more **coordinate adjectives**—adjectives that modify the same word or word group—unless they are joined by a conjunction.

> She brushed her <u>long</u>, <u>shining</u> hair.
>
> The baby was <u>tired</u> and <u>cranky</u> and <u>wet</u>. (adjectives joined by conjunctions; no commas required)

Checklist: Punctuating Adjectives in a Series

☐ If you can reverse the order of the adjectives or insert *and* between the adjectives without changing the meaning, the adjectives are coordinate, and you should use a comma.

She brushed her <u>long</u>, <u>shining</u> hair.

She brushed her <u>shining</u>, <u>long</u> hair.

She brushed her <u>long</u> [and] <u>shining</u> hair.

☐ If you cannot reverse the order of the adjectives or insert *and*, the adjectives are not coordinate, and you should not use a comma.

<u>Ten red</u> balloons fell from the ceiling.

<u>Red ten</u> balloons fell from the ceiling.

<u>Ten</u> [and] <u>red</u> balloons fell from the ceiling.

ESL Tip

If you have difficulty determining the order of two or more adjectives, **see 48d5** for tips to help you with this problem.

Exercise 30.2

Correct the use of commas in the following sentences, adding or deleting commas where necessary. If a sentence is punctuated correctly, mark it with a *C*.

Example: Neither dogs, snakes, bees, nor dragons frighten her.

▸ 1. Seals, whales, dogs, lions, and horses, all are mammals.

▸ 2. Mammals are warm-blooded vertebrates that bear live young, nurse them, and usually have fur.

3. Seals are mammals, but lizards, and snakes, and iguanas are reptiles, and salamanders are amphibians.
4. Amphibians also include frogs, and toads and newts.
5. Eagles geese ostriches turkeys chickens and ducks are classified as birds.

30c Setting Off Introductory Elements

(1) Dependent Clauses

An introductory dependent clause is generally set off from the rest of the sentence by a comma.

> <u>Although the CIA used to call undercover agents *penetration agents*</u>, they now routinely refer to them as *moles*.

> <u>When war came to Baghdad</u>, many victims were children.

If a dependent clause is short and designates time, you may omit the comma—provided the sentence will be clear without it.

> <u>When I exercise</u> I drink plenty of water.

NOTE: Do not use a comma to set off a dependent clause at the *end* of a sentence.

(2) Verbal and Prepositional Phrases

An introductory verbal phrase is usually set off by a comma.

> <u>Thinking that this might be his last chance</u>, Peary struggled toward the North Pole. (participial phrase)

> <u>To write well</u>, one must read a lot. (infinitive phrase)

An introductory prepositional phrase is also usually set off by a comma.

> <u>During the Depression</u>, movie attendance rose. (prepositional phrase)

However, if an introductory prepositional phrase is short and no ambiguity is possible, you may omit the comma.

> <u>After the exam</u> I took a four-hour nap.

See
13b1

Close-up: Using Commas with Verbal Phrases

A <u>verbal phrase</u> that serves as the subject of a sentence is not set off by a comma.

Laughing out loud, can release tension. (gerund phrase)

To know him, is to love him. (infinitive phrase)

(3) Transitional Words and Phrases

A <u>transitional word or phrase</u> that begins a sentence is usually set off from the rest of the sentence with a comma.

> However⸴ any plan that is enacted must be fair.
>
> In other words⸴ we cannot act hastily.

Exercise 30.3

Add commas in the following paragraph where necessary to set off an introductory element from the rest of a sentence.

> ►While childhood is shrinking adolescence is expanding. ►Whatever the reason girls are maturing earlier. ►The average onset of puberty is now two years earlier than it was only forty years ago. ►What's more both boys and girls are staying in the nest longer. ►At present, it is not unusual for children to stay in their parents' home until they are twenty or twenty-one, delaying adulthood and extending adolescence. To some who study the culture this increase in adolescence portends dire consequences. With teenage hormones running amuck for longer the problems of teenage pregnancy and sexually transmitted diseases loom large. Young boys' spending long periods of their lives without responsibilities is also a recipe for disaster. However others see this "youthing" of American culture in a more positive light. Without a doubt adolescents are creative, lively, and more willing to take risks. If we channel their energies carefully they could contribute, even in their extended adolescence, to American culture and technology.

30d Setting Off Nonessential Material

Sometimes words, phrases, or clauses *contribute* to the meaning of a sentence but are not *essential* for conveying the sentence's main point or emphasis. Use commas to set off such nonessential material whether it appears at the beginning, in the middle, or at the end of a sentence.

(1) Nonrestrictive Modifiers

Use commas to set off **nonrestrictive modifiers,** which supply information that is not essential to the meaning of the word or word group they modify. (Do *not* use commas to set off **restrictive modifiers,** which supply information that is essential to the meaning of the word or word group they modify.)

> **Nonrestrictive (commas required):** Actors⸴ <u>who have inflated egos⸴</u> are often insecure. (*All* actors—not just those with inflated egos—are insecure.)

Restrictive (no commas): Actors <u>who have inflated egos</u> are often insecure. (Only those actors with inflated egos—not all actors—are insecure.)

Adjective Clauses

Nonrestrictive: He ran for the bus, <u>which was late as usual</u>.

Restrictive: Speaking in public is something <u>that most people fear</u>.

Prepositional Phrases

Nonrestrictive: The clerk, <u>with a nod</u>, dismissed me.

Restrictive: The man <u>with the gun</u> demanded their money.

Verbal Phrases

Nonrestrictive: The marathoner, <u>running her fastest</u>, beat her previous record.

Restrictive: The candidates <u>running for mayor</u> have agreed to a debate.

Appositives

Nonrestrictive: *Citizen Kane*, Orson Welles's first film, made him famous.

Restrictive: The film <u>*Citizen Kane*</u> made Orson Welles famous.

Checklist: Restrictive and Nonrestrictive Modifiers

To determine whether a modifier is restrictive or nonrestrictive, ask yourself these questions:

☐ Is the modifier essential to the meaning of the noun it modifies (*The man <u>with the gun</u>*, not just any man)? If so, it is restrictive and does not take commas.

☐ Is the modifier introduced by *that* (*something <u>that most people fear</u>*)? If so, it is restrictive. *That* cannot introduce a nonrestrictive clause.

☐ Can you delete the relative pronoun without causing ambiguity or confusion (*something <u>[that] most people fear</u>*)? If so, the clause is restrictive.

☐ Is the appositive more specific than the noun that precedes it (*the film* <u>Citizen Kane</u>)? If so, it is restrictive.

Close-up: Using Commas with *That* and *Which*

• *That* introduces only restrictive clauses, which are not set off by commas.

I bought a used car <u>that</u> cost $2,000.

- *Which* can introduce both restrictive and nonrestrictive clauses.

  Restrictive (no comma): I bought a used car <u>which</u> cost $2,000.

  Nonrestrictive (commas needed): The used car I bought, <u>which</u> cost $2,000, broke down after a week.

  NOTE: Many writers prefer to use *which* only to introduce nonrestrictive clauses.

http://kirsznermandell.wadsworth.com

Computer Tip: *That* or *Which*

Your word processor's grammar checker may identify *which* as an error when it introduces a restrictive clause. It will prompt you to add commas, using *which* to introduce a nonrestrictive clause, or to change *which* to *that*. Review the meaning of your sentence, and revise accordingly.

Exercise 30.4

Insert commas where necessary to set off nonrestrictive modifiers.

▸The Statue of Liberty which was dedicated in 1886 has undergone extensive renovation. ▸Its supporting structure whose designer was the French engineer Alexandre Gustave Eiffel is made of iron. The Statue of Liberty created over a period of nine years by sculptor Frédéric-Auguste Bartholdi stands 151 feet tall. The people of France who were grateful for American help in the French Revolution raised the money to pay the sculptor who created the statue. The people of the United States contributing over $100,000 raised the money for the pedestal on which the statue stands.

(2) Transitional Words and Phrases

<u>Transitional words and phrases</u>—which include conjunctive adverbs like *however, therefore, thus,* and *nevertheless* as well as expressions like *for example* and *on the other hand*—qualify, clarify, and make connections. Because they are not essential to meaning, they are always set off by commas when they interrupt a clause or when they begin or end a sentence.

See 5b2

The Outward Bound program, for example, is considered safe.

In fact, Outward Bound has an excellent reputation.

Other programs are not so safe, however.

Close-up: Transitional Words and Phrases

When a transitional word or phrase joins two independent clauses, it must be preceded by a semicolon and followed by a comma.

Laughter is the best medicine ; of course , penicillin also comes in handy sometimes.

(3) Contradictory Phrases

A phrase that expresses contradiction is usually set off by commas.

This medicine is taken after meals , never on an empty stomach .

Mark McGwire , not Sammy Sosa , was the first to break Roger Maris's home-run record.

(4) Absolute Phrases

An **absolute phrase,** which includes a noun or pronoun and a participle and modifies an entire independent clause, is always set off by a comma from the clause it modifies.

His fear increasing , he waited to enter the haunted house.

Many soldiers were lost in Southeast Asia , their bodies never recovered .

(5) Miscellaneous Nonessential Material

Other nonessential material usually set off by commas includes tag questions, names in direct address, mild interjections, and *yes* and *no*.

This is your first day on the job , isn't it ?

I wonder , Mr. Honeywell , whether Mr. Albright deserves a raise.

Well , it's about time.

Yes , we have no bananas.

Exercise 30.5

Set off the nonessential elements in these sentences with commas. If a sentence is correct, mark it with a *C*.

Example: Piranhas , like sharks , will attack and eat almost anything if the opportunity arises.

▸ 1. Kermit the Frog is a Muppet a cross between a marionette and a puppet.

▸ 2. The common cold a virus is frequently spread by hand contact not by mouth.

▸ 3. The account in the Bible of Noah's Ark and the forty-day flood may be based on an actual deluge.

▸ 4. Many US welfare recipients, such as children, the aged, and the severely disabled, are unable to work.

▸ 5. The submarine *Nautilus* was the first to cross under the North Pole wasn't it?

6. The 1958 Ford Edsel was advertised with the slogan "Once you've seen it, you'll never forget it."

7. Superman was called Kal-El on the planet Krypton; on earth however he was known as Clark Kent not Kal-El.

8. Its sales topping any of his previous singles "Heartbreak Hotel" was Elvis Presley's first million-seller.

9. Two companies Nash and Hudson joined in 1954 to form American Motors.

10. A firefly is a beetle not a fly and a prairie dog is a rodent not a dog.

30e Using Commas in Other Conventional Contexts

(1) With Direct Quotations

In most cases, use commas to set off a direct quotation from the **identifying tag**—the phrase that identifies the speaker (*he said, she answered,* and so on).

Emerson said to Whitman, "I greet you at the beginning of a great career."

"I greet you at the beginning of a great career," Emerson said to Whitman.

"I greet you," Emerson said to Whitman, "at the beginning of a great career."

When the identifying tag comes between two complete sentences, however, the tag is introduced by a comma but followed by a period.

"Winning isn't everything," Vince Lombardi said. "It's the only thing."

If the first sentence of an interrupted quotation ends with a question mark or exclamation point, do not use commas.

"Should we hold the front page over?" she asked. "After all, it's a slow news day."

"Hold the front page over!" he cried. "This is the biggest story of the decade."

(2) With Titles or Degrees Following a Name

Hamlet, prince of Denmark, is Shakespeare's most famous character.

Michael Crichton, MD, wrote *Jurassic Park*.

(3) In Addresses and Dates

When a date or an address falls within a sentence, use a comma after the last element.

On August 30, 1983, the space shuttle *Challenger* was launched.

Do not use a comma to separate the street number from the street or the state name from the ZIP code.

Her address is 600 West End Avenue, New York, NY 10024.

NOTE: Do not use a comma to separate the month from the year: August 1983.

(4) In Salutations and Closings

In informal correspondence, use commas following salutations and closings.

Dear John,   Love,

Dear Aunt Sophie,   Sincerely,

Also use commas in both informal and business correspondence following the complimentary close.

NOTE: In business letters, always use a colon, not a comma, after the salutation.

(5) In Long Numbers

For a number of four digits or more, place a comma before every third digit, counting from the right.

1,200   120,000

12,000   1,200,000

NOTE: Commas are not used in long page and line numbers, address numbers, telephone numbers, or ZIP codes (or in four-digit year numbers).

Exercise 30.6

Add commas where necessary to set off quotations, names, dates, addresses, and numbers.

- 1. India became independent on August 15 1947.
- 2. The UAW has more than 1500000 dues-paying members.
- 3. Nikita Khrushchev, former Soviet premier, once said "We will bury you!"
- 4. Mount St. Helens, northeast of Portland Oregon, began erupting on March 27 1980 and eventually killed at least thirty people.
- 5. Located at 1600 Pennsylvania Avenue Washington DC, the White House is a popular tourist attraction.
6. In 1956, playing before a crowd of 64519 fans in Yankee Stadium in New York New York, Don Larsen pitched the first perfect game in World Series history.
7. Lewis Thomas MD was born in Flushing New York and attended Harvard Medical School in Cambridge Massachusetts.
8. In 1967 2000000 people worldwide died of smallpox, but in 1977 only about twenty people died.
9. "The reports of my death" Mark Twain remarked "have been greatly exaggerated."
10. The French explorer Jean Nicolet landed at Green Bay Wisconsin in 1634, and in 1848 Wisconsin became the thirtieth state; it has 10355 lakes and a population of more than 4700000.

30f Using Commas to Prevent Misreading

In some cases, you need to use a comma to avoid ambiguity. Consider the following sentence.

Those who can, sprint the final lap.

Without the comma, *can* appears to be an auxiliary verb ("Those who can sprint . . ."), and the sentence seems incomplete. Because the comma tells readers to pause, it eliminates confusion.

Also use a comma to acknowledge the omission of a repeated word, usually a verb, and to separate words repeated consecutively.

Pam carried the box; Tim, the suitcase.

Everything bad that could have happened, happened.

Exercise 30.7

Add commas where necessary to prevent misreading.

Example: Whatever will be, will be.

- 1. According to Bob Frank's computer is obsolete.
- 2. Da Gama explored Florida; Pizarro Peru.
- 3. By Monday evening students must begin preregistration for fall classes.

▸ 4. Whatever they built they built with care.
   5. When batting practice carefully.
   6. Brunch includes warm muffins topped with whipped butter and freshly brewed coffee.
   7. Students go to school to learn not to play sports.
   8. Technology has made what once seemed not possible possible.

30g Editing Misused Commas

Do not use commas in the following situations.

(1) To Join Two Independent Clauses

A comma alone cannot join two independent clauses; it must be followed by a coordinating conjunction. Using just a comma to connect two independent clauses creates a **comma splice**.

See
Ch. 25

but
The season was unusually cool,⌃the orange crop was not
seriously harmed.

(2) To Set Off Restrictive Modifiers

See
30d1

Commas are not used to set off **restrictive modifiers**.

Women⁄ who seek to be equal to men⁄ lack ambition.

The film⁄ *Malcolm X*⁄ was directed by Spike Lee.

(3) Between Inseparable Grammatical Constructions

Do not place a comma between grammatical elements that cannot be logically separated: a subject and its predicate, a verb and its complement or direct object, a preposition and its object, or an adjective and the word or phrase it modifies.

A woman with dark red hair⁄ opened the door. (comma incorrectly placed between subject and predicate)

Louis Braille developed⁄ an alphabet of raised dots for the blind. (comma incorrectly placed between verb and object)

They relaxed somewhat during⁄ the last part of the obstacle course. (comma incorrectly placed between preposition and object)

Wind-dispersed weeds include the well-known and plentiful⁄ dandelions, milkweed, and thistle. (comma incorrectly placed between adjective and words it modifies)

(4) Between a Verb and an Indirect Quotation or Indirect Question

Do not use commas between verbs and indirect quotations or between verbs and indirect questions.

General Douglas MacArthur vowed⸝ that he would return. (comma incorrectly placed between verb and indirect quotation)

The landlord asked⸝ if we would sign a two-year lease. (comma incorrectly placed between verb and indirect question)

(5) Between Phrases Linked by Correlative Conjunctions

Commas are not used to separate two phrases linked by <u>correlative conjunctions</u>.

See 20g

Forty years ago, most college students had access to neither photocopiers⸝ nor pocket calculators.

Both typewriters⸝ and tape recorders were generally available, however.

(6) In Compounds That Are Not Composed of Independent Clauses

Do not use commas before coordinating conjunctions like *and* or *but* when they join two elements of a compound subject, predicate, object, complement, or auxiliary verb.

Plagues⸝ and pestilence were common during the Middle Ages. (compound subject)

Many women thirty-five and older are returning to college⸝ and tend to be good students. (compound predicate)

Mattel has marketed a doctor's lab coat⸝ and an astronaut suit for its Barbie doll. (compound object)

People buy bottled water because it is pure⸝ and fashionable. (compound complement)

She can⸝ and will be ready to run in the primary. (compound auxiliary verb)

(7) Before a Dependent Clause at the End of a Sentence

Commas are generally not used before a dependent clause that falls at the end of a sentence.

Jane Addams founded Hull House⸝ because she wanted to help Chicago's poor.

Exercise 30.8

Unnecessary commas have been intentionally added to some of the sentences that follow. Delete any unnecessary commas. If a sentence is correct, mark it with a *C*.

Example: Spring fever, is a common ailment.

▸ 1. A book is like a garden, carried in the pocket. (Arab proverb)
▸ 2. Like the iodine content of kelp, air freight, is something most Americans have never pondered. (*Time*)
  3. Charles Rolls, and Frederick Royce manufactured the first Rolls-Royce Silver Ghost, in 1907.
  4. The hills ahead of him were rounded domes of grey granite, smooth as a bald man's pate, and completely free of vegetation. (Wilbur Smith, *Flight of the Falcon*)
  5. Food here is scarce, and cafeteria food is vile, but the great advantage to Russian raw materials, when one can get hold of them, is that they are always fresh and untampered with. (Andrea Lee, *Russian Journal*)

Chapter 31   Using Semicolons

The **semicolon** is used only between items of equal grammatical rank: two independent clauses, two phrases, and so on.

31a Separating Independent Clauses

Use a semicolon between closely related independent clauses that convey parallel or contrasting information but are not joined by a coordinating conjunction.

> Paul Revere's *The Boston Massacre* is traditional American protest art; Edward Hicks's paintings are socially conscious art with a religious strain.

NOTE: Using only a comma or no punctuation at all between independent clauses creates a <u>comma splice</u> or <u>fused sentence</u>.

See
Ch. 25

Exercise 31.1

Add semicolons where necessary to separate independent clauses. Then, reread the paragraph to make certain no comma splices or fused sentences remain.

Example: *Birth of a Nation* was one of the earliest epic movies ⁏it was based on the book *The Klansman*.

▶During the 1950s movie attendance declined because of the increasing popularity of television. ▶As a result, numerous gimmicks were introduced to draw audiences into theaters. ▶One of the first of these was Cinerama, in this technique three pictures were shot side by side and projected onto a curved screen. ▶Next came 3-D, complete with special glasses, *Bwana Devil* and *The Creature from the Black Lagoon* were two early 3-D ventures. ▶*The Robe* was the first picture filmed in Cinemascope in this technique a shrunken image was projected on a screen twice as wide as it was tall. Smell-O-Vision (or Aroma-rama) was a short-lived gimmick that enabled audiences to smell what they were viewing problems developed when it became impossible to get one odor out of the theater in time for the next smell to be introduced. William Castle's *Thirteen Ghosts* introduced special glasses for cowardly viewers who wanted to be able to control what they saw, the red part of the glasses was the "ghost viewer" and the green part was the "ghost remover." Perhaps the ultimate in movie gimmicks accompanied the film *The Tingler* when this film was shown seats in the theater were wired to generate mild electric shocks. Unfortunately, the shocks set off a chain reaction that led to hysteria in the theater. During the 1960s, such gimmicks all but disappeared, viewers were able once again to simply sit back and enjoy a movie. In 1997, *Mr. Payback*, a short interactive film that contained elements of a videogame, brought back the gimmick, it allowed viewers to vote on how they wanted the plot to unfold.

31b Separating Independent Clauses Introduced by Transitional Words and Phrases

Use a semicolon before a **transitional word or phrase** that joins two independent clauses. (The transitional element is followed by a comma.)

See 5b2

Thomas Jefferson brought two hundred vanilla beans and a recipe for vanilla ice cream back from France ⁏ <u>thus</u>, he gave America its all-time favorite ice-cream flavor.

Exercise 31.2

Combine each of the following sentence groups into one sentence that contains only two independent clauses. Use a semicolon and the transitional word or phrase in parentheses to join the two clauses, adding commas within clauses where necessary. You will need to add, delete, relocate, or change some words. There is no one correct version; keep experimenting until you find the arrangement you feel is most effective.

Example: The Aleutian Islands, ~~are~~ located off the west coast of
Alaska, ~~They~~ are an extremely remote chain of islands, ; in fact, they
~~They~~ are sometimes called America's Siberia. (in fact)

▸ 1. The Aleutians lie between the North Pacific Ocean and the
Bering Sea. The weather there is harsh. Dense fog, 100-mph
winds, and even tidal waves and earthquakes are not uncommon.
(for example)
▸ 2. These islands constitute North America's largest network of active volcanoes. The Aleutians boast some beautiful scenery. The
islands are relatively unexplored. (still)
3. The Aleutians are home to a wide variety of birds. Numerous animals, such as fur seals and whales, are found there. These islands
may house the largest concentration of marine animals in the
world. (in fact)
4. During World War II, thousands of American soldiers were stationed on Attu Island. They were stationed on Adak Island. The
Japanese eventually occupied both islands. (however)
5. The islands' original population of native Aleuts was drastically
reduced in the eighteenth century by Russian fur traders. Today
the total population is only about 8,500. US military employees
comprise more than half of this. (consequently)
(Adapted from *National Geographic*)

31c Separating Items in a Series

Use semicolons between items in a series when one or more of these
items include commas.

Three papers are posted on the bulletin board outside the building: a description of the exams; a list of appeal procedures for
students who fail; and an employment ad from an automobile
factory, addressed specifically to candidates whose appeals are
turned down. (Andrea Lee, *Russian Journal*)

Laramie, Wyoming; Wyoming, Delaware; and Delaware, Ohio,
were three of the places they visited.

Exercise 31.3

Replace commas with semicolons where necessary to separate internally punctuated items in a series. (For information on use of semicolons with quotation marks, **see 33e2.**)

Example: Luxury automobiles have some strong selling points: they
are status symbolsͅ some, such as the Corvette, appreciate
in valueͅ and they are comfortable and well appointed.

▶ 1. The history of modern art seems at times to be a collection of
"isms": Impressionism, a term that applies to painters who
attempted to depict contemporary life by reproducing an "impression" of what the eye sees, Abstract Expressionism, which
applies to artists who stress emotion and the unconscious in their
nonrepresentational works, and, more recently, Minimalism,
which applies to painters and sculptors whose work reasserts the
physical reality of the object.

▶ 2. Although the term *Internet* is widely used to refer only to the
World Wide Web and email, the Internet consists of a variety of
discrete elements, including newsgroups, which allow users to
post and receive messages on an unbelievably broad range of topics, interactive communication forums, such as blogs, discussion
forums, and chat rooms, and FTP, which allows users to download material from remote computers.

3. Three of rock and roll's best-known guitar heroes played with the
"British Invasion" group The Yardbirds: Eric Clapton, the group's
first lead guitarist, went on to play with John Mayall's Bluesbreak-
ers, Cream, and Blind Faith, and is now a popular solo act, Jeff
Beck, the group's second guitarist, though not as visible as Clapton, made rock history with the Jeff Beck Group and inventive
solo albums, and Jimmy Page, the group's third and final guitarist,
transformed the remnants of the original group into the premier
heavy metal band, Led Zeppelin.

4. Some of the most commonly confused words in English are
aggravate, which means "to worsen," and *irritate*, which means
"to annoy," *continual*, which means "recurring at intervals," and
continuous, which means "an action occurring without interruption," *imply*, which means "to hint, suggest," and *infer*, which
means "to conclude from," and *compliment*, which means "to
praise," and *complement*, which means "to complete or add to."

5. Tennessee Williams wrote *The Glass Menagerie*, which is about
Laura Wingfield, a disabled young woman, and her family, *A
Streetcar Named Desire*, which starred Marlon Brando, and *Cat on
a Hot Tin Roof*, which won a Pulitzer Prize.

31d **Editing Misused Semicolons**

Do not use semicolons in the following situations.

(1) Between a Dependent and an Independent Clause

Use a comma, not a semicolon, between a dependent and an independent clause.

Because new drugs can now suppress the body's immune reaction; fewer organ transplants are rejected by the body.

http://kirsznermandell.wadsworth.com

> **Computer Tip: Editing Misused Semicolons**
>
> Your word processor's grammar checker will highlight certain misused semicolons and frequently offer suggestions for revision.

(2) Between a Phrase and a Clause

Use a comma, not a semicolon, between a phrase and a clause.

Increasing rapidly; computer crime poses a challenge for government, financial, and military agencies.

(3) To Introduce a List

Use a colon, not a semicolon, to introduce a <u>list</u>.

Despite the presence of CNN and Fox News, the evening news remains a battleground for the three major television networks; CBS, NBC, and ABC.

NOTE: Always use a complete sentence followed by a colon to introduce a list.

(4) To Introduce a Quotation

Do not use a semicolon to introduce <u>quoted speech or writing</u>.

Marie Antoinette may not have said; "Let them eat cake."

> **Exercise 31.4**
>
> Read the following paragraph carefully. Then, add semicolons where necessary, and delete incorrectly used ones, substituting other punctuation where necessary.
>
> ►Barnstormers were aviators; who toured the country after World War I, giving people short airplane rides and exhibitions of stunt flying, in fact, the name *barnstormer* was derived from the use of barns as airplane hangars. ►Americans' interest in airplanes had all but disappeared after the war. ►The barnstormers helped

popularize flying; especially in rural areas. ►Some were pilots who had flown in the war; others were just young men with a thirst for adventure. They gave people rides in airplanes; sometimes charging a dollar a minute. For most passengers, this was their first ride in an airplane, in fact, sometimes it was their first sight of one. After Lindbergh's 1927 flight across the Atlantic; Americans suddenly needed no encouragement to embrace aviation. The barnstormers had outlived their usefulness; and an era ended. (Adapted from William Goldman, *Adventures in the Screen Trade*)

| Chapter 32 | Using Apostrophes |

Use an apostrophe to form the possessive case, to indicate omissions in contractions, and to form certain plurals.

32a Forming the Possessive Case

The possessive case indicates ownership. In English, the possessive case of nouns and indefinite pronouns is indicated either with a phrase that includes the word *of* (the hands *of* the clock) or with an apostrophe and, in most cases, an *s* (the clock's hands).

(1) Singular Nouns and Indefinite Pronouns

To form the possessive case of singular nouns and indefinite pronouns, add *'s*.

"The Monk's Tale" is one of Chaucer's *Canterbury Tales*.

When we would arrive was anyone's guess.

(2) Singular Nouns Ending in *-s*

To form the possessive case of singular nouns that end in *-s*, add *'s* in most cases.

Reading Henry James's *The Ambassadors* was not Maris's idea of fun.

The class's time was changed to 8 a.m.

NOTE: With some singular nouns that end in *-s*, pronouncing the possessive ending as a separate syllable can sound awkward. In such cases, it is acceptable to use just an apostrophe: Crispus Attucks' death, Aristophanes' *Lysistrata*.

Do not use an apostrophe to form the possessive case of a title that already contains an 's ending; use a phrase instead.

Awkward: *A Midsummer Night's Dream's* staging

Revised: the staging of *A Midsummer Night's Dream*

(3) Plural Nouns Ending in -s

To form the possessive case of regular plural nouns (those that end in -s or -es), add only an apostrophe.

The Readers' Guide to Periodical Literature is available online.

Laid-off employees received two weeks' severance pay and three months' medical benefits.

The Lopezes' three children are triplets.

(4) Irregular Plural Nouns

To form the possessive case of nouns that have irregular plurals, add 's.

Long after they were gone, the geese's honking could still be heard.

The Children's Hour is a play by Lillian Hellman; *The Women's Room* is a novel by Marilyn French.

The two oxen's yokes were securely attached to the cart.

(5) Compound Nouns or Groups of Words

To form the possessive case of compound nouns or of word groups, add 's to the last word.

The editor-in-chief's position is open.

He accepted the secretary of state's resignation under protest.

This is someone else's responsibility.

(6) Two or More Items

To indicate individual ownership of two or more items, add 's to each item.

Ernest Hemingway's and Gertrude Stein's writing styles have some similarities. (Hemingway and Stein have two separate writing styles.)

To indicate joint ownership, add 's only to the last item.

Gilbert and Sullivan's operettas include *The Pirates of Penzance* and *The Mikado*. (Gilbert and Sullivan collaborated on both operettas.)

Exercise 32.1

Change each word or phrase in parentheses to its possessive form. In some cases, you may have to use a phrase to indicate the possessive.

Example: The (children) toys were scattered all over their (parents) bedroom.

The children's toys were scattered all over their parents' bedroom.

▸ 1. Jane (Addams) settlement house was called Hull House.
▸ 2. (*A Room of One's Own*) popularity increased with the rise of feminism.
  3. The (chief petty officer) responsibilities are varied.
  4. Vietnamese (restaurants) numbers have grown dramatically in ten (years) time.
  5. (Charles Dickens) and (Mark Twain) works have sold millions of copies.

32b Indicating Omissions in Contractions

(1) Omitted Letters

Apostrophes replace omitted letters in contractions that combine a pronoun and a verb (*he* + *will* = *he'll*) or the elements of a verb phrase (*do* + *not* = *don't*).

Frequently Used Contractions

it's (it is, it has)	let's (let us)
he's (he is, he has)	we've (we have)
she's (she is, she has)	they're (they are)
who's (who is, who has)	we'll (we will)
isn't (is not)	I'm (I am)
wouldn't (would not)	we're (we are)
couldn't (could not)	you'd (you would)
don't (do not)	we'd (we would)
won't (will not)	they'd (they had)

NOTE: Contractions are generally too informal for use in college writing.

http://kirsznermandell.wadsworth.com

Computer Tip: Revising Contractions

If you set your word processor's writing style to Formal or Technical, the grammar checker will highlight contractions and offer suggestions for revision.

Close-up: Using Apostrophes

Be careful not to confuse contractions (which always include apostrophes) with the possessive forms of personal pronouns (which never include apostrophes).

Contractions	Possessive Forms
Who's on first?	Whose book is this?
They're playing our song.	Their team is winning.
It's raining.	Its paws were muddy.
You're a real pal.	Your résumé is very impressive.

(2) Omitted Numbers

In informal writing, an apostrophe may be used to represent the century in a year.

Crash of '29   class of '06   '57 Chevy

In college writing, however, write out the year in full: *the Crash of 1929, the class of 2006, a 1957 Chevrolet.*

Exercise 32.2

In the following sentences, correct any errors in the use of apostrophes. (Remember, apostrophes are used in contractions but not in possessive pronouns.) If a sentence is correct, mark it with a *C*.

Example: *Whose*
            ~~Who's~~ troops were sent to Korea?

▶ 1. Its never easy to choose a major; whatever you decide, your bound to have second thoughts.
▶ 2. Olive Oyl asked, "Whose that knocking at my door?"
▶ 3. Their watching too much television; in fact, they're eyes are glazed.
▶ 4. Whose coming along on the backpacking trip?
▶ 5. The horse had been badly treated; it's spirit was broken.
   6. Your correct in assuming its a challenging course.
   7. Sometimes even you're best friends won't tell you your boring.
   8. They're training had not prepared them for the hardships they faced.
   9. It's too early to make a positive diagnosis.
  10. Robert Frost wrote the poem that begins, "Who's woods these are I think I know."

32c Forming Plurals

In a few special situations, add *'s* to form plurals.

Forming Plurals with Apostrophes

Plurals of Letters

The Italian language has no *j*'s or *k*'s.

Plurals of Words Referred to as Words

The supervisor would accept no *if*'s, *and*'s, or *but*'s.

NOTE: Elements spoken of as themselves (letters, numerals, or words) are set in italic type; the plural ending, however, is not.

See
37c

NOTE: Apostrophes are not used in plurals of abbreviations (including acronyms) or numbers.

DVDs   WACs   1960s

Exercise 32.3

In the following sentences, form correct plurals for the letters and words in parentheses. Underline to indicate italics where necessary.

Example: The word *bubbles* contains three (b).

The word *bubbles* contains three *b*'s.

▸ 1. She closed her letter with a row of (x) and (o) to indicate kisses and hugs.
▸ 2. The three (R) are reading, writing, and 'rithmetic.
  3. The report included far too many (maybe) and too few (definitely).
  4. The word bookkeeper contains two (o), two (k), and three (e).
  5. His letter included many (please) and (thank you).

32d Editing Misused Apostrophes

Do not use apostrophes with plural nouns that are not possessive.

The Thompson/s are not at home.

Down vest/s are very warm.

The Philadelphia Seventy Sixer/s are exciting to watch.

Do not use apostrophes to form the possessive case of personal pronouns.

This ticket must be your/s or her/s.

The next turn is their/s.

Her doll had lost it/s right eye.

The next great moment in history is our/s.

See
32b1

NOTE: Be especially careful not to confuse the possessive forms of personal pronouns with <u>contractions</u>.

Exercise 32.4

In the following sentences, correct all errors in the use of apostrophes to form noun plurals or the possessive case of personal pronouns.

Example: Dr. Sampson's lecture/s were more interesting than her/s.

▸ 1. The Schaefer's seats are right next to our's.
▸ 2. Most of the college's in the area offer computer courses open to outsider's as well as to their own students.
▸ 3. The network completely revamped it's daytime programming.
▸ 4. Is the responsibility for the hot dog concession Cynthia's or your's?
▸ 5. Romantic poets are his favorite's.
  6. Debbie returned the books to the library, forgetting they were her's.
  7. Cultural revolution's do not occur very often, but when they do they bring sweeping change's.
  8. Roll-top desk's are eagerly sought by antique dealer's.
  9. A flexible schedule is one of their priorities, but it isn't one of our's.
 10. Is your's the red house or the brown one?

Chapter 33 Using Quotation Marks

Use quotation marks to set off brief passages of quoted speech or writing, to set off certain titles, and to set off words used in special ways. Do not use quotation marks when quoting long passages of prose or poetry.

33a Setting Off Quoted Speech or Writing

When you quote a word, phrase, or brief passage of someone else's speech or writing, enclose the quoted material in a pair of quotation marks.

Gloria Steinem said, "We are becoming the men we once hoped to marry."

In an essay about advertising in women's magazines, Gloria Steinem wrote, "When *Ms.* began, we didn't even consider *not* taking ads."

Close-up: Using Quotation Marks with Dialogue

When you record **dialogue** (conversation between two or more people), enclose the quoted words in quotation marks. Begin a new paragraph each time a new speaker is introduced.

When you are quoting several paragraphs of dialogue by one speaker, begin each new paragraph with quotation marks. However, use closing quotation marks only at the end of the *entire quoted passage*, not at the end of each paragraph.

Special rules govern the punctuation of a quotation when it is used with an **identifying tag,** a phrase (such as *he said*) that identifies the speaker or writer. Punctuation guidelines for various situations involving identifying tags are outlined below.

(1) Identifying Tag in the Middle of a Quoted Passage

Use a pair of commas to set off an identifying tag that interrupts a quoted passage.

> "In the future**,**" pop artist Andy Warhol once said**,** "everyone will be world famous for fifteen minutes."

If the identifying tag follows a completed sentence but the quoted passage continues, use a period after the tag, and begin the new sentence with a capital letter and quotation marks.

> "Be careful**,**" Erin warned**.** "Reptiles can be tricky**.**"

(2) Identifying Tag at the Beginning of a Quoted Passage

Use a comma after an identifying tag that introduces quoted speech or writing.

> The Raven repeated**,** "Nevermore."

Use a <u>colon</u> instead of a comma before a quotation if the identifying tag is a complete sentence.

See
34a3

> She gave her final answer**:** "No."

Computer Tip: Checking Punctuation with **Quotation Marks**

Your word processor's grammar checker will often highlight missing punctuation in sentences containing quotation marks and offer suggestions for revision.

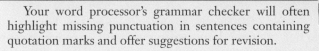

(3) Identifying Tag at the End of a Quoted Passage

Use a comma to set off a quotation from an identifying tag that follows it.

"Be careful out there, " the sergeant warned.

If the quotation ends with a question mark or an exclamation point, use that punctuation mark instead of the comma. In this situation, the tag begins with a lowercase letter even though it follows end punctuation.

"Is Ankara the capital of Turkey?" she asked.

"Oh boy!" he cried.

NOTE: Commas and periods are always placed *inside* quotation marks. For information on placement of other punctuation marks with quotation marks, **see 33e.**

Exercise 33.1

Add quotation marks to these sentences where necessary to set off quotations from identifying tags.

Example: Wordsworth's phrase "splendour in the grass" was used as the title of a movie about young lovers.

▸ 1. Few people can explain what Descartes's words I think, therefore I am actually mean.
▸ 2. Gertrude Stein said, You are all a lost generation.
  3. Freedom of speech does not guarantee anyone the right to yell fire in a crowded theater, she explained.
  4. There's no place like home, Dorothy insisted.
  5. If everyone will sit down the teacher announced the exam will begin.

33b Setting Off Long Prose Passages and Poetry

(1) Long Prose Passages

When you quote a short prose passage, set it off in quotation marks, and run it into the text.

    Galsworthy describes Aunt Juley as "prostrated by the
    blow" (329).

However, do not enclose a **long prose passage** (a passage of more than four lines) in quotation marks. Instead, set it off by indenting the entire passage one inch (or ten spaces) from the left-hand margin. Double-space above and below the quoted passage, and double-space between lines within it. Introduce the passage with a colon.

> The following portrait of Aunt Juley illustrates
> several of the devices Galsworthy uses throughout <u>The</u>
> <u>Forsyte Saga</u>, such as a journalistic detachment that is
> almost cruel in its scrutiny, a subtle sense of the
> grotesque, and an ironic stance:
>
> > Aunt Juley stayed in her room, prostrated by the
> > blow. Her face, discoloured by tears, was divided
> > into compartments by the little ridges of pouting
> > flesh which had swollen with emotion. . . . At
> > fixed intervals she went to her drawer, and took
> > from beneath the lavender bags a fresh pocket-
> > handkerchief. Her warm heart could not bear the
> > thought that Ann was lying there so cold. (329)
>
> Many similar portraits of characters appear throughout the
> novel.

NOTE: With long prose passages, parenthetical documentation is placed one space *after* the end punctuation. (With short prose passages, parenthetical documentation goes *before* the end punctuation.)

Close-up: Quoting Long Prose Passages

When you quote a long prose passage that is a single paragraph, do not indent the first line. When quoting two or more paragraphs, however, indent the first line of each paragraph (including the first) *three* additional spaces. If the first sentence of the quoted passage does not begin a paragraph in the source, do not indent—but do indent the first line of each subsequent paragraph. If the passage you are quoting includes material set in a pair of quotation marks, keep the quotation marks.

---

(2) Poetry

Treat one line of poetry like a short prose passage: enclose it in quotation marks and run it into the text.

> One of John Donne's best-known poems begins with
> the line, "Go and catch a falling star."

See
34e2
If you quote two or three lines of poetry, separate the lines with slashes (/), and run the quotation into the text. (Leave one space before and one space after the slash.)

> Alexander Pope writes, "True Ease in Writing comes
> from Art, not Chance, / As those move easiest who
> have learned to dance."

See
33b1
If you quote more than three lines of poetry, set them off like a long prose passage. (For special emphasis, you may set off fewer lines in this manner.) Do not use quotation marks, and be sure to reproduce punctuation, spelling, capitalization, and indentation *exactly* as they appear in the poem.

> Wilfred Owen, a poet who was killed in action in World
> War I, expressed the horrors of war with vivid imagery:
>> Bent double, like old beggars under sacks.
>> Knock-kneed, coughing like hags, we cursed
>>> through sludge.
>> Till on the haunting flares we turned our backs
>> And towards our distant rest began to trudge.
>> (lines 1-4)

33c Setting Off Titles

Titles of short works and titles of parts of long works are enclosed in quotation marks. Other titles are italicized.

Titles Requiring Quotation Marks

Articles in Magazines, Newspapers, and Professional Journals
"Why Johnny Can't Write"

Essays, Short Stories, Short Poems, and Songs
"Fenimore Cooper's Literary Offenses"   "Flying Home"
"The Road Not Taken"   "The Star-Spangled Banner"

Chapters or Sections of Books
"Miss Sharp Begins to Make Friends"

Episodes of Radio or Television Series
"Lucy Goes to the Hospital"

See 37a for a list of titles that require italics.

See
37a
NOTE: MLA style recommends underlining to indicate italics.

33d Setting Off Words Used in Special Ways

Enclose a word used in a special or unusual way in quotation marks. (If you use the phrase *so-called* before an unusual usage, do not also use quotation marks.)

It was clear that adults approved of children who were "readers," but it was not at all clear why this was so. (Annie Dillard)

Also enclose a **coinage**—an invented word—in quotation marks.

After the twins were born, the minivan became a "babymobile."

33e Using Quotation Marks with Other Punctuation

At the end of a quotation, punctuation is sometimes placed inside and sometimes outside quotation marks.

(1) With Final Commas or Periods

At the end of a quotation, place a comma or period *inside* the quotation marks.

Many, like the poet Robert Frost, think about "the road not taken," but not many have taken "the one less traveled by."

(2) With Final Semicolons or Colons

At the end of a quotation, place a semicolon or colon *outside* the quotation marks.

Students who do not pass the test receive "certificates of completion"; those who pass are awarded diplomas.

Taxpayers were pleased with the first of the candidate's promised "sweeping new reforms": a balanced budget.

(3) With Question Marks, Exclamation Points, and Dashes

If a question mark, exclamation point, or dash is part of the quotation, place the punctuation mark *inside* the quotation marks.

"Who's there?" she demanded.

"Stop!" he cried.

"Should we leave now, or—" Vicki paused, unable to continue.

If a question mark, exclamation point, or dash is *not* part of the quotation, place the punctuation mark *outside* the quotation marks.

Did you finish reading "The Black Cat"?

Whatever you do, don't yell "Uncle"!

The first story—Updike's "*A & P*"—provoked discussion.

If both the quotation and the sentence are questions or exclamations, place the punctuation mark *outside* the quotation marks.

Who asked, "Is Paris burning"?

Close-up: Quotations within Quotations

Use *single* quotation marks to enclose a quotation within a quotation.

Claire noted, "Liberace always said, 'I cried all the way to the bank.'"

Also use single quotation marks within a quotation to indicate a title that would normally be enclosed in double quotation marks.

I think what she said was, "Play it, Sam. Play 'As Time Goes By.'"

Use double quotation marks around quotations or titles within a long prose passage.

See
33b1

33f Editing Misused Quotation Marks

Quotation marks should not be used in the following situations.

(1) To Convey Emphasis

Do not use quotation marks to convey emphasis.

William Randolph Hearst's "fabulous" home is a castle called San Simeon.

(2) To Set Off Slang or Technical Terms

Do not use quotation marks to set off slang or technical terms. (Note that slang is almost always inappropriate in college writing.)

Dawn is "into" running.
           very involved in

"Biofeedback" is sometimes used to treat migraine headaches.

(3) To Enclose Titles of Long Works

See
37a

Titles of long works are italicized (or underlined to indicate italics), not set in quotation marks.

The classic novel "War and Peace" is even longer than the epic poem "Paradise Lost."

NOTE: Do not use quotation marks (or italics) to set off titles of your own papers.

(4) To Set Off Terms Being Defined

Terms being defined are italicized (or underlined to indicate italics).

The word "tintinnabulation," meaning the ringing sound of bells, was used by Poe in his poem "The Bells."

(5) To Set Off Indirect Quotations

Quotation marks should not be used to set off **indirect quotations** (someone else's written or spoken words that are not quoted exactly).

Freud wondered "what a woman wanted."

Exercise 33.2

Correct the use of quotation marks in the following sentences. If a sentence is correct, mark it with a *C*.

Example: The "Watergate" incident brought many new expressions into the English language.

▸ 1. Kilroy was here and Women and children first are two expressions *Bartlett's Familiar Quotations* attributes to "Anon."
▸ 2. Neil Armstrong said he was making a small step for man but a giant leap for mankind.
▸ 3. "The answer, my friend", Bob Dylan sang, "is blowin' in the wind".
▸ 4. The novel was a real "thriller," complete with spies and counter-spies, mysterious women, and exotic international chases.
▸ 5. The sign said, Road liable to subsidence; it meant that we should look out for potholes.
   6. One of William Blake's best-known lines—To see a world in a grain of sand—opens his poem Auguries of Innocence.
   7. In James Thurber's short story The Catbird Seat, Mrs. Barrows annoys Mr. Martin by asking him silly questions like Are you tearing up the pea patch? Are you scraping around the bottom of the pickle barrel? and Are you lifting the oxcart out of the ditch?
   8. I'll make him an offer he can't refuse, promised "the godfather" in Mario Puzo's novel.
   9. What did Timothy Leary mean by "Turn on, tune in, drop out?"
   10. George, the protagonist of Bernard Malamud's short story, A Summer's Reading, is something of an "underachiever."

34a Using Colons

The **colon** is a strong punctuation mark that points readers ahead.

(1) Introducing Lists or Series

Colons set off lists or series, including those introduced by phrases like *the following* or *as follows*.

Waiting tables requires three skills: memory, speed, and balance.

NOTE: When a colon introduces a list or series, explanatory material, or a quotation, it must be preceded by a complete sentence.

(2) Introducing Explanatory Material

Use a colon to introduce material that explains, exemplifies, or summarizes. Frequently, this material is presented as an **appositive,** a word group that identifies or renames an adjacent noun or pronoun.

Diego Rivera painted a controversial mural: the one commissioned for Rockefeller Center in the 1930s.

She had one dream: to play professional basketball.

Sometimes a colon separates two independent clauses, the second illustrating or explaining the first.

A *U.S. News & World Report* survey revealed a surprising fact: Americans spend more time at malls than anywhere else except at home and at work.

Close-up: Using Colons

When a complete sentence follows a colon, it may begin with either a capital or a lowercase letter. However, if the sentence is a quotation, the first word is always capitalized (unless it was not capitalized in the source).

(3) Introducing Quotations

See
33b1 When you quote a <u>long prose passage</u>, always introduce it with a colon. Also use a colon before a short quotation when it is introduced by a complete sentence.

With dignity, Bartleby repeated the familiar words: "I prefer not to."

> ### Other Conventional Uses of Colons
>
> **To Separate Titles from Subtitles**
> *Family Installments: Memories of Growing Up Hispanic*
>
> **To Separate Minutes from Hours**
> 6:15 a.m.
>
> **After Salutations in Business Letters**
> Dear Dr. Evans:
>
> **To Separate Place of Publication from Name of Publisher in a <u>Works-Cited</u> List**
> Boston: Wadsworth, 2005

See
46a2

(4) Editing Misused Colons

Do not use colons in the following situations.

After Expressions Like **Such As** *and* **For Example** Do not use colons after the expressions *such as, namely, for example,* and *that is.* (Remember that when a colon introduces a list or series, a complete sentence must precede the colon.)

The Eye Institute treats patients with a wide variety of conditions, such as: myopia, glaucoma, and cataracts.

In Verb and Prepositional Constructions Do not place colons between verbs and their objects or complements or between prepositions and their objects.

James A. Michener wrote: *Hawaii, Centennial, Space,* and *Poland.*

Hitler's armies marched through: the Netherlands, Belgium, and France.

Exercise 34.1

Add colons where appropriate in the following sentences, and delete any misused colons.

Example: There was one thing he really hated: getting up at 7:00 every morning.

▸ 1. Books about the late John F. Kennedy include the following: *A Hero for Our Time; Johnny, We Hardly Knew Ye; One Brief Shining Moment;* and *JFK: Reckless Youth.*

▸ 2. Only one task remained: to tell his boss he was quitting.

3. The story closed with a familiar phrase: "And they all lived happily ever after."

4. The sergeant requested: reinforcements, medical supplies, and more ammunition.
5. She kept only four souvenirs a photograph, a matchbook, a theater program, and a daisy pressed between the pages of *William Shakespeare The Complete Works*.

34b Using Dashes

(1) Setting Off Nonessential Material

See
30d

Like commas, **dashes** can set off <u>nonessential material</u>, but unlike commas, dashes call attention to the material they set off. Indicate a dash with two unspaced hyphens (which most word-processing programs will automatically convert to a dash).

For emphasis, you may use dashes to set off explanations, qualifications, examples, definitions, and appositives.

> Neither of the boys—both nine-year-olds—had any history of violence.

> Too many parents learn the dangers of swimming pools the hard way—after their toddler has drowned.

(2) Introducing a Summary

Use a dash to introduce a statement that summarizes a list or series before it.

> "Study hard," "Respect your elders," "Don't talk with your mouth full"—Sharon had often heard her parents say these things.

(3) Indicating an Interruption

In dialogue, a dash can mark a hesitation or an unfinished thought.

> "I think—no, I know—this is the worst day of my life," Julie sighed.

NOTE: Because too many dashes can make a passage seem disorganized and out of control, be careful not to overuse them.

Exercise 34.2

Add dashes where needed in the following sentences. If a sentence is correct, mark it with a *C*.

Example: World War I called "the war to end all wars" was, unfortunately, no such thing.

▸ 1. Tulips, daffodils, hyacinths, lilies all these flowers grow from bulbs.
▸ 2. St. Kitts and Nevis two tiny island nations are now independent after 360 years of British rule.
  3. "But it's not" She paused and thought about her next words.
  4. He considered several different majors history, English, political science, and business before deciding on journalism.
  5. The two words added to the Pledge of Allegiance in the 1950s "under God" remain part of the Pledge today.

34c Using Parentheses

(1) Setting Off Nonessential Material

Use parentheses to enclose material that expands, clarifies, illustrates, or supplements.

In some European countries (notably Sweden and France), high-quality day care is offered at little or no cost to parents.

When a complete sentence set off by parentheses falls within another sentence, it should not begin with a capital letter or end with a period.

Because the area is so cold (temperatures average in the low twenties), it is virtually uninhabitable.

NOTE: When parentheses fall within a sentence, punctuation never precedes the opening parenthesis. Punctuation may follow the closing parenthesis, however.

When the parenthetical sentence does *not* fall within another sentence, it must begin with a capital letter and end with appropriate punctuation.

The area is very cold. (Temperatures average in the low twenties.)

(2) Using Parentheses in Other Situations

Parentheses are used around letters and numbers that identify points on a list, dates, cross-references, and documentation.

All reports must include the following components: (1) an opening summary, (2) a background statement, and (3) a list of conclusions.

Russia defeated Sweden in the Great Northern War (1700–1721).

Other scholars also make this point (see p. 54).

One critic has called the novel "puerile" (Arvin 72).

Exercise 34.3

Add parentheses where appropriate in the following sentences. If a sentence is correct, mark it with a *C*.

Example: The greatest battle of the War of 1812 (the Battle of New Orleans) was fought after the war was declared over.

▸ 1. During the Great War 1914–1918, Britain censored letters written from the front lines.
▸ 2. Those who lived in towns on the southern coast like Dover could often hear the mortar shells across the channel in France.
   3. Wilfred Owen wrote his most famous poem "Dulce et Decorum Est" in the trenches in France.
   4. The British uniforms with bright red tabs right at the neck were responsible for many British deaths.
   5. It was difficult for the War Poets as they are now called to return to writing about subjects other than the horrors of war.

34d Using Brackets

(1) Setting Off Comments within Quotations

Brackets within quotations tell readers that the enclosed words are yours and not those of your source. You can bracket an explanation, a clarification, a correction, or an opinion.

> "Even at Princeton he [F. Scott Fitzgerald] felt like an outsider."

If a quotation contains an error, indicate that the error is not yours by following the error with the Latin word *sic* ("thus") in brackets.

> "The octopuss [sic] is a cephalopod mollusk with eight arms."

NOTE: Use brackets to indicate changes that you make in order to fit a <u>quotation</u> smoothly into your sentence.

See
44d1

(2) Replacing Parentheses within Parentheses

When one set of parentheses falls within another, use brackets in place of the inner set.

> In her study of American education between 1945 and 1960 (*The Troubled Crusade* [New York: Basic, 1963]), Diane Ravitch

addresses issues like progressive education, race, educational reforms, and campus unrest.

34e Using Slashes

(1) Separating One Option from Another

When separating one option from another with a slash, do not leave
a space before or after the slash.

> The either/or fallacy is a common error in logic.
>
> Writer/director Spike Lee will speak at the film festival.

(2) Separating Lines of Poetry Run Into the Text

When separating lines of poetry run into the text, leave one space
before and one space after the slash.

> The poet James Schevill writes, "I study my defects / And learn
> how to perfect them."

34f Using Ellipses

Use ellipses in the following situations.

(1) Indicating an Omission in Quoted Prose

An **ellipsis**—three *spaced* periods—indicates that you have omitted
words from a prose quotation. Note that an ellipsis in the middle of
a quoted passage can indicate the omission of a word, a sentence or
two, or even a whole paragraph or more. When deleting material
from a quotation, be careful not to change the meaning of the original passage.

> **Original:** "When I was a young man, being anxious to distin-
> guish myself, I was perpetually starting new propositions."
> (Samuel Johnson)
>
> **With Omission:** "When I was a young man, ... I was perpetu-
> ally starting new propositions."

Note that when you delete words immediately after an internal
punctuation mark (such as the comma in the above example), you
retain the punctuation before the ellipsis.

When you delete material at the end of a sentence, place the sentence's period or other end punctuation before the ellipsis.

According to humorist Dave Barry, "from outer space Europe appears to be shaped like a large ketchup stain. ..." (period followed by ellipses)

NOTE: Never begin a quoted passage with an ellipsis.

When you delete material between sentences, any punctuation should precede the ellipsis.

Deletion from Middle of One Sentence to End of Another
According to Donald Hall, "Everywhere one meets the idea that reading is an activity desirable in itself. ... People surround the idea of reading with piety and do not take into account the purpose of reading." (period followed by ellipses)

Deletion from Middle of One Sentence to Middle of Another
"When I was a young man, ... I found that generally what was new was false." (Samuel Johnson) (comma followed by ellipses)

NOTE: If a quoted passage already contains ellipses, MLA recommends that you enclose your own ellipses in brackets to distinguish them from those that appear in the original quotation.

Close-up: Using Ellipses

If a quotation ending with an ellipsis is followed by parenthetical documentation, the final punctuation *follows* the documentaton.

As Jarman argues, "Compromise was impossible . . ." (161).

(2) Indicating an Omission in Quoted Poetry

Use an ellipsis when you omit a word or phrase from a line of poetry. When you omit one or more lines of poetry, use a line of spaced periods. (The length may be equal either to the line above it or to the missing line—but it should not be longer than the longest line of the poem.)

Original:
> Stitch! Stitch! Stitch!
> In poverty, hunger, and dirt,
> And still with a voice of dolorous pitch,
> Would that its tone could reach the Rich,
> She sang this "Song of the Shirt"!
>
> (Thomas Hood)

With Omission:
> Stitch! Stitch! Stitch!
> In poverty, hunger, and dirt,
> . . . .
> She sang this "Song of the Shirt"!

Exercise 34.4

Read the following paragraph, and follow the instructions after it, taking care in each case not to delete essential information.

The most important thing about research is to know when to stop. How does one recognize the moment? When I was eighteen or thereabouts, my mother told me that when out with a young man I should always leave a half-hour before I wanted to. Although I was not sure how this might be accomplished, I recognized the advice as sound, and exactly the same rule applies to research. One must stop *before* one has finished; otherwise, one will never stop and never finish. (Barbara Tuchman, *Practicing History*)

▸ 1. Delete a phrase from the middle of one sentence, marking the omission with ellipses.

▸ 2. Delete words from the middle of one sentence to the middle of another, marking the omission with ellipses.

3. Delete words at the end of any sentence, marking the omission with ellipses.

4. Delete one complete sentence from the middle of the passage, marking the omission with ellipses.

Exercise 34.5

Add appropriate punctuation—colons, dashes, parentheses, brackets, or slashes—to the following sentences. If a sentence is correct, mark it with a *C*.

Example: There was one thing she was sure of ː if she did well at the interview, the job would be hers.

▸ 1. Mark Twain Samuel L. Clemens made the following statement "I can live for two months on a good compliment."

▸ 2. Liza Minnelli, the actress singer who starred in several films, is the daughter of Judy Garland.

▸ 3. Saudi Arabia, Oman, Yemen, Qatar, and the United Arab Emirates all these are located on the Arabian Peninsula.

▸ 4. John Adams 1735–1826 was the second president of the United States; John Quincy Adams 1767–1848 was the sixth.

▸ 5. The sign said "No tresspassing sic."

6 *Checkmate* a term derived from the Persian phrase meaning "the king is dead" announces victory in chess.

7. The following people were present at the meeting the president of the board of trustees, three trustees, and twenty reporters.

8. Before the introduction of the potato in Europe, the parsnip was a major source of carbohydrates in fact, it was a dietary staple.

9. In the well-researched book *Crime Movies* (New York Norton, 1980), Carlos Clarens studies the gangster genre in film.

10. I remember reading though I can't remember where that Upton Sinclair sold plots to Jack London.

Spelling and Grammar: English (U.S.)

Compound Words:

Self reliance is a concept Emerson explores
his famous essay with the same name.

PART 6

Understanding Spelling and Mechanics

Most people can spell even difficult words "almost correctly"; usually only a letter or two are wrong. For this reason, memorizing a few rules and their exceptions and learning the correct spelling of the most commonly misspelled words can make a big difference. Knowing when and how to use a dictionary can also help you improve your spelling, and it can help you learn to use words more appropriately.

35a Using Your Dictionary

Every writer should own a dictionary and use it to check the spelling, meaning, and usage of unfamiliar words. The most widely used type of dictionary is a one-volume **desk dictionary** or **college dictionary.**

To fit a lot of information into a small space, dictionaries use a system of symbols, abbreviations, and typefaces. Each dictionary uses a slightly different system, so consult the preface of your dictionary to determine how its system operates.

As Figure 35.1 illustrates, a typical dictionary entry includes a number of different elements, each of which is explained in the pages that follow.

(1) Entry Word, Pronunciation Guide, and Part-of-Speech Label

The **entry word,** which appears in boldface at the beginning of the entry, gives the spelling of a word and indicates how the word is divided into syllables.

> **col · or** *n.* Also chiefly British **col · our**

The **pronunciation guide** appears in parentheses or between slashes after the main entry. Dictionaries use symbols to represent sounds, and an explanation of these symbols usually appears at the bottom of each page or across the bottom of facing pages throughout the alphabetical listing.

Abbreviations called **part-of-speech labels** indicate parts of speech and grammatical forms.

See
22a

If a verb is <u>regular,</u> the entry provides only the base form of the verb. If a verb is <u>irregular,</u> the part-of-speech label indicates the irregular principal parts of the verb.

> **with · draw** . . . *v.* -drew, -drawn, -drawing

Part-of-speech labels also indicate the plural form of irregular nouns. (When the plural form is regular, it is not shown.)

> **child** . . . *n. pl.* chil · dren

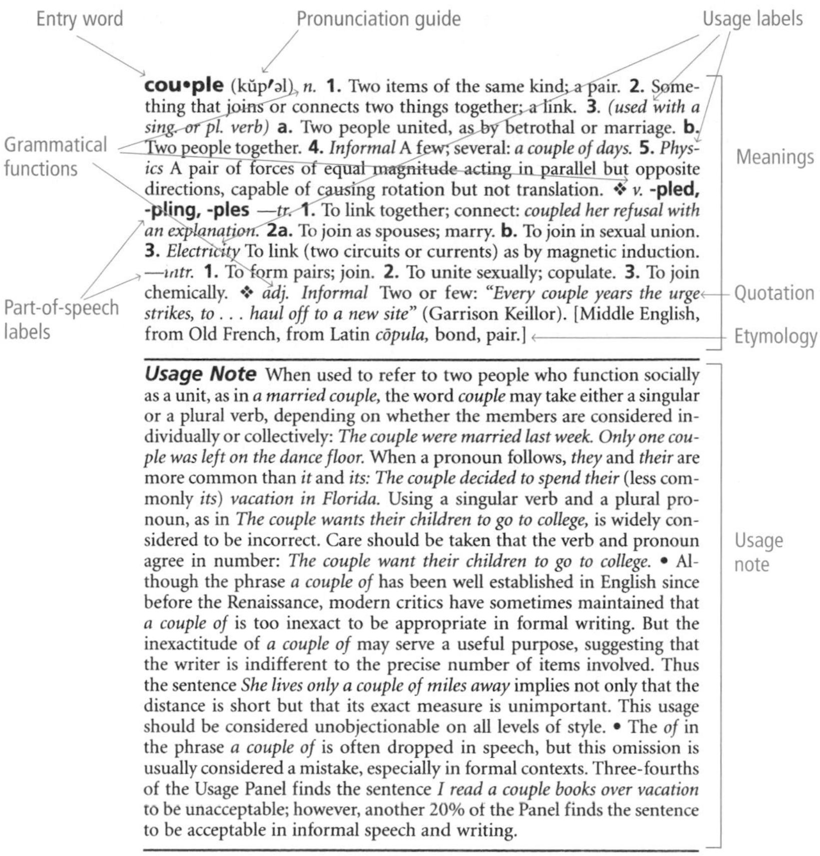

Entry word   Pronunciation guide   Usage labels

cou•ple (kŭp′əl), *n.* **1.** Two items of the same kind; a pair. **2.** Something that joins or connects two things together; a link. **3.** *(used with a sing. or pl. verb)* **a.** Two people united, as by betrothal or marriage. **b.** Two people together. **4.** *Informal* A few; several: *a couple of days.* **5.** *Physics* A pair of forces of equal magnitude acting in parallel but opposite directions, capable of causing rotation but not translation. ❖ *v.* **-pled, -pling, -ples** —*tr.* **1.** To link together; connect: *coupled her refusal with an explanation.* **2a.** To join as spouses; marry. **b.** To join in sexual union. **3.** *Electricity* To link (two circuits or currents) as by magnetic induction. —*intr.* **1.** To form pairs; join. **2.** To unite sexually; copulate. **3.** To join chemically. ❖ *adj. Informal* Two or few: *"Every couple years the urge strikes, to . . . haul off to a new site"* (Garrison Keillor). [Middle English, from Old French, from Latin *cōpula,* bond, pair.]

Grammatical functions — | Meanings

Part-of-speech labels | Quotation / Etymology

Usage Note When used to refer to two people who function socially as a unit, as in *a married couple,* the word *couple* may take either a singular or a plural verb, depending on whether the members are considered individually or collectively: *The couple were married last week. Only one couple was left on the dance floor.* When a pronoun follows, *they* and *their* are more common than *it* and *its: The couple decided to spend their* (less commonly *its*) *vacation in Florida.* Using a singular verb and a plural pronoun, as in *The couple wants their children to go to college,* is widely considered to be incorrect. Care should be taken that the verb and pronoun agree in number: *The couple want their children to go to college.* • Although the phrase *a couple of* has been well established in English since before the Renaissance, modern critics have sometimes maintained that *a couple of* is too inexact to be appropriate in formal writing. But the inexactitude of *a couple of* may serve a useful purpose, suggesting that the writer is indifferent to the precise number of items involved. Thus the sentence *She lives only a couple of miles away* implies not only that the distance is short but that its exact measure is unimportant. This usage should be considered unobjectionable on all levels of style. • The *of* in the phrase *a couple of* is often dropped in speech, but this omission is usually considered a mistake, especially in formal contexts. Three-fourths of the Usage Panel finds the sentence *I read a couple books over vacation* to be unacceptable; however, another 20% of the Panel finds the sentence to be acceptable in informal speech and writing.

Usage note

Figure 35.1 Entry from *The American Heritage Dictionary of the English Language*, **Fourth Edition.**

Finally, part-of-speech labels indicate the <u>comparative</u> and <u>superlative</u> forms of both regular and irregular adjectives and adverbs.

See 23d

red . . . *adj.* red · der; red · dest

(2) Meanings

Some dictionaries give the most common meaning first and then list less common ones. Others begin with the oldest meaning and move to the most current ones. Check the preface of your dictionary to find out how its entries are arranged.

(3) Etymology

The **etymology** of a word—its history, its evolution over the years—appears in brackets either before or after the list of meanings. For example, *The American Heritage Dictionary of the English Language* shows that *couple* came into Middle English (ME) from Old French (OFr.) and into Old French from Latin (Lat.).

(4) Synonyms and Antonyms

A dictionary entry often lists synonyms (and occasionally antonyms) in addition to definitions. **Synonyms** are words that have similar meanings, such as *well* and *healthy*. **Antonyms** are words that have opposite meanings, such as *courage* and *cowardice*.

Close-up: Using a Thesaurus

When you consult a print or online **thesaurus,** a list of synonyms and antonyms, remember that no two words have exactly the same meanings. Use synonyms carefully, checking your dictionary to make sure the connotation of the synonym is very close to that of the original word.

---

(5) Usage Labels

Dictionaries use **usage labels** to indicate in what contexts words are acceptable. (Where such labels involve value judgments, dictionaries differ.) Among these labels are *nonstandard* (in wide use but not considered standard usage); *informal/colloquial* (part of the language of conversation and acceptable in informal writing); *slang* (appropriate only in extremely informal situations); *dialect/regional* (limited to a certain geographical region); *obsolete* (no longer in use); *archaic/rare* (once common but now seldom used); and *poetic* (common only in poetry).

35b Understanding Spelling and Pronunciation

Because pronunciation often provides few clues to English spelling, you need to pay particular attention to the three problem areas that cause the most misspellings.

(1) Words That Are Often Pronounced Carelessly

Most of us pronounce words rather carelessly in everyday speech. Consequently, when spelling, we may leave out, add, or transpose letters.

candidate	library	recognize
environment	lightning	specific
February	nuclear	supposed to
government	perform	surprise
hundred	quantity	used to

(2) American and British Spellings

Some words are spelled one way in the United States and another way in Great Britain and the Commonwealth nations.

American	British
color	colour
defense	defence
judgment	judgement
theater	theatre
toward	towards
traveled	travelled

(3) Homophones

Homophones are words—such as *accept* and *except*—that are pronounced alike but spelled differently.

accept	to receive
except	other than
affect	to have an influence on (*verb*)
effect	result (*noun*); to cause (*verb*)
its	possessive of *it*
it's	contraction of *it is*
principal	most important (*adjective*); head of a school (*noun*)
principle	a basic truth; rule of conduct

For a full list of these and other homophones, along with their meanings and sentences illustrating their use, **see the Glossary of Usage.**

http://kirsznermandell.wadsworth.com

Computer Tip: Running a Spell Check

You should always run a spell check, but remember that a spell checker will not identify a word that is spelled correctly but used incorrectly—*then* for *than* or *its* for *it's*, for example—or a typo that creates another word, such as *form* for *from*. For this reason, you still need to proofread your papers—even after you run a spell check.

35c Learning Spelling Rules

Knowing a few reliable rules and their most common exceptions can help you overcome problems caused by the inconsistency between pronunciation and spelling.

(1) The *ie/ei* Combinations

The old rule still stands: use *i* before *e* except after *c* (or when pronounced *ay*, as in *neighbor*).

i before *e*	*ei* after *c*	*ei* pronounced *ay*
belief	ceiling	weigh
chief	deceit	freight
niece	receive	eight

Exceptions: *either, neither, foreign, leisure, weird,* and *seize*. In addition, if the *ie* combination is not pronounced as a unit, the rule does not apply: *atheist, science*.

Exercise 35.1

Fill in the blanks with the proper *ie* or *ei* combination. After completing the exercise, use your dictionary or spell checker to check your answers.

Example: conc__*ei*__ve

▸ 1. rec_____pt
▸ 2. var_____ty
▸ 3. caff_____ne
▸ 4. ach_____ve
▸ 5. kal_____doscope
  6. misch_____f
  7. effic_____nt
  8. v_____n
  9. spec_____s
 10. suffic_____nt

(2) Doubling Final Consonants

The only words that double their consonants before a suffix that begins with a vowel (*-ed, -ing*) are those that pass the following three tests:

1. They have one syllable or are stressed on the last syllable.
2. They contain only one vowel in the last syllable.
3. They end in a single consonant.

The word *tap* satisfies all three conditions: it has only one syllable, it contains only one vowel (*a*), and it ends in a single consonant (*p*). Therefore, the final consonant doubles before a suffix beginning with a vowel (*tapped, tapping*). The word *relent* meets two of the three conditions: it is stressed on the last syllable, and it has one vowel in the last syllable, but it does not end in a single consonant. Therefore, its final consonant is not doubled (*relented, relenting*).

(3) Prefixes

The addition of a prefix never affects the spelling of the root (*mis + spell = misspell*). Some prefixes can cause spelling problems, however, because they are pronounced alike although they are not spelled alike: *ante-/anti-, en-/in-, per-/pre-,* and *de-/di-*.

antebellum	antiaircraft
encircle	integrate
perceive	prescribe
deduct	direct

(4) Silent e before a Suffix

When a suffix that begins with a consonant is added to a word ending in silent *e*, the *e* is generally kept: *hope/hopeful; lame/lamely; bore/boredom*. **Exceptions:** *argument, truly, ninth, judgment,* and *acknowledgment*.

When a suffix that starts with a vowel is added to a word that ends in a silent *e*, the *e* is generally dropped: *hope/hoping; trace/traced; grieve/grievance; love/lovable*. **Exceptions:** *changeable, noticeable,* and *courageous*.

Exercise 35.2

Combine the following words with the suffixes in parentheses. Keep or drop the silent *e* as you see fit; be prepared to explain your choices.

Example: fate (al)
　　　　　　fatal

- ▶ 1. surprise (ing)
- ▶ 2. sure (ly)
- ▶ 3. force (ible)
- ▶ 4. manage (able)
- ▶ 5. due (ly)
- 6. outrage (ous)
- 7. service (able)
- 8. awe (ful)
- 9. shame (ing)
- 10. shame (less)

(5) *y* before a Suffix

When a word ends in a consonant plus *y*, the *y* generally changes to an *i* when a suffix is added (*beauty + ful = beautiful*). The *y* is kept, however, when the suffix *-ing* is added (*tally + ing = tallying*) and in some one-syllable words (*dry + ness = dryness*).

When a word ends in a vowel plus *y*, the *y* is retained (*joy + ful = joyful; employ + er = employer*). **Exception:** *day + ly = daily*.

Exercise 35.3

Add the endings in parentheses to the following words. Change or keep the final *y* as you see fit; be prepared to explain your choices.

Example: party (ing)
            partying

- ▸ 1. journey (ing)   6. sturdy (ness)
- ▸ 2. study (ed)   7. merry (ment)
- ▸ 3. carry (ing)   8. likely (hood)
- ▸ 4. shy (ly)   9. plenty (ful)
- ▸ 5. study (ing)   10. supply (er)

(6) *seed* Endings

Endings with the sound *seed* are nearly always spelled *cede*, as in *precede*, *intercede*, *concede*, and so on. **Exceptions:** *supersede*, *exceed*, *proceed*, and *succeed*.

(7) *-able, -ible*

If the root of a word is itself an independent word, the suffix *-able* is most often used. If the root of a word is not an independent word, the suffix *-ible* is most often used.

  *comfort*able   *compat*ible
  *agree*able   *incred*ible
  *dry*able   *plaus*ible

(8) Plurals

Most nouns form plurals by adding *s: savage/savages, tortilla/tortillas, boat/boats*. There are, however, a number of exceptions.

***Words Ending in* -f *or* -fe** Some words ending in *-f* or *-fe* form plurals by changing the *f* to *v* and adding *es* or *s: life/lives, self/selves*. Others add just *s: belief/beliefs, safe/safes*. Words ending in *-ff* take *s* to form plurals: *tariff/tariffs*.

***Words Ending in* -y** Most words that end in a consonant followed by *y* form plurals by changing the *y* to *i* and adding *es: baby/babies*. **Exceptions:** proper nouns, such as the *Kennedys* (never the *Kennedies*).
    Words that end in a vowel followed by a *y* form plurals by adding *s: day/days, monkey/monkeys*.

***Words Ending in* -o** Words that end in a vowel followed by *o* form the plural by adding *s: radio/radios, stereo/stereos, zoo/zoos*. Most words that end in a consonant followed by *o* add *es* to form the plural: *tomato/tomatoes, hero/heroes*. **Exceptions:** *silo/silos, piano/pianos, memo/memos,* and *soprano/sopranos*.

***Words Ending in* -s, -ss, -sh, -ch, -x, *and* -z** These words form plurals by adding *es: Jones/Joneses, mass/masses, rash/rashes, lunch/lunches, box/boxes, buzz/buzzes.* **Exceptions:** Some one-syllable words that end in *-s* or *-z* double their final consonants when forming plurals: *quiz/quizzes.*

Compound Nouns **Compound nouns**—nouns formed from two or more words—usually form the plural with the last word in the compound construction: *welfare state/welfare states; snowball/snowballs.* However, where the first word of the compound noun is more important than the others, form the plural with the first word: *sister-in-law/sisters-in-law, attorney general/attorneys general, hole in one/holes in one.*

Foreign Plurals Some words, especially those borrowed from Latin or Greek, keep their foreign plurals. Look up a foreign word's plural form in a dictionary if you do not know it.

Singular	**Plural**
basis	bases
criterion	criteria
datum	data
larva	larvae
medium	media
memorandum	memoranda
stimulus	stimuli

Chapter 36   Knowing When to Capitalize

http://kirsznermandell.wadsworth.com

Computer Tip: Revising Capitalization Errors

In *Microsoft Word*, the AutoCorrect tool will automatically capitalize certain words—such as the first word of a sentence or the days of the week. Be sure to proofread your documents after using the AutoCorrect tool, though, since it can actually introduce capitalization errors into your writing.

36a   Capitalizing the First Word of a Sentence

Capitalize the first word of a sentence, including a sentence of quoted speech or writing.

As Shakespeare wrote, "Who steals my purse steals trash."

Do not capitalize a sentence set off within another sentence by dashes or parentheses.

Finding the store closed—it was a holiday—they went home.

The candidates are Frank Lester and Jane Lester (they are not related).

See 34a   Capitalization is optional when a complete sentence is introduced by a colon.

Close-up: Using Capital Letters in Poetry

The first word of a line of poetry is generally capitalized. If the poet uses a lowercase letter to begin a line, however, you should follow that style when you quote the line.

36b Capitalizing Proper Nouns

Proper nouns—the names of specific persons, places, or things—are capitalized, and so are adjectives formed from proper nouns.

ESL Tip

Do not capitalize a word simply because you want to emphasize its importance. If you are not sure whether a noun should be capitalized, look it up in a dictionary.

---

(1) Specific People's Names

Eleanor Roosevelt   Medgar Evers

Capitalize a title when it precedes a person's name (Senator Olympia Snowe) or is used instead of the name (Dad). Do not capitalize titles that *follow* names (Olympia Snowe, the senator from Maine) or those that refer to the general position, not the particular person who holds it (a stay-at-home dad).

You may, however, capitalize titles that indicate very high-ranking positions even when they are used alone or when they follow a name: the Pope; George W. Bush, President of the United States. Never capitalize a title denoting a family relationship when it follows an article or a possessive pronoun (an uncle, his mom).

Capitalize titles that represent academic degrees or abbreviations of those degrees even when they follow a name: Dr. Benjamin Spock; Benjamin Spock, MD.

(2) Names of Particular Structures, Special Events, Monuments, and So On

the Brooklyn Bridge   the Taj Mahal

the Eiffel Tower   Mount Rushmore

the World Series   the *Titanic*

NOTE: Capitalize a common noun, such as *bridge*, *river*, *county*, or *lake*, when it is part of a proper noun (Lake Erie, Kings County).

(3) Places and Geographical Regions

Saturn   the Straits of Magellan

Budapest   the Fiji Islands

Walden Pond   the Western Hemisphere

Capitalize *north*, *south*, *east*, and *west* when they denote particular geographical regions, but not when they designate directions.

There are more tornadoes in Kansas than in the <u>East</u>. (*East* refers to a specific region.)

Turn <u>west</u> at Broad Street and continue <u>north</u> to Market. (*West* and *north* refer to directions, not specific regions.)

(4) Days of the Week, Months, and Holidays

Saturday   Cinco de Mayo

January   Rosh Hashanah

(5) Historical Periods, Events, Documents, and Names of Legal Cases

the Industrial Revolution   the Treaty of Versailles

the Reformation   the Voting Rights Act

the Battle of Gettysburg   *Brown* v. *Board of Education*

NOTE: Names of court cases are italicized (or underlined to indicate italics) in the text of your papers but not in works-cited entries.

(6) Philosophic, Literary, and Artistic Movements

Naturalism   Dadaism

Neoclassicism   Expressionism

(7) Races, Ethnic Groups, Nationalities, and Languages

African American   Korean

Latino/Latina   Dutch

NOTE: When the words *black* and *white* denote races, they have traditionally not been capitalized. Current usage is divided on whether to capitalize *black*.

(8) Religions and Their Followers; Sacred Books and Figures

Islam   the Koran   Buddha

the Talmud   the Scriptures   God

NOTE: It is not necessary to capitalize pronouns referring to God (although some people do so as a sign of respect).

(9) Political, Social, Athletic, Civic, and Other Groups and Their Members

the Democratic Party

the International Brotherhood of Electrical Workers

the New York Yankees

the American Civil Liberties Union

the National Council of Teachers of English

the Rolling Stones

See 39b
NOTE: When the name of a group or institution is abbreviated, the abbreviation uses capital letters in place of the capitalized words.

IBEW   ACLU   NCTE

(10) Businesses, Government Agencies, and Other Institutions

Bank of America   Lincoln High School

the Environmental Protection   the University of Maryland
Agency

(11) Brand Names and Words Formed from Them

Velcro   Coke   Post-it   Rollerblades   Astroturf

NOTE: In general, use generic references, not brand names, in college writing—*photocopy*, not *Xerox*, for example. These generic names are not capitalized.

(12) Specific Academic Courses

Sociology 201   English 101

NOTE: Do not capitalize a general subject area (sociology, zoology) unless it is the name of a language (English, Spanish).

(13) Adjectives Formed from Proper Nouns

Freudian slip   Elizabethan era

Platonic ideal   Shakespearean sonnet

Aristotelian logic   Marxist ideology

When words derived from proper nouns have lost their original associations, do not capitalize them: china bowl, french fries.

36c Capitalizing Important Words in Titles

In general, capitalize all words in titles with the exception of articles (*a*, *an*, and *the*), prepositions, coordinating conjunctions, and the *to* in infinitives (unless they are the first or last word in the title or subtitle).

"Dover Beach"   *On the Waterfront*

The Declaration of Independence *Madame Curie: A Biography*

Across the River and into the Trees   *What Friends Are For*

36d Capitalizing the Pronoun *I*, the Interjection *O*, and Other Single Letters in Special Constructions

Always capitalize the pronoun *I* even if it is part of a contraction (*I'm*, *I'll*, *I've*).

Sam and I finally went to the Grand Canyon, and I'm glad we did.

Always capitalize the interjection *O*.

Give us peace in our time, O Lord.

However, capitalize the interjection *oh* only when it begins a sentence.

NOTE: Many other single letters are capitalized in certain usages: U-boat, D day, Model T, vitamin B, an A in history, C major. Consult your dictionary to determine whether or not to use a capital letter.

36e Capitalizing Salutations and Closings of Letters

Always capitalize the first word of the salutation of a personal or business letter.

D̲ear Fred,   D̲ear Mr. Reynolds:

Always capitalize the first word of the complimentary close.

S̲incerely,   V̲ery truly yours,

36f Editing Misused Capitals

Do not capitalize words for emphasis or as an attention-getting strategy. If you are uncertain about whether or not a word should be capitalized, consult a dictionary.

(1) Seasons

Do not capitalize the names of the seasons—summer, fall, winter, spring—unless they are personified, as in *Old Man Winter.*

(2) Centuries and Loosely Defined Historical Periods

Do not capitalize the names of centuries or general historical periods.

s̲eventeenth-century p̲oetry   the a̲utomobile a̲ge

Do, however, capitalize names of specific historical, anthropological, and geological periods.

I̲ron A̲ge   P̲aleozoic E̲ra

(3) Diseases and Other Medical Terms

Do not capitalize names of diseases or medical tests or conditions unless a proper noun is part of the name or unless the name of the disease is an **acronym**.

See 29a2

smallpox	Apgar test	AIDS
Lyme disease	mumps	SIDS

Exercise 36.1

Capitalize words where necessary in these sentences.

Example: John F. Kennedy won the p̲ulitzer p̲rize for his book p̲rofiles in c̲ourage.

▸ 1. Two of the brontë sisters wrote *jane eyre* and *wuthering heights,* nineteenth-century novels that are required reading in many english classes that focus on victorian literature.

▸ 2. It was a beautiful day in the spring—it was april 15, to be exact— but all Ted could think about was the check he had to write to the internal revenue service and the bills he had to pay by friday.

▸ 3. Traveling north, they hiked through british columbia, planning a leisurely return on the cruise ship *canadian princess.*

▸ 4. Alice liked her mom's apple pie better than aunt nellie's rhubarb pie, but she liked grandpa's punch best of all.

▸ 5. A new elective, political science 30, covers the vietnam war from the gulf of tonkin to the fall of saigon, including the roles of ho chi minh, the viet cong, and the buddhist monks; the positions of presidents johnson and nixon; and the influence of groups like the student mobilization committee and vietnam veterans against the war.

6. When the central high school drama club put on a production of shaw's *pygmalion,* the director xeroxed extra copies of the parts for eliza doolittle and professor henry higgins so he could give them to the understudies.

7. Shaking all over, Bill admitted, "driving on the los angeles freeway is a frightening experience for a kid from brooklyn, even in a bmw."

8. The new united federation of teachers contract guarantees teachers many paid holidays, including columbus day, veterans day, and washington's birthday; a week each at christmas and easter; and two full months (july and august) in the summer.

9. The sociology syllabus included the books *beyond the best interests of the child, regulating the poor: the functions of public welfare,* and *a welfare mother;* in anthropology, we were to begin by studying the stone age; and in geology, we were to focus on the Mesozoic era.

10. Winners of the nobel peace prize include lech walesa, former leader of the polish trade union solidarity; the reverend dr. martin luther king jr., founder of the southern christian leadership conference; and archbishop desmond tutu of south africa.

Chapter 37   **Using Italics**

37a   Setting Off Titles and Names

Use italics for the titles and names listed in the following box. Most other titles are set off with **quotation marks**.

See
33c

Titles and Names Set in Italics

Books: *David Copperfield, The Bluest Eye*

Newspapers: the *Washington Post*, the *Philadelphia Inquirer* (According to MLA style, introductory articles are not italicized in titles of newspapers.)

Magazines and Journals: *Rolling Stone, Scientific American*

Online Magazines and Journals: *salon.com, theonion.com*

Web Sites or Home Pages: *urbanlegends.com, movie-mistakes.com*

Pamphlets: *Common Sense*

Films: *The Matrix, Citizen Kane*

Television Programs: *60 Minutes, The Bachelor, Fear Factor*

Radio Programs: *All Things Considered, A Prairie Home Companion*

Long Poems: *John Brown's Body, The Faerie Queen*

Plays: *Macbeth, A Raisin in the Sun*

Long Musical Works: *Rigoletto, Eroica*

Software Programs: *Microsoft Word, PowerPoint*

Search Engines and Web Browsers: *Google, Netscape Communicator*

Databases: *Academic Search Premier, Expanded Academic ASAP Plus*

Paintings and Sculpture: *Guernica, Pietà*

Ships: *Lusitania,* U.S.S. *Saratoga* (S.S. and U.S.S. are not italicized.)

Trains: *City of New Orleans, The Orient Express*

Aircraft: *The Hindenburg, Enola Gay* (Only particular aircraft, not makes or types such as Piper Cub or Boeing 757, are italicized.)

Spacecraft: *Challenger, Enterprise*

NOTE: Names of sacred books, such as the Bible and the Koran, and well-known documents, such as the Constitution and the Declaration of Independence, are neither italicized nor placed within quotation marks.

Close-up: Using Italics

MLA guidelines recommend that you underline to indicate italics. However, you may italicize if your instructor prefers. (Note that style guides in other disciplines may require italics.)

37b Setting Off Foreign Words and Phrases

Italics are often used to set off foreign words and phrases that have not become part of the English language.

"*C'est la vie*," Madeline said when she saw the long line for the concert.

Spirochaeta plicatilis is a corkscrewlike bacterium.

If you are not sure whether a foreign word has been assimilated into English, consult a dictionary.

37c Setting Off Elements Spoken of as Themselves and Terms Being Defined

Use italics to set off letters, numerals, and words that refer to the letters, numerals, and words themselves.

Is that a *p* or a *g*?

I forget the exact address, but I know it has a *3* in it.

Does *through* rhyme with *cough*?

Also use italics to set off words and phrases that you go on to define.

A *closet drama* is a play meant to be read, not performed.

NOTE: When you quote a dictionary definition, put the word you are defining in italics and the definition itself in quotation marks.

To *infer* means "to draw a conclusion"; to *imply* means "to suggest."

37d Using Italics for Emphasis

Italics may occasionally be used for emphasis.

Initially, poetry might be defined as a kind of language that says *more* and says it *more intensely* than does ordinary language. (Lawrence Perrine, *Sound and Sense*)

However, overuse of italics is distracting. Instead of italicizing, try to indicate emphasis with word choice and sentence structure.

Using Hyphens

Underline to indicate italics where necessary, and delete any italics that are incorrectly used. If a sentence is correct, mark it with a *C*.

Example: <u>However</u> is a conjunctive adverb, not a coordinating conjunction.

▸ 1. I said Carol, not Darryl.
▸ 2. A *deus ex machina*, an improbable device used to resolve the plot of a fictional work, is used in Charles Dickens's novel Oliver Twist.
▸ 3. He dotted every i and crossed every t.
▸ 4. The Metropolitan Opera's production of Carmen was a tour de force for the principal performers.
▸ 5. *Laissez-faire* is a doctrine holding that government should not interfere with trade.
6. Antidote and anecdote are often confused because their pronunciations are similar.
7. Hawthorne's novels include Fanshawe, The House of the Seven Gables, The Blithedale Romance, and The Scarlet Letter.
8. Words like mailman, policeman, and fireman have been replaced by nonsexist terms like letter carrier, police officer, and firefighter.
9. A classic black tuxedo was considered de rigueur at the charity ball, but Jason preferred to wear his *dashiki*.
10. Thomas Mann's novel Buddenbrooks is a bildungsroman.

Chapter 38   Using Hyphens

Hyphens have two conventional uses: to break a word at the end of a line and to link words in certain compounds.

38a Breaking a Word at the End of a Line

A computer never breaks a word at the end of a line; if the full word will not fit, it is brought down to the next line. Sometimes, however, you will want to break a word with a hyphen—for example, to fill in space at the end of a line. When you break a word at the end of a line, divide it only between syllables, consulting a dictionary if necessary. Never divide a word at the end of a page, and never hyphenate a one-syllable word. In addition, never leave a single letter at the end of a line or carry only one or two letters to the next line.

If you divide a <u>compound word</u> at the end of a line, put the hyphen between the elements of the compound (*snow-mobile*, not *snowmo-bile*).   See 38b

http://kirsznermandell.wadsworth.com

Computer Tip: Dividing Electronic Addresses (URLs)

Never insert a hyphen to divide an electronic address (URL) at the end of a line. (Readers might think the hyphen is part of the address.) MLA style recommends that you break the URL after a slash. If this is not possible, break it in a logical place—after a period, for example—or avoid the problem altogether by moving the entire URL to the next line.

38b Dividing Compound Words

A **compound word** consists of two or more words. Some familiar compound words are always hyphenated: *no-hitter, helter-skelter.* Other compounds are always written as one word: *fireplace, peacetime.* Finally, some compounds are always written as two separate words: *labor relations, bunk bed.* Your dictionary can tell you whether a particular compound requires a hyphen.

http://kirsznermandell.wadsworth.com

Computer Tip: Hyphenating Compound Words

Your word processor's grammar checker will highlight certain compound words with incorrect or missing hyphenation and offer suggestions for revision.

---

(1) Hyphenating with Compound Adjectives

A **compound adjective** is a series of two or more words that function together as an adjective. When a compound adjective *precedes* the noun it modifies, use hyphens to join its elements.

> The research team tried to use <u>nineteenth-century</u> technology to design a <u>space-age</u> project.

When a compound adjective *follows* the noun it modifies, do not use hyphens to join its elements.

> The three government-operated programs were run smoothly, but the one that was not <u>government operated</u> was short of funds.

NOTE: A compound adjective formed with an adverb ending in *-ly* is not hyphenated, even when it precedes the noun: Many <u>upwardly mobile</u> families are on tight budgets.

Use **suspended hyphens**—hyphens followed by a space or by appropriate punctuation and a space—in a series of compounds that have the same principal elements.

Graduates of two= and four=year colleges were eligible for the grants.

The exam called for sentence=, paragraph=, and essay=length answers.

(2) Hyphenating with Certain Prefixes and Suffixes

Use a hyphen between a prefix and a proper noun or proper adjective.

mid=July   pre=Columbian

Use a hyphen to connect the prefixes *all-*, *ex-*, *half-*, *quarter-*, *quasi-*, and *self-* and the suffix *-elect* to a noun.

ex=senator   self=centered   president=elect

NOTE: The words *selfhood*, *selfish*, and *selfless* do not include hyphens. In these cases, *self* is the root, not a prefix.

(3) Hyphenating in Compound Numerals and Fractions

Hyphenate compounds that represent numbers below one hundred (even if they are part of a larger number).

the twenty=first century   three hundred sixty=five days

Also hyphenate the written form of a fraction when it modifies a noun.

a two=thirds share of the business

(4) Hyphenating for Clarity

Hyphenate to prevent readers from misreading one word for another.

Before we can reform criminals, we must re=form our ideas about prisons.

Hyphenate to avoid hard-to-read combinations, such as two *i*'s (*semi=illiterate*).

In most cases, hyphenate between a capital initial and a word when the two combine to form a compound: *A=frame*, *T=shirt*.

(5) Hyphenating in Coined Compounds

A **coined compound,** one that uses a new combination of words as a unit, requires hyphens.

He looked up with a who‑do‑you‑think‑you‑are expression.

Exercise 38.1

Add hyphens to the compounds in these sentences wherever they are required. Consult a dictionary if necessary.

Example: Alaska was the forty-ninth state to join the United States.

▸ 1. One of the restaurant's blue plate specials is chicken fried steak.
▸ 2. Virginia and Texas are both right to work states.
▸ 3. He stood on tiptoe to see the near perfect statue, which was well hidden by the security fence.
▸ 4. The five and ten cent store had a self service makeup counter and stocked many up to the minute gadgets.
▸ 5. The so called Saturday night special is opposed by pro gun control groups.
  6. He ordered two all beef patties with special sauce, lettuce, cheese, pickles, and onions on a sesame seed bun.
  7. The material was extremely thought provoking, but it hardly presented any earth shattering conclusions.
  8. The Dodgers Phillies game was rained out, so the long suffering fans left for home.
  9. Bone marrow transplants carry the risk of what is known as a graft versus host reaction.
  10. The state funded child care program was considered a highly desirable alternative to family day care.

Chapter 39 Using Abbreviations

Generally speaking, **abbreviations** are not appropriate in college writing except in tables, charts, and works-cited lists. Some abbreviations are only acceptable in scientific, technical, or business writing, or only in a particular discipline. If you have any questions about the appropriateness of a particular abbreviation, check a style manual in your field.

39a Abbreviating Titles

Titles before and after proper names are usually abbreviated.

Mr. Homer Simpson   Rep. Chaka Fattah

Henry Kissinger, PhD   Prof. Elie Wiesel

Do not, however, use an abbreviated title without a name.

   doctor

The ~~Dr.~~ diagnosed hepatitis.

39b Abbreviating Organization Names and Technical Terms

See 29a2

Well-known businesses and government, social, and civic organizations are frequently referred to by capitalized initials. These **abbreviations** fall into two categories: those in which the initials are pronounced as separate units (MTV) and **acronyms,** in which the initials are pronounced as a word (NATO).

To save space, you may use accepted abbreviations for complex technical terms that are not well known, but be sure to spell out the full term the first time you mention it, followed by the abbreviation in parentheses.

Citrus farmers have been using ethylene dibromide (EDB), a chemical pesticide, for more than twenty years. Now, however, EDB has contaminated water supplies.

See 46a

Close-up: Abbreviations in MLA Documentation

MLA documentation style requires abbreviations of publishers' company names—for example, `Columbia UP` for *Columbia University Press*—in the works-cited list. Do not, however, use such abbreviations in the body of your paper. MLA style also permits the use of abbreviations that designate parts of written works (`ch. 3`, `sec. 7`)—but only in the works-cited list and parenthetical documentation. MLA also recommends abbreviating literary works and books of the Bible: `Oth`. (*Othello*), `Exod`. (*Exodus*). These words should not be abbreviated in the text of your paper.

39c Abbreviating Dates, Times of Day, and Temperatures

Dates, times of day, and temperatures are often abbreviated.

50 BC (*BC* follows the date.)   AD 432 (*AD* precedes the date.)

6 a.m.   3:03 p.m.

20°C (Centigrade or Celsius)   180°F (Fahrenheit)

Always capitalize *BC* and *AD*. (The more neutral alternatives *BCE*, for "before the common era," and *CE*, for "common era," are also capitalized.) Use lowercase letters for a.m. and p.m., but use these abbreviations only when they are accompanied by numbers.

                         morning.

We will see you in the ~~a.m.~~

NOTE: Avoid the abbreviation *no.* (written either *no.* or *No.*), except in technical writing, and then use it only before a specific number.

39d Editing Misused Abbreviations

In college writing, abbreviations are not used in the following cases.

(1) Names of Days, Months, or Holidays

Do not abbreviate days of the week, months, or holidays.

    Saturday, December   *Christmas*

On ~~Sat., Dec.~~ 23, I started my ~~Xmas~~ shopping.

(2) Names of Streets and Places

In general, do not abbreviate names of streets and places.

                        Drive   *New York City.*

He lives on Riverside ~~Dr.~~ in ~~NYC.~~

Exceptions: The abbreviation *US* is often acceptable (*US Coast Guard*), as is *DC* in *Washington, DC*. Also permissible are *Mt.* before the name of a mountain (*Mt. Etna*) and *St.* in a place name (*St. Albans*).

(3) Names of Academic Subjects

Do not abbreviate names of academic subjects.

    Psychology   *literature*

~~Psych.~~ and English ~~lit.~~ are required courses.

(4) Names of Businesses

Write company names exactly as the firms themselves write them, including the distinction between the ampersand (&) and the word *and*: *AT&T, Charles Schwab & Co., Inc.* Abbreviations for *company, corporation*, and the like are used only along with a company name.

    corporation   *company*

The ~~corp.~~ merged with a ~~co.~~ in Ohio.

(5) Latin Expressions

Abbreviations of the common Latin phrases *i.e.* ("that is"), *e.g.* ("for example"), and *etc.* ("and so forth") are not appropriate in college writing.

for example,
Other musicians (~~e.g.,~~ Bruce Springsteen) have also been influenced by Bob Dylan.

and other poems.
Poe wrote "The Raven," "Annabel Lee," ~~etc.~~

(6) Units of Measurement

In technical and business writing, some units of measurement are abbreviated when they are preceded by a numeral.

The hurricane had winds of 35 mph.

One new Honda gets over 50 mpg.

NOTE: MLA style requires that you write out units of measurement and spell out words such as *inches, feet, years, miles, pints, quarts,* and *gallons.*

(7) Symbols

The symbols =, +, and # are acceptable in technical and scientific writing but not in nontechnical college writing. The symbols % and $ are acceptable only when used with <u>numerals</u> (15%, $15,000), not with spelled-out numbers.

Exercise 39.1

Correct any incorrectly used abbreviations in the following sentences, assuming that all are intended for a college audience. If a sentence is correct, mark it with a *C*.

and
Example: *Romeo ~~&~~ Juliet* is a play by Shakespeare.

▸ 1. The committee meeting, attended by representatives from Action for Children's Television (ACT) and NOW, Sen. Putnam, & the pres. of ABC, convened at 8 A.M. on Mon. Feb. 24 at the YWCA on Germantown Ave.

▸2. An econ. prof. was suspended after he encouraged his students to speculate on securities issued by a corp. under investigation by the SEC.

▸ 3. Benjamin Spock, the MD who wrote *Baby and Child Care*, was a respected dr. known throughout the USA.

▸ 4. The FDA banned the use of Red Dye no. 2 in food in 1976, but other food additives are still in use.

▶ 5. The Rev. Dr. Martin Luther King Jr., leader of the SCLC, led the famous Selma, Ala., march.

6. Wm. Golding, a novelist from the U.K., won the Nobel Prize in lit.

7. The adult education center, financed by a major computer corp., offers courses in basic subjects like introductory bio. and tech. writing as well as teaching HTML and XML.

8. All the bros. in the fraternity agreed to write to Pres. Dexter appealing their disciplinary probation under Ch. 4, Sec. 3, of the IFC constitution.

9. A 4 qt. (i.e., 1 gal.) container is needed to hold the salt solution.

10. According to Prof. Morrison, all those taking the exam should bring two sharpened no. 2 pencils to the St. Joseph's University auditorium on Sat.

Chapter 40 Using Numbers

Convention determines when to use a **numeral** (22) and when to spell out a number (twenty-two). Numerals are commonly used in scientific and technical writing and in journalism, but they are used less often in the humanities.

NOTE: The guidelines in this chapter are based on the *MLA Handbook for Writers of Research Papers*, 6th ed. (2003). APA style, however, requires that all numbers below ten be spelled out if they do not represent specific measurements and that numbers ten and above be expressed in numerals.

40a Spelled-Out Numbers versus Numerals

Unless a number falls into one of the categories listed in 40b, spell it out if you can do so *in one or two words*.

The Hawaiian alphabet has only twelve letters.

Class size stabilized at twenty-eight students.

The subsidies are expected to total about two million dollars.

Numbers *more than two words* long are expressed in figures.

The dietitian prepared 125 sample menus.

The developer of the community purchased 300,000 doorknobs and 153,000 faucets.

Never begin a sentence with a numeral. If necessary, reword the sentence.

Faulty: 250 students are currently enrolled in World History 106.

Revised: Current enrollment in World History 106 is 250 students.

NOTE: When one number immediately precedes another in a sentence, spell out the first, and use a numeral for the second: *five 3-quart containers.*

http://kirsznermandell.wadsworth.com

Computer Tip: Spelled-Out Numbers versus Numerals

Your word processor's grammar checker will often highlight numerals in your writing and suggest that you spell them out. Before clicking Change, be sure that the number does not fall into one of the categories listed in 40b.

40b Conventional Uses of Numerals

(1) Addresses

111 Fifth Avenue, New York, NY 10003

(2) Dates

January 15, 1929   1914–1919

(3) Exact Times

9:16   10 a.m. (or 10:00 a.m.)

Exceptions: Spell out times of day when they are used with *o'clock: eleven o'clock*, not *11 o'clock.* Also spell out times expressed in quarter and half hours: *half-past eight, a quarter to ten.*

(4) Exact Sums of Money

$25.11 $6,752.00

NOTE: Always use a numeral (not a spelled-out number) with a $ symbol. You may spell out a round sum of money if you use sums infrequently in your paper, provided you can do so in two or three words.

five dollars   two thousand dollars

(5) Divisions of Written Works

Use arabic (not roman) numerals for chapter and volume numbers; acts, scenes, and lines of plays; chapters and verses of the Bible; and line numbers of long poems.

(6) Measurements before an Abbreviation or Symbol

12″	55 mph
32°	15 cc

(7) Percentages and Decimals

80%	3.14

NOTE: You may spell out a percentage (*eighty percent*) if you use percentages infrequently in your paper, provided the percentage can be expressed in two or three words. Always use a numeral (not a spelled-out number) with a % symbol.

(8) Ratios, Scores, and Statistics

In a paper that follows APA style, use numerals for numbers presented as a comparison.

See Ch. 47

> Children preferred Fun Flakes over Graino by a ratio of 20 to 1.
> The Orioles defeated the Phillies 6 to 0.
> The median age of the voters was 42; the mean age was 40.

(9) Identification Numbers

Route 66	Track 8	Channel 12

NOTE: When writing out large numbers, insert a comma every three digits from the right, beginning after the third digit.

3,000	25,000	6,751,098

Do not, however, use commas in four-digit page and line numbers, addresses, or year numbers.

page 1202	3741 Laurel Ave.	1968

Exercise 40.1

Following MLA guidelines, revise the use of numbers in these sentences, making sure usage is correct and consistent. If a sentence uses numbers correctly, mark it with a *C*.

Example: The Empire State Building is ~~one hundred and two~~ *102* stories high.

▸ 1. *1984*, a novel by George Orwell, is set in a totalitarian society.

▸ 2. The English placement examination included a 30-minute personal-experience essay, a 45-minute expository essay, and a 150-item objective test of grammar and usage.

▸ 3. In a control group of two hundred forty-seven patients, almost three out of four suffered serious adverse reactions to the new drug.

▸ 4. Before the Thirteenth Amendment to the Constitution, slaves were counted as $^3/_5$ of a person.

▸ 5. The intensive membership drive netted 2,608 new members and additional dues of over 5 thousand dollars.

6. They had only 2 choices: either they could take the yacht at Pier Fourteen, or they could return home to the penthouse at Twenty-seven Harbor View Drive.

7. The atomic number of lithium is three.

8. Approximately 3 hundred thousand schoolchildren in District 6 were given hearing and vision examinations between May third and June 26.

9. The United States was drawn into the war by the Japanese attack on Pearl Harbor on December seventh, 1941.

10. An upper-middle-class family can spend over 250,000 dollars to raise each child up to age 18.

Doing Research and Documenting Sources

Research is the systematic investigation of a topic outside your own knowledge and experience. However, doing research means more than just reading other people's ideas. When you undertake a research project, you become involved in a process that requires you to **think critically**: to evaluate and interpret the ideas explored in your sources and to formulate ideas of your own. Your research will be most efficient if you follow a systematic process such as the one outlined below.

See
Ch. 6

The Research Process

Activity	Date Due	Date Completed
Move from a General Assignment to a Narrow Topic, **41a**	_____	_____
Map Out a Search Strategy, **41b**	_____	_____
Do Exploratory Research and Formulate a Research Question, **41c**	_____	_____
Assemble a Working Bibliography, **41d**	_____	_____
Develop a Tentative Thesis, **41e**	_____	_____
Do Focused Research, **41f**	_____	_____
Take Notes, **41g**	_____	_____
Fine-Tune Your Thesis, **41h**	_____	_____
Outline Your Paper, **41i**	_____	_____
Draft Your Paper, **41j**	_____	_____
Revise Your Paper, **41k**	_____	_____
Prepare Your Final Draft, **41l**	_____	_____

41a Moving from Assignment to Topic

(1) Understanding Your Assignment

Every research paper begins with an assignment. Before you can find a direction for your research, you must be sure you understand the exact requirements of this assignment.

Checklist: Understanding Your Assignment

☐ Has your instructor provided a list of possible topics, or are you expected to select a topic on your own?

☐ Is your purpose to explain, to persuade, or to do something else?

☐ Is your audience your instructor? Your fellow students? Both? Someone else?

☐ Can you assume your audience knows a lot (or just a little) about your topic?

☐ When is the completed research paper due?

☐ About how long should it be?

☐ Will you be given a specific research schedule to follow, or are you expected to set your own schedule?

☐ Is collaborative work permitted? Is it encouraged? If so, at what stages of the research process?

☐ Does your instructor expect you to keep your notes on note cards? In a computer file?

☐ Does your instructor expect you to prepare a formal outline?

☐ Are instructor–student conferences required?

☐ Will your instructor review notes, outlines, or drafts with you at regular intervals?

☐ Does your instructor require you to keep a research notebook?

☐ What manuscript guidelines and documentation style are you to follow?

☐ What help is available to you—from your instructor, other students, experts on your topic, community resources, your library staff?

Kimberly Romney, the student whose writing process you followed in Chapters 2–4, was given the following assignment in a second-semester composition class:

> Write a ten- to fifteen-page research paper that takes a position on any issue related to the Internet. Keep a research notebook that traces your progress.

Throughout this chapter, you will see examples of the work Kimberly did as she completed this assignment.

(2) Choosing a Topic

Once you understand the requirements and scope of your assignment, you need to decide on a topic. In many cases, your instructor will help you choose a topic, either by providing a list of suitable topics or by suggesting a general subject area—for example, a famous trial, an event that happened on the day you were born, a problem on college campuses. Keep in mind, though, that you may still need to narrow your topic to one you can write about: one trial, one event, one problem.

If your instructor prefers that you select a topic on your own, you should consider a number of possible topics and weigh both their suitability for research and your interest in them. You decide on a topic for your research paper in much the same way you decide on a topic for a short essay: you read, brainstorm, talk to people, and ask questions. Specifically, you talk to friends and family, coworkers, and perhaps your instructor; read magazines and newspapers; take stock of your interests; consider possible topics suggested by your other courses (historical events, scientific developments, and so on); and, of course, browse the Internet. (Your search engine's <u>subject guides</u> can be particularly helpful to you as you look for a promising topic for your research or try to narrow a broad subject.)

Checklist: Choosing a Research Topic

As you look for a suitable research topic, keep the following guidelines in mind:

☐ **Are you genuinely interested in your research topic?**

☐ **Is your topic suitable for research?** Topics limited to your personal experience and those based on value judgments are not suitable for research.

☐ **Are the boundaries of your research topic appropriate?** A research topic should be neither too broad nor too narrow.

☐ **Can your topic be researched in a library to which you have access?**

---

(3) Starting a Research Notebook

Keeping a **research notebook,** a combination journal of your reactions and log of your progress, is an important part of the research process. A research notebook maps out your direction and keeps you on track; throughout the research process, it helps you define and redefine the boundaries of your assignment.

In this notebook, you can record lists of things to do, sources to check, leads to follow up on, appointments, possible community contacts, questions to which you would like to find answers, stray ideas, possible thesis statements or titles, and so on. (Be sure to date your entries and to check off and date work completed.)

See 2c

See 43b2

Here is an example of an entry from Kimberly's research note-book in which she discusses how she chose a topic for her research paper.

Excerpt from Research Notebook

```
          Last semester, I wrote a personal essay about
my difficulties using computers and the Internet
when I arrived at college. In class, we'd read an
essay by Henry Louis Gates Jr. that confirmed what
I thought: not everyone feels comfortable using
computers and the Internet. Gates says that the
Internet threatens to create two societies—one that
is tapped into the digital economy and one that is
not, and he refers to this problem as the "digital
divide." For this paper, I'd like to expand the
paper I wrote for my first-semester composition
course and talk more broadly about the digital
divide. I asked my comp professor if I could, and
she gave me permission. (I'll check with Professor
Wilson too.)
          I've been thinking about how far I've come in
terms of improving my computer skills. I feel much
more proficient using word-processing programs and
using the Internet for research. For that reason, I
think this paper will be much better than the one I
wrote last semester.
```

Exercise 41.1

Using your own instructor's guidelines for selecting a research topic, choose a topic for your paper. Then, start a research notebook by entering information about your assignment, schedule, and topic.

41b Mapping Out a Search Strategy

Once you have found a topic to write about, you should plan your **search strategy,** the process you will use to help you locate and evaluate source material. This process reflects the way research works: you begin by doing **exploratory research,** looking at general reference works that give you a broad overview of your topic, and progress to **focused research,** consulting more specialized reference works as well as books and articles (in print or online) on your topic.

The diagram in Figure 41.1 on page 338 is a general model of a search strategy that you can customize to suit the research project you are working on.

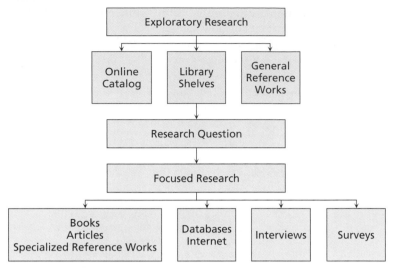

Figure 41.1 Search strategy.

41c Doing Exploratory Research and Formulating a Research Question

During **exploratory research,** you develop an overview of your topic, searching the Internet and looking through general reference works such as encyclopedias, bibliographies, and specialized dictionaries (either in print or online). Your goal at this stage is to formulate a **research question** that you want your research paper to answer. A research question helps you to decide which sources to seek out, which to examine first, which to examine in depth, and which to skip entirely. (The answer to your research question will be your paper's thesis statement.)

After doing some exploratory research, Kimberly decided on the following research question: "Do all Americans have equal access to the Internet?"

41d Assembling a Working Bibliography

During your exploratory research, you begin to assemble a **working bibliography** for your paper. (This working bibliography will be the basis for your <u>works-cited list</u>, which will include all the sources you cite in your paper.)

As you consider each potential source, keep track of your sources by recording full and accurate bibliographic information in a separate computer file designated "Bibliography" (or, if you prefer, on individual index cards). Keep records of interviews (including telephone and email interviews), meetings, lectures, films, and electronic sources as well as books and articles. For each source, include not only basic identifying details—such as the date of an interview, the call number of a library book, the URL of an Internet source and the date you downloaded it, or the author of an article accessed from a database— but also a brief evaluation that includes comments about the kind of information the source contains, the amount of information offered, its relevance to your topic (and, perhaps, its limitations).

Close-up: Assembling a Working Bibliography

As you record bibliographic information for your sources, include the following information:

Book author(s); title (underlined or in italics); call number (for future reference); city of publication; publisher; date of publication; brief evaluation

Article author(s); title of article (in quotation marks); title of journal (underlined or in italics); volume number; date; inclusive page numbers; URL (if applicable); date downloaded (if applicable); brief evaluation

---

As you go about collecting sources and building your working bibliography, be careful to monitor the quality and relevance of all the materials you examine. Making informed choices early in the research process will save you a lot of time in the long run. For more information on evaluating library sources, **see 42c;** for guidelines on evaluating Internet sources, **see 43d.**

Following are examples of records Kimberly kept for her working bibliography. In the library, she copied her source information on index cards. When she returned to her dorm room, she transferred the information from her cards into a computer file.

Information for a Working Bibliography (on Index Card)

Norris, Pippa	—— Author
Digital Divide: Civic Engagement, Information Poverty, and the Internet Worldwide	—— Title
Cambridge: Cambridge UP, 2001	—— Publication information
A book about the digital divide that explains its history and its relationship to economics and class.	—— Evaluation

Information for a Working Bibliography (in Computer File)

Author —	CBS AP
Title —	"Digital Divide Debated"
Publication —	http://www.cbsnews.com/stories/2002/05/30/tech/main510589.shtml
information	May 30, 2002
	Accessed March 2, 2003
Evaluation —	Reports on Bush administration's argument that the digital divide is no longer a significant problem. Cites the findings of the February 2002 Commerce report.

Exercise 41.2

Consulting Figure 41.1 on page 338, map out a search strategy for your research project (by hand or with your computer). Next, do exploratory research to find a research question for your paper, carefully evaluating the relevance and usefulness of each source. Then, compile your working bibliography. When you have finished, reevaluate your sources and plan additional research if necessary.

41e Developing a Tentative Thesis

See
41h

Your **tentative thesis** is a preliminary statement of the main point you think your research will support. This statement, which you will eventually refine into your paper's **thesis statement**, should answer your research question.

Developing a Tentative Thesis

Subject Area	Topic	Research Question	Tentative Thesis
Issue related to the Internet	Access to the Internet	Do all Americans have equal access to the Internet?	Not all Americans have equal access to the Internet, and this is a potentially serious problem.

Because it suggests the specific direction your research will take as well as the scope and emphasis of your argument, your tentative thesis can help you generate a list of the main points you plan to develop in your paper. This list can help you narrow the focus of your research so you can zero in on a few specific categories to explore as you read and take notes.

> **Listing Your Points**
>
> Tentative Thesis: Not all Americans have equal access to the Internet, and this is a potentially serious problem.
> • Give background about the Internet; tell why it's important
> • Identify groups that don't have access to the Internet
> • Explain problems this creates
> • Suggest possible solutions

Exercise 41.3

Following your instructor's guidelines, develop a tentative thesis for your research paper and a tentative list of the points you plan to develop.

41f Doing Focused Research

With exploratory research, you look at general reference works to get an overview of your topic. With **focused research,** however, you look for the specific information—facts, examples, statistics, definitions, quotations—you need to support your points. Once you have decided on a tentative thesis and made a list of the points you plan to explore, you are ready to begin your focused research.

(1) Reading Sources

As you look for information, try to explore as many sources as possible. It makes sense to examine more sources than you actually intend to use so you can proceed even if one or more of your sources turns out to be biased, outdated, unreliable, superficial, or irrelevant—in other words, not suitable. You should also make sure you try to explore different viewpoints. After all, if you read only those sources that agree on a particular issue, you will have difficulty understanding the full range of opinion about your topic.

As you explore various sources, quickly evaluate each source's potential usefulness. For example, if your source is a book, skim the table of contents and the index; if your source is a journal article, read the abstract. Then, if an article or a section of a book seems useful, photocopy it for future reference. Similarly, when you find an online source that looks promising, print it out (or send it to yourself as an email attachment) so you can evaluate it further later on. (For information on evaluating print and electronic sources, **see 42c.**)

See
Ch. 45

NOTE: Do not paste online source material directly into your paper. This can lead to plagiarism.

(2) Balancing Primary and Secondary Sources

See
42b4

During your focused research, you will encounter both primary sources (original documents and observations) and secondary sources (interpretations of original documents and observations).

For some research projects, primary sources are essential; most research projects, however, rely heavily on secondary sources, which provide scholars' insights and interpretations. Remember, though, that the further you get from the primary source, the more chances exist for inaccuracies caused by misinterpretations or distortions.

41g Taking Notes

As you locate information in the library and on the Internet, take notes (either by hand or on a computer) to create a record of exactly what you found and where you found it.

(1) Recording Source Information

See
Ch. 44

Each piece of information you record in your notes (whether summarized, paraphrased, or quoted from your sources) should be accompanied by a short descriptive heading that indicates its relevance to one of the points you will develop in your paper. Because you will use these headings to guide you as you organize your notes, you should make them as specific as possible. Labeling every note for a paper on the "digital divide" created by the Internet `digital divide` or `Internet`, for example, will not prove very helpful later on. More focused headings—for instance, `dangers of digital divide` or `government's steps to narrow the gap`—will be much more useful.

Also include brief comments that make clear your reasons for recording the information. These comments (enclosed in brackets so you will know they express your own ideas, not those of your source) should establish the purpose of your note—what you think it can explain, support, clarify, describe, or contradict—and perhaps suggest its relationship to other notes or other sources. Any questions you have about the information or its source can also be included in your comment.

Finally, each note should accurately identify the source of the information you are recording. You need not write out the complete citation, but you must include enough information to identify your source. For example, `Gates 499` would be enough to send you back to your working bibliography card or file, where you would be able to find the complete documentation for Henry Louis Gates's essay "One Internet, Two Nations." (If you use more than one source by the same author, you need a more complete reference.)

Close-up: Taking Notes

When you take notes, your goal is flexibility: you want to be able to arrange and rearrange information easily and efficiently as your paper takes shape. If you take notes on your computer, type each individual note (accompanied by source information) under a specific heading rather than listing all information from a single source under the same heading. (Later on, you can move notes around so notes on the same topic are grouped together.) If you take notes by hand, use the time-tested index-card system, taking care to write on only one side of the card and to use a separate index card for each individual note rather than running several notes together on a single card.

Following are examples of notes that Kimberly kept. For sources that she read in the library, Kimberly used index cards to record notes. When she returned to her dorm room, she entered this information into a computer file that she created for this purpose.

Notes (on Index Card)

Short heading   Source

Initiatives questioned   Schwartz, "Lack"

As a result of the dot.com bust, organizations like PowerUp, which created 1,000 community-based technology centers, have disbanded. According to a PowerUp spokesperson, "The model that was launched in late 1999. . . was a model that had its bloodlines in different economic times. The model isn't necessarily the best one for these economic times." —— Note

[Is there a new model to replace these organizations?] —— Comments

Notes (in Computer File)

Short heading

Problems of digital divide

Rangel-King, Houston Chronicle, 12/6/01 — Source

"African-Americans make up only 11 percent — Note (quotation) of the information technology workforce and account for less than 1 percent of the doctorate level computer science degrees conferred, according to a recent study performed by Data Source Associates."

Efforts to close gap

Rangel-King, Houston Chronicle, 12/6/01

Houston-based Association of Minority — Note (paraphrase) Information Technology Professionals (AMITP) works to close digital divide by providing networking opportunities to African Americans in technology industry. [How successful have — Comment they been? How many members?]

Checklist: Taking Notes

☐ **Identify the source of each piece of information.**
☐ **Include everything now that you will need later** to understand your note—names, dates, places, connections with other notes—and to remember why you recorded it.
☐ **Distinguish quotations from paraphrases and summaries and your own ideas from those of your sources.** If you copy a source's words, place them in quotation marks. (If you take notes by hand, circle the quotation marks; if you type your notes, put the quotation marks in boldface.) If you write down your own ideas, enclose them in brackets—and, if you are typing, italicize them as well. These techniques will help you avoid accidental plagiarism in your paper.

See Ch. 45

☐ **Put an author's comments into your own words whenever possible,** summarizing and paraphrasing material as well as adding your own observations and analyses.
☐ **Copy an author's comments accurately,** using the exact words, spelling, punctuation marks, and capitalization.

(2) Managing Photocopies and Printouts

Much of the information you gather will be in the form of photocopies (of articles, book sections, and so on) and material downloaded or printed out from the Internet. Learning to manage this source information efficiently will save you a lot of time.

First, be careful not to allow the ease of copying and downloading to encourage you to postpone decisions about the usefulness of your sources. Remember, you can easily accumulate so many pages that it will be almost impossible for you to keep track of all your information.

You should also keep in mind that photocopies and printouts are just raw information, not information that has already been interpreted and evaluated. Making copies of sources is only the first step in the process of taking thorough, careful notes. You still have to paraphrase and summarize your source's ideas and make connections among them.

Moreover, photocopies and printouts do not have much flexibility. For example, a single page of text may include information that should be earmarked for several different sections of your paper. This lack of flexibility makes it difficult for you to arrange source material into any meaningful order. Just as you would with any source, you have to transcribe your notes into your computer or onto index cards. These notes will give you the flexibility you need to write your paper.

Remember, you should approach photocopies and material you download or print out just as you approach any other source: as material that you will read, highlight, annotate, and then take notes about.

Close-up: Avoiding Plagiarism

To avoid the possibility of accidental plagiarism, be sure to keep all downloaded material in a separate file—not in your notes file. After you read this material and decide how to use it, you can move the notes you take into your notes file (along with full source information).

See
Ch. 45

Exercise 41.4

Begin focused research for your paper, reading sources carefully and taking notes as you read. Your notes should include paraphrase, summary, and your own observations and analysis as well as quotations.

41h Fine-Tuning Your Thesis

After you have finished your focused research and note-taking, you should be ready to refine your tentative thesis into a carefully

See
3a–c
worded statement that expresses a conclusion your research can support. This **thesis statement** should be more precise than your tentative thesis, accurately conveying the direction, emphasis, and scope of your paper.

Fine-Tuning Your Thesis

Tentative Thesis

Not all Americans
have equal access
to the Internet,
and this is a
potentially serious
problem.

Thesis Statement

Although the Internet has
changed our lives for the
better, it threatens to
leave many people behind,
creating two distinct
classes—those who have
access and those who do not.

If your thesis statement does not express a conclusion your research can support, you will need to revise it. Reviewing your notes carefully, perhaps grouping information in different ways, may help you decide on a more suitable thesis. Or, you may try other techniques—for instance, using your research question as a starting point for additional brainstorming or freewriting.

Exercise 41.5

Carefully read over all the notes you have collected during your focused research, and develop a thesis statement for your paper.

41i Constructing an Outline

Once you have a thesis, you are ready to make an outline to guide you as you write your rough draft.

To make sense out of all the notes you have accumulated, you need to sort and organize them. As you organize and reorganize your notes into categories and subcategories, you will begin to see the ideas in your paper take shape. Your outline will reflect this shape.

A formal outline is different from a list of the main points you tentatively plan to develop in your paper. A **formal outline**—which
See
4c4
may be either a **topic outline** or a **sentence outline**—includes all the points you will develop. It indicates both the exact order in which you will present your ideas and the relationship between main points and supporting details.

NOTE: The outline you construct at this stage is only a guide for you to follow as you draft your paper; you are likely to change it as you draft and revise. The final outline, which you may be required to hand in with your finished paper, will reflect what you have written and serve as a guide for your readers. (For an example of a formal sentence outline, **see 46c.**)

Following is Kimberly's topic outline.

Formal (Topic) Outline

<u>Thesis statement</u>: Although the Internet has changed our lives for the better, it threatens to leave many people behind, creating two distinct classes—those who have access and those who do not.

    I. Internet during the 1990s

        A. Empowering tool

        B. Source of knowledge and prosperity

   II. Problems of digital divide

        A. Lack of access by many groups

        B. Educational and economic disadvantages

        C. Widening gap

  III. Efforts by government and others to close gap

        A. Community Technology Centers Program

        B. Commerce Department's Technology Opportunities Program

        C. Bill and Melinda Gates Foundation

        D. <u>The Digital Divide Network</u> and <u>The Civil Rights Forum</u>

   IV. Initiatives questioned

        A. Bush administration's view

        B. Worsening economy

        C. Challenges by minority groups

    V. Recommendations for the future

        A. Improve access to technology, especially the Internet

        B. Redefine "digital divide" to make it more inclusive

        C. Continue federal funding

Checklist: Constructing a Formal Outline

☐ Write your thesis statement at the top of the page.

☐ Review your notes to make sure each note expresses only one general idea. If this is not the case, recopy any unrelated information, creating a separate note.

☐ Check that the heading for each note specifically characterizes that note's information. If it does not, change the heading.

☐ Sort your notes according to their headings, keeping a miscellaneous file for notes that do not seem to fit into any category. Irrelevant notes, those unrelated to your paper's thesis, should be set aside (but not discarded).

☐ Check your categories for balance. If most of your notes fall into just one or two categories, revise some of your headings to create narrower, more focused categories. If you have only one or two notes in a category, you may need to do additional research or treat that topic only briefly (or not at all).

☐ Organize the individual notes within each group, adding more specific subheads to your headings as needed. Arrange your notes in an order that highlights the most important points and subordinates lesser ones.

☐ Decide on a logical order in which to discuss your paper's major points.

See
4c4

☐ Construct your <u>formal outline</u>, using divisions and subdivisions that correspond to your headings.

☐ Review your completed outline to make sure you have not placed too much emphasis on a relatively unimportant idea, ordered ideas illogically, or created sections that overlap with others.

http://kirsznermandell.wadsworth.com

Computer Tip: Outlining

Before you begin writing, create a separate file for each major section of your outline. Then, copy your notes into these files in the order in which you intend to use them. You can print out each file as you need it and use it for a guide as you write.

Exercise 41.6

Review your notes carefully. Then, sort and group them into categories, and construct a topic outline for your paper.

41j Writing a Rough Draft

When you are ready to write your <u>rough draft</u>, check to be sure you have arranged your notes in the order in which you intend to use them. Follow your outline as you write, using your notes as needed.

As you move along, leave space for material you plan to add, and bracket phrases or whole sections that you think you may later decide to move or delete. In other words, lay the groundwork for a major revision.

As your draft takes shape, be sure to supply transitions between sentences and paragraphs to indicate how your points are related. To make it easy for you to revise later on, triple-space your draft. Be careful to copy source information fully and accurately on this and every subsequent draft, placing the documentation as close as possible to the material it identifies.

(1) Shaping the Parts of the Paper

Like any other essay, a research paper has an introduction, a body, and a conclusion. In your rough draft, as in your outline, you focus on the body of your paper. Do not spend time planning your introduction or conclusion at this stage; your ideas will change as you write, and you will need to revise your opening and closing paragraphs later to reflect those changes.

Introduction In your **introduction,** you identify your topic and establish how you will approach it. Your <u>introduction</u> also includes your thesis statement, which presents the position you will support in the rest of the paper.

Body As you draft the **body** of your paper, lead readers through your discussion with strong <u>topic sentences</u> that correspond to the divisions of your outline.

```
    In the late 1990s, many argued that the Internet had
ushered in a new age, one in which instant communication
would bring people closer together and eventually eliminate
national boundaries.'
```

You can also use <u>headings</u> if they are a convention of the discipline in which you are writing.

```
Responses to Digital Divide

    In response, the government, corporations, nonprofit
organizations, and public libraries made efforts to bridge
the gap between the "haves" and the "have-nots."
```

Even in your rough draft, carefully worded topic sentences and headings will help you keep your discussion under control.

See 5d
Use different patterns of development to shape the individual sections of your paper, and be sure to connect ideas with clear transitions. If necessary, connect two sections of your paper with a transitional paragraph that shows their relationship.

See 5e1

Conclusion The **conclusion** of a research paper often restates your thesis. This is especially important in a long paper because by the time your readers get to the end, they may have lost sight of your paper's main idea. Your conclusion can also include a summary of your key points, a call for action, or perhaps an apt quotation. In your rough draft, however, your concluding paragraph is usually very brief.

See 5e3

(2) Working Source Material into Your Paper

In the body of your paper, you evaluate and interpret your sources, comparing different ideas and assessing conflicting points of view. As a writer, your job is to draw your own conclusions, blending information from various sources into a paper that coherently and forcefully presents your own original viewpoint to your readers.

See 44d
Be sure to integrate source material smoothly into your paper, clearly and accurately identifying the relationships among various sources (and between those sources' ideas and your own). If two sources present conflicting interpretations, you should be especially careful to use precise language and accurate transitions to make the contrast apparent (for instance, "`Although the Bush administra-` `tion remains optimistic, some studies suggest . . .`"). When two sources agree, you should make this clear (for example, "`Like Young, McPherson believes . . .`" or "`Department of` `Commerce statistics confirm Gates's point`"). Such phrasing will provide a context for your own comments and conclusions. If different sources present complementary information about a subject, blend details from the sources carefully, keeping track of which details come from which source.

Following is an excerpt from Kimberly's draft. It includes her instructor's comments, inserted with *Microsoft Word*'s Comment tool.

Rough Draft with Instructor's Comments (Excerpt)

|The| `Bill and Melinda Gates Foundation,`

`for example, has provided libraries across`

`the country with funding that allows them to`

> **Comment:** You need a transition sentence before this one to show that this paragraph is about a new idea. See 5b6.

purchase computers and connect them to the Internet (Egan)

[Add page number?]. The Digital Divide Network is a Web

site that posts stories about the digital divide from a

variety of perspectives. |By posting information on the Web

site that they created|, the site's sponsor

> Comment: Wordy. See 17a.

hopes to raise awareness of the problems that

the digital divide causes. The Civil Rights Forum is a Web

site that focuses on the digital divide. This

> Comment: Pronoun-antecedent agreement. See 26b.

site says that|their|goal is to "bring civil

rights organizations and community groups into the debate

over the future of our media environment."

> Comment: This should begin a new paragraph. See 5a.

[Add source] |Recently|, however, many of

|those|initiatives have been questioned for a

> Comment: Incorrect pronoun reference. See 21c.

variety of reasons. Many people, for example,

argue that the digital divide is no longer a significant

problem. In 2001, a phone survey of more than 350,000

Americans conducted by the company Media Audit determined

that 44 percent of African-American households were

accessing the Internet, |"an increase of over 41 percent

over the last three years."|Further, the company found that

Latino households were also increasingly

> Comment: Who said this? See 44c.

accessing the Internet. In fact, 42 percent of Latino

households were using the Internet in 2001 (Roach).

In February 2002, the Department of Commerce published

its annual digital divide report. Using the most recent

US Census data, the report argues that from 1998 to

2001 . . .

Exercise 41.7

Write a rough draft of your paper, being careful to incorporate source material and visuals smoothly and to record source information accurately. Begin drafting with the section for which you have the most material.

41k Revising Your Drafts

You should begin revising by making an outline of your rough draft and comparing it to the outline you made before you began the draft. If you find significant differences, you will have to revise your thesis statement or rewrite sections of your paper. The checklists in 4c5 can guide your revisions of your paper's overall structure and its individual paragraphs, sentences, and words.

See 4b–c

As you review your drafts, follow the **revision** procedures that apply to any paper. In addition, focus on the questions in the following checklist, which apply specifically to research papers.

Checklist: Revising a Research Paper

- ☐ Should you do more research to find support for certain points?
- ☐ Do you need to reorder the major sections of your paper?
- ☐ Should you rearrange the order in which you present your points within those sections?
- ☐ Do you need to add section headings? transitional paragraphs?

See 44d

- ☐ Have you **integrated source material** smoothly into your paper?
- ☐ Have you chosen visuals carefully and integrated them smoothly into your paper?
- ☐ Are quotations blended with paraphrase, summary, and your own observations and reactions?

See Ch. 45

- ☐ Have you avoided **plagiarism** by carefully documenting all borrowed ideas?
- ☐ Have you analyzed and interpreted the ideas of others rather than simply stringing those ideas together?
- ☐ Do your own ideas—not those of your sources—define the focus of your discussion?

NOTE: You will probably take your paper through several drafts, changing different parts of it each time or working on one part over and over again. After revising each draft thoroughly, print out a corrected version and make additional corrections by hand on that draft before typing the next version.

Following are two versions of an excerpt from Kimberly's paper. The first version includes comments (inserted with *Microsoft Word*'s Comment tool) from two peer reviewers. The second uses the Track Changes tool to show the revisions Kimberly made in response to these comments.

Rough Draft with Peer Reviewers' Comments (Excerpt)

||A recent article| observes that many

African-American and other minority groups

argue that digital divide rhetoric might

actually stereotype minorities. The article

says that digital divide rhetoric "could

discourage businesses or academics from creating content or

services tailored for minority communities—ultimately

making the digital divide a self-fulfilling

prophecy." |By talking as if there is a

digital divide, many scholars and leaders in the African-

American community fear that this idea will be accepted as

a fact rather than a condition. Tara L.

McPherson |says| that "the idea of challenging

the digital divide is not about denying its

existence. But it is to ensure that the focus

on the digital divide doesn't naturalize a

kind of exclusion of investment."|

> **Comment:** You need a transition sentence here!

> **Comment:** Ditto, this is really awk. ☺

> **Comment:** Tell us the name and where this came from.

> **Comment:** Do you need a p. #?

> **Comment:** Use a stronger word—*asserts, claims,* etc. Wilson doesn't like us to keep using "says." ☺

> **Comment:** I think you're supposed to have the author's last name here.

Revision with Track Changes

In other cases, the groups targeted by digital divide

programs argue that they might do more harm than good. A

recent article in the Chronicle of Higher Education

observes that many African-American and other minority

groups argue that digital divide rhetoric might actually

stereotype minorities. The article says that digital divide

rhetoric "could discourage businesses or academics from

creating content or services tailored for minority

communities—ultimately making the digital divide a self-

fulfilling prophecy" (Young). By talking as if there is a

digital divide, many scholars and leaders in the African-

American community fear that this idea will be accepted as

a fact rather than a condition. Tara L. McPherson ~~says~~ argues that "the idea of challenging the digital divide is not about denying its existence. But it is to ensure that the focus on the digital divide doesn't naturalize a kind of exclusion of investment~~.~~" (qtd. in Young).

Exercise 41.8

Following the guidelines in 41k and 4b, revise your research paper until you are ready to prepare your final draft.

41l Preparing a Final Draft

See 4d

Before you print out the final version of your paper, **edit and proofread** hard copy of your outline and your works-cited list as well as of the paper itself. Next, consider (or reconsider) your paper's title. It should be descriptive enough to tell your readers what your paper is about, and it should create interest in your subject. Your title should

See 1a

also be consistent with the **purpose** and tone of your paper. (You would hardly want a humorous title for a paper about the death penalty or world hunger.) Finally, your title should be engaging and to the point—and perhaps even provocative. Often, a quotation from one of your sources will suggest a likely title.

When you are satisfied with your title, read your paper through again, proofreading for grammar, spelling, or typing errors you may have missed. Pay particular attention to parenthetical documentation and works-cited entries. (Remember that every error undermines your credibility.) Once you are satisfied that your paper is as accurate as you can make it, print it out one last time. Then, fasten the pages with a paper clip (do not staple the pages or fold the corners together), and hand it in. (For the final draft of Kimberly's research paper, along with a sentence outline and a works-cited list, see **46c**.)

Exercise 41.9

Prepare a sentence outline and a works-cited list for your research paper. (Section 4c4 explains and illustrates the specific conventions of sentence outlines; 46a2 illustrates MLA works-cited list format.) Then, edit and proofread your paper, outline, and works-cited list; decide on a title; and type your paper according to the format your instructor requires. Proofread your typed copy carefully before you hand it in.

http://kirsznermandell.wadsworth.com

> **Computer Tip: Useful Web Sites**
>
> A variety of different Web sites may be useful to you as you go through the research process. For an extensive list, see *The Concise Wadsworth Handbook* Web site, http://kirsznermandell.wadsworth.com.

Chapter 42 | Doing Library and Field Research

A modern, networked college library offers you resources that you cannot find anywhere else—even on the Internet. In the long run, you will save a great deal of time and effort, as well as gain a deeper understanding of your topic, if you begin your research with a survey of the library's print and electronic resources.

42a Doing Exploratory Library Research

You should begin your <u>exploratory research</u> in the library by consulting general encyclopedias, dictionaries, and bibliographies. (You can also find in the library the many resources you will use during <u>focused research</u>—for example, periodical indexes, articles, and books.)

See 41c

See 42b

During exploratory research, your goal is to find a research question—the question you want your paper to answer. You can begin this process by searching your college or university library's **online catalog** to see what kind of information is available about your topic. You can then look at general reference works and consult the library's electronic databases.

(1) Using Online Catalogs

Most college and university libraries—and a growing number of regional and community libraries—have abandoned print catalog systems in favor of **online catalogs**—computer databases that list all the books, articles, and other materials held by the library.

You access an online catalog (as well as other electronic library resources) by using one of the computer terminals located throughout the library and typing in certain words or phrases that enable you to find the information you need. If you have never used an online catalog, ask your reference librarian for help before you begin.

When you search the online catalog for information about your topic, you may conduct either a *keyword search* or a *subject search*. Later on in the research process, when you know more precisely what you are looking for, you can search for a particular book by entering its title, author, or call number.

Conducting a Keyword Search When you carry out a **keyword search,** you enter into the Search box of the online catalog a term or terms associated with your topic. The screen then displays a list of articles that contain those words in their bibliographic citations or abstracts. The more precise your search terms are, the more specific and useful the information you retrieve will be. (Combining keywords with AND, OR, and NOT allows you to narrow or broaden

See 43b3

your search. This technique is called conducting a <u>Boolean search</u>.)

Checklist: Keyword Dos and Don'ts

When conducting a keyword search, remember the following hints:

- ☐ Use precise, specific keywords to distinguish your topic from similar topics.
- ☐ Enter both singular and plural keywords when appropriate— *printing press* and *printing presses,* for example.
- ☐ Enter both abbreviations and their full-word equivalents (for example, *US* and *United States*).
- ☐ Try variant spellings (for example, *color* and *colour*).
- ☐ Don't use too long a string of keywords. (If you do, you will retrieve large amounts of irrelevant material.)

Conducting a Subject Search When you carry out a **subject search,** you enter specific subject headings into the online catalog. The subject categories in a library are most often arranged according to headings established in the five-volume manual *Library of Congress Subject Headings,* held at the reference desk of your library. Although it may be possible to guess at a subject heading, your search will be more successful if you consult these volumes to help you identify the exact words you need.

NOTE: Many college and university libraries have Web sites that enable users to access their online catalogs from a dorm room or from any computer connected to the Internet. Ask at your library for the appropriate Web address and password.

(2) Consulting General Reference Works

General reference works—encyclopedias, bibliographies, and so on—which provide broad overviews of particular subjects, can be helpful when you are doing exploratory research. From these sources, you can learn key facts and specific terminology as well as find dates, places, and people. In addition, general reference works often include bibliographies that you can use later on when you do focused research.

NOTE: Articles in general encyclopedias are usually not detailed enough for a college-level research paper. Articles in specialized encyclopedias, dictionaries, and bibliographies, however, are more likely to be appropriate for your research.

(3) Using Electronic Resources

Today's libraries have electronic resources that enable you to find a wide variety of sources. The same computer terminals that enable you to access the online catalog may also enable you to access this source material.

Online databases are collections of digital information—citations of books; reports; journal, magazine, and newspaper articles (and sometimes the articles themselves)—arranged for easy access and retrieval by computer. Different libraries offer different databases and make them available in different ways. Many libraries have implemented Web-based systems that make it easy for them to network their databases (and online catalogs) beyond the library's walls. Some libraries may acquire databases on CD-ROM or DVD, but most subscribe to information service companies, such as DIALOG or Gale, that provide access to hundreds of databases not otherwise available to you. One of your first tasks should be to determine what subscription databases your library has access to. Visit your library's Web site, or ask a reference librarian for more information.

General and Specialized Subscription Databases Some library databases, called **bibliographic databases,** include references to articles published in magazines and scholarly journals and may also be available in print. They provide information about each article but do not usually include the full text of the article itself. (**Full-text** databases include the entire text of articles, online encyclopedias, or other works.) These databases are **proprietary,** which means that libraries must subscribe to them in order to make them available to students and faculty. Licensing and copyright agreements generally restrict the use of these subscription databases; they are not available from outside the library to those who are not affiliated with the school.

Some library databases for articles cover many subject areas (*Expanded Academic ASAP* or *LexisNexis Academic Universe*, for example); others cover just one subject area in great detail (*PsycINFO* or *Sociological Abstracts*, for example). The choices available to you may seem overwhelming at first. Assuming that your library offers a variety of databases (some libraries subscribe to hundreds), how do you know which ones will be best for your research topic? One strategy is to begin by searching a general database that includes full-text articles and then move on to a more specialized database that covers your subject in more detail. The specialized databases are more likely to include scholarly and professional sources, but they are also less likely to include the full text. They will, however, include **abstracts** (short summaries) that can help you determine the usefulness of a source. If you are in doubt about which databases would be most useful to you, ask a librarian for suggestions. (Figure 42.1 shows a printout from a library subscription database.)

| Date | Volume | Issue number | First page of article | Total number of pages |

Title: The Supply Side of the Digital Divide: Is There Equal Availability in the Broadband Internet Access Market?

Periodical: *Economic Inquiry,* April 2003 v41 i2 p346(18).

Author: James E. Prieger

Author's Abstract: The newest dimension of the digital divide is access to broadband (high-speed) Internet service. Using comprehensive US data covering all forms of access technology (chiefly DSL and cable modem), I look for evidence of unequal broadband availability in areas with high concentrations of poor, minority, or rural households. There is little evidence of unequal availability based on income or on black or Hispanic concentration. There is mixed evidence concerning availability based on Native American or Asian concentration. Other findings: Rural location decreases availability; market size, education, Spanish language use, commuting distance, and Bell presence increase availability. (JEL L96, J78, L51)

Subjects: Digital Divide (Technology) = Demographic Aspects

Internet = Usage

Features: tables; figures

Figure 42.1 Library subscription database printout.

Searching Databases There are two ways to search library databases for information on a topic: by subject headings and by keyword(s). **Subject headings** are taken from a list of terms recognized by that database. Sometimes it is easy to choose a subject heading, but sometimes, it is harder to choose an appropriate term. For example, what do you call older people? Are they senior citizens? elderly? the aged? (Some databases provide a print or online thesaurus to help you pick subject headings.)

The other option is **keyword searching,** which allows you to type in any significant term likely to be found in the title, subject headings, abstract, or (if the full text is available) text of an article. Keyword searching also allows you to link terms using **boolean operators** (AND, OR, NOT). For example, *elderly* AND *abuse* would retrieve only articles that mention both elderly people and abuse; *elderly* OR *aged* OR *senior citizens* would retrieve articles that mention any of these terms. Keyword searching is particularly helpful when you need to narrow or expand the focus of your search.

Both subject heading and keyword searches are useful ways to find information on your topic. The most important thing is to be persistent. One good source often leads to another because abstracts and text may suggest other terms you can use. References and footnotes may suggest additional sources as well.

42b Doing Focused Library Research

Once you have completed your exploratory research and formulated your research question, it is time to move to focused research. During **focused research,** you examine the specialized reference works, books, and articles devoted specifically to your topic. At this stage, you may also need to make use of the special services that many college libraries provide.

If your library has a Web site (and most libraries do), you may find it enables you to access more than just the library catalog or the various periodicals to which it subscribes. In fact, many library Web sites are gateways to a vast amount of information, including research guides on a wide variety of topics; electronic journals and newspapers to which the library subscribes; and links to recommended Internet resources. Many library Web sites also include online forms that you can use to ask a question electronically, and some even include an online chat service that enables you to contact a librarian from your home or residence hall computer.

http://kirsznermandell.wadsworth.com

Computer Tip: Web Resources for
Focused Library Research

General Reference Resources (Carnegie-Mellon U.)
    http://eserver.org/reference/
How to Find Articles (U. of Toronto)
    http://library.scar.utoronto.ca/Bladen_Library/
    Research101/findart.htm

(continued)

Web resources for focused library research (continued)

Finding Books (U. of Dayton Libraries—some restrictions)
http://www.udayton.edu/~library/daynet
Internet Public Library—Newspapers
http://aristotle.ipl.org/cgi-bin/reading/news.out.p1
Internet Public Library—Magazines
http://aristotle.ipl.org/reading/serials/
Primary vs. Secondary Sources (U. of Toronto)
http://library.scar.utoronto.ca/Bladen_Library/
Research101/primary.htm
Library Catalogs—Terminology
http://www.nucat.library.nwu.edu
Library Catalogs—Dewey Decimal System
http://www.oclc.org/fp/

(1) Consulting Specialized Reference Works

During your exploratory research, you used general reference works to help you narrow your topic and formulate your research question. Now, you can access **specialized reference works**—unabridged dictionaries, special dictionaries, yearbooks, almanacs, atlases, and so on—to find facts, examples, statistics, definitions, and expert opinion.

(2) Consulting Books

The online catalog gives you the information you need—specifically, the call numbers—for locating specific titles. A **call number** is like a book's address in the library: it tells you exactly where to find the book you are looking for. (Figure 42.2 shows an online catalog entry for a book.)

Once you become familiar with the physical layout of the library and the classification system your library uses, you should find it quite simple to locate the books you need.

Checklist: Tracking Down a Missing Book

Problem
Book has been checked out of library.
Book is not in library's collection.

Possible Solution
☐ Consult person at circulation desk.
☐ Check other nearby libraries.
☐ Ask instructor if he or she owns a copy.
☐ Arrange for interlibrary loan (if time permits).

Problem	Possible Solution
Journal is not in library's collection/article is ripped out of journal.	☐ Arrange for interlibrary loan (if time permits). ☐ Check to see whether article is available in a full-text database. ☐ Ask librarian whether article has been reprinted as part of a collection.

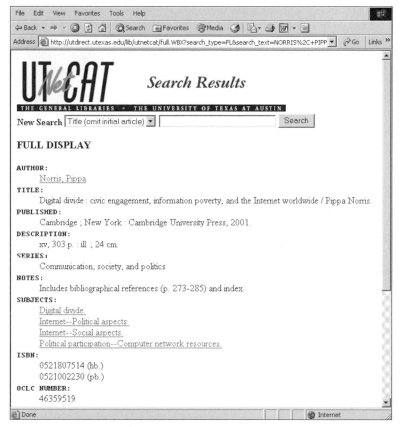

Figure 42.2 Online catalog entry for a book.

(3) Consulting Articles

A **periodical** is a newspaper, magazine, scholarly journal, or other publication published at regular intervals (weekly, monthly, or quarterly). Articles in scholarly journals can be the best, most reliable sources you can find on a subject; they provide current information and are written by experts on the topic. And, because these journals focus on a particular subject area, they can provide in-depth analysis.

NOTE: You cannot access most scholarly journals on the free Internet. Although you may occasionally find individual articles on the Internet, the easiest and most reliable way to access scholarly journals is through one of the subscription databases in your college library.

Periodical indexes are databases that list articles from a selected group of magazines, newspapers, or scholarly journals. These subscription databases may be available in bound volumes, on microfilm or microfiche, and on CD-ROM or DVD; however, most libraries now offer them online. They are updated frequently and provide the most current information available.

Close-up: Frequently Used Subscription Databases

The following subscription databases are found in most academic libraries. (Be sure to check your library's Web site or ask a librarian about those available to you.)

General Indexes	Description
Ebscohost	Database system for thousands of periodical articles on many subjects
Expanded Academic ASAP	A largely full-text database covering all subjects in thousands of magazines and scholarly journals
FirstSearch	Full-text articles from many popular and scholarly periodicals
LexisNexis Academic Universe	Includes full-text articles from national, international, and local newspapers. Also includes large legal and business sections.
Readers' Guide to Periodical Literature	Index to popular periodicals

Specialized Indexes	Description
Dow Jones Interactive	Full text of articles from US newspapers and trade journals
ERIC	Largest database of education-related journal articles and reports in the world
General BusinessFile ASAP	A full-text database covering business topics
PubMed (MEDLINE)	Covers articles in medical journals. Some may be available in full text.
PsycINFO	Covers psychology and related fields
Sociological Abstracts	Covers the social sciences

(4) Finding Primary and Secondary Sources

Primary sources give firsthand accounts of topics or events. They include diaries, letters, speeches, manuscripts, memoirs, autobiographies, records of governments or organizations, newspaper articles, and even books written at the time an event occurred. Primary sources also include photographs, maps, films, tape recordings, novels, short stories, poems, or plays.

Checklist: Finding Primary Sources

☐ Do a keyword search of your online catalog. Use keywords that combine your topic with additional terms that describe the format of the primary source—for example, *slaves* AND *narratives*.

☐ See if the online catalog lists any bibliographies that might include primary sources. For example, a bibliography on an author might list works *by* the author (primary sources) as well as works *about* the author (secondary sources).

☐ Check with a reference librarian to see if your library subscribes to any databases that contain full-text primary sources.

☐ Check with a reference librarian to see if your library houses government publications that may include primary sources.

☐ Check with a reference librarian to see if your library houses any manuscripts.

☐ Use the Internet to find digitized collections of primary source materials—for example, documents that relate to US history, transcripts of television shows, or video clips.

Secondary sources are accounts or interpretations of topics or events. In many cases, their purpose is to interpret or analyze primary sources. Secondary sources include textbooks, literary criticism, and encyclopedias.

Checklist: Finding Secondary Sources

☐ Search your library's online catalog for books. Combine a term that describes your topic with terms such as *interpretation, criticism,* or *bibliography.*

☐ Search the library's subscription databases for articles in scholarly journals, popular magazines, and newspapers that discuss the causes, effects, and interpretation of events.

☐ Check the notes, bibliographies, and works-cited lists at the end of books and articles.

☐ Do a keyword search on the Internet—but be sure to critically evaluate any information you find.

NOTE: The US Government publishes information on a wide variety of topics, much of it available on the Web—for example, statistical information collected by government agencies; reports issued by government agencies such as the Environmental Protection Agency, the Department of Education, and NASA; US Supreme Court decisions; and presidential papers, political speeches, treaties, and US patents.

Exercise 42.1

Which library research sources would you consult to find the following information?

▸ 1. A discussion of Monica Ali's novel *Brick Lane* (2003)
▸ 2. A government publication about how to heat your home with solar energy
▸ 3. Biographical information about the American anthropologist Margaret Mead
▸ 4. Books about Margaret Mead and her work
▸ 5. Organizational literature about what is being done to prevent the killing of wolves in North America
  6. Information about the theories of Albert Einstein
  7. Current information about the tobacco lobby
  8. The address at which to contact Edward P. Jones, an American writer
  9. Whether your college library has *The Human Use of Human Beings* by Norbert Wiener
  10. Current information about AmeriCorps

42c Evaluating Library Sources

Whenever you find a source (print or electronic), take the time to **evaluate** it—to assess its usefulness and its reliability. To determine the usefulness of a library source, ask the following questions:

1. **Does the source treat your topic in enough detail?** To be of any real help, a book should include a section or chapter on your topic, not simply a footnote or brief reference. For articles, either read the abstract or skim the entire article for key facts, looking closely at section headings, information set in boldface type, and topic sentences. An article should have your topic as its central subject (or at least one of its main concerns).

2. **Is the source current?** The date of publication tells you whether the information in a book or article is up to date. A source's currency is particularly important for scientific and technological

subjects, but even in the humanities, new discoveries and new ways of thinking lead scholars to reevaluate and modify their ideas.

3. **Is the source respected?** A contemporary review of a source can help you make this assessment. *Book Review Digest*, available in the reference section of your library, lists popular books that have been reviewed in at least three newspapers or magazines and includes excerpts from representative reviews.

4. **Is the source reliable?** Is a piece of writing largely fact or unsubstantiated opinion? Does the author support his or her conclusions? Does the author include documentation? Is the author objective, or does he or she have a particular agenda to advance? Compare a few statements with a neutral source—a textbook or an encyclopedia, for instance—to see whether an author seems to be slanting facts.

In general, **scholarly publications**—books and journals aimed at an audience of expert readers—are more respected and reliable than **popular publications**—books, magazines, and newspapers aimed at an audience of general readers. However, assuming they are current, written by reputable authors, and documented, articles from some popular publications may be appropriate for your research. Check with your instructor or librarian to be sure.

Exercise 42.2

Read the following paragraphs carefully, paying close attention to the information provided about their sources and authors as well as to their content. Decide which sources would be most useful and reliable in supporting the thesis "Winning the right to vote has (or has not) significantly changed the role of women in national politics." Which sources, if any, should be disregarded? Which would you examine first? Why?

▶ 1. Almost forty years after the adoption of the Nineteenth Amendment, a number of promised or threatened events have failed to materialize. The millennium has not arrived, but neither has the country's social fabric been destroyed. Nor have women organized a political party to elect only women candidates to public office. . . . Instead, women have shown the same tendency to divide along orthodox party lines as male voters. (Eleanor Flexner, *Century of Struggle*, Atheneum, 1968. *A scholarly treatment of women's roles in America since the Mayflower, this book was well reviewed by historians.*)

▶ 2. Nineteen eighty-two was the year that time ran out for the proposed equal rights amendment. Eleanor Smeal, president of the

National Organization for Women, the group that headed the intense 10-year struggle for the ERA, conceded defeat on June 24. Only 24 words in all, the ERA read simply: "Equality of rights under the law shall not be denied or abridged by the United States or by any state on account of sex." Two major opinion polls had reported just weeks before the ERA's defeat that a majority of Americans continued to favor the amendment. (June Foley, "Women 1982: The Year That Time Ran Out," *The World Almanac & Book of Facts*, 1983.)

3. When you think about it, right-wing victories have almost always depended on *turning on* the conservative minority, and *turning off* everybody else. This was done categorically by denying suffrage to black men and to women of all races; physically, by implementing poll taxes and literacy tests; and procedurally, by creating barriers that still make registration and voting a more daunting task here than in any other democracy. It's interesting that the psychological turnoff—the idea that politics is a dirty game, and voting doesn't matter—began to be pushed just as the 1960s civil rights movement was showing the nation that voting could be meaningful. (Gloria Steinem, "Voting as Rebellion," *Ms.* Sept./Oct. 1996.)

4. It won't happen this year. But the next chance at the White House is only four years away, and more women than you might think are already laying the groundwork for their own presidential bids. Bolstered by changing public attitudes, women in politics no longer assume that the Oval Office will always be a male bastion. In 1936, when George Gallup first asked people whether they would "vote for a woman for president if she qualified in every other respect," 65 percent said they would not. Back then, women were only slightly more open to the idea than men. Things are far different today. A recent poll shows that 90 percent of Americans, men included, say they could support a woman for president. (Eleanor Clift and Tom Brazaitis, *Madam President. The authors profile the women who they say are positioning themselves to be president.*)

42d Doing Field Research

In addition to the research you do in the library and on the Internet, some projects may require you to conduct an interview. An **interview** often gives you material that you cannot get by any other means—for instance, biographical information, a firsthand account of an event, or the opinions of an expert.

Computer Tip: Conducting an Email Interview

Using email to conduct an interview can save you a great deal of time. Before you send your questions, make sure the person is willing to cooperate. If the person agrees, send a short list of specific questions. After you have received the answers, send a response thanking the person for his or her cooperation.

The kinds of questions you ask in an interview depend on the information you want. **Open-ended questions**—questions designed to elicit general information—allow a respondent great flexibility in answering: *"Do you think students today are motivated? Why or why not?"* **Closed-ended questions**—questions intended to elicit specific information—enable you to zero in on a particular detail about a subject: *"How much money did the government's cost-cutting programs actually save?"*

Checklist: Conducting an Interview

☐ Always make an appointment.
☐ Prepare a list of specific questions tailored to the subject matter and the time limit of your interview.
☐ Do background reading about your topic. (Do not ask for information that you can easily find elsewhere.)
☐ Have paper and a pen with you. If you want to record the interview, get your subject's permission in advance.
☐ Allow the person you are interviewing to complete an answer before you ask another question.
☐ Take notes, but continue to pay attention as you do so.
☐ Pay attention to the reactions of your interview subject.
☐ Be willing to depart from your prepared list of questions to ask follow-up questions.
☐ At the end of the interview, thank your subject for his or her time and cooperation.
☐ Send a brief note of thanks.

43a Understanding the Internet

The **Internet** is a vast system of networks that links millions of computers. Because of its size and diversity, the Internet allows people from all over the world to communicate quickly and easily.

Even with all its advantages, however, the Internet does not give you access to the specialized print and electronic resources found in a typical college library. For this reason, you should consider the Internet to be a supplement to your library research, not a substitute for it.

Close-up: Limitations of Internet Research

- Many important and useful publications are available only in print or through the library's subscription databases and not on the Internet.
- The information in your college library will almost always be more focused and more useful than much of what you will find on the Internet.
- The information you see on an Internet site—unlike information in your library's subscription databases—may not be there when you try to access it at a later time.
- Anyone can publish on the Internet, so sites can vary greatly in quality. Because librarians screen the material in your college library, it is likely to meet academic standards of reliability.
- Although the authorship and affiliation of Internet documents can often be difficult or impossible to determine, this is not usually the case with the sources in your college library.

43b Using the World Wide Web for Research

When most people refer to the Internet, they actually mean the **World Wide Web,** which is just a part of the Internet. (**See 43c** for other components of the Internet that you can use in your research.) The Web relies on **hypertext links,** keywords highlighted in blue (and often underlined). By clicking your mouse on these links, you can move easily from one **Web page** (a single document) to another or from one **Web site** (a collection of Web pages) to another.

To carry out a Web search, you need a **Web browser,** a tool that enables you to view information on the Web. Two of the most popular browsers—*Microsoft Internet Explorer* and *Netscape Navigator*—

display the full range of text, photos, sound, and video available in Web documents.

Once you are connected to the Internet, you use your browser to access a **search engine,** a program that searches for and retrieves documents available on the Internet.

There are three ways to use search engines to find the information you want: *entering an electronic address, using subject guides,* and *doing a keyword search.*

(1) Entering an Electronic Address

The most basic way to access information on the Web is to go directly to a specific electronic address, called a **URL** (uniform resource locator). Search engines and Web browsers display a dialog box that enables you to enter the URL of a particular Web site. You may also type the URL directly into the Location text field on your browser's **home page** (the page you see when you open your browser). (Figure 43.1 shows a dialog box and a location field.) Once you type in a URL and click on Open or Search (or hit Enter or the return key), you will be connected to the Web site you want. Make sure to type the URL exactly as it appears—without adding spaces or adding or deleting punctuation marks. Remember that omitting (or adding)

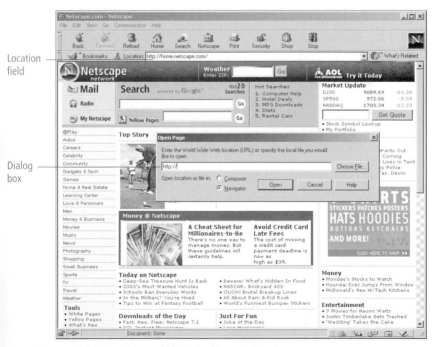

Figure 43.1 Entering an address in *Netscape Navigator.*

just a single letter or punctuation mark will send you to the wrong site—or to no site at all.

http://kirsznermandell.wadsworth.com

> **Computer Tip: Understanding URLs**
>
> The first section of a URL indicates the type of file being accessed. In the address http://www.google.com/ images, *http* indicates that the file is in hypertext transfer protocol. After the colon and the two slashes is the name of the host site where the file is stored (www.google.com). The *www* tells the user that the Web site is on the World Wide Web, *google* is the domain name, and *com* shows that this is a commercial institution. Following this section is the directory path to the file (*images*).

See 42a–b

For links to Web sites for <u>exploratory and focused research</u>, go to http://kirsznermandell.wadsworth.com ▶ *The Concise Wadsworth Handbook* ▶ Chapter 43 ▶ Web Sites for Exploratory and Focused Research.

(2) Using Subject Guides

You can also use subject guides to help you locate information. Some search engines, such as *Yahoo!*, *About.com*, and *Look Smart*, contain a **subject guide**—a list of general categories (*Arts, Business, Computers,* and so on) from which you can choose. (Figure 43.2 shows the home page of the search engine *Yahoo!* with a subject guide.) Each of these categories will lead you to a more specific list of categories and subcategories until, eventually, you get to the topic you want. For example, clicking on *Society* would lead you to *Activism* and then to *Animal Rights* and eventually to an article concerning cruelty to animals on factory farms. Although using subject guides is a time-consuming strategy for finding specific information, it can be an excellent tool during <u>exploratory research</u>, when you want to find or narrow a topic.

See 42a

(3) Doing a Keyword Search

Finally, you can locate information by doing a **keyword search.** You do this by entering a keyword (or words) into your search engine's search field. (Figure 43.3 shows a keyword search page of the search engine *Google.*) The search engine will identify any site in its database on which the keyword (or words) you have typed appears. (These sites are called **hits.**) If, for example, you simply type *Civil War* (say, in hope of finding information on Fort Sumter during the Civil War), the search engine will generate an enormous list of hits—well over a million. This list will likely include, along with sites that might be relevant to your research, the Civil War Reenactors home page as well as sites that focus on Civil War music.

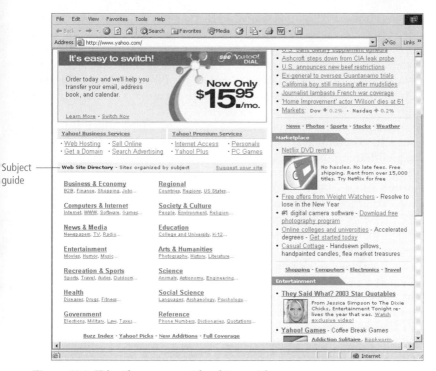

Figure 43.2 *Yahoo!* home page with subject guide.

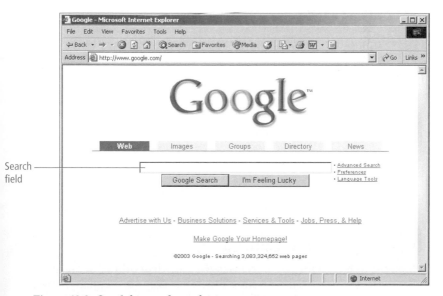

Figure 43.3 *Google* keyword search page.

Because searching this way is inefficient and time consuming, you need to *focus* your search by using **search operators,** words and symbols that tell a search engine how to interpret your keywords. One way to focus your search is to put quotation marks around your search term (type *"Fort Sumter"* rather than *Fort Sumter*). This will direct the search engine to locate only documents containing this phrase.

Another way to focus your search is to carry out a **Boolean search,** combining keywords with AND, OR, NOT (typed in all capital letters), or a plus or minus sign to eliminate irrelevant hits from your search. (To do this type of search, you may have to select a search engine's Advanced Search option.) For example, to find Web pages that focus on the battle of Fort Sumter in the Civil War, type *Civil War* AND *Fort Sumter.* If you do, your search will yield only items that contain *both* terms. (If you typed in *Civil War* OR *Fort Sumter,* your search will yield items that contain *either* term.) Some search engines allow you to search using three or more keywords—*Civil War* AND *Fort Sumter* NOT *national monument,* for example. In this case, your search would yield items that contained both the terms *Civil War* and *Fort Sumter,* but not the term *national monument.* By limiting your search in this way, you would just get items that discussed Fort Sumter and the Civil War and eliminate items that discussed Fort Sumter's current use as a national monument. Focusing your search in this way enables you to avoid irrelevant Web pages.

http://kirsznermandell.wadsworth.com

Computer Tip: Using Search Operators

" " (quotation marks) Use quotation marks to search for a specific phrase: *"Baltimore Economy"*

AND Use AND to search for sites that contain both words: *Baltimore* AND *Economy*

OR Use OR to search for sites that contain either word: *Baltimore* OR *Economy*

NOT Use NOT to exclude the word that comes after the NOT: *Baltimore* AND *Economy* NOT *Agriculture*

+ (plus sign) Use a plus sign to include the word that comes after it: *Baltimore + Economy*

− (minus sign) Use a minus sign to exclude the word that comes after it: *Baltimore + Economy − Agriculture*

(4) Finding the Right Search Engine

Some search engines are more user-friendly than others; some allow for more sophisticated searching functions; some are updated more frequently; and some are more comprehensive than others. As you try out various search engines, you will probably settle on a favorite that you will turn to first whenever you need to find information.

Close-up: Popular Search Engines

AllTheWeb (www.alltheweb.com): This excellent search engine provides comprehensive coverage of the Web. Many users think that this search engine is as good as *Google*. In addition to generating Web page results, *AllTheWeb* has the ability to search for news stories, pictures, video clips, MP3s, and FTP files.

AltaVista (www.altavista.com): Good, precise engine for focused searches. Fast and easy to use.

Ask Jeeves (www.ask.com): Good beginner's site. Allows you to narrow your search by asking questions, such as *Are dogs smarter than pigs?*

Excite (www.excite.com): Good for general topics. Because it searches over 250 million Web sites, you often get more information than you need.

Go (http://infoseek.go.com): Enables you to access information in a directory of reviewed sites, news stories, and Usenet groups.

Google (www.google.com): Arguably, the best search engine available. Accesses a large database that includes both text and graphics. It is easy to navigate, and searches usually yield a high percentage of useful hits.

HotBot (www.hotbot.com): Excellent, fast search engine for locating specific information. Good search options allow you to fine-tune your searches.

Lycos (www.lycos.com): Enables you to search for specific media (graphics, for example). A somewhat small index of Web pages.

Teoma (www.teoma.com): Teoma is a search engine owned by *Ask Jeeves*. Although it has a smaller index of the Web than *Google* and *AllTheWeb*, it is very effective when it comes to answering questions. It contains a Refine feature that offers suggested topics to explore after you do a search. It also has a Resources section of results that will point you to linked resources about various topics.

WebCrawler (www.webcrawler.com): Good for beginners. Easy to use.

Yahoo! (www.yahoo.com): Good for exploratory research. Enables you to search using either subject headings or keywords. Searches its own indexes as well as the Web.

Because even the best search engines search only a fraction of what is on the Web, if you use only one search engine, you will most likely miss much valuable information. It is therefore a good idea to repeat each search with several different search engines or to use one of the **metasearch** or **metacrawler** engines that uses several search engines simultaneously.

NOTE: It is a good idea to begin a search by checking your library's Web site for a list of recommended Web sites, arranged by topic.

Close-up: Metasearch Engines

Dogpile (www.dogpile.com)
Ixquick (www.ixquick.com)
Metacrawler (www.metacrawler.com)
Profusion (www.profusion.com)
Zworks (www.zworks.com)

In addition to the popular general-purpose search engines and metasites, there are also numerous search engines devoted entirely to specific subject areas, such as literature, business, sports, and women's issues. Hundreds of such specialized search engines are indexed at *Allsearchengines.com* (www.allsearchengines.com). These sites are especially useful during <u>**focused research**</u>, when you are looking for in-depth information about your topic.

See
42b

Close-up: Specialized Search Engines

Voice of the Shuttle (humanities search engine)
http://vos.ucsb.edu/

Pilot-Search.com (literary search engine)
http://www.pilot-search.com/

FedWorld (US government database and report search engine)
http://www.fedworld.gov/

HealthFinder (health, nutrition, and diseases information for consumers)
http://www.healthfinder.gov/default.htm

The Internet Movie Database (search engine and database for film facts, reviews, and so on)
http://www.imdb.com

SportQuest (sports search engine)
http://www.sportquest.com/

FindLaw (legal search engine)
http://www.findlaw.com/

NOTE: *Search Engine Watch* at www.searchenginewatch.com maintains an extensive, comprehensive, and up-to-date list of the latest search engines. Not only does this site list search engines by category, but it also reviews them.

Checklist: Tips for Effective Searching

☐ **Choose your keywords carefully.** A search engine is only as good as the keywords you use. Use quotation marks and Boolean search operators to make your searches more productive. Review the Computer Tip box on page 372 before you use any search engine.

☐ **Include enough terms.** If you are looking for information on housing, for example, search for several different variations of your keyword: *housing, houses, house buyer, buying houses, residential real estate,* and so on. Some search engines, like *Infoseek,* automatically search plurals; others do not. Some, like *AltaVista,* automatically search variants of your keyword; others require you to think of the variants by yourself.

☐ **Choose the right search engine.** No one all-purpose search site exists. Make sure you review the tips for choosing a search engine on pages 372–75.

☐ **Use more than one search engine.** Because different search engines index different sites, try several. If one does not yield results after a few tries, switch to another. Also, do not forget to do a metasearch with a search engine like *Metacrawler.*

☐ **Add useful sites to your bookmarks or favorites list.** Whenever you find a particularly useful Web site, **bookmark** it by selecting this option on the menu bar of your browser (with some browsers, such as *Internet Explorer,* this option is called *Favorites*). If you add a site to your bookmark list, you can return to the site whenever you want to by opening the Bookmark menu and selecting it.

43c Using Other Internet Tools

In addition to the World Wide Web, the Internet contains a number of other components that you can use to help you gather information for your research.

(1) Using Email

Email can be useful as you do research because it enables you to exchange ideas with classmates, ask questions of your instructors, and even conduct long-distance interviews. You can follow email links in Web documents, and you can also transfer word-processing documents or other files (as email attachments) from one computer to another.

(2) Using Listservs

Listservs (sometimes called **discussion lists**), electronic mailing lists to which you must subscribe, enable you to communicate with groups of people interested in particular topics. (Many schools and even individual courses have their own listservs.) Individuals in a listserv send emails to a main email address, and these messages are routed to all members of the group. Some listserv subscribers may be experts who can answer your queries. Keep in mind, however, that you must evaluate any information you get from a listserv before you use it in your research.

(3) Using Newsgroups

Like listservs, **newsgroups** are discussion groups. Unlike listserv messages, which are sent to you as email, newsgroup messages are collected on the **Usenet** system, a global collection of news servers, where anyone can access them. In a sense, newsgroups function as gigantic bulletin boards where users post messages that others can read and respond to. Thus, newsgroups can provide specific information as well as suggestions about where to look for further information. Just as you would with a listserv, you should evaluate information you get from a newsgroup before you use it.

(4) Using MUDS, MOOS, IRCS, and Instant Messaging

With emails and listservs, there is a delay between the time a message is sent and the time it is received. **MUDS, MOOS, IRCS,** and **instant messaging** enable you to send and receive messages in real time. In other words, communication is **synchronous**; that is, messages are sent and received as they are typed. Synchronous communication programs are being used more and more in college settings—for class discussions, online workshops, and collaborative projects.

43d Evaluating Web Sites

Most of the information you get on the Internet will be from the Web. For this reason, it is important to keep in mind that Web sites vary greatly in quality and reliability. Because it is so easy for anyone to operate a Web site and thereby publish anything, regardless of quality, critical evaluation of material that appears on the Web is more important than evaluation of more traditional sources of information, such as books and articles in print journals.

Determining the quality of a Web site is crucial if you plan to use material from it for your research. If you are using such materials for personal information or entertainment, it is probably enough just to be aware of what is legal and what is illegal (for example, you should not download copyrighted material, such as software or music, illegally posted on a Web site). However, if you are using information from a Web site—for example, articles, interviews, reviews, commentary—in a research project, you need to be much more careful. Central to your assessment of such materials is your evaluation of the Web site on which they appear. To make sure a Web site is reliable, you must check it for *accuracy, credibility, objectivity, currency*, and *coverage*.

NOTE: If you can answer "yes" to most of the following questions, your Web site is most likely reliable.

Accuracy **Accuracy** refers to the reliability of the material itself and to the use of proper documentation. Keep in mind that factual errors should cause you to question the reliability of the material you are reading.

- Is the text free of errors in sentence structure, usage, and grammar?
- Does the site provide a list of references?
- Are links available to other references?
- Has the author identified himself or herself and provided an email or traditional address?
- Does the author encourage questions and comments?
- Can information be verified in other resources?

Credibility **Credibility** refers to the credentials of the person or organization responsible for the site. Web sites vary greatly in quality and reliability. Those operated by well-known institutions (the Smithsonian or the US Department of Health and Human Services, for example) tend to provide highly reliable information and therefore have built-in credibility. Those operated by individuals (personal Web pages, for example) are often less reliable. Before using information that you access from a Web site, consider the credibility of the sponsoring organization as well as of the author of the material.

- Can you verify the credentials of the author or authors?
- Is the author an authority in his or her field?
- Does the site claim to be **refereed?** In other words, does an editorial board or a group of experts determine what material appears on the Web site, or is this an individual decision?
- Does the sponsoring organization exist apart from its Web presence?

- Does the site display a corporate logo? Does the content of the site have the official approval of the organization?
- Can you determine how long the Web site has existed?

Checklist: Determining the Legitimacy of an Anonymous Web Source

When a Web source is anonymous, you have to take special measures to determine its legitimacy. The following strategies can help you get the information you need to assess the legitimacy of an anonymous source.

☐ **Post a query.** If you get information from a newsgroup or a listserv, ask others in the group what they know about the source and its author.

☐ **Follow the links.** Follow the hypertext links in a document to other documents. If the links take you to legitimate sources, you know that the author is aware of these sources of information.

☐ **Do a keyword search.** Do a search using the name of the organization or the article as keywords. Other documents (or citations in other works) may identify the author, and this will help you assess the legitimacy of your source.

Objectivity **Objectivity** refers to the degree to which a Web site exhibits bias. Some Web sites make no secret of their biases. They openly advocate a particular point of view or action, or they are clearly trying to sell something. The biases of other Web sites may be harder to identify. For example, a Web site may present itself as a source of factual information when it is actually advocating a specific point of view. You need to determine a site's biases before you use material as a resource for academic work.

- Does advertising appear in the text?
- Does a corporation, political organization, or special-interest group sponsor the site?
- Does the site provide links to sites with a political purpose?
- Does the site have an expressed policy concerning the advertising that it exhibits?
- Does the site express a particular viewpoint?

Currency **Currency** refers to how up to date a Web site is. The easiest way to assess a site's currency is to determine when it was last updated. Keep in mind, however, that even if the date on the site is current, the information that the site includes may not be.

- Are all the links to other sites still functioning?
- Is the actual information on the page up to date?
- Does the site clearly identify the date it was created and revised?

Coverage or Scope **Coverage,** or **scope,** refers to the comprehensiveness of the information on a Web site.

- Does the site clearly state what points it intends to address?
- Does the site provide in-depth coverage?
- Are points well supported?
- Does the site identify a target audience, particularly by age or grade level? Does the target audience suggest the site is appropriate for your research needs?

Chapter 44	Summarizing, Paraphrasing, Quoting, and Synthesizing Sources

Simply copying down the words of a source is the least efficient way of <u>taking notes</u>. Experienced researchers know that a better strategy is to take notes that combine summary and paraphrase with direct quotation. By doing so, they make sure they understand both the material and its relevance to their research. This, in turn, makes it possible for them to <u>synthesize sources</u>, combining borrowed material with their own original ideas in a coherent piece of writing.

44a Writing a Summary

A **summary** is a brief restatement, *in your own words*, of the main idea of a passage or an article. When you write a summary, you condense the author's ideas into a few concise sentences. A summary is always much shorter than the original because it omits the examples, asides, analogies, and rhetorical strategies that writers use to add emphasis and interest. If you think it is necessary to include a distinctive word or phrase from your source, place it in quotation marks; otherwise, you will be committing <u>plagiarism</u>. Remember that your summary should accurately represent the author's ideas and should include only the ideas of your source, not your own interpretations or opinions. Finally, be sure to document all quoted words and paraphrases as well as the summary itself.

Close-up: Summaries

- **Summaries are original.** They should use your own language and phrasing, not the language and phrasing of your source.
- **Summaries are concise.** They should always be much shorter than the original.
- **Summaries are accurate.** They should precisely express the main idea of your source.
- **Summaries are objective.** They should not include your opinions.
- **Summaries are complete.** They should reflect the entire source, not just one part of it.

Compare the following three passages. The first is an original source; the second, an acceptable summary; and the third, an unacceptable summary.

Original Source:
Today, the First Amendment faces challenges from groups who seek to limit expressions of racism and bigotry. A growing number of legislatures have passed rules against "hate speech"—[speech] that is offensive on the basis of race, ethnicity, gender, or sexual orientation. The rules are intended to promote respect for all people and protect the targets of hurtful words, gestures, or actions.

Legal experts fear these rules may wind up diminishing the rights of all citizens. "The bedrock principle [of our society] is that government may never suppress free speech simply because it goes against what the community would like to hear," says Nadine Strossen, president of the American Civil Liberties Union and professor of constitutional law at New York University Law School. In recent years, for example, the courts have upheld the right of neo-Nazis to march in Jewish neighborhoods; protected cross-burning as a form of free expression; and allowed protesters to burn the American flag. The offensive, ugly, distasteful, or repugnant nature of expression is not reason enough to ban it, courts have said.

But advocates of limits on hate speech note that certain kinds of expression fall outside of First Amendment protection. Courts have ruled that "fighting words"—words intended to provoke immediate violence—or speech that creates a clear and present danger are not protected forms of expression. As the classic argument goes, freedom of speech does not give you the right to yell "Fire!" in a crowded theater. (Sudo, Phil. "Freedom of Hate Speech?" *Scholastic Update* 124.14 [1992]: 17–20)

Acceptable Summary: The right to freedom of speech, guaranteed by the First Amendment, is becoming more difficult to defend. Some people think that stronger

laws against the use of "hate speech" weaken the First
Amendment. But others argue that some kinds of speech
remain exempt from this protection (Sudo 17).

The preceding acceptable summary presents an accurate, objective overview of the original without using its exact language or phrasing. (The one distinctive phrase borrowed from the source is placed within quotation marks.)

Compare the acceptable summary with the following unacceptable summary. Notice that the unacceptable summary uses words and phrases from the original without placing them in quotation marks. This use constitutes <u>plagiarism</u>. In addition, the unacceptable summary expresses the writer's opinion ("Other people have the sense to realize . . .").

See
Ch. 45

Unacceptable Summary: Today, the First Amendment faces
challenges from lots of people. Some of these people are
legal experts who want to let Nazis march in Jewish
neighborhoods. Other people have the sense to realize
that some kinds of speech fall outside of First Amendment
protection because they create a clear and present danger
(Sudo 17).

44b Writing a Paraphrase

A summary conveys just the main idea of a source; a **paraphrase** gives a *detailed* restatement of a source's important ideas in their entirety. It not only indicates the source's main points, but it also reflects its order, tone, and emphasis. Consequently, a paraphrase can sometimes be as long as the source itself.

Close-up: Paraphrases

- **Paraphrases are original.** They should use your original language and phrasing, not the language and phrasing of your source.
- **Paraphrases are accurate.** They should precisely reflect both the ideas and the emphasis of your source.
- **Paraphrases are objective.** They should not include your opinions.
- **Paraphrases are complete.** They should include all the important ideas in your source.

When you paraphrase, make certain that you use your own words, except when you want to quote to give readers a sense of the original. If you include quotations, circle the quotation marks in your notes so that you will not forget to document them later. Try not to look at the source as you write, use language and syntax that come naturally to you, and avoid duplicating the wording or sentence structure of the original. Whenever possible, use synonyms that accurately convey the meaning of the original word or phrase. If you cannot think of a synonym for an important term, quote—but remember to document all direct quotations from your source as well as the entire paraphrase. Finally, be sure that your paraphrase reflects only the ideas of your source—not your analysis or interpretation of those ideas.

Following are an original passage, an acceptable paraphrase, and an unacceptable paraphrase.

Original Passage:
   When you play a video game, you enter into the world of the programmers who made it. You have to do more than identify with a character on a screen. You must act for it. Identification through action has a special kind of hold. Like playing a sport, it puts people into a highly focused and highly charged state of mind. For many people, what is being pursued in the video game is not just a score, but an altered state.
   The pilot of a race car does not dare to take . . . attention off the road. The imperative of total concentration is part of the high. Video games demand the same level of attention. They can give people the feeling of being close to the edge because, as in a dangerous situation, there is no time for rest and the consequences of wandering attention [are] dire. With pinball, a false move can be recuperated. The machine can be shaken, the ball repositioned. In a video game, the program has no tolerance for error, no margin for safety. Players experience their every movement as instantly translated into game action. The game is relentless in its demand that all other time stop and in its demand that the player take full responsibility for every act, a point that players often sum up [with] the phrase "One false move and you're dead." (Turkle, Sherry. *The Second Self: Computers and the Human Spirit.* New York: Simon & Schuster, 1984. 83–84.)

Acceptable Paraphrase: The programmer defines the reality of the video game. The game forces a player to merge with the character who is part of the game. The character becomes an extension of the player, who determines how he or she will think and act. According to Turkle, like sports, video games put a player into a very intense "altered state" of mind that is the most important part of the activity (83).
   The total involvement they demand is what attracts many people to video games. These games can simulate the thrill of participating in a dangerous activity without any of the risks. There is no time for rest and no opportunity to correct errors of judgment. Unlike video games, pinball games are forgiving. A player can—within certain limits—manipulate a pinball game to correct minor mistakes. With video games, however, every move has

immediate consequences. The game forces a player to adapt
to its rules and to act carefully. One mistake can cause
the death of the character on the screen and the end of
the game (Turkle 83-84).

Although the preceding acceptable paraphrase follows the order and
emphasis of the original—and even quotes a key phrase—its wording
and sentence structure are very different from those of the source.
Still, it conveys the key ideas of the source and maintains an objective tone.

The following unacceptable paraphrase simply echoes the phrasing and syntax of the original, borrowing words and expressions
without enclosing them in quotation marks. This constitutes <u>plagia-</u>
<u>rism</u>. In addition, the paraphrase digresses into a discussion of the
writer's own views about the relative merits of pinball and video
games ("That is why I like . . .").

See
Ch. 45

Unacceptable Paraphrase: Playing a video game, you enter
into a new world—one the programmer of the game made.
You can't just play a video game; you have to identify
with it. Your mind goes to a new level, and you are put
into a highly focused state of mind.
    Just as you would if you were driving a race car or
piloting a plane, you must not let your mind wander.
Video games demand complete attention. But the sense that
at any time you could make one false move and lose is
their attraction—at least for me. That is why I like
video games more than pinball. Pinball is just too easy.
You can always recover. By shaking the machine or quickly
operating the flippers, you can save the ball. Video
games, however, are not so easy to control. Usually, one
slip and you're dead (Turkle 83-84).

44c Quoting Sources

When you **quote,** you copy a writer's statements exactly as they appear in a source, word for word and punctuation mark for punctuation mark, enclosing the borrowed material in quotation marks. As a
rule, you should not quote extensively in a research paper. Numerous
quotations interrupt the flow of your discussion and give readers the
impression that your paper is just a collection of other people's ideas.

Checklist: When to Quote
☐ Quote when a source's wording or phrasing is so distinctive that a summary or paraphrase would diminish its impact.

(continued)

When to quote (continued)

☐ Quote when a source's words—particularly those of a recognized expert on your subject—will lend authority to your presentation.

☐ Quote when an author's words are so concise that paraphrasing would create a long, clumsy, or incoherent phrase or would change the meaning of the original.

☐ Quote when you plan to disagree with a source. Using a source's exact words helps convince readers you are being fair.

NOTE: Remember to document all quotations that you use in your paper.

Exercise 44.1

Assume that in preparation for a paper on the effects of the rise of the suburbs, you read the following paragraph from the book *Great Expectations: America and the Baby Boom Generation* by Landon Y. Jones. Reread the paragraph, and write a brief summary. Then, paraphrase the paragraph, quoting only those words and phrases you consider especially distinctive.

As an internal migration, the settling of the suburbs was phenomenal. In the twenty years from 1950 to 1970, the population of the suburbs doubled from 36 million to 72 million. No less than 83 percent of the total population growth in the United States during the 1950s was in the suburbs, which were growing fifteen times faster than any other segment of the country. As people packed and moved, the national mobility rate leaped by 50 percent. The only other comparable influx was the wave of European immigrants to the United States around the turn of the century. But as *Fortune* pointed out, more people moved to the suburbs every year than had ever arrived on Ellis Island.

44d Integrating Source Material into Your Writing

Weave paraphrases, summaries, and quotations smoothly into your discussion, adding your own analysis or explanation to show the relevance of your source material to the points you are making.

Close-up: Integrating Source Material into Your Writing

To make sure your sentences do not all sound the same, experiment with different methods of integrating source material into your paper.

- Vary the verbs you use to introduce a source's words or ideas (instead of repeating *says*).

acknowledges	discloses	implies
suggests	observes	notes
concludes	believes	comments
insists	explains	claims
predicts	summarizes	illustrates
reports	finds	proposes
warns	concurs	speculates
admits	affirms	indicates

- Vary the placement of the **identifying tag** (the phrase that identifies the source), putting it in the middle or at the end of the quoted material instead of always at the beginning.

Quotation with Identifying Tag in Middle: "A serious problem confronting Amish society from the viewpoint of the Amish themselves," observes Hostetler, "is the threat of absorption into mass society through the values promoted in the public school system" (193).

Paraphrase with Identifying Tag at End: The Amish are also concerned about their children's exposure to the public school system's values, notes Hostetler (193).

(1) Integrating Quotations

Be sure to work quotations smoothly into your sentences. Quotations should never be awkwardly dropped into your paper, leaving the relationship between the quoted words and your point unclear. Instead, use a brief introductory remark to provide a context for the quotation, and quote only those words you need to make your point.

Acceptable: For the Amish, the public school system is a problem because it represents "the threat of absorption into mass society" (Hostetler 193).

Unacceptable: For the Amish, the public school system represents a problem. "A serious problem confronting Amish society from the viewpoint of the Amish themselves is the threat of absorption into mass society through the values promoted in the public school system" (Hostetler 193).

Whenever possible, use an **identifying tag** to introduce the source of the quotation.

Identifying Tag: As John Hostetler points out, the Amish see the public school system as a problem because it represents "the threat of absorption into mass society" (193).

> ### Close-up: Punctuating Identifying Tags
>
> Whether or not to use a comma with an identifying tag depends on where you place the tag in the sentence. If the identifying tag immediately precedes a quotation, use a comma. If the identifying tag does not immediately precede a quotation, do not use a comma.
>
> As Hostetler points out, "The Amish are successful in maintaining group identity" (56).
>
> Hostetler points out that the Amish frequently "use severe sanctions to preserve their values" (56).
>
> Never use a comma after *that*.
>
> Hostetler says that/ Amish society is "defined by religion" (76).

Substitutions or Additions within Quotations When you make changes or additions to fit a quotation into your paper, indicate these changes by enclosing them in brackets.

Original Quotation: "Immediately after her wedding, she and her husband followed tradition and went to visit almost everyone who attended the wedding" (Hostetler 122).

Quotation Revised to Make Verb Tenses Consistent:
Nowhere is the Amish dedication to tradition more obvious than in the events surrounding marriage. Right after the wedding celebration, the Amish bride and groom "visit almost everyone who [has] attended the wedding" (Hostetler 122).

Quotation Revised to Supply an Antecedent for a Pronoun:
"Immediately after her wedding, [Sarah] and her husband followed tradition and went to visit almost everyone who attended the wedding" (Hostetler 122).

Quotation Revised to Change an Uppercase to a Lowercase Letter: The strength of the Amish community is illustrated by the fact that "[i]mmediately after her wedding, she and her husband followed tradition and went to visit almost everyone who attended the wedding" (Hostetler 122).

See 34f1

Omissions within Quotations When you delete unnecessary or irrelevant words, substitute an ellipsis (three spaced periods) for the deleted words.

Original Quotation: "Not only have the Amish built and staffed their own elementary and vocational schools, but they have gradually organized on local, state, and national levels to cope with the task of educating their children" (Hostetler 206).

Quotation Revised to Eliminate Unnecessary Words:
"Not only have the Amish built and staffed their own elementary and vocational schools, but they have gradually organized . . . to cope with the task of educating their children" (Hostetler 206).

Close-up: Omissions within Quotations

Be sure you do not misrepresent or distort the meaning of quoted material when you shorten it. For example, do not say, "the Amish have managed to maintain . . . their culture" when the original quotation is "the Amish have managed to maintain *parts of* their culture."

NOTE: If the passage you are quoting already contains ellipses, MLA style requires that you place brackets around any ellipses you add.

Long Quotations Set off a quotation of more than four typed lines of prose (or more than three lines of poetry) by indenting it one inch (ten spaces) from the margin. Double-space, and do not use quotation marks. If you are quoting a single paragraph, do not indent the first line. If you are quoting more than one paragraph, indent the first line of each complete paragraph an additional one-quarter inch (three spaces). Integrate the quotation into your paper by introducing it with a complete sentence followed by a colon. Place parenthetical documentation one space after the end punctuation.

See 33b

> According to Hostetler, the Amish were not always hostile to public education:
>
> > The one-room rural elementary school served the Amish community well in a number of ways. As long as it was a public school, it stood midway between the Amish community and the world. Its influence was tolerable, depending upon the degree of influence the Amish were able to bring to the situation. (196)

(2) Integrating Paraphrases and Summaries

Introduce your paraphrases and summaries with identifying tags, and end them with appropriate documentation. By doing so, you make certain that your readers are able to differentiate your own ideas from those of your sources.

Correct (Identifying Tag Differentiates Ideas of Source from Ideas of Writer): Art can be used to uncover many problems

```
that children have at home, in school, or with their
friends. For this reason, many therapists use art therapy
extensively. According to William Alschuler in Art and
Self-Image, children's views of themselves in society are
often reflected by their art style. For example, a
cramped, crowded art style using only a portion of the
paper shows a child's limited role (260).
```

Misleading (Ideas of Source Blend with Ideas of Writer): Art
can be used to uncover many problems that children have
at home, in school, or with their friends. For this
reason, many therapists use art therapy extensively.
Children's views of themselves in society are often
reflected by their art style. For example, a cramped,
crowded art style using only a portion of the paper shows
their limited role (Alschuler 260).

Exercise 44.2

Look back at the summary and paraphrase that you wrote for Exercise
44.1. Write three possible identifying tags for each, varying the verbs
you use for attribution and the placement of the identifying tag. Be
sure to include appropriate documentation at the end of each passage.

(3) Synthesizing Sources

When you write a **synthesis,** you use paraphrase, summary, and
quotation to combine material from two or more sources, along with
your own ideas, in order to express an original viewpoint. (In this
sense, an entire research paper is a synthesis.) You begin synthesizing
material by comparing your sources and determining how they are
alike and different, where they agree and disagree, and whether they
reach the same conclusions. As you identify connections between
one source and another or between a source and your own ideas, you
develop your own perspective on your subject. It is this viewpoint,
summarized in a thesis statement (in the case of an entire paper) or
in a topic sentence (in the case of a paragraph), that becomes the
focus of your synthesis.

As you write your synthesis, make your points one at a time, and
use material from your sources to support these points. Be certain
you use identifying tags as well as the transitional words and phrases
that your readers will need to follow your discussion. Finally, remember that your ideas, not the ideas of your sources, should be
central to your discussion.

The following synthesis was written by a student as part of a research paper.

```
Computers have already changed our lives. They carry
out (at incredible speed) many of the everyday tasks that
```

make our way of life possible. For example, computer
billing, with all its faults, makes modern business
possible, and without computers we would not have access to
the telephone services or television reception that we take
for granted. But computers are more than fast calculators.
According to one computer expert, they are well on their way
to learning, creating, and someday even thinking (Raphael
21). Another computer expert, Douglas Hofstadter, agrees,
saying that someday a computer will have both "will . . .
and consciousness" (423). It seems likely, then, that as a
result of the computer, our culture will change profoundly
(Turkle 15).

Exercise 44.3

Choose a debatable issue from the following list.

- Illegal immigrants' rights to free public education
- Helmet requirements for motorcycle riders
- Community service requirements for college students

Write a one-sentence summary of your own position on the issue;
then, interview a classmate and write a one-sentence summary of his
or her position on the same issue. Next, locate a source that discusses
your issue, and write a paraphrase of the writer's position. Finally,
write a paragraph that synthesizes the three positions.

Chapter 45	Avoiding Plagiarism

45a Defining Plagiarism

Plagiarism occurs when you present another person's ideas or words
as if they were your own. In this case, you not only cheat yourself by
losing an opportunity to learn, but you also cheat your instructors
and your fellow students by undercutting the trust and intellectual
honesty that is necessary if education is to take place.

Most plagiarism that occurs is **unintentional plagiarism**—for
example, inadvertently pasting a quoted passage from a downloaded
file directly into a paper and forgetting to include the quotation
marks and documentation. But there is a difference between an honest mistake and **intentional plagiarism**—for example, copying sentences from a journal article or submitting a paper that someone else
has written. The penalties for unintentional plagiarism may sometimes be severe, but intentional plagiarism is almost always dealt

with harshly: students who intentionally plagiarize can receive a failing grade for the paper (or the course) or even be expelled from school. For this reason, the words and ideas of others—whether borrowed from a print source or from an electronic source—must always be properly documented.

http://kirsznermandell.wadsworth.com

> **Computer Tip: Avoiding Plagiarism**
>
> The same technology that has made plagiarism easier to commit has also made it easier to detect. By doing a *Google* search, an instructor can quickly find the source of a phrase that has been plagiarized from a Web site. Other products search subscription databases and identify plagiarized passages in student papers.

45b Avoiding Unintentional Plagiarism

The most common cause of unintentional plagiarism is sloppy research habits. To avoid this problem, start your research paper early, choose a topic that interests you, and understand that the skills you learn now will help you in other courses as well as after you graduate. Do not cut and paste text from a Web site or full-text database directly into your paper. Never use sources that you have not actually read or invent sources that do not exist. If you paraphrase, do so correctly by following the examples in 45c; changing a few words here and there is not enough.

See
Chs.
46–47

Another cause of intentional plagiarism is failure to use proper documentation. In general, you must document any words or ideas that you borrow from your sources (whether print or electronic). Of course, certain items need not be documented: **common knowledge** (information every reader probably knows), facts available from a variety of reference sources, familiar sayings and well-known quotations, and your own original research (interviews and surveys, for example). Information that is another writer's original contribution, however, must be acknowledged. So, although you do not have to document the fact that John F. Kennedy graduated from Harvard in 1940 or that he was elected president in 1960, you do have to document a historian's evaluation of his presidency. The best rule to follow is if you have doubts, document.

45c Revising to Eliminate Plagiarism

You can avoid plagiarism by using documentation whenever it is required and by adhering to the following guidelines.

(1) Enclose Borrowed Words in Quotation Marks

Original: Historically, only a handful of families have dominated the fireworks industry in the West. Details such as chemical recipes and mixing procedures were cloaked in secrecy and passed down from one generation to the next. . . . One effect of familial secretiveness is that, until recent decades, basic pyrotechnic research was rarely performed, and even when it was, the results were not generally reported in scientific journals. (Conkling, John A. "Pyrotechnics." *Scientific American* July 1990: 96)

Plagiarism: John A. Conkling points out that until recently, little scientific research was done on the chemical properties of fireworks, and when it was, the results were not generally reported in scientific journals (96).

Even though the writer documents the source of his information, he uses the source's exact words without placing them in quotation marks.

Correct (Borrowed Words in Quotation Marks): John A. Conkling points out that until recently, little scientific research was done on the chemical properties of fireworks, and when it was, "the results were generally not reported in scientific journals" (96).

Correct (Paraphrase): John A. Conkling points out that the little research conducted on the chemical composition of fireworks was seldom reported in the scientific literature (96).

http://kirsznermandell.wadsworth.com

Computer Tip: Plagiarism and Internet Sources

Any time you download text from the Internet, you run the risk of committing unintentional plagiarism. To avoid the possibility of plagiarism, follow these guidelines:

- Download information into individual files so that you can keep track of your sources.
- Do not simply cut and paste blocks of downloaded text into your paper; summarize or paraphrase this material first.
- If you record the exact words of your source, enclose them in quotation marks.
- Whether your information is from emails, online discussion groups, listservs, or Web sites, give proper credit by providing appropriate documentation.
- Always document figures, tables, charts, and graphs obtained from the Internet or from any other electronic source.

(2) Do Not Imitate a Source's Syntax and Phrasing

Original: Let's be clear: this wish for politically correct casting goes only one way, the way designed to redress the injuries of centuries. When Pat Carroll, who is a woman, plays Falstaff, who is not, casting is considered a stroke of brilliance. When Josette Simon, who is black, plays Maggie in *After the Fall*, a part Arthur Miller patterned after Marilyn Monroe and which has traditionally been played not by white women, but by blonde white women, it is hailed as a breakthrough.

But when the pendulum moves the other way, the actors' union balks. (Quindlen, Anna. "Error, Stage Left." *New York Times* 12 Aug. 1990, sec. 1: 21)

Plagiarism: Let us be honest. The desire for politically appropriate casting goes in only one direction, the direction intended to make up for the damage done over hundreds of years. When Pat Carroll, a female, is cast as Falstaff, a male, the decision is a brilliant one. When Josette Simon, a black woman, is cast as Maggie in *After the Fall*, a role that Arthur Miller based on Marilyn Monroe and that has usually been played by a woman who is not only white but also blonde, it is considered a major advance.

But when the shoe is on the other foot, the actors' union resists (Quindlen 21).

Although this writer does not use the exact words of her source, she closely imitates the original's syntax and phrasing, simply substituting synonyms for the author's words.

Correct (Paraphrase; One Distinctive Phrase Placed in Quotation Marks): According to Anna Quindlen, the actors' union supports "politically correct casting" (21) only when it means casting a woman or minority group member in a role created for a male or a Caucasian. Thus, it is acceptable for actress Pat Carroll to play Falstaff or for black actress Josette Simon to play Marilyn Monroe; in fact, casting decisions such as these are praised. But when it comes to casting a Caucasian in a role intended for an African American, Asian, or Hispanic, the union objects (21).

NOTE: Although the parenthetical documentation at the end identifies the passage's source, the quotation requires separate documentation.

(3) Document Statistics Obtained from a Source

Although many people assume that statistics are common knowledge, they are usually the result of original research and must therefore be documented. Moreover, providing the source of the statistics helps readers to assess their reliability.

Correct: According to one study, male drivers between the ages of sixteen and twenty-four accounted for the majority of accidents. Of 303 accidents recorded almost one half took place before the drivers were legally allowed to drive at eighteen (Schuman et al. 1027).

(4) Differentiate Your Words and Ideas from Those of the Source

Original: At some colleges and universities traditional survey courses of world and English literature . . . have been scrapped or diluted. At others they are in peril. At still others they will be. What replaces them is sometimes a mere option of electives, sometimes "multicultural" courses introducing material from Third World cultures and thinning out an already thin sampling of Western writings, and sometimes courses geared especially to issues of class, race, and gender. Given the notorious lethargy of academic decision-making, there has probably been more clamor than change; but if there's enough clamor, there will be change. (Howe, Irving. "The Value of the Canon." *The New Republic* 2 Feb. 1991: 40–47)

Plagiarism: Debates about expanding the literary canon take place at many colleges and universities across the United States. At many universities, the Western literature survey courses have been edged out by courses that emphasize minority concerns. These courses are "thinning out an already thin sampling of Western writings" in favor of courses geared especially to issues of "class, race, and gender" (Howe 40).

Because the writer does not differentiate his ideas from those of his source, it appears that only the quotations in the last sentence are borrowed when, in fact, the first sentence also owes a debt to the original. The writer should have clearly identified the boundaries of the borrowed material by introducing it with an identifying tag and ending with documentation. (Note that a quotation *always* requires separate documentation.)

Correct: Debates about expanding the literary canon take place at many colleges and universities across the United States. According to critic Irving Howe, at many universities the Western literature survey courses have been edged out by courses that emphasize minority concerns (41). These courses, says Howe, are "thinning out an already thin sampling of Western writings" in favor of "courses geared especially to issues of class, race, and gender" (40).

Checklist: Avoiding Plagiarism

☐ **Take careful notes.** Be sure you have recorded information from your sources carefully and accurately.
☐ **In your notes, clearly identify borrowed material.** In handwritten notes, put all words borrowed from your
sources inside circled quotation marks, and enclose your own
comments within brackets. If you are taking notes on a computer, boldface all quotation marks.
☐ **In your paper, differentiate your ideas from those of your
sources** by clearly introducing borrowed material with an
identifying tag and by following it with documentation.
☐ **Enclose all direct quotations** used in your paper within
quotation marks.
☐ **Review all paraphrases and summaries** in your paper to
make certain they are in your own words and that any distinctive words and phrases from a source are quoted.
☐ **Document all quoted material and all paraphrases and
summaries** of your sources.
☐ **Document all information** that is open to dispute or that is
not common knowledge.
☐ **Document all opinions, conclusions, figures, tables, statistics, graphs, and charts** taken from a source.
☐ **Never submit the work of another person as your own.**
Do not buy a paper from an online paper mill or use a paper
given to you by a friend. In addition, do not include in your
paper passages that have been written by a friend, relative, or
writing tutor.

Exercise 45.1

The following student paragraph uses material from three sources,
but its author has neglected to cite them. After reading the paragraph
and the three sources that follow it, identify the material that has been
quoted directly from a source. Compare the wording to the original
for accuracy, and insert quotation marks where necessary, making sure
the quoted passages fit smoothly into the paragraph. Differentiate the
ideas of the student from those of each of the three sources by using
identifying tags to introduce any quotations. (If you think the student
did not need to quote a passage, paraphrase it instead.) Finally, add
parenthetical documentation for each piece of information that requires it.

Student Paragraph

     Oral history is an important way of capturing certain
aspects of the past that might otherwise be lost. While
history books relate the stories of great men and great

events, rarely do they include the experiences of ordinary people—slaves, concentration camp survivors, and the illiterate, for example. By providing information about the people and emotions of the past, oral history makes sense of the present and gives a glimpse of the likely future. But because any particular rendition of a life history relies heavily on personal memory, great care must be taken to evaluate and explain the context of an oral history. Like any other historical account, oral history is just one of many possible versions of an individual's past.

Source 1

Oral history relies heavily on memory, a notoriously malleable entity; people remake the past in light of present concerns and knowledge. Yet not all memories are false, and oral history gives us testimony that might otherwise be lost—stories of slaves, of concentration camp survivors, of the illiterate and the obscure, of the legion "ordinary people" who rarely find their way into the history books. Oral history gives us the human element, the thoughts and emotions and confusions that lie beneath the calm surface of written documents. Even when people remake the past because memories are faulty or unbearable, we can learn much about the ways in which the past affects the present. (Freedman, Jean R. "Never Underestimate the Power of a Bus: My Journey to Oral History." *Oral History Review* 29.2 [2002]: 30.)

Source 2

[There is a] widely held view that history belongs to great men and great events, not ordinary people or ordinary life. Yet we know that "ordinary" people in our local districts have important stories to tell. . . . Local histories tell us, on the one hand, that things were done differently in the past, but on the other hand, that in essence people and emotions were much the same. We need to learn from the past to make sense of the present, and get a glimpse of the likely future. (Gregg, Alison. "Planning and Managing an Oral History Collection." *Aplis* 13.4 [Dec. 2000]: 174.)

Source 3

One aspect of oral history . . . concerns the way in which any particular rendition of a life history is a product of the personal present. It is well-recognized that chronicles of the past are invariably a product of the present, so that different "presents" inspire different versions of the past. Just as all historical accounts—the very questions posed or the interpretive framework imposed—are informed by the historian's present, so, too, is a life history structured by both the interviewer's and the narrator's present. . . . [O]ral history cannot be treated as a source of some narrative truth, but rather as one of many possible versions of an individual's past. . . . [and] the stories told in an oral history are not simply the source of explanation, but rather require explanation. (Honig, Emily. "Getting to the Source: Striking Lives: Oral History and the Politics of Memory." *Journal of Women's History* 9.1 [1997]: 139.)

18. More than one work from the same anthology (p. 409)
19. An article in a reference book (signed/unsigned) (p. 409)

Dissertations, Pamphlets, Government Publications

20. A dissertation (published/unpublished) (p. 409)
21. A pamphlet (p. 410)
22. A government publication (p. 410)

Entries for Articles

Scholarly Journals

23. An article in a scholarly journal with continuous pagination through an annual volume (p. 411)
24. An article in a scholarly journal with separate pagination in each issue (p. 411)

Magazines and Newspapers

25. An article in a weekly magazine (signed/unsigned) (p. 411)
26. An article in a monthly magazine (p. 411)
27. An article that does not appear on consecutive pages (p. 411)
28. An article in a newspaper (signed/unsigned) (p. 412)
29. An editorial in a newspaper (p. 412)
30. A letter to the editor of a newspaper (p. 412)
31. A book review in a newspaper (p. 412)
32. An article with a title within its title (p. 412)

Entries for Miscellaneous Print and Nonprint Sources

Lectures and Interviews

33. A lecture (p. 413)
34. A personal interview (p. 413)
35. A published interview (p. 413)

Letters

36. A personal letter (p. 413)
37. A letter published in a collection (p. 413)
38. A letter in a library's archives (p. 413)

Films, Videotapes, Radio and Television Programs, Recordings

39. A film (p. 413)
40. A videotape, DVD, or laser disc (p. 414)
41. A radio or television program (p. 414)
42. A recording (p. 414)

Paintings, Photographs, Cartoons, Advertisements

43. A painting (p. 414)
44. A photograph (p. 414)

Chapter 46	MLA Documentation Style

Documentation, the formal acknowledgment of the sources you use in your paper, enables your readers to judge the quality and originality of your work. This chapter explains and illustrates the documentation style recommended by the Modern Language Association (MLA). Chapter 47 discusses the documentation style of the American Psychological Association (APA).

46a Using MLA Style

MLA style* is required by many teachers of English and other languages as well as by teachers in other humanities disciplines. This method of documentation has three parts: *parenthetical references in the body of the paper* (also known as *in-text citations*), *a works-cited list,* and *content notes.*

(1) Parenthetical References in the Text

MLA documentation uses **parenthetical references** in the body of the paper keyed to a works-cited list at the end of the paper. A typical parenthetical reference consists of the author's last name and a page number.

```
The colony's religious and political freedom appealed to

many idealists in Europe (Ripley 132).
```

*MLA documentation style follows the guidelines set in the *MLA Handbook for Writers of Research Papers,* 6th ed. New York: MLA, 2003.

Close-up: Placing Parenthetical References

To make sure each parenthetical reference in your paper clearly refers to the information it documents, follow these guidelines.

- Place documentation after each quotation as well as at the end of each passage of paraphrase or summary. Avoid using a single parenthetical reference to cover several pieces of information from a variety of different sources.
- Place documentation so that it will not interrupt your discussion—ideally, at the end of a sentence.
- To differentiate your ideas from those of your sources, place an identifying tag before, and documentation after, each piece of borrowed material.

See
44d

To distinguish two or more sources by the same author, include an appropriate shortened title in the parenthetical reference after the author's name.

```
Penn emphasized his religious motivation (Kelley, William

Penn 116).
```

If you state the author's name or the title of the work in your discussion, do not include it in the parenthetical reference.

```
Penn's political motivation is discussed by Joseph J.

Kelley in Pennsylvania, The Colonial Years, 1681-1776

(44).
```

Close-up: Punctuating with MLA Parenthetical References

Paraphrases and Summaries   Parenthetical references are placed *before* the sentence's end punctuation.

```
Penn's writings epitomize seventeenth-century

religious thought (Dengler and Curtis 72).
```

Quotations Run In with the Text   Parenthetical references are placed *after* the quotation but *before* the end punctuation.

```
As Ross says, "Penn followed his conscience in all

matters" (127).

According to Williams, "Penn's utopian vision was

informed by his Quaker beliefs . . ." (72).
```

Quotations Set Off from the Text   When you quote more than
four lines of <u>prose</u> or more than three lines of <u>poetry</u>, parenthetical references are placed one space after the end punctuation.

See
33b

> According to Arthur Smith, William Penn envisioned a
> state based on his religious principles:
>
>> Pennsylvania would be a commonwealth in
>> which all individuals would follow God's
>> truth and develop according to God's law.
>> For Penn, this concept of government was
>> self-evident. It would be a mistake to see
>> Pennsylvania as anything but an expression
>> of Penn's religious beliefs. (314)

SAMPLE MLA PARENTHETICAL REFERENCES

1. A Work by a Single Author

Fairy tales reflect the emotions and fears of children
(Bettelheim 23).

2. A Work by Two or Three Authors

The conventions of the ancient Greek theater reflect the
culture in which they developed (Watson and McKernie 17).

With the advent of behaviorism, psychology began a new
phase of inquiry (Cowen, Barbo, and Crum 31-34).

3. A Work by More Than Three Authors
List only the first author, followed by et al. ("and others").

The European powers believed they could change the
fundamentals of Muslim existence (Bull et al. 395).

4. A Work in Multiple Volumes
If you list more than one volume of a multivolume work in your
works-cited list, include the appropriate volume and page number
(separated by a colon followed by a space).

The French Revolution had a great influence on William
Blake (Raine 1: 52-53).

5. A Work without a Listed Author
Use a shortened version of the title in the parenthetical reference, beginning with the word by which it is alphabetized in the works-cited list.

> In spite of political unrest, Soviet television remained
>
> fairly conservative, ignoring all challenges to the
>
> system ("Soviet" 3).

6. A Work That Is One Page Long
Do not include a page reference for a one-page article.

> Sixty percent of Arab Americans work in white-collar jobs
>
> (El-Badru).

7. An Indirect Source
If you must use a statement by one author that is quoted in the work of another author, indicate that the material is from an indirect source with the abbreviation qtd. in ("quoted in").

> Wagner stated that myth and history stood before him
>
> "with opposing claims" (qtd. in Thomas 65).

8. More Than One Work
Cite each work as you normally would, separating one from the other with a semicolon.

> The Brooklyn Bridge has been used as a subject by many
>
> American artists (McCullough 144; Tashjian 58).

NOTE: Long parenthetical references distract readers. Whenever possible, present them as <u>content notes</u>.

9. A Literary Work
When citing a work of prose, it is often helpful to include more than the author's name and the page number in the parenthetical citation. Follow the page number with a semicolon, and then add any additional information that might be necessary.

> In <u>Moby-Dick</u>, Melville refers to a whaling expedition
>
> funded by Louis XIV of France (151; ch. 24).

Parenthetical references to poetry do not include page numbers. In parenthetical references to long poems, cite division and line numbers, separating them with a period.

> In the <u>Aeneid</u>, Virgil describes the ships as cleaving the
>
> "green woods reflected in the calm water" (8.124).

(In this citation, the reference is to book 8, line 124 of the *Aeneid*.)

When citing short poems, identify the poet and the poem in the text of the paper and use line numbers in the citation.

```
In "A Song in the Front Yard," Brooks says, "I've stayed

in the front yard all my life / I want a peek at the

back" (lines 1-2).
```

NOTE: When citing lines of a poem, include the word `line` (or `lines`) in the first parenthetical reference; use just numbers in subsequent references.

In citing plays, include the act, scene, and line numbers (in arabic numerals), separated by periods; titles of well-known literary works are often abbreviated (<u>Mac</u>. 2.2.14-16).

10. The Bible

MLA style requires a biblical citation to include the version of the Bible (underlined) and the book (abbreviated if longer than four letters, but not underlined or enclosed in quotation marks), followed by the chapter and verse numbers (separated by a period).

```
The cynicism of the speaker is apparent when he says,

"All things are wearisome; no man can speak of them all"

(New England Bible, Eccles. 1.8).
```

NOTE: The first time you use a biblical citation, give the version in your parenthetical reference; after that, only include the book. If you are using more than one version, however, include the version in each in-text citation.

11. An Entire Work

When citing an entire work, include the author's name and the work's title in the text of your paper rather than in a parenthetical reference.

```
Herbert Gans's The Urban Villagers is a study of an

Italian-American neighborhood in Boston.
```

12. Two or More Authors with the Same Last Name

To distinguish authors with the same last name, include their initials in the parenthetical references.

```
Recent increases in crime have caused thousands of urban

homeowners to install alarms (L. Cooper, 115). Some of

these alarms use sophisticated sensors that were

developed by the army (D. Cooper, 76).
```

13. A Government Document or a Corporate Author

Cite such works using the organization's name followed by the page number (American Automobile Association 34). You can avoid long parenthetical references by working the organization's name into your paper.

> According to the President's Commission for the Study of
>
> Ethical Problems in Medicine and Biomedical and
>
> Behavioral Research, the issues relating to euthanasia
>
> are complicated (76).

14. An Electronic Source

If a reference to an electronic source includes paragraph numbers rather than page numbers, use the abbreviation par. or pars. followed by the paragraph number or numbers.

> The earliest type of movie censorship came in the form of
>
> licensing fees, and in Deer River, Minnesota, "a
>
> licensing fee of $200 was deemed not excessive for a town
>
> of 1000" (Ernst, par. 20).

If the electronic source has no page or paragraph numbers, try to cite the work in your discussion rather than in a parenthetical reference. By consulting your works-cited list, readers will be able to determine that the source is electronic and may therefore not have page numbers.

> In her article "Limited Horizons," Lynne Cheney says that
>
> schools do best when students read literature not for
>
> practical information but for its insights into the human
>
> condition.

(2) Works-Cited List

The **works-cited list**, which appears at the end of your paper, is an alphabetical listing of all the research materials you cite. Double-space within and between entries on the list, and indent the second and subsequent lines of each entry one-half inch (five spaces). (**See 46b** for full manuscript guidelines.)

SAMPLE MLA WORKS-CITED LIST ENTRIES

Print Sources

Entries for Books

Book citations include the author's name; book title (underlined); and publication information (place, publisher, date). Capitalize all major words of the title except articles, coordinating conjunctions, prepositions, and the *to* of an infinitive (unless such a word is the first or last word of the title or subtitle). Do not underline the period that follows a book's title.

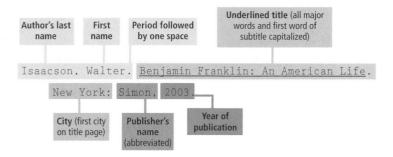

Author's last name | First name | Period followed by one space | Underlined title (all major words and first word of subtitle capitalized)

Isaacson, Walter. Benjamin Franklin: An American Life.
    New York: Simon, 2003.

City (first city on title page) | Publisher's name (abbreviated) | Year of publication

Authors

1. A Book by One Author
Use a short form of the publisher's name; *Alfred A. Knopf, Inc.*, for example, is shortened to *Knopf*, and *Oxford University Press* becomes *Oxford UP.*

> Bettelheim, Bruno. The Uses of Enchantment: The Meaning
>   and Importance of Fairy Tales. New York: Knopf, 1976.

2. A Book by Two or Three Authors
List the first author last name first. List subsequent authors first name first in the order in which they appear on the title page.

> Watson, Jack, and Grant McKernie. A Cultural History of
>   the Theater. New York: Longman, 1993.

3. A Book by More Than Three Authors
You may either list the first author only, followed by et al. ("and others"), or you may include all the authors in the order in which they appear on the title pages.

> Bull, Henry, et al. The Near East. New York: Oxford UP,
>   1990.

Bull, Henry, George Carr, Kim Hoffman, and Gordon Forbes.

The Near East. New York: Oxford UP, 1990.

4. Two or More Books by the Same Author

List books by the same author in alphabetical order by title. After the first entry, use three unspaced hyphens followed by a period in place of the author's name.

Thomas, Lewis. The Lives of a Cell: Notes of a Biology

Watcher. New York: Viking, 1974.

---. The Medusa and the Snail: More Notes of a Biology

Watcher. New York: Viking, 1979.

If the author is the editor or translator of the second entry, place a comma and the appropriate abbreviation after the hyphens (---, ed.). See entry 6 for more on edited books and entry 13 for more on translated books.

5. A Book by a Corporate Author

A book is cited by its corporate author when individual members of the association, commission, or committee that produced it are not identified on the title page.

American Automobile Association. Western Canada and

Alaska. Heathrow: AAA Publishing, 1999.

Editions, Multivolume Works, Forewords, Translations

6. An Edited Book

An edited book is a work prepared for publication by a person other than the author. If your focus is on the *author's* work, begin your citation with the author's name. After the title, include the abbreviation Ed. ("Edited by") followed by the name of the editor or editors.

Bartram, William. The Travels of William Bartram. Ed.

Mark Van Doren. New York: Dover, 1955.

If your focus is on the *editor's* work, begin your citation with the editor's name followed by the abbreviation ed. ("editor") if there is one editor or eds. ("editors") if there is more than one. After the title, give the author's name preceded by the word By.

Van Doren, Mark, ed. The Travels of William Bartram. By

William Bartram. New York: Dover, 1955.

7. A Subsequent Edition of a Book

When citing an edition other than the first, indicate the edition number that appears on the work's title page.

```
Gans, Herbert J. The Urban Villagers. 2nd ed. New York:

    Free, 1982.
```

8. A Republished Book
Include the original publication date after the title of a republished book—for example, a paperback version of a hardcover book.

```
Wharton, Edith. The House of Mirth. 1905. New York:

    Scribner's, 1975.
```

9. A Book in a Series
If the title page indicates that the book is a part of a series, include the series name, neither underlined nor enclosed in quotation marks, and the series number, followed by a period, before the publication information.

```
Davis, Bertram H. Thomas Percy. Twayne's English Authors

    Ser. 313. Boston: Twayne, 1981.
```

10. A Multivolume Work
When all volumes of a multivolume work have the same title, include the number of the volume you are using.

```
Raine, Kathleen. Blake and Tradition. Vol. 1. Princeton:

    Princeton UP, 1968.
```

When you use two or more volumes, cite the entire work.

```
Raine, Kathleen. Blake and Tradition. 2 vols. Princeton:

    Princeton UP, 1968.
```

If the volume you are using has an individual title, you may cite the title without mentioning any other volumes.

```
Durant, Will, and Ariel Durant. The Age of Napoleon. New

    York: Simon, 1975.
```

If you wish, however, you may include supplemental information such as the number of the volume, the title of the entire work, the total number of volumes, and the inclusive publication dates.

11. The Foreword, Preface, or Afterword of a Book

```
Taylor, Telford. Preface. Less Than Slaves. By Benjamin

    B. Ferencz. Cambridge: Harvard UP, 1979. xiii-xxii.
```

12. A Book with a Title within Its Title
If the book you are citing contains a title that is normally underlined to indicate italics (a novel, play, or long poem, for example), do *not* underline the interior title.

```
Knoll, Robert E., ed. Storm over The Waste Land. Chicago:
     Scott, 1964.
```

If the book you are citing contains a title that is normally enclosed within quotation marks, keep the quotation marks.

```
Herzog, Alan, ed. Twentieth Century Interpretations of
     "To a Skylark." Englewood Cliffs: Prentice, 1975.
```

13. A Translation

```
García Márquez, Gabriel. One Hundred Years of Solitude.
     Trans. Gregory Rabassa. New York: Avon, 1991.
```

14. The Bible

Underline the title and give all publication information.

```
The New English Bible with the Apocrypha: Oxford Study
     Edition. New York: Oxford UP, 1976.
```

Parts of Books

15. A Short Story, Play, or Poem in an Anthology

```
Chopin, Kate. "The Storm." Literature: Reading, Reacting,
     Writing. Ed. Laurie G. Kirszner and Stephen R.
     Mandell. 5th ed. Boston: Wadsworth, 2004. 176-79.
Shakespeare, William. Othello, The Moor of Venice.
     Shakespeare: Six Plays and the Sonnets. Ed. Thomas
     Marc Parrott and Edward Hubler. New York:
     Scribner's, 1956. 145-91.
```

See entry 18 for guidelines about how to cite more than one work from the same anthology.

16. A Short Story, Play, Poem, or Essay in a Collection of an Author's Work

```
Walcott, Derek. "Nearing La Guaira." Selected Poems. New
     York: Farrar, 1964. 47-48.
```

17. An Essay in an Anthology

Even if you cite only one page of the essay in your paper, supply inclusive page numbers for the entire essay.

```
Lloyd, G. E. R. "Science and Mathematics." The Legacy of
     Greece. Ed. Moses I. Finley. New York: Oxford UP,
     1981. 256-300.
```

18. More Than One Work from the Same Anthology

List each work from the same anthology separately, followed by a cross-reference to the entire anthology. List complete publication information for the anthology itself.

Bolgar, Robert R. "The Greek Legacy." Finley 429-72.

Finley, Moses I., ed. The Legacy of Greece. New York:

Oxford UP, 1981.

Williams, Bernard. "Philosophy." Finley 202-55.

19. An Article in a Reference Book (Signed/Unsigned)

For a signed article, begin with the author's name. For unfamiliar reference books, include full publication information.

Drabble, Margaret. "Expressionism." The Oxford Companion

to English Literature. 5th ed. New York: Oxford UP,

1985.

If the article is unsigned, begin with the title. For familiar reference books, do not include publication information.

"Cubism." The Encyclopedia Americana. 1994 ed.

NOTE: You may omit page numbers if the reference book lists entries alphabetically.

If you are listing one definition among several from a dictionary, include the abbreviation Def. ("Definition") along with the letter or number that corresponds to the definition.

"Justice." Def. 2b. The Concise Oxford Dictionary. 10th

ed. 1999.

Dissertations, Pamphlets, Government Publications

20. A Dissertation (Published/Unpublished)

Cite a published dissertation the same way you would cite a book, but add relevant dissertation information before the publication information. For dissertations published by University Microfilms International (UMI), include the order number at the end of the entry.

Peterson, Shawn. Loving Mothers and Lost Daughters:

Images of Female Kinship Relations in Selected

Novels of Toni Morrison. Diss. U of Oregon, 1993.

Ann Arbor: UMI, 1994. ATT 9322935.

NOTE: University Microfilms, which publishes most of the dissertations in the United States, also publishes in CD-ROM. For the proper format for citing CD-ROMs, see entries 74 and 75.

Use quotation marks for the title of an unpublished dissertation.

Romero, Yolanda Garcia. "The American Frontier Experience
    in Twentieth-Century Northwest Texas." Diss. Texas
    Tech U, 1993.

21. A Pamphlet
If no author is listed, begin with the underlined title.

Existing Light Photography. Rochester: Kodak, 1989.

22. A Government Publication
If the publication has no listed author, begin with the name of the government followed by the name of the agency; you may use an abbreviation if its meaning is clear: United States. Cong. Senate.

United States. Office of Consumer Affairs. 2003
    Consumer's Resource Handbook. Washington: GPO, 2003.

NOTE: GPO is the abbreviation for Government Printing Office.

When citing two or more publications by the same government, use three unspaced hyphens in place of the name for the second and subsequent entries. If you also cite more than one work from the same agency of that government, use an additional set of unspaced hyphens in place of the agency name.

United States. FAA. Passenger Airline Safety in the
    Twenty-First Century. Washington: GPO, 2003.

---. ---. Recycled Air in Passenger Airline Cabins.
    Washington: GPO, 2002.

Entries for Articles
Article citations include the author's name; the title of the article (in quotation marks); the title of the periodical (underlined); the month (abbreviated except for May, June, and July) and the year; and the pages on which the full article appears, without the abbreviations *p.* or *pp.*

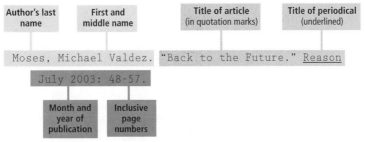

Scholarly Journals

23. An Article in a Scholarly Journal with Continuous Pagination through an Annual Volume

For an article in a journal with continuous pagination—for example, one in which an issue ends on page 172 and the next issue begins with page 173—include the volume number, followed by the date of publication (in parentheses). Follow the publication date with a colon, a space, and the inclusive page numbers.

Huntington, John. "Science Fiction and the Future."

College English 37 (1975): 340-58.

24. An Article in a Scholarly Journal with Separate Pagination in Each Issue

For a journal in which each issue begins with page 1, include the volume number, a period, and the issue number.

Sipes, R. G. "War, Sports, and Aggression: An Empirical

Test of Two Rival Theories." American Anthropologist

4.2 (1973): 65-84.

Magazines and Newspapers

25. An Article in a Weekly Magazine (Signed/Unsigned)

For signed articles, start with the author, last name first. In dates, the day precedes the month.

Traub, James. "The Hearts and Minds of City College." New

Yorker 7 June 1993: 42-53.

For unsigned articles, start with the title of the article.

"Solzhenitsyn: A Candle in the Wind." Time 23 Mar.

1970: 70.

26. An Article in a Monthly Magazine

Roll, Lori. "Careers in Engineering." Working Woman

Nov. 1982: 62.

27. An Article That Does Not Appear on Consecutive Pages

When, for example, an article begins on page 120 and then skips to page 186, include only the first page number and a plus sign.

Griska, Linda. "Stress and Job Performance." Psychology

Today Nov.-Dec. 1995: 120+.

28. An Article in a Newspaper (Signed/Unsigned)

```
Oates, Joyce Carol. "When Characters from the Page Are
     Made Flesh on the Screen." New York Times 23 Mar.
     1986, late ed.: C1+.

"Soviet Television." Los Angeles Times 13 Dec. 1990,
     sec. 2: 3+.
```

NOTE: Omit the article *the* from the title of a newspaper even if the actual title includes the article.

29. An Editorial in a Newspaper

```
"Tough Cops, Not Brutal Cops." Editorial. New York Times
     5 May 1994, late ed.: A26.
```

30. A Letter to the Editor of a Newspaper

```
Chang, Paula. Letter. Philadelphia Inquirer 10 Dec. 2003,
     suburban ed.: A17.
```

31. A Book Review in a Newspaper

```
Fox-Genovese, Elizabeth. "Big Mess on Campus." Rev. of
     Illiberal Education: The Politics of Race and Sex on
     Campus, by Dinesh D'Souza. Washington Post 15 Apr.
     1991, ntnl. weekly ed.: 32.
```

32. An Article with a Title within Its Title
If the article you are citing contains a title that is normally enclosed within quotation marks, use single quotation marks for the interior title.

```
Nash, Robert. "About 'The Emperor of Ice Cream.'"
     Perspectives 7 (1954): 122-24.
```

If the article you are citing contains a title that is normally underlined to indicate italics, underline it in your works-cited entry.

```
Leicester, H. Marshall, Jr. "The Art of Impersonation: A
     General Prologue to The Canterbury Tales." and PMLA
     95 (1980): 213-24.
```

Entries for Other Miscellaneous Print and Nonprint Sources

Lectures and Interviews

33. A Lecture

Sandman, Peter. "Communicating Scientific Information."

     Communications Seminar, Dept. of Humanities and

     Communications. Drexel U, 26 Oct. 1999.

34. A Personal Interview

West, Cornel. Personal interview. 28 Dec. 2002.

Tannen, Deborah. Telephone interview. 8 June 2003.

35. A Published Interview

Stavros, George. "An Interview with Gwendolyn Brooks."

     Contemporary Literature 11.1 (Winter 1970):

     1-20.

Letters

36. A Personal Letter

Tan, Amy. Letter to the author. 7 Apr. 2001.

37. A Letter Published in a Collection

Joyce, James. "Letter to Louis Gillet." 20 Aug. 1931.

     James Joyce. By Richard Ellmann. New York: Oxford

     UP, 1965. 631.

38. A Letter in a Library's Archives

Stieglitz, Alfred. Letter to Paul Rosenberg. 5 Sept.

     1923. Stieglitz Archive. Yale U Arts Lib., New Haven.

Films, Videotapes, Radio and Television Programs, Recordings

39. A Film

Include the title of the film (underlined), the distributor, and the date, along with other information of use to readers, such as the names of the performers, the director, and the writer.

Citizen Kane. Dir. Orson Welles. Perf. Welles, Joseph

     Cotten, Dorothy Comingore, and Agnes Moorehead. RKO,

     1941.

If you are focusing on the contribution of a particular person, begin with that person's name.

    Welles, Orson, dir. Citizen Kane. Perf. Welles, Joseph

        Cotten, Dorothy Comingore, and Agnes Moorehead. RKO,

        1941.

40. A Videotape, DVD, or Laser Disc
Cite a videotape, DVD (digital videodisc), or laser disc like a film, but include the medium before the name of the distributor.

    Miller, Arthur. Interview. The Crucible. Dir. William

        Schiff. Videocassette. The Mosaic Group, 1987.

41. A Radio or Television Program

    "Prime Suspect 3." By Lynda La Plante. Perf. Helen

        Mirren. Mystery! PBS. WNET, New York. 28 Apr. 1994.

42. A Recording
List the composer, conductor, or performer (whichever you are focusing on), followed by the title (and, when citing jacket notes, a description of the material), manufacturer, and year of issue.

    Boubill, Alain, and Claude-Michel Schönberg. Miss Saigon.

        Perf. Lea Salonga, Claire Moore, and Jonathan Pryce.

        Cond. Martin Koch. Geffen, 1989.

    Marley, Bob. "Crisis." Lyrics. Bob Marley and the

        Wailers. Kava Island Records, 1978.

Paintings, Photographs, Cartoons, Advertisements

43. A Painting

    Hopper, Edward. Railroad Sunset. 1929. Whitney Museum of

        American Art, New York.

44. A Photograph
Cite a photograph in a museum's collection in the same way you cite a painting.

    Stieglitz, Alfred. The Steerage. 1907. Los Angeles County

        Museum of Art.

To cite a personal photograph, begin with a descriptive title (neither underlined nor set within quotation marks), followed by the place the photograph was taken, the photographer, and the date.

```
Rittenhouse Square, Philadelphia. Personal photograph by

    author. 6 May 2003.
```

45. A Cartoon or Comic Strip

```
Trudeau, Garry. "Doonesbury." Comic strip. Philadelphia

    Inquirer 19 July 1999, late ed.: E13.
```

46. An Advertisement

```
Microsoft. Advertisement. National Review 28 June 1999:

    11.
```

Electronic Sources

Entries from Internet Sites

The documentation style for Internet sources presented here conforms to the most recent guidelines published in the *MLA Handbook for Writers of Research Papers* (6th ed.) and found online at <http://www.mla.org>.

MLA style recognizes that full source information for Internet sources is not always available. Include in your citation whatever information you can reasonably obtain: the title of the Internet site (underlined); the editor of the site (if available); the version number of the source (if applicable); the date of electronic publication (or update); the number or range of pages, paragraphs, or sections (if available); the name of any institution or sponsor; the date of access to the source; and the URL.

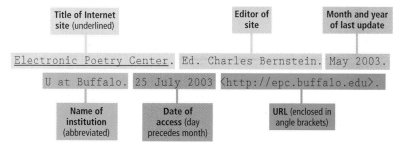

MLA requires that you enclose the electronic address (URL) within angle brackets to distinguish the address from the punctuation in the rest of the citation. If a URL will not fit on a line, the computer will carry the entire URL over to the next line. If you prefer to divide the URL, divide it after a slash. (Do not insert a hyphen.) If it is excessively long, give just the URL of the site's search page. Readers can then access the document by entering the author's name or the source's title.

Internet-Specific Sources

47. An Entire Web Site

<u>Philadelphia Writers Project</u>. Ed. Miriam Kotzen Green.

  May 1998. Drexel U. 12 June 2001 <http://

  www.Drexel.edu/letrs/wwp>.

48. A Document within a Web Site

"D Day: June 7th, 1944." <u>The History Channel Online</u>.

  1999. History Channel. 7 June 2002 <http://

  historychannel.com/thisday/today/997690.html>.

49. A Home Page for a Course

Mulry, David. Composition and Literature. Course home

  page. Jan. 2003-Apr. 2003. Dept. of English, Odessa

  College. 6 Apr. 2003 <http:// www.odessa.edu/

  dept/english/dmulryEnglish_1302.html>.

50. A Personal Home Page

Gainor, Charles. Home page. 22 July 2003. 10 Nov. 2003

  <http://www.chass.utoronto.ca:9094/~char>.

51. A Linked Site

If you get information from a linked site—that is, if you connect from one site to another—include the title of the document you cite (followed by its date) and the abbreviation Lkd. (followed by the original site from which you accessed your document). Follow this with the date of access and the URL.

Schnell, Eric H. <u>Writing for the Web: A Primer for

  Librarians</u>. Vers. 11. Jan. 2003. Lkd. <u>OWL at Purdue

  U</u>. 24 July 2003 <http://owl.english.purdue.edu/

  internet/resources/writetech.html#web>.

52. A Radio Program Accessed from an Internet Archive

Edwards, Bob. "Country Music's First Family." <u>Morning

  Edition</u>. 16 July 2002. <u>NPR Archives</u>. 2 Oct. 2002

  <http://www.npr.org/programs/morning/index.html>.

53. An Email

Smith, Karen. Email to the author. 28 June 2001.

54. An Online Posting (Newsgroup or Online Forum)

Gilford, Mary. "Dog Heroes in Children's Literature."

Online posting. 17 Mar. 1999. 12 Apr. 1999

<news:alt.animals.dogs>.

Schiller, Stephen. "Paper Cost and Publishing Costs."

Online posting. 24 Apr. 1999. 11 May 1999. Book

Forum. 17 May 1999 <www.nytimes.com/webin/

webx?13A^41356.ee765e/0>.

55. A Synchronous Communication (MOO or MUD)
MOOs (multiuser domain, object oriented) and MUDs (multi-user domain) are Internet programs that enable users to communicate in real time. To cite a communication obtained on a MOO or a MUD, give the name (or names) of the writer(s), a description of the event, the date of the event, the forum (LinguaMOO, for example), the date of access, and the URL (starting with `telnet://`).

Guitar, Gwen. Online discussion of Cathy in Emily

Brontë's <u>Wuthering Heights</u>. 17 Mar. 1999. LinguaMOO.

17 Mar. 1999 <telnet://lingua.utdallas.edu:8888>.

Books, Articles, Reviews, Letters, and Reference Works on the Internet

56. A Book

Douglass, Frederick. <u>My Bondage and My Freedom</u>. Boston,

1855. 8 June 2000 <gopher://gopher.vt.edu:10024/

22/178/3>.

57. An Article in a Scholarly Journal
When you cite information from an electronic source that has a print version, include the publication information for the printed source, the number of pages or paragraphs (if available), and the date you accessed it.

Dekoven, Marianne. "Utopias Limited: Post-Sixties and

Postmodern American Fiction." <u>Modern Fiction Studies</u>

41.1 (1995): 13 pp. 17 Mar. 1999 <http://muse.jhu.edu/

journals/mfs.v041/41.1dwkovwn.html>.

58. An Article in a Magazine

Weiser, Jay. "The Tyranny of Informality." <u>Time</u> 26 Feb.

1996. 1 Mar. 2002 <http://www.enews.com/

magazines.tnr/current/022696.3.html>.

59. An Article in a Newspaper

Lohr, Steve. "Microsoft Goes to Court." New York Times
    on the Web 19 Oct. 1998. 29 Apr. 1999 <http://
    www.nytimes.com/web/docroot/library.ciber/
    week/1019business.html>.

60. An Article in a Newsletter

"Unprecedented Cutbacks in History of Science Funding."
    AIP Center for History of Physics 27.2 (Fall 1995).
    26 Feb. 1996 <http://www.aip.org/history/fall95.html>.

61. A Review

Ebert, Roger. Rev. of Star Wars: Episode I—The Phantom
    Menace, dir. George Lucas. Chicago Sun-Times Online
    8 June 2000. 22 June 2000 <http://www.suntimes.com/
    output/ebert1/08show.html>.

62. A Letter to the Editor

Chen-Cheng, Henry H. Letter. New York Times on the Web 19
    July 1999. 19 July 1999 <http://www.nytimes.com/hr/
    mo/day/letters/ichen-cheng.html>.

63. An Article in an Encyclopedia
Include the article's title, the title of the database (underlined), the version number (if available), the date of electronic publication, the sponsor, and the date of access as well as the URL.

"Hawthorne, Nathaniel." Encyclopaedia Britannica Online.
    2002. Encyclopaedia Britannica. 16 May 2002
    <http://www.search.eb.com>.

64. A Government Publication
Cite an online government publication the same way you would a print version; end with the information required for an electronic source.

United States. Dept. of Justice. Bureau of Justice
    Statistics. Violence against Women: Estimates from
    the Redesigned National Crime Victimization Survey.
    Jan. 1995. 10 July 2003 <www.ojp.usdoj.gov/bjs/
    020131.pdf>.

Paintings, Photographs, Cartoons, and Maps on the Internet

65. A Painting

```
Seurat, Georges-Pierre. Evening, Honfleur. 1886. Museum
     of Mod. Art, New York. 8 Jan. 2004 <http://
     www.moma.org/collection/depts/paint_sculpt/
     blowups/paint_sculpt_002.html>.
```

66. A Photograph

```
Brady, Mathew. Ulysses S. Grant 1822-1885. Mathew Brady's
     National Portrait Gallery. 2 Oct. 2002 <http://
     www.npg.si.edu/exh/brady/gallery/56gal.html>.
```

67. A Cartoon

```
Stossel, Sage. "Star Wars: The Next Generation." Cartoon.
     Atlantic Unbound 2 Oct. 2002. 14 Nov. 2002 <http://
     www.theatlantic.com/unbound/sage/ss990519.htm>.
```

68. A Map

```
"Philadelphia, Pennsylvania." Map. U.S. Gazetteer. US
     Census Bureau. 17 July 2000 <http://www.census.gov/
     cgi-bin/gazetteer>.
```

Entries from Subscription Services

Subscription services can be divided into those to which you subscribe (**personal subscription services**), such as America Online, and those to which your library subscribes (**library subscription services**), such as Gale Group Databases, LexisNexis, and ProQuest Direct.

To cite information from a **personal subscription service,** include the name of the database (underlined) as well as the name of the subscription service. If the personal subscription service provides a URL for a specific document, follow the examples in entries 47–55. Personal subscription services usually supply information without a URL, however. If the subscription service enables you to use a **keyword** to access material, type Keyword followed by a colon and the keyword (after the date of access).

```
"Kafka, Franz." Compton's Encyclopedia Online. Vers. 3.1.
     2000. America Online. 8 June 2003. Keyword:
     Compton's.
```

If instead of using a keyword you follow a series of **topic labels,** type the word `Path` followed by a colon and then the sequence of topics (separated by semicolons) you followed to get to the material.

> "Elizabeth Adams." <u>History Resources</u>. 28 Apr. 2002.
>
>   America Online. 11 Nov. 2002. Path: Research;
>
>   Biography; Women in Science; Biographies.

To cite information from a **library subscription service,** supply the publishing information (including page numbers, if available) followed by the name of the database (underlined), the name of the subscription service, the library at which you accessed the database, the date of access, and the URL of the service's home page.

> Luckenbill, Trent. "Environmental Litigation: Down the
>
>   Endless Corridor." <u>Environment</u> 8 June 2001: 34-42.
>
>   <u>ABI/INFORM Global</u>. ProQuest Direct. Drexel U Lib.,
>
>   Philadelphia, PA. 12 Oct. 2001 <http://www.umi.com/
>
>   proquest>.

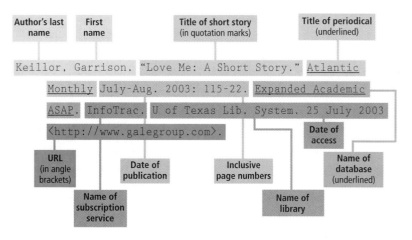

Journal Articles, Magazine Articles, and News Services from Subscription Services

69. A Scholarly Journal Article with Separate Pagination in Each Issue

> Schaefer, Richard J. "Editing Strategies in Television
>
>   News Documentaries." <u>Journal of Communication</u> 47.4
>
>   (1997): 69-89. <u>InfoTrac OneFile Plus</u>. Gale Group
>
>   Databases. Augusta R. Kolwyck Lib., Chattanooga, TN.

Databases. Augusta R. Kolwyck Lib., Chattanooga, TN.

2 Oct. 2002 <http://www.galegroup.com>.

NOTE: Along with the name of the library, you may include the city and state if you think they would be of use.

70. A Scholarly Journal Article with Continuous Pagination Throughout an Annual Volume

Hudson, Nicholas. "Samuel Johnson, Urban Culture, and the

Geography of Postfire London." <u>Studies in English</u>

<u>Literature</u> 42 (2002): 557-80. <u>MasterFILE Premier</u>.

EBSCOhost. Augusta R. Kolwyck Lib., Chattanooga, TN.

15 Sept. 2003 <http://www.epnet.com>.

71. A Monthly Magazine Article

Livermore, Beth. "Meteorites on Ice." <u>Astronomy</u> July

1993: 54-58. <u>Expanded Academic ASAP Plus</u>. Gale Group

Databases. Augusta R. Kolwyck Lib., Chattanooga, TN.

12 Nov. 2003 <http://www.galegroup.com>.

Wright, Karen. "The Clot Thickens." <u>Discover</u> Dec. 1999.

<u>MasterFILE Premier</u>. EBSCOhost. Augusta R.

Kolwyck Lib., Chattanooga, TN. 10 Oct. 2003

<http://www.epnet.com>.

72. A News Service

Ryan, Desmond. "Some Background on the Battle of

Gettysburg." <u>Knight Ridder/Tribune News Service</u>

7 Oct. 1993. <u>InfoTrac OneFile Plus</u>. Gale Group

Databases. Augusta R. Kolwyck Lib., Chattanooga, TN.

16 Nov. 2003 <http://www.galegroup.com>.

73. A Newspaper Article

Meyer, Greg. "Answering Questions about the West Nile

Virus." <u>Dayton Daily News</u> 11 July 2002: Z3-7.

<u>Academic Universe News</u>. LexisNexis. Augusta R.

Kolwyck Lib., Chattanooga, TN. 17 Feb. 2003

<http://web.lexis-nexis.com>.

Other Electronic Sources
DVDs and CD-ROMs

74. A Nonperiodical Publication on DVD, CD-ROM, or Diskette Database

Cite a nonperiodical publication on DVD, CD-ROM, or diskette the same way you would cite a book, but also include a description of the medium of publication.

"Windhover." The Oxford English Dictionary. 2nd ed. DVD.

Oxford: Oxford UP, 2001.

"Whitman, Walt." DiskLit: American Authors. CD-ROM.

Boston: Hall, 2000.

75. A Periodical Publication on a DVD or CD-ROM Database

Zurbach, Kate. "The Linguistic Roots of Three Terms."

Linguistic Quarterly 37 (1994): 12-47. InfoTrac:

Magazine Index Plus. CD-ROM. Information Access.

Jan. 2001.

(3) Content Notes

Content notes—multiple bibliographical citations or other material that does not fit smoothly into the text—are indicated by a **superscript** (raised numeral) in the paper. Notes can appear either as footnotes at the bottom of the page or as endnotes on a separate sheet entitled Notes (or Note, if there is only one endnote), placed after the last page of the paper and before the works-cited list. Content notes are double-spaced within and between entries. The first line is indented one-half inch (five spaces), and subsequent lines are typed flush left.

For Multiple Citations
In the Paper

Many researchers emphasize the necessity of having dying

patients share their experiences.[1]

In the Note

> [1]Kübler-Ross 27; Stinnette 43; Poston 70; Cohen and
> Cohen 31-34; Burke 1: 91-95.

For Other Material
In the Paper

> The massacre during World War I is an event the survivors
> could not easily forget.[2]

In the Note

> [2]For a firsthand account of these events, see
> Bedoukian 178-81.

46b MLA Manuscript Guidelines

Although MLA papers do not usually include abstracts, internal headings, tables, or graphs, this situation is changing. If you want to use any of these elements in your paper, be sure to check with your instructor.

The guidelines in the following checklists are based on the latest version of the *MLA Handbook for Writers of Research Papers.*

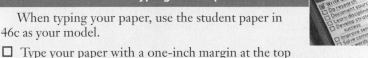

Checklist: Typing Your Paper

When typing your paper, use the student paper in 46c as your model.

☐ Type your paper with a one-inch margin at the top and bottom and on both sides. Double-space your paper throughout.

☐ Type your name, your instructor's name, the course title, and the date on separate lines against the upper-left margin. Double-space, center, and type the title. Double-space again, and begin typing the text of the paper.

☐ Capitalize all important words in your title, but not prepositions, articles, coordinating conjunctions, or the *to* in infinitives (unless they begin or end the title or subtitle). Do not underline your title or enclose it in quotation marks. Never put a period after the title, even if it is a sentence.

☐ Set off more than four lines of prose or more than three lines of poetry by indenting the whole quotation one inch (or ten

(continued)

Typing your paper (continued)

spaces). If you quote a single paragraph or part of a paragraph, do not indent the first line beyond one inch. If you quote two or more paragraphs, indent the first line of each paragraph an additional quarter inch. (If the first sentence does not begin a paragraph, do not indent it. Indent the first line only in successive paragraphs.)

☐ Number all pages of your paper consecutively—including the first—in the upper right-hand corner, one-half inch from the top, flush right. Type your name followed by a space before the page number on every page.

See 46a
☐ If you use source material in your paper, follow **MLA documentation style**.

See 11d

Checklist: Using Visuals

☐ Insert **visuals** into the text as close as possible to where they are discussed.

☐ Label each table with the word `Table` followed by an arabic numeral (for instance, `Table 1`). Double-space, and type a descriptive caption, with the first line flush left with the left-hand margin; indent subsequent lines one-quarter inch. Capitalize the caption as if it were a title. (Both the table number and descriptive caption should appear above the table.) Type the word `Source` below the table, followed by a colon and all source information. Type the first line of the source note flush with the left-hand margin; indent subsequent lines one-quarter inch.

☐ Label other types of visual material—graphs, charts, photographs, clip art, drawings, and so on—`Fig.` (Figure) followed by an arabic numeral (for example, `Fig. 2`). Type each label and a title or caption on the same line, followed by source information, directly below the visual. Type all lines flush with the left-hand margin.

☐ Do not include the source of the visual in the works-cited list unless you use other material from that source elsewhere in the paper.

Checklist: Preparing the MLA Works-Cited List

See 46a3
☐ Begin the works-cited list on a new page after the last page of text or **content notes**, numbered as the next page of the paper.

☐ Center the title Works Cited one inch from the top of the page. Double-space between the title and the first entry.
☐ Each entry on the works-cited list has three divisions: author, title, and publication information. Separate divisions with a period and one space.
☐ List entries alphabetically, last name first. Use the author's full name as it appears on the title page. If a source has no listed author, alphabetize it by the first word of the title (not counting the article).
☐ Type the first line of each entry flush with the left-hand margin; indent subsequent lines one-half inch (or five spaces).
☐ Double-space within and between entries.
☐ Enclose URLs in angle brackets. If a URL carries over to the next line, break the URL after a slash; do not insert a hyphen. If your word-processing program automatically converts URLs to hotlinks, turn off this feature. (You can do this with *Microsoft Word* by opening the AutoCorrect function under the Tools menu, and then selecting AutoFormat.)

46c Sample MLA-Style Research Paper

The paper that follows was written by Kimberly Romney, a student in a second-semester composition class. Kimberly's research paper is an expansion of an essay that she wrote in her first-semester composition class (see pp. 57–62). Examples of Kimberly's writing and research process appear throughout Chapter 41. The following paper includes a sentence outline, MLA-style in-text citations, a notes page, a works-cited list, and a graph.

NOTE: Not all instructors ask students to submit a formal outline along with the final draft of their papers.

1″   ½″

Romney i

Outline

<u>Thesis statement</u>: Although the Internet has changed

1″ our lives for the better, it threatens to leave many 1″

people behind, creating two distinct classes—those

who have access and those who do not.

   I. In the late 1990s, many argued that the

      Internet had ushered in a new age.

      A. Former Vice President Al Gore saw the

         Internet as an empowering tool.

      B. Gore believed the Internet would bring

         knowledge and prosperity to the entire world.

  II. Others questioned the benefits of the Internet.

      A. They argued that the Internet was out of

         reach for many Americans.

         1. Low-income and minority households were

            less likely than others to have computers.

         2. For minorities, Internet content was as

            much of a problem as economics.

      B. They argued that those without Internet

         access had difficulties at school, trouble

         obtaining jobs, and fewer opportunities to

         save money and time as consumers.

      C. They argued that the Internet was widening

         the economic and social divide that already

         separated Americans.

 III. In response, the government, corporations,

      nonprofit organizations, and public libraries

1″

made efforts to bridge the gap between the
"haves" and "have-nots."

A. The federal government has launched programs
like the Community Technology Centers
Program (CTC), which helps finance computer
activity centers for students and adults.

B. The Department of Commerce's Technology
Opportunities Program (TOP) provided money
and services to organizations that needed a
technology boost.

C. The Bill and Melinda Gates Foundation funded
libraries trying to provide patrons with
Internet access.

D. Nonprofit organizations sponsor Web sites
like The Digital Divide Network and The
Civil Rights Forum, which continue to raise
public awareness on a global scale.

IV. Recently, however, the need for many of these
initiatives has been questioned.

A. Recent surveys have found that the Internet
is being used by minorities and the
impoverished.

1. A Media Audit phone survey found an
increase in Internet use among
minorities.

2. A Department of Commerce report also
found an increase in Internet access.

3. The Bush administration argues that the
   digital divide is no longer a problem and
   wants to discontinue federal funding to
   programs like CTC and TOP.

B. Since the dot.com bust, many companies have
   discontinued funding for programs like
   PowerUp, which aimed to broaden Internet
   access.

C. Some groups targeted by digital divide
   programs argue that they might do more harm
   than good.

V. While the digital divide may be narrowing,
   problems remain.

A. The poor, the elderly, the disabled, and
   minorities still have difficulty accessing
   the Internet.

B. The digital divide applies not just to
   Internet access, but to access to technology
   in general.

   1. Technological illiteracy presents
      obstacles to voting.

   2. African Americans are not well
      represented in technology fields.

   3. Children in rural areas lack access to
      technology.

VI. Clearly, much still needs to be done.

A. The Internet must be made available to the
   widest possible audience.

B. Training must be provided to people
   unfamiliar with the new technology.
C. The most likely "have-nots" must be
   targeted.

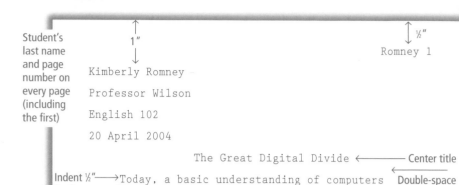

Student's last name and page number on every page (including the first)

1"

½"

Romney 1

Kimberly Romney

Professor Wilson

English 102

20 April 2004

The Great Digital Divide ←——— Center title

Indent ½"——→Today, a basic understanding of computers   Double-space
(or five spaces)
     1"   and how to use them is necessary for success. For this   1"
     ←——→
        reason, those who are unfamiliar with modern digital

technology find themselves at a great disadvantage

when it comes to education and employment. One of the

most exciting digital technologies available is the

information superhighway—better known as the

Internet. The Internet, with its accompanying

software and services, is rapidly changing the way we

access and see information. Clearly, the Internet

offers great promise, but some argue that it is

creating many problems as well. Although the Internet

Thesis statement   has changed our lives for the better, it threatens to

leave many people behind, creating two distinct

classes—those who have access and those who do not.

In the late 1990s, many argued that the Internet

had ushered in a new age, one in which instant

communication would bring people closer together and

eventually eliminate national boundaries. In

Material from Internet source, introduced by author's name, does   "Building a Global Community," former Vice President

Al Gore took this optimistic view, seeing the

Internet as a means "to deepen and extend our oldest

1"

Romney 2

and most cherished global values: rising standards
of living and literacy, an ever-widening circle of
freedom, and individual empowerment." Gore went on
to say that he could envision the day when we would
"extend our knowledge and our prosperity to our most
isolated inner cities, to the barrios, the favelas,
the colonias, and our most remote rural villages."

    Others, however, argued that for many people the
benefits of the Internet were not nearly this obvious
or far-reaching. They maintained that the Internet
was creating what many have called a "digital divide"
(Civil Rights Forum), which excludes a large
percentage of the poor, elderly, disabled, and
members of many minority groups from current
technological advancements. A survey conducted by the
US Department of Commerce in 1999 showed that people
with higher annual household incomes and whites were
more likely to own computers than minorities and
people from low-income households. Approximately 80
percent of households with incomes of $75,000 or
above had computers, compared to 16 percent of
households earning $10,000-$15,000. The survey also
found that in households with incomes between $15,000
and $34,999, only 23 percent of African-American and
26 percent of Hispanic households had computers,
compared to 47 percent of white households (US Dept.
of Commerce).

Side notes (right margin):

not include a parenthetical reference with a paragraph or page number because this information was not provided in the electronic text

Parenthetical documentation refers to material accessed from a Web site

Romney 3

¶ synthesizes information from a Commerce Department study and a newspaper article

Superscript number identifies content note

      While the Department of Commerce study suggested
that financial circumstances were responsible for the
"digital divide," the gap in computer ownership
across incomes indicated that other factors might be
contributing to the disparity. In a 1999 New York
Times op-ed article, Henry Louis Gates Jr. argued
that bridging the digital divide would "require more
than cheap PC's"; it would "involve content" (500).[1]
African Americans were not interested in the
Internet, Gates wrote, because the content rarely
appealed to them. Gates compared the lack of interest
in the Internet with the history of African
Americans' relationship to the recording industry:
"Blacks began to respond to this new medium only when
mainstream companies like Columbia Records introduced
so-called race records, blues and jazz discs aimed at
a nascent African American market" (501). Gates
believed that Web sites that address the needs of
African Americans could play the same role that race
records did for the music industry. Ignoring the race
problem, Gates warned, would lead to a form of cybersegregation that would devastate the African-American
community (501).

Student's original conclusions; no documentation necessary

      It was clear to many that people without
Internet access had difficulty at school, trouble
obtaining jobs, and fewer opportunities to save
money and time as consumers. They also lacked access
to educational materials and to jobs posted on the

Romney 4

Internet. With access to only a portion of available goods and services, people who were offline did not have the advantages that people who were online could routinely get. The Internet was clearly widening the economic and social divide that already separated people in this country.

In response, the government, corporations, nonprofit organizations, and public libraries made efforts to bridge the gap between the "haves" and "have-nots." For example, the Education Department's Community Technology Centers Program (CTC) helped finance computer activity centers for students and adults. Also, the Department of Commerce's Technology Opportunities Program (TOP) provided money and services to organizations that needed more technology to operate efficiently. One recipient was America's Second Harvest, which used the funds to track donations to its national network of food banks (Schwartz, "Report").

Nonprofit organizations also worked to bridge the digital divide. The Bill and Melinda Gates Foundation, for example, has provided libraries across the country with funding that allows them to purchase computers and connect to the Internet (Egan). Nonprofit organizations also sponsor Web sites. The Digital Divide Network is a Web site that posts stories about the digital divide from a variety of perspectives. By posting information, the site's

Parenthetical documentation includes abbreviated title when two or more works by the same author are cited

Romney 5

sponsor hopes to raise awareness of the problems
that the digital divide causes. Similarly, <u>The Civil
Rights Forum</u> is a Web site that focuses on the
digital divide from the perspective of minorities and
people of color. This site says that its goal is to
"bring civil rights organizations and community
groups into the debate over the future of our media
environment."

  Recently, however, the need for many of these
initiatives has been questioned for a variety of
reasons. Some people, for example, argue that the
digital divide is no longer a significant problem. In
2001, a phone survey of more than 350,000 Americans
conducted by the company Media Audit determined that
44 percent of African-American households were
accessing the Internet, "an increase of over 41
percent over the last three years" (Roach). Further,
the company found that Latino households were also
increasingly accessing the Internet. In fact, 42
percent of Latino households were using the Internet
in 2001 (Roach). In February 2002, the US Department
of Commerce published its annual digital divide
report. Using the most recent US Census data, the
report argues that from 1998 to 2001, Internet access
in homes increased significantly. Moreover, as
illustrated in fig. 1, computer use by young people
between the ages of 3 and 24 rose dramatically
between 1998 and 2001.

Romney 6

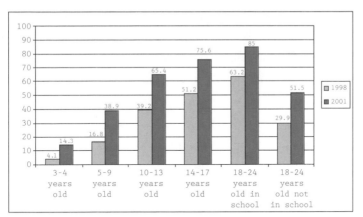

Graph summarizes relevant data. Source information is typed directly below the figure. This information does not appear in the works-cited list because the source is not used elsewhere in the paper.

Fig. 1. United States, Dept. of Commerce, Economics and Statistics Admin., Natl. Telecommunications and Information Admin., A Nation Online: How Americans Are Expanding Their Use of the Internet (Washington, DC: US Dept. of Commerce, 2002) 43, 22 Feb. 2004 <http://www.ntia.doc.gov/ntiahome/dn/anationonline2.pdf>.

Arguing that significant strides have been made to bridge the digital divide, the Bush administration believes that programs like CTC and TOP are no longer needed ("Digital Divide Debated"). At the same time, as the result of the dot.com bust, private industry has withdrawn some support for efforts to bridge the digital divide. One organization, called PowerUp, worked with corporations to create community-based technology centers. In places like Austin, Texas, PowerUp worked to establish a computer center in the

Romney 7

city's impoverished neighborhood by collaborating

with AOL Time Warner and the Austin Urban League

(Doggett). Despite its initial success, the

organization was hard hit by an economic downturn.

According to a PowerUp spokesperson, "The model that

was launched in late 1999 . . . was a model that had

its bloodlines in different economic times. The model

isn't necessarily the best one for these economic

times" (Schwartz, "Lack"). In 2002, PowerUp closed

its offices, leaving the community centers they

created to find funding on their own.

In other cases, the groups targeted by digital

divide programs argue that they might do more harm

than good. A recent article in the Chronicle of

Higher Education observes that many African-American

and other minority groups argue that digital divide

rhetoric might actually stereotype minorities. The

article says that digital divide rhetoric "could

discourage businesses or academics from creating

content or services tailored for minority

communities—ultimately making the digital divide a

self-fulfilling prophecy" (Young). Many scholars and

leaders in the African-American community fear that a

focus on the digital divide will lead to its being

seen as a fact to be accepted rather than as a

problem to be solved. Tara L. McPherson agrees,

arguing that "the idea of challenging the digital

divide is not about denying its existence. But it is

Ellipses indi-
cate that the
student has
deleted
words from
the quotation

Romney 8

to ensure that the focus on the digital divide

doesn't naturalize a kind of exclusion of investment"

(qtd. in Young).

"Qtd. in"
indicates that
McPherson's
comments
were quoted
in Young's
article

     Despite the appearance that the digital divide

is closing and the claims that digital divide

rhetoric may actually be counterproductive, many

public officials and private interest groups continue

to voice their concerns that gaps in technological

literacy and availability remain a problem among

many populations and communities. In fact, a 2002

report published by the Benton Foundation disagrees

with the US Department of Commerce's findings. This

report, <u>Bringing a Nation Online: The Importance of</u>

<u>Federal Leadership</u>, contends that federal funding is

key in continuing to bring more people into the

digital age. While the Department of Commerce report

maintains that most people have access to computers

in their homes, <u>Bringing a Nation Online</u> uses the

same statistics to argue that many people continue

to have difficulty accessing the Internet. The

authors found that 75 percent of people with

household incomes less than $15,000 and 66 percent

with incomes between $15,000 and $35,000 are not yet

using the Internet (Benton Foundation). Wealthier

Americans, however, have significantly greater

access to the Internet. Of the Americans with

incomes of $50,000-$75,000 a year, 67.3 percent

use the Internet (Benton Foundation). Thus,

Romney 9

the authors strongly disagree with the Bush

administration's recommendation to cut programs

like the Department of Commerce's Technology

Opportunities Program and the Community Technology

Centers Program:

Quotation of
more than
four lines is
typed as
a block,
indented 1"
(or ten
spaces), and
double-
spaced, with
no quotation
marks. Paren-
thetical docu-
mentation is
placed one
space after
end punctua-
tion.

> TOP and CTC are important engines of
> digital opportunity. They are emblematic
> of the importance of federal leadership
> in the effort to bridge the digital divide.
> Federal leadership brings the power of
> information to underserved communities. A
> federal retreat from that leadership role
> would undermine innovative efforts to
> bring digital opportunity to underserved
> communities and jeopardize many successful
> community programs. Rather than walking
> away from the investment, the federal
> government should build upon the success of
> these programs to bring digital opportunity
> to the entire nation. (Benton Foundation)

Other evidence also suggests that the digital

divide is not only a problem of Internet access, but

a problem of access to technology in general. The

election reform bill of 2001, for example, allocated

billions of dollars to create better voting

technology in poor and minority areas. William

Kennard observes that in areas where punch card

machines were used, voters were seven times more

likely to have their ballots discarded than in areas that used other types of ballots. For this reason, minorities and the poor are not only disconnected from technology, "they are also disconnected from our democracy" (Kennard). Similarly, a Houston Chronicle article refers to the small number of African Americans working in the information technology field, citing a study by a company called Data Source Associates that found that African Americans make up only 11 percent of workers in technology fields (Rangel-King).[2]

Superscript number identifies content note

It is not only minorities and the impoverished who are affected by the digital divide. Many people know that children in inner-city schools lack access to computer technology and to the Internet, but few know that children attending schools in rural areas are also at risk. Vicky Wellborn, a high school English teacher in a small town, reports that her school only recently instituted a computer literacy program. As they ordered computers, the instructors realized that one of their biggest challenges would be training themselves. Although the computer literacy program has been helpful to many students, the difficulties of teaching an unfamiliar subject continue to challenge teachers at the school (Wellborn).

Although many strides have been made in closing the gap between those who have access to the Internet

Romney 11

and technology and those who do not, problems and new challenges remain. Steps must be taken to solve these problems. First, we must continue efforts to make the Internet available to the widest possible audience.

Conclusion recommends solutions for problem of "digital divide." Because ¶ introduces no new material (it summarizes material already discussed and presents student's original conclusions), no documentation is necessary.

We must also ensure that the rhetoric surrounding the term <u>digital divide</u> is used to close this gap, not to create a new one by establishing or reinforcing stereotypes about minorities. A broader definition of what the digital divide is might help us to see that it has the potential to marginalize many groups of people—the poor, the elderly, the disabled, and rural schoolchildren, for example—not just members of minority groups. On a practical level, the federal government should continue to fund programs that increase access to computer technology in general, and to the Internet in particular. Unless we take steps to make these resources available to all, we will quickly become two separate and unequal societies: one "plugged-in" and privileged and one "unplugged" and marginalized.

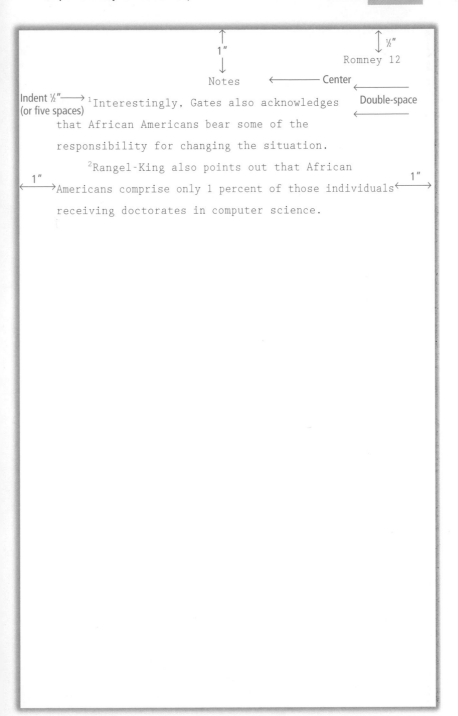

↑
1″
↓

↑ ½″
↓
Romney 12

Notes   ←——— Center

Indent ½″——→ ¹Interestingly, Gates also acknowledges   Double-space
(or five spaces)

that African Americans bear some of the

responsibility for changing the situation.

²Rangel-King also points out that African

1″
←——→Americans comprise only 1 percent of those individuals←——→
1″

receiving doctorates in computer science.

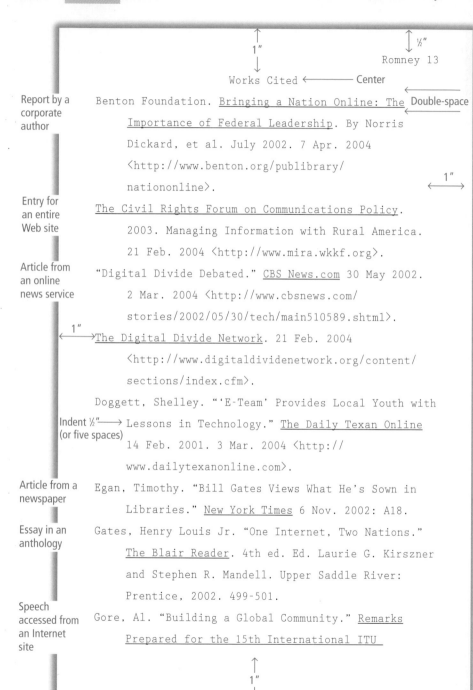

Romney 13

Works Cited ←——— Center

1″

Report by a corporate author Benton Foundation. <u>Bringing a Nation Online: The</u> Double-space
<u>Importance of Federal Leadership</u>. By Norris
Dickard, et al. July 2002. 7 Apr. 2004
〈http://www.benton.org/publibrary/
nationonline〉.   1″

Entry for an entire Web site <u>The Civil Rights Forum on Communications Policy</u>.
2003. Managing Information with Rural America.
21 Feb. 2004 〈http://www.mira.wkkf.org〉.

Article from an online news service "Digital Divide Debated." <u>CBS News.com</u> 30 May 2002.
2 Mar. 2004 〈http://www.cbsnews.com/
stories/2002/05/30/tech/main510589.shtml〉.

1″
←——→<u>The Digital Divide Network</u>. 21 Feb. 2004
〈http://www.digitaldividenetwork.org/content/
sections/index.cfm〉.

Doggett, Shelley. "'E-Team' Provides Local Youth with
Indent ½″——→ Lessons in Technology." <u>The Daily Texan Online</u>
(or five spaces) 14 Feb. 2001. 3 Mar. 2004 〈http://
www.dailytexanonline.com〉.

Article from a newspaper Egan, Timothy. "Bill Gates Views What He's Sown in
Libraries." <u>New York Times</u> 6 Nov. 2002: A18.

Essay in an anthology Gates, Henry Louis Jr. "One Internet, Two Nations."
<u>The Blair Reader</u>. 4th ed. Ed. Laurie G. Kirszner
and Stephen R. Mandell. Upper Saddle River:
Prentice, 2002. 499-501.

Speech accessed from an Internet site Gore, Al. "Building a Global Community." <u>Remarks</u>
<u>Prepared for the 15th International ITU</u>

1″

Romney 14

Conference. 12 Oct. 1998. 12 Mar. 2004

<http://clinton3.nara.gov/WH/EOP/OVP/speeches/

itu.html>.

Kennard, William E. "Democracy's Digital Divide."

Christian Science Monitor 7 Mar. 2002. Academic

Universe: News. LexisNexis. U of Texas Lib.

System, TX. 17 Mar. 2004 <http://

web.lexis-nexis.com>.

Rangel-King, Kristi. "Tech Group Aims to Close

'Digital Divide.'" Houston Chronicle 6 Dec.

2001. Academic Universe: News. LexisNexis. U of

Texas Lib. System, TX. 12 Mar. 2004 <http://

web.lexis-nexis.com>.

Roach, Ronald. "More Minority Households Gain

Internet Access." Black Issues in Higher

Education 5 July 2001. InfoTrac College Edition.

InfoTrac. 21 Mar. 2004 <http://

infotrac.thomsonlearning.com>.

Schwartz, John. "A Lack of Money Forces Computer

Initiative to Close." New York Times 30 Oct.

2002. Expanded Academic ASAP. Gale Group

Databases. U of Texas Lib. System, TX. 20 Mar.

2004 <http://www.galegroup.com>.

---. "Report Disputes Bush Approach to Bridging

'Digital Divide.'" New York Times 11 July 2002.

Expanded Academic ASAP. Gale Group Databases.

U of Texas Lib. System, TX. 19 Mar. 2004

<http://www.galegroup.com>.

Newspaper article accessed from a library subscription database

Three unspaced hyphens used instead of repeating author's name

Romney 15

Government document accessed from the Internet

United States. Dept. of Commerce. Economics and

Statistics Admin. Natl. Telecommunications and

Information Admin. <u>Falling through the Net:</u>

<u>Defining the Digital Divide: A Report on the</u>

<u>Telecommunications and Information Technology</u>

<u>Gap in America</u>. Washington: GPO, 1999. 20 Mar.

2004 <http://www.ntia.doc.gov/ntiahome/fttn99/

FTTN.pdf>.

Wellborn, Vicky. "Re: Computer Literacy." Email to

the author. 23 Sept. 2003.

Young, Jeffrey R. "Does 'Digital Divide' Rhetoric Do

More Harm Than Good?" <u>Chronicle of Higher</u>

<u>Education</u> 9 Nov. 2001. 20 Mar. 2004

<http://chronicle.com>.

DIRECTORY OF APA IN-TEXT CITATIONS

1. A work by a single author (p. 448)
2. A work by two authors (p. 448)
3. A work by three to five authors (p. 448)
4. A work by six or more authors (p. 448)
5. Works by authors with the same last name (p. 448)
6. A work by a corporate author (p. 449)
7. A work with no listed author (p. 449)
8. A personal communication (p. 449)
9. An indirect source (p. 449)
10. A specific part of a source (p. 449)
11. An electronic source (p. 449)
12. Two or more works within the same parenthetical reference (p. 450)
13. A table (p. 450)

DIRECTORY OF APA REFERENCE LIST ENTRIES

Print Sources

Entries for Books

Authors

1. A book with one author (p. 451)
2. A book with more than one author (p. 451)
3. A book with no listed author or editor (p. 451)
4. A book with a corporate author (p. 451)

Editions, Multivolume Works, Forewords

5. An edited book (p. 452)
6. A work in several volumes (p. 452)
7. The foreword, preface, or afterword of a book (p. 452)

Parts of Books

8. A selection from an anthology (p. 452)
9. An article in a reference book (p. 452)

Government Reports

10. A government report (p. 452)

Entries for Articles

Scholarly Journals

11. An article in a scholarly journal with continuous pagination through an annual volume (p. 453)

47a Using APA Style

APA style* is used extensively in the social sciences in disciplines such as psychology, sociology, and economics. APA documentation has three parts: *in-text citations*, a *reference list*, and optional *content footnotes*.

(1) In-Text Citations

APA documentation uses short in-text citations in the body of the paper. These citations are keyed to an alphabetical list of references that follows the paper. A typical in-text citation consists of the author's last name (followed by a comma) and the year of publication in parentheses.

```
Many people exhibit symptoms of depression after the

death of a pet (Russo, 2000).
```

If the author's name appears in the introductory phrase, the in-text citation includes just the year of publication.

```
According to Russo (2000), many people exhibit symptoms

of depression after the death of a pet.
```

NOTE: You may include the author's name and the date either in the introductory phrase or in parentheses at the end of the borrowed material.

When quoting directly, include the page number in parentheses after the quotation.

```
According to Weston (1996), children from one-parent

homes read at "a significantly lower level than those

from two-parent homes" (p. 58).
```

NOTE: A long quotation (forty words or more) is not set in quotation marks. It is set as a block, and the entire quotation is double-spaced and indented one-half inch (or five to seven spaces) from the left margin. The citation is placed in parentheses one space after the final punctuation.

---

*APA documentation style follows the guidelines set in the *Publication Manual of the American Psychological Association*, 5th ed. Washington, DC: APA, 2001.

SAMPLE APA IN-TEXT CITATIONS

1. A Work by a Single Author

Many college students suffer from sleep deprivation

(Anton, 1999).

2. A Work by Two Authors

There is growing concern over the use of psychological

testing in elementary schools (Albright & Glennon, 1982).

3. A Work by Three to Five Authors

If a work has more than two but fewer than six authors, mention all names in the first reference; in subsequent references in the same paragraph, cite only the first author followed by et al. ("and others"). When the reference appears in later paragraphs, include the year.

First Reference

(Sparks, Wilson, & Hewitt, 2001)

Subsequent References in the Same Paragraph

(Sparks et al.)

Reference in Later Paragraphs

(Sparks et al., 2001)

4. A Work by Six or More Authors

When a work has six or more authors, cite the name of the first author followed by et al. and the year in all references.

(Miller et al., 1995)

> #### Close-up: Citing Works by Multiple Authors
>
> When referring to multiple authors in your discussion, join the last two names with and.
>
> According to Rosen, Wolfe, and Ziff
>
> (1988). . . .
>
> In-text citations, however, require an **ampersand.**
>
> (Rosen, Wolfe, & Ziff, 1988)

5. Works by Authors with the Same Last Name

If your reference list includes works by two or more authors with the same last name, use each author's initials in all in-text citations.

F. Bor (2001) and S. D. Bor (2000) concluded that no

further study is needed.

6. A Work by a Corporate Author

If the name of a corporate author is long, abbreviate it after the first citation.

First Reference

(National Institute of Mental Health [NIMH], 2001)

Subsequent Reference

(NIMH, 2001)

7. A Work with No Listed Author

If a work has no listed author, cite the first two or three words of the title and the year. Use quotation marks around titles of periodical articles and chapters of books; use italics for titles of books, periodicals, brochures, reports, and the like.

("New Immigration," 2000)

8. A Personal Communication

Cite letters, memos, telephone conversations, personal interviews, emails, messages from electronic bulletin boards, and so on only in the text—*not* in the reference list.

(R. Takaki, personal communication, October 17, 2001)

9. An Indirect Source

Cogan and Howe offer very different interpretations of

the problem (cited in Swenson, 2000).

10. A Specific Part of a Source

Use abbreviations for the words *page* (p.), *pages* (pp.), *chapter* (chap.), and *section* (sec.).

These theories have an interesting history (Lee, 1966,

chap. 2).

11. An Electronic Source

For an electronic source that does not show page numbers, use the paragraph number preceded by a ¶ symbol or the abbreviation para.

Conversation at the dinner table is an example of a

family ritual (Kulp, 2001, ¶ 3).

In the case of an electronic source that has neither page nor paragraph numbers, cite the heading in the source and the number of the paragraph (following the heading) in which the material is located.

Healthy eating is a never-ending series of free choices

(Shapiro, 2001, Introduction section, para. 2).

If the source has no headings, you may not be able to specify an exact location.

12. Two or More Works within the Same Parenthetical Reference
List works by different authors in alphabetical order, separated by semicolons.

This theory is supported by several studies (Barson &

Roth, 1995; Rose, 2001; Tedesco, 2002).

List works by the same author or authors in order of date of publication, with the earliest date first.

This theory is supported by several studies (Rhodes &

Dollek, 2000, 2002, 2003).

For works by the same author published in the same year, designate the work whose title comes first alphabetically *a*, the one whose title comes next *b*, and so on; repeat the year in each citation.

This theory is supported by several studies (Shapiro,

2003a, 2003b).

13. A Table
If you use a table from a source, give credit to the author in a note at the bottom of the table. Do not include this information in the reference list.

Note. From "Predictors of Employment and Earnings Among

JOBS Participants," by P. A. Neenan and D. K. Orthner,

1996, *Social Work Research, 20* (4), p. 233.

(2) Reference List

The **reference list** gives the publication information for all the sources you cite. It should appear at the end of your paper on a new numbered page titled References. Entries on the reference list should be arranged alphabetically. Double-space within and between reference list entries, and indent the second and subsequent lines of each entry one-half inch (five spaces). (**See 47b** for manuscript guidelines.)

SAMPLE APA REFERENCE LIST ENTRIES

Print Sources

Entries for Books

Book citations include the author's name; the year of publication (in parentheses); the book title (italicized); and publication information.

Capitalize only the first word of the title and subtitle and any proper nouns. Include any additional necessary information—edition, report number, or volume number, for example—in parentheses after the title.

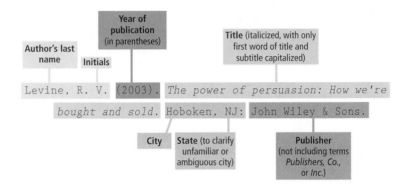

Author's last name / Initials / Year of publication (in parentheses) / Title (italicized, with only first word of title and subtitle capitalized)

Levine, R. V. (2003). *The power of persuasion: How we're bought and sold.* Hoboken, NJ: John Wiley & Sons.

City / State (to clarify unfamiliar or ambiguous city) / Publisher (not including terms *Publishers, Co.,* or *Inc.*)

1. A Book with One Author

Use a short form of the publisher's name. Write out the names of associations, corporations, and university presses. Include the words Book and Press, but do not include terms such as Publishers, Co., or Inc.

Maslow, A. H. (1974). *Toward a psychology of being.*

Princeton: Van Nostrand.

2. A Book with More Than One Author

List up to six authors—by last name and initials. For more than six authors, add et al. after the sixth name.

Wolfinger, D., Knable, P., Richards, H. L., & Silberger,

R. (1990). *The chronically unemployed.* New York:

Berman Press.

3. A Book with No Listed Author or Editor

Writing with a computer. (2000). Philadelphia: Drexel

Press.

4. A Book with a Corporate Author

When the author and the publisher are the same, include the word Author at the end of the citation instead of repeating the publisher's name.

League of Women Voters of the United States. (2001).

Local league handbook. Washington, DC: Author.

Editions, Multivolume Works, Forewords

5. An Edited Book

Lewin, K., Lippitt, R., & White, R. K. (Eds.). (1985).

    Social learning and imitation. New York: Basic Books.

6. A Work in Several Volumes

Jones, P. R., & Williams, T. C. (Eds.). (1990–1993).

    Handbook of therapy (Vols. 1–2). Princeton:

    Princeton University Press.

7. The Foreword, Preface, or Afterword of a Book

Taylor, T. (1979). Preface. In B. B. Ferencz, *Less than*

    slaves (pp. ii–ix). Cambridge: Harvard University

    Press.

Parts of Books

8. A Selection from an Anthology
Give inclusive page numbers preceded by pp. (in parentheses) after the title of the anthology. The title of the selection is not enclosed in quotation marks.

Lorde, A. (1984). Age, race, and class. In P. S.

    Rothenberg (Ed.), *Racism and sexism: An integrated*

    study (pp. 352–360). New York: St. Martin's Press.

NOTE: If you cite two or more selections from the same anthology, give the full citation for the anthology in each entry.

9. An Article in a Reference Book

Edwards, P. (Ed.). (1987). Determinism. In *The*

    encyclopedia of philosophy (Vol. 2, pp. 359–373).

    New York: Macmillan.

Government Reports

10. A Government Report

National Institute of Mental Health. (1987). *Motion*

    pictures and violence: A summary report of

    research (DHHS Publication No. ADM 91-22187).

    Washington, DC: U.S. Government Printing

    Office.

Entries for Articles

Article citations include the author's name; the date of publication (in parentheses); the title of the article; the title of the periodical (italicized); the volume number (italicized); the issue number, if any (in parentheses); and the inclusive page numbers (including all digits). Capitalize only the first word of the article's title and subtitle. Do not underline or italicize the title of the article or enclose it in quotation marks. Give the periodical title in full, and capitalize all words except articles, prepositions, and conjunctions of fewer than four letters. Use p. or pp. when referring to page numbers in newspapers, but omit this abbreviation when referring to page numbers in journals and popular magazines.

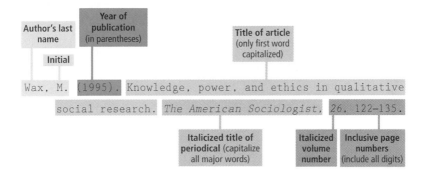

Scholarly Journals

11. An Article in a Scholarly Journal with Continuous Pagination through an Annual Volume

Miller, W. (1969). Violent crimes in city gangs. *Journal of Social Issues, 27,* 581–593.

12. An Article in a Scholarly Journal with Separate Pagination in Each Issue

Williams, S., & Cohen, L. R. (1984). Child stress in early learning situations. *American Psychologist, 21*(10), 1–28.

Magazines and Newspapers

13. A Magazine Article

McCurdy, H. G. (1983, June). Brain mechanisms and intelligence. *Psychology Today, 46,* 61–63.

14. A Newspaper Article

If an article appears on nonconsecutive pages, give all page numbers, separated by commas (for example, A1, A14). If the article appears on consecutive pages, indicate the full range of pages (for example, A7–A9).

James, W. R. (1993, November 16). The uninsured and

health care. *Wall Street Journal*, pp. A1, A14.

15. A Letter to the Editor of a Newspaper

Williams, P. (2000, July 19). Self-fulfilling stereotypes

[Letter to the editor]. *Los Angeles Times*, p. A22.

Entries for Miscellaneous Print Sources

Letters

16. A Personal Letter

References to unpublished personal letters, like references to all other personal communications, should be included only in the text of the paper, not in the reference list.

17. A Published Letter

Joyce, J. (1931). Letter to Louis Gillet. In Richard

Ellmann, *James Joyce* (p. 631). New York: Oxford

University Press.

Entries for Other Sources

Television Broadcasts, Films, CDs, Audiocassette Recordings, Computer Software

18. A Television Broadcast

Murphy J. (Executive Producer). (2002, March 4). *The CBS

evening news* [Television broadcast]. New York:

Columbia Broadcasting Service.

19. A Television Series

Sorkin, A., Schlamme, T., & Wells, J. (Executive

Producers). (2002). *The west wing* [Television

series]. Los Angeles: Warner Bros. Television.

20. A Film

Spielberg, S. (Director). (1994). *Schindler's list*

[Motion picture]. United States: Universal.

21. A CD Recording

Marley, B. (1977). Waiting in vain. On *Exodus* [CD]. New

York: Island Records.

22. An Audiocassette Recording

Skinner, B. F. (Speaker). (1972). *Skinner on*

Skinnerism [Cassette recording]. Hollywood, CA:

Center for Cassette Studies.

23. Computer Software

Sharp, S. (1995). Career Selection Tests (Version 5.0)

[Computer software]. Chico, CA: Avocation Software.

Electronic Sources

[Search]

APA guidelines for documenting electronic sources focus on Web sources, which often do not include all the bibliographic information that print sources do. For example, Web sources may not include page numbers or a place of publication. At a minimum, a Web citation should have a title, a date (the date of publication, update, or retrieval), and an electronic address (URL). If possible, also include the author(s) of a source. When you need to break the URL at the end of a line, break it after a slash or before a period (do not add a hyphen). Do not add a period at the end of the URL. (Current guidelines for electronic sources can be found on the APA Web site at www.apa.org.)

Entries from Internet Sites

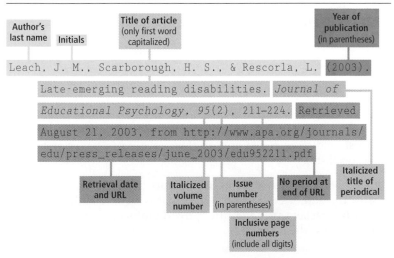

| Author's last name | Initials | Title of article (only first word capitalized) | | Year of publication (in parentheses) |

Leach, J. M., Scarborough, H. S., & Rescorla, L. (2003).

Late-emerging reading disabilities. *Journal of*

Educational Psychology, 95(2), 211–224. Retrieved

August 21, 2003, from http://www.apa.org/journals/

edu/press_releases/june_2003/edu952211.pdf

| Retrieval date and URL | Italicized volume number | Issue number (in parentheses) | No period at end of URL | Italicized title of periodical |

Inclusive page numbers (include all digits)

Internet-Specific Sources

24. An Internet Article Based on a Print Source

If you have seen the article only in electronic format, include the phrase `Electronic version` in brackets after the title.

> Winston, E. L. (2000). The role of art therapy in
>
> treating chronically depressed patients [Electronic
>
> version]. *Journal of Bibliographic Research, 5,*
>
> 54–72.

NOTE: If you have reason to believe the article you retrieved is different from the print version, add the date you retrieved it and the URL.

25. An Article in an Internet-Only Journal

> Hornaday, J., & Bunker, C. (2001). The nature of the
>
> entrepreneur. *Personal Psychology, 23,* Article
>
> 2353b. Retrieved November 21, 2001, from
>
> http://journals.apa.org/volume23/pre002353b.html

26. A Document from a University Web Site

> Beck, E. (1997, July). *The good, the bad & the ugly: Or,*
>
> *why it's a good idea to evaluate web sources.*
>
> Retrieved January 7, 2002, from New Mexico State
>
> University Library Web site: http://lib.nmsu.edu/
>
> instruction/evalcrit.html

27. A Web Document (No Author Identified, No Date)

> *The stratocaster appreciation page.* (n.d.). Retrieved
>
> July 27, 2002, from http://members.tripod.com/~AFH/

NOTE: The abbreviation `n.d.` stands for "no date."

28. An Email

As with all other personal communication, references to personal email should be included only in the text of your paper, not in the reference list.

29. A Message Posted to a Newsgroup

List the author's full name—or, if that is not available, the screen name. In brackets after the title, provide information that will help readers access the message.

Shapiro, R. (2001, April 4). Chat rooms and interpersonal
communication [Msg 7]. Message posted to
news://sci.psychology.communication

30. A Searchable Database

Nowroozi, C. (1992). What you lose when you miss sleep.
Nation's Business, 80(9), 73–77. Retrieved April 22,
2001, from Expanded Academic ASAP database.

Abstracts, Newspaper Articles

31. An Abstract

Guinot, A., & Peterson, B. R. (1995). *Forgetfulness and
partial cognition* (Drexel University Cognitive
Research Report No. 21). Abstract retrieved December
4, 2001, from http://www.Drexel.edu/~guinot/
deltarule-abstract.html

32. An Article in a Daily Newspaper

Farrell, P. D. (1997, March 23). New high-tech stresses
hit traders and investors on the information
superhighway. *Wall Street Journal.* Retrieved
April 4, 1999, from http://wall-street.news.com/
forecasts/stress/stress.html

(3) Content Footnotes

APA format permits content notes, indicated by **superscripts** (raised numerals) in the text. The notes are listed on a separate numbered page, titled Footnotes, following the appendixes (or after the reference list if there are no appendixes). Double-space all notes, indenting the first line of each note one-half inch (or five to seven spaces) and beginning subsequent lines flush left. Number the notes with superscripts that correspond to the numbers in your text.

47b APA Manuscript Guidelines

Social science papers have internal headings (internal sections include an untitled introduction, Method, Results, and Discussion). Each section of a social science paper is a complete unit with a beginning and an end so it can be read separately and still make sense out of context. The body of the paper may include charts, graphs, maps, photographs, flowcharts, or tables.

The following guidelines are based on the latest version of the *Publication Manual of the American Psychological Association.*

Checklist: Typing Your Paper

When typing your paper, use the student paper in 47c as your model.

☐ Leave one-inch margins at the top and bottom and on both sides. Double-space your paper throughout.

☐ Indent the first line of every paragraph and the first line of every content footnote one-half inch (or five to seven spaces) from the left-hand margin.

☐ Set off a **long quotation** (more than forty words) in a block format by indenting the entire quotation five to seven spaces (or one-half inch) from the left-hand margin.

☐ Number all pages consecutively. Each page should include a **page header** (an abbreviated title) and a page number typed one-half inch from the top and one inch from the right-hand edge of the page. Leave five spaces (or one-half inch) between the page header and the page number.

See 11b
☐ Center and type major <u>headings</u> with uppercase and lowercase letters. Place minor headings flush left, typed with uppercase and lowercase letters and italicized.

See 11c
☐ Format items in a series as a numbered <u>list</u>.

☐ Arrange the pages of the paper in the following order:
  • Title page (page 1) includes a page header, **running head,** title, and **byline** (your name)
  • Abstract (page 2)
  • Text of paper (beginning on page 3)
  • Reference List (new page)
  • Appendixes (start each on a new page)
  • Content footnotes (new page)

See 47a
☐ If you use source material in your paper, citations should be consistent with **<u>APA documentation style</u>**.

Checklist: Using Visuals

APA distinguishes between two types of visuals: **tables** and **figures** (charts, graphs, photographs, and diagrams). In manuscripts not intended for publication, tables and figures are included in the text. A short table or figure should appear on the page where it is discussed; a long table or figure should be placed on a separate page just after the page where it is discussed.

☐ Number all **tables** consecutively. Each table should have a *label* and a *title*.
- The **label** consists of the word `Table` (not in italics), along with an arabic numeral, typed flush left above the table.
- Double-space and type a brief explanatory **title** for each table (in italics) flush left below the label. Capitalize the first letters of principal words of the title.

`Table 7`

Frequency of Negative Responses of Dorm Students to

Questions Concerning Alcohol Consumption

☐ Number all **figures** consecutively. Each figure should have a *label* and a *caption*.
- The **label** consists of the word `Figure` (typed flush left below the figure) followed by the figure number (both in italics).
- The **caption** explains the figure and serves as a title. Double-space the caption, but do not italicize it. Capitalize only the first word, and end the caption with a period. The caption follows the label (on the same line).

Figure 1. `Duration of responses measured in seconds.`

NOTE: If you use a table or figure from an outside source, include full source information in a note at the bottom of the table or figure. This information does not appear in your reference list.

Checklist: Preparing the APA Reference List

☐ Begin the reference list on a new page after the last page of text, numbered as the next page of the paper.
☐ Center the title `References` at the top of the page.
☐ List the items on the reference list alphabetically (with author's last name first).
☐ Type the first line of each entry at the left-hand margin. Indent subsequent lines one-half inch (or five to seven spaces).
☐ Separate the major divisions of each entry with a period and one space.
☐ Double-space the reference list within and between entries.

Checklist: Arranging Entries in the APA Reference List

☐ Single-author entries precede multiple-author entries that begin with the same name.

```
Field, S. (1987)

Field, S., & Levitt, M. P. (1984)
```

☐ Entries by the same author or authors are arranged according to date of publication, starting with the earliest date.

```
Ruthenberg, H., & Rubin, R. (1985)

Ruthenberg, H., & Rubin, R. (1987)
```

☐ Entries with the same author or authors and date of publication are arranged alphabetically according to title. Lowercase letters (*a*, *b*, *c*, and so on) that indicate the order of publication are placed within parentheses.

```
Wolk, E. M. (1996a). Analysis . . .

Wolk, E. M. (1996b). Hormonal . . .
```

47c Sample APA-Style Research Paper

The following student paper, "Sleep Deprivation in College Students," uses APA documentation style. It includes a title page, an abstract, a reference list, a table, and a bar graph.

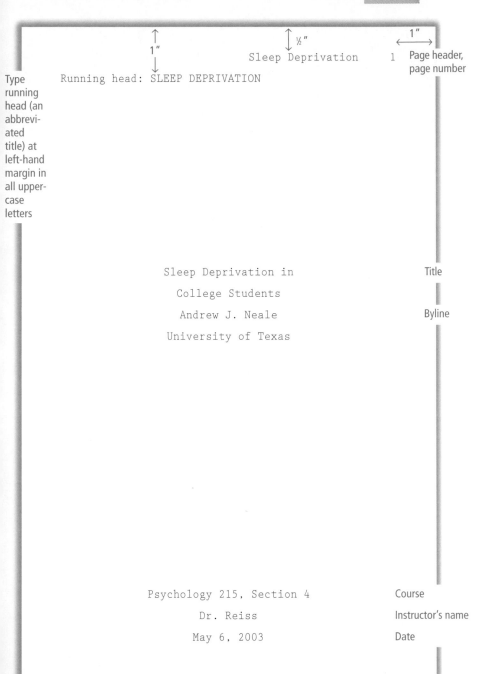

Type running head (an abbreviated title) at left-hand margin in all uppercase letters

Running head: SLEEP DEPRIVATION

Sleep Deprivation   1   Page header, page number

Sleep Deprivation in   Title
College Students
Andrew J. Neale   Byline
University of Texas

Psychology 215, Section 4   Course
Dr. Reiss   Instructor's name
May 6, 2003   Date

Sleep Deprivation   2

Center heading

                                Abstract

A survey of 50 first-year college students in an
introductory biology class was conducted. The survey
consisted of 5 questions regarding the causes and
results of sleep deprivation and specifically
addressed the students' study methods and the
grades they received on the fall midterm. The
study's hypothesis was that although students
believe that forgoing sleep to study will yield
better grades, sleep deprivation actually causes a
decrease in performance. In support of this
hypothesis, 43% of the students who received either
an A or a B on the fall midterm deprived themselves
of sleep in order to cram for the test, whereas 90%
of those who received a C or a D were sleep
deprived.

Abstract typed
as a single
paragraph in
block format

Page
header
and
number
on every
page

Sleep Deprivation   3

Full title ——→ Sleep Deprivation in College Students
(centered)

   For many college students, sleep is a luxury
that they feel they cannot afford. Bombarded with
tests and assignments and limited by a 24-hour day,
students often attempt to make up time by forgoing
sleep. Ironically, students may actually impair
their scholastic performance by failing to get
adequate sleep. According to several psychological
and medical studies, sleep deprivation can lead to
memory loss and health problems, both of which are
more likely to harm a student's academic performance
than to help it.

   Sleep is often overlooked as an essential
component of a healthy lifestyle. Millions of
Americans wake up daily to alarm clocks because their
bodies have not gotten a sufficient amount of sleep.
This indicates that for many people, sleep is viewed
as a luxury rather than a necessity. As National Sleep
Foundation Executive Director Richard L. Gelula
observes, "Some of the problems we face as a society—
from road rage to obesity—may be linked to lack of
sleep or poor sleep" (National Sleep Foundation,
2002, ¶ 3). In fact, according to the National
Sleep Foundation, "excessive sleepiness is associated
with reduced short-term memory and learning
ability, negative mood, inconsistent performance,
poor productivity and loss of some forms of behavioral
control" (2000, ¶ 2).

Margin notes:

1″

Double-space

Introduction

Thesis statement

1″

Literature review (¶s 2–7)

Quotation requires its own documentation and a page number. A ¶ number is used for Internet sources.

1″

Sleep Deprivation 4

Focus shifts to student sleep deprivation

Sleep deprivation is particularly common among college students, many of whom maintain busy lifestyles and are required to memorize a great deal of material before their exams. It is common for college students to take a quick nap between classes or fall asleep while studying in the library because they are sleep deprived. Approximately 44% of young adults experience daytime sleepiness at least a few days a month (National Sleep Foundation, 2002). Many students face daytime sleepiness on the day of an exam because they stayed up all night studying. These students believe that if they read and review immediately before taking a test—even though this usually means losing sleep—they will remember more information and thus get better grades. However, this is not the case.

Student uses past tense when discussing other researchers' studies

A study conducted by professors Mary Carskadon at Brown University in Providence, Rhode Island, and Amy Wolfson at the College of the Holy Cross in Worcester, Massachusetts, showed that high school students who got adequate sleep were more likely to do well in their classes (Carpenter, 2001). According to their study of the correlation between grades and sleep, students who went to bed earlier on both weeknights and weekends earned mainly A's and B's. The students who received D's and F's averaged about 35 minutes less sleep per day than the high achievers (cited in Carpenter). Apparently,

cited in indicates an indirect source

then, sleep is essential to high academic
achievement.

Once students reach college and have the
freedom to set their own schedules, however, many
believe that sleep is expendable. For example,
students believe that if they use the time they
would normally sleep to study, they will do better
on exams. A recent survey of 144 undergraduate
students in introductory psychology classes
contradicted this assumption. According to this
study, long sleepers, or those individuals who slept
9 or more hours out of a 24-hour day, had
significantly higher grade point averages (GPAs)
than short sleepers, or individuals who slept less
than 7 hours out of a 24-hour day. Therefore,
contrary to the belief of many college students,
more sleep is often required to achieve a high GPA
(Kelly, Kelly, & Clanton, 2001).

Many students believe that sleep deprivation
is not the cause of their poor performance, but
rather that a host of other factors might be to
blame. A study in the *Journal of American College
Health* tested the effect that several factors
have on a student's performance in school, as
measured by students' GPAs. Some of the factors
considered included exercise, sleep, nutritional
habits, social support, time management
techniques, stress management techniques, and

Sleep Deprivation   6

First reference
includes all
three authors;
et al. replaces
second and
third authors in
subsequent ref-
erence in same
paragraph

spiritual health (Trockel, Barnes, & Egget,
2000). The most significant correlation
discovered in the study was between GPA and the
sleep habits of students. Sleep deprivation had
a more negative impact on GPAs than any other
factor did (Trockel et al.).

Despite these findings, numerous students
continue to believe that they will be able to
remember more material if they do not sleep at
all before an exam. They fear that sleeping
will interfere with their ability to retain
information. Pilcher & Walters (1997), however,
showed that sleep deprivation actually impaired
learning skills. In this study, one group of
students was sleep-deprived, while the other got 8
hours of sleep before the exam. Each group estimated
how well they had performed on the exam. The
students who were sleep-deprived believed their
performance on the test was better than did those
who were not sleep-deprived, but actually the
performance of the sleep-deprived students was
significantly worse than that of those who got 8
hours of sleep prior to the test (Pilcher & Walters,
1997, cited in Bubolz, Brown, & Soper, 2001). This
study confirms that sleep deprivation harms
cognitive performance and reveals that many students
believe that the less sleep they get, the better
they will do.

Sleep Deprivation   7

A survey of students in an introductory biology

class at the University of Texas demonstrated the

effects of sleep deprivation on scholastic

performance and supported the hypothesis that

despite students' beliefs, forgoing sleep does not

lead to better test scores.

Student uses past tense when discussing his own research study

Method

To ascertain the causes and results of sleep

deprivation, a study of the relationship between

sleep and test performance was conducted. A survey

of 50 first-year college students in an introductory

biology class was completed, and their performance

on the fall midterm was analyzed.

Each student was asked to complete a survey

composed of the following five questions about their

sleep patterns and their performance on the fall

midterm.

1. Did you deprive yourself of sleep when
   studying for the fall midterm?

2. Do you regularly deprive yourself of sleep
   when studying for an exam?

3. What was your grade on the exam?

4. Do you feel your performance was helped or
   harmed by the amount of sleep you had?

5. Will you deprive yourself of sleep when you
   study for the final exam?

List is indented ½" (or five to seven spaces) and treated as long block quotation

To maintain confidentiality, the students were

not asked to put their names on the survey. Also, to

determine whether the students answered question 3
accurately, the group grade distribution from the
surveys was compared to the number of A's, B's, C's,
and D's shown in the instructor's record of the test
results. The two frequency distributions were
identical.

Results

Analysis of the survey data indicated a
significant difference between the grades of
students who were sleep deprived and the grades of
those who were not. The results of the survey are

presented in Table 1.

Table 1 introduced

Table 1

*Results of Survey of Students in University of
Texas Introduction to Biology Class Examining the
Relationship between Sleep Deprivation and Academic
Performance*

Table placed on page where it is discussed

Grade Totals	Sleep-Deprived	Not Sleep-Deprived	Usually Sleep-Deprived	Improved	Harmed	Continue Sleep Deprivation?
A = 10	4	6	1	4	0	4
B = 20	9	11	8	8	1	8
C = 10	10	0	6	5	4	7
D = 10	8	2	2	1	3	2
Total	31	19	17	18	8	21

The grades in the class were curved so that out
of 50 students, 10 received A's, 20 received B's, 10

Sleep Deprivation   9

received C's, and 10 received D's. For the purposes
of this survey, an A or B on the exam indicates that
the student performed well. A grade of C or D on the
exam is considered a poor grade.

Of the 50 students in the class, 31 (or 62%)
said they deprived themselves of sleep when studying
for the fall midterm. Of these students, 17 (or 34%
of the class) answered yes to the second question,
reporting they regularly deprive themselves of sleep
before an exam.

Statistical
findings in
table reported

Of the 31 students who said they deprived
themselves of sleep when studying for the fall
midterm, only 4 earned A's, and the majority of the
A's in the class were received by those students who
were not sleep-deprived. Even more significant was
the fact that of the 4 students who were sleep-
deprived and got A's, only one student claimed
usually to be sleep-deprived on the day of an exam.
Thus, assuming the students who earn A's in a class
do well in general, it is possible that sleep
deprivation did not help or harm these students'
grades. Not surprisingly, of the 4 students who
received A's and were sleep-deprived, all said they
would continue to use sleep deprivation to enable
them to study for longer hours.

The majority of those who used sleep
deprivation in an effort to obtain a higher grade
received B's and C's on the exam. A total of 20

Sleep Deprivation   10

students earned a grade of B on the exam. Of
those students, only 9, or 18% of the class, said
they were deprived of sleep when they took the
test.

Students who said they were sleep-deprived when
they took the exam received the majority of the poor
grades. Ten students got C's on the midterm, and of
these 10 students, 100% said they were sleep-
deprived when they took their test. Of the 10
students (20% of the class) who got D's, 8 said they
were sleep deprived. Figure 1 shows the significant
relation that was found between poor grades on the
exam and sleep deprivation.

Figure 1 introduced

Figure placed on page where it is discussed

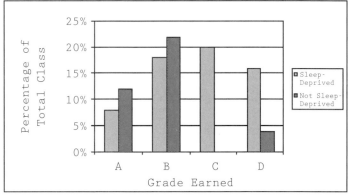

Label

Caption

No source information needed for student's original graph

Figure 1. Results of survey of students in University
of Texas introduction to biology class examining the
relationship between sleep deprivation and academic
performance.

Sleep Deprivation   11

Discussion

For many students, sleep is viewed as a luxury rather than as a necessity. Particularly during the exam period, students use the hours in which they would normally sleep to study. However, this method does not seem to be effective. The survey discussed here reveals a clear correlation between sleep deprivation and lower exam scores. In fact, the majority of students who performed well on the exam, earning either an A or a B, were not deprived of sleep. Therefore, students who choose studying over sleep should rethink their approach and consider that sleep deprivation may actually lead to impaired academic performance.

1"
Sleep Deprivation   12

References   ← Center

Bubolz, W., Brown, F., & Soper, B. (2001). Sleep Double-space
habits and patterns of college students: A
preliminary study. *Journal of American College
Health, 50,* 131–135.

Carpenter, S. (2001). Sleep deprivation may be

Indent ½"→undermining teen health. *Monitor on Psychology,*
(or five spaces) *32*(9). Retrieved March 9, 2003, from

http://www.apa.org/monitor/oct01/sleepteen.html

Entries
listed in   Kelly, W. E., Kelly, K. E., & Clanton, R. C. (2001).
alphabetical   The relationship between sleep length and grade-
order   point average among college students. *College
Student Journal, 35*(1), 84–90.

National Sleep Foundation. (2000). *Adolescent sleep
needs and patterns: Research report and resource
guide.* Retrieved March 16, 2003, from
http://www.sleepfoundation.org/publications/
sleep_and_teens_report1.pdf

National Sleep Foundation. (2002, April). *Epidemic of
daytime sleepiness linked to increased feelings
of anger, stress, and pessimism.* Retrieved March
14, 2003, from http://www.sleepfoundation.org/
nsaw/pk_pollresultsmood.html

Trockel, M., Barnes, M., & Egget, D. (2000). Health-
related variables and academic performance among
first-year college students: Implications for
sleep and other behaviors. *Journal of American
College Health, 49,* 125–131.

PART 8

Bilingual and ESL Writers

48a Solving Verb-Related Problems

See
Ch. 22

Although <u>verbs</u> in all languages perform similar functions, they differ in form and usage from language to language—perhaps more than any other part of speech or grammatical unit. The most common ESL errors related to verbs involve *subject-verb agreement* and *verb tense*.

(1) Subject-Verb Agreement

English verbs change their form according to *person, number,* and *tense.* The verb in a sentence must agree with the subject in person and number. **Person** refers to *who* or *what* is performing the action of the verb (for example, *I, you,* or someone else). **Number** refers to *how many* people or things are performing the action (one or more than one).

See
26a

In English, the rules for <u>subject-verb agreement</u> are fairly straightforward. With **regular verbs** in the present tense, for third-person singular subjects (for example, *he, she, it, the dog, Mary*), add *s* or *es* to the base form of the verb. If you are not sure whether to add *s* or *es,* consult a dictionary. For all other subjects (for example, *I, you, we, they, the dogs*), use the base form of the verb.

I *write*	we *write*
you (singular) *write*	you (plural) *write*
he, she, it *writes*	they *write*

Two very common **irregular verbs** are *be* and *have,* which take the following forms in the present tense.

I *am*	we *are*
you (singular) *are*	you (plural) *are*
he, she, it *is*	they *are*

I *have*	we *have*
you (singular) *have*	you (plural) *have*
he, she, it *has*	they *have*

Close-up: Modal Auxiliaries

Certain verbs, called **modal auxiliaries**—*can, could, may, might, must, shall, should, will,* and *would*—do not change their form to agree with the subject.

I <u>*can*</u> buy the props, and then <u>Myria and Emma</u> <u>*can*</u> paint them tomorrow.

> Mr. Lam and Ms. Boyer *might* be able to attend, but
> Mr. Esposito *might* not be able to make it.
>
> Roisin *would* enjoy law school, but his brothers probably *would* not.

(2) Forming Past, Present, and Future Verbs

In English, the form of a verb changes according to *when* the action of the verb takes place—in the **past, present,** or **future.** For example, adding *ed* to many English verbs creates a past tense and places the action of the verb in the past. One problem that many nonnative English speakers have with English **verb tenses** results from the large number of irregular verbs in English: for example, the first-person singular simple past form of the verb *to sing* is not "I singed," but "I sang," and the first-person singular simple past form of the verb *to fight* is not "I fighted," but "I fought."

> See
> 22b

Close-up: Choosing the Simplest Verb Forms

Some nonnative English speakers use verb forms that are more complicated than they need to be. They may do this because their native language uses more complicated verb forms than English does or because they "overcorrect" their verbs into complicated forms. Specifically, nonnative speakers tend to use progressive and perfect verb forms instead of simple verb forms. To communicate your ideas clearly to an English-speaking audience, choose the simplest possible verb form.

(3) Using Auxiliary Verbs to Form Past, Present, and Future Verbs

The **auxiliary verbs** (also known as **helping verbs**) *be, have,* and *do* are used to create some present, past, and future forms of verbs in English: "Julio *is taking* a vacation"; "I *have been* tired lately"; "He *does* not *need* a license." The auxiliary verbs *be, have,* and *do* change form to reflect the time frame of the action or situation and to agree with the subject; however, the main verb remains in simple present or simple past form.

> I *am* ready to go to the meeting.
>
> They *were* ready to go to the meeting.
>
> Mr. Chuen *has lived* in that house for eight years.
>
> They *have lived* near downtown for only one year.

Ms. Trepagnier _does_ not _like_ the opera.

My brothers _do_ not _want_ to see a Broadway musical.

NOTE: Remember, only auxiliary verbs, not the verbs they "help," change form to indicate person, number, and tense.

Present: We <u>have</u> to eat.

Past: We <u>had</u> to eat. (not "We had to ate.")

Exercise 48.1

A student wrote the following two paragraphs as part of a paper for his ESL composition I class. He was asked to write about several interviews he conducted with people in his future profession, hotel management. The paragraphs contain errors in subject-verb agreement and verb tense, which the student's instructor underlined. Correct the underlined verbs by changing their form: begin by considering when the action took place, and then choose the simplest appropriate verb form to express that time. (Be sure to pay attention to the meaning and context of the sentences to determine which verb form is appropriate.)

> In the past, when someone ▸(1) <u>ask</u> me why I was interested in the hotel business, I always ▸(2) <u>have</u> a hard time answering that question. I do not know exactly when and why I ▸(3) <u>decide</u> to be a hotel manager. The only reason I can think of is my father. In his current job, he ▸(4) <u>travel</u> a lot, and I have had a few chances to follow him and see other cities. Every time I went with him on a business trip, we ▸(5) <u>spended</u> the night in a hotel, and I was surprised at how much hotels ▸(6) <u>does</u> to satisfy their customers. All the employees are always friendly and polite. This gave me a positive image of hotels that made me ▸(7) <u>decided</u> that the hotel business would be right for me.
>
> For this paper, I (8) <u>spended</u> almost two weeks interviewing department heads at a local Hilton Hotel. Mr. Andrew Plain, the person who (9) <u>spend</u> the most time with me, (10) <u>share</u> an experience related to when he first got into the business. One of his first jobs was to plan a wedding, and he (11) <u>feel</u> a lot of responsibility because he (12) <u>believe</u> that a wedding is a one-time life experience for most people. So he wanted to take care of everything and make sure that everything was on track. To prepare for the wedding, he (13) <u>need</u> to work almost every Sunday, and one night he

even (14) <u>have</u> to sleep in his office to attend the
early wedding ceremony the next morning. From my
experience with this interview, I realized that the
people who are interested in the hotel business (15)
<u>needs</u> great dedication to their career.

(4) Negative Verbs

The meaning of a verb may be made **negative** in English in a variety
of ways, chiefly by adding the words *not* or *does not* to the verb (is, *is
not;* can ski, *cannot* ski; drives a car, *does not* drive a car).

Nonnative English speakers (and some native speakers) sometimes
use double negatives. A <u>double negative</u> is an error that occurs when
the meaning of a verb is made negative not just once but twice in
a single sentence. In some languages, a double structure is actually
required in order to negate a verb; for example, the French phrase *je
ne <u>sais</u> pas* ("<u>I</u> <u>don</u>'t <u>know</u>") uses the double structure *ne/pas* around
the verb *sais*. However, a double negative is incorrect in written Eng-
lish.

> *any*
> Henry doesn't have <s>no</s> friends at all. (*or* Henry <s>doesn't have</s> no
> friends at all.)

> *any*
> I looked for articles in the library, but there weren't <s>none</s>.
> (*or* I looked for articles in the library, but there weren't none.)

(5) Phrasal Verbs

Many verbs in English are composed of two or more words—for example, *check up on*, *run for*, *turn into*, and *wait on*. These verbs are
called **phrasal verbs.** It is important to become familiar with phrasal
verbs and their definitions so you will recognize these verbs as
phrasal verbs instead of as verbs that are followed by prepositions.
Knowing the definitions of the individual words that make up these
verbs is not always enough to enable you to define the phrasal verbs
accurately. Even after consulting a dictionary, you will need to pay
close attention to the use of these verbs in speech and writing.

Sometimes the words that make up a phrasal verb can be separated from each other by a direct object. In these **separable phrasal
verbs,** the object can come either before or after the preposition.
For example, "<u>Ellen</u> *<u>turned down</u>* the job offer" and "<u>Ellen</u> *<u>turned</u>*
the job offer *<u>down</u>*" are both correct. However, when the object is a
pronoun, the pronoun must come before the preposition. There-
fore, "<u>Ellen</u> <u>turned</u> *it* <u>down</u> " is correct; "<u>Ellen</u> <u>turned down</u> *it*" is
incorrect.

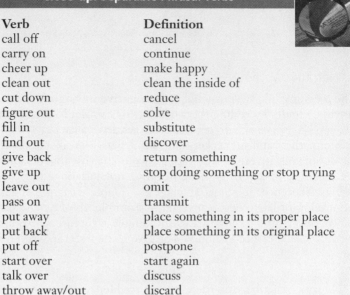

Close-up: Separable Phrasal Verbs

Verb	Definition
call off	cancel
carry on	continue
cheer up	make happy
clean out	clean the inside of
cut down	reduce
figure out	solve
fill in	substitute
find out	discover
give back	return something
give up	stop doing something or stop trying
leave out	omit
pass on	transmit
put away	place something in its proper place
put back	place something in its original place
put off	postpone
start over	start again
talk over	discuss
throw away/out	discard
touch up	repair

However, some phrasal verbs—such as *look into, make up for,* and *break into*—consist of words that can never be separated. With these **inseparable phrasal verbs,** you do not have a choice about where to place the object; the object must always follow the preposition. For example, "Anna *cared for* her niece" is correct, but "Anna *cared* her niece *for*" is incorrect.

Close-up: Inseparable Phrasal Verbs

Verb	Definition
come down with	develop an illness
come up with	produce
do away with	abolish
fall behind in	lag
get along with	be congenial with
get away with	avoid punishment
keep up with	maintain the same achievement or speed
look up to	admire
make up for	compensate
put up with	tolerate
run into	meet by chance

see to	arrange
show up	arrive
stand by	wait *or* remain loyal to
stand up for	support
watch out for	beware of *or* protect

(6) Voice

Verbs may be in either active or passive <u>voice</u>. When the subject of a sentence performs the action of the verb, the verb is in **active voice.** When the action of the verb is performed on the subject, the verb is in **passive voice.**

See 22d

> <u>Karla and Miguel</u> <u>purchased</u> the plane tickets. (active voice)
>
> <u>The plane tickets</u> <u>were purchased</u> by Karla and Miguel. (passive voice)

Because your writing will usually be clearer and more concise if you use the active voice, you should use the passive voice only when you have a good reason to do so. For example, in scientific writing, it is common for writers to use the passive voice in order to convey the idea of scientific objectivity (lack of bias).

(7) Using Infinitives and Gerunds as Nouns

In English, two verb forms may be used as nouns: **infinitives,** which always begin with *to* (as in *to work, to sleep, to eat*), and **gerunds,** which always end in *-ing*, (as in *working, sleeping, eating*).

> <u>*To bite into this steak*</u> <u>requires</u> better teeth than mine. (infinitive used as a noun)
>
> <u>*Cooking*</u> <u>is</u> one of my favorite hobbies. (gerund used as a noun)

Sometimes the gerund and the infinitive form of the same verb can be used interchangeably. For example, "He continued *to sleep*" and "He continued *sleeping*" convey the same meaning. However, this is not always the case. Saying, "Marco and Lisa stopped *to eat* at Julio's Café" is not the same as saying, "Marco and Lisa stopped *eating* at Julio's Café." In this example, the meaning of the sentence changes depending on whether a gerund or infinitive is used.

(8) Using Participles as Adjectives

In English, verb forms called **present participles** and **past participles** are frequently used as adjectives. Present participles usually end in *-ing*, as in *working, sleeping,* and *eating,* and past participles usually end in *-ed, -t,* or *-en,* as in *worked, slept,* and *eaten.*

According to the Bible, God spoke to Moses from a *burning* bush. (present participle used as an adjective)

Some people think raw fish is healthier than *cooked* fish. (past participle used as an adjective)

A **participial phrase** is a group of words consisting of the participle plus the noun phrase that functions as the object or complement of the action being expressed by the participle. To avoid confusion, the participial phrase must be placed as close as possible to the noun it modifies.

Having visited San Francisco last week, Jim and Lynn showed us pictures from their vacation. (The participial phrase is used as an adjective that modifies *Jim and Lynn*.)

(9) Transitive and Intransitive Verbs

Many nonnative English speakers find it difficult to decide whether or not a verb needs an object and in what order direct and indirect objects should appear in a sentence. Learning the difference between transitive verbs and intransitive verbs can help you with such problems.

A **transitive verb** is a verb that has a direct object: "My father asked a question" (subject + verb + direct object). In this example, *asked* is a transitive verb; it needs an object to complete its meaning.

An **intransitive verb** is a verb that does not take an object: "The doctor smiled" (subject + verb). In this example, *smiled* is an intransitive verb; it does not need an object to complete its meaning.

A transitive verb may be followed by a direct object or by both an indirect object and a direct object. (An indirect object answers the question "To whom?" or "For whom?") The indirect object may come before or after the direct object. If the indirect object follows the direct object, the preposition *to* or *for* must precede the indirect object.

    s   v   do

Keith wrote a letter. (subject + verb + direct object)

    s   v   io   do

Keith wrote his friend a letter. (subject + verb + indirect object + direct object)

    s   v   do   io

Keith wrote a letter *to* his friend. (subject + verb + direct object + *to/for* + indirect object)

Some verbs in English look similar and have similar meanings, except that one is transitive and the other is intransitive. For example, *lie* is intransitive, *lay* is transitive; *sit* is intransitive, *set* is transitive;

rise is intransitive, *raise* is transitive. Knowing whether a verb is transitive or intransitive will help you with troublesome verb pairs like these and help you place the words in the correct order.

NOTE: It is also important to know whether a verb is transitive or intransitive because only transitive verbs can be used in the <u>passive voice</u>. To determine whether a verb is transitive or intransitive—that is, to determine whether or not it needs an object—consult the example phrases in a dictionary.

See
22d

(10) Verbs Formed from Nouns

In English, nouns can sometimes be used as verbs, with no change in form (other than the addition of an *s* for agreement with third-person singular subjects or the addition of past tense endings). For example, the nouns *chair, book, frame,* and *father* can all be used as verbs.

She *chairs* a committee on neighborhood safety.

We *booked* a flight to New York for next week.

I will *frame* my daughter's diploma after she graduates.

He *fathered* several children out of wedlock.

48b Solving Noun-Related Problems

<u>Nouns</u> name things: people, objects, places, feelings, and ideas. In English, most nouns have different forms for **singular** and **plural** number (such as singular *star* and plural *stars*), but there are exceptions to this rule. In English, two or more nouns may be used to form a single **compound noun:** "She ate a *cheese sandwich.*"

See
20a

The most common ESL errors related to nouns involve the singular-plural distinction and the use of articles with nouns.

(1) The Singular-Plural Distinction

In English, nouns may have **number;** that is, they may change in form according to whether they name one thing or more than one thing. If a noun names one thing, it is a singular noun; if a noun names more than one thing, it is a plural noun.

To change most singular nouns to plural, add *s* or *es* to the singular form. For example, *pencil* changes to *pencils*, and *bench* changes to *benches*.

However, many nouns in English are irregular. To change an irregular noun from singular to plural, you need to change the spelling of the word instead of just adding a suffix to the word. For example, *mouse* changes to *mice, tooth* changes to *teeth,* and *child* changes to *children*.

> ### Close-up: Noncount Nouns
>
> Some English nouns do not have a plural form. These are called **noncount nouns** because what they name cannot be counted. (**Count nouns** name items that can be counted, such as *woman* or *desk*.) The following commonly used nouns are noncount nouns. These words have no plural forms. Therefore, you should never add *s* or *es* to them.
>
> | | | |
> |---|---|---|
> | advice | evidence | knowledge |
> | clothing | furniture | luggage |
> | education | homework | merchandise |
> | enthusiasm | information | revenge |
> | equipment | | |

NOTE: Some noncount nouns—such as *luggage* or *furniture*—seem like items that can be counted. To avoid confusion, consult the example phrases in a dictionary in order to determine whether a noun takes a regular plural form or an irregular plural form and to determine whether it is a count or a noncount noun.

Exercise 48.2

An ESL student wrote the following paragraph as part of a composition paper about her experiences learning English. Read the paragraph, and decide which of the underlined words need to be made plural and which should remain unchanged. If a word should be made plural, make the necessary correction. If a word is correct as is, mark it with a *C*. If you are not sure whether or not a noun is countable, look it up in a dictionary.

```
            Visiting Ireland for three ▶(1) month expanded my
▶(2) knowledge of English. I took a part-time English
▶(3) course, which was the key to improving my writing.
The ▶(4) course helped me understand the essential
▶(5) rule of English, and I learned a lot of new
(6) vocabulary and expressions. In the first three
(7) lecture, the teacher, Mr. Nelson, explained the
fundamentals of writing in English. My (8) enthusiasm
for the English language increased because I realized
the importance of this (9) language for my (10) future.
Mr. Nelson recommended that I read more English (11)
book. I took his advice, and my English got better.
```

(2) Using Articles with Nouns

English has two types of **articles,** indefinite and definite. Use an **indefinite article** (*a* or *an*) with a noun when readers are not familiar with the noun you are naming—for example, when you are introducing a noun for the first time. To say, "Jatin entered *a* building," signals to the audience that you are introducing the idea of the building into your speech or writing for the first time. The building is unspecific, or indefinite, until it has been identified.

The indefinite article *a* is used when the word following it (which may be a noun or an adjective) begins with a consonant or with a consonant sound: *a tree, a onetime offer.* The indefinite article *an* is used if the word following it begins with a vowel (*a, e, i, o,* or *u*) or with a vowel sound: *an apple, an honor.*

Use the **definite article** (*the*) when the noun you are naming has already been introduced, when the noun is already familiar to readers, or when the noun to which you refer is specific. To say, "Jatin entered *the* building," signals to readers that you are referring to the same building you mentioned earlier. The building has now become specific and may be referred to by the definite article.

Close-up: Using Articles with Nouns

There are three main exceptions to the rules governing the use of articles with nouns:

1. A **plural noun** does not require an **indefinite article:** "I love horses," not "I love *a* horses." (A plural noun does, however, require a definite article when you have already introduced the noun to your readers or when you are referring to a specific plural noun: "I love *the* horses in the national park near my house.")

2. A **noncount noun** may or may not require an article.

   "Love conquers all," not "*A* love conquers all" or "*The* love conquers all."

   "*A* good education is important," not "Good education is important."

   "*The* homework is difficult" or "Homework is difficult," not "*A* homework is difficult."

   To help determine whether or not a noncount noun requires an article, look up that noun in a dictionary and consult the sample sentences provided.

3. A **proper noun,** which names a particular person, place, or thing, sometimes takes an article and sometimes does not. When you use an article with a proper noun, do not capitalize the article unless the article is the first word of the sentence.

   "*The* Mississippi River is one of the longest rivers in the world," not "Mississippi River is one of the longest rivers in the world."

   (continued)

> *Using articles with nouns (continued)*
>
> "Teresa was born in *the* United States," not "Teresa was born in United States."
>
> "China is the most populous nation on earth," not "*The* China is the most populous nation on earth."
>
> To find out whether or not a proper noun requires an article, look up that noun in a dictionary, and consult the sample sentences provided.

NOTE: The rules for article usage outlined in this section may be helpful, but they will not work all the time. For people who speak first languages that do not have an article system (or that have an article system that works very differently from that of English), articles are one of the hardest aspects of the English language to acquire.

Exercise 48.3

The following introductory paragraph of a paper about renewable energy power sources was written for an ESL composition course. Read the paragraph, and decide whether or not each of the underlined noun phrases requires an article. If a noun phrase is correct as is, mark it with a *C*. If a noun phrase needs an article, indicate whether that article should be *a*, *an*, or *the*.

▸(1) <u>Use of electrical power</u> has increased dramatically over ▸(2) <u>last thirty years</u> and continues to rise. ▸(3) <u>Most ordinary sources</u> of ▸(4) <u>electricity</u> require ▸(5) <u>oil</u>, ▸(6) <u>gas</u>, or ▸(7) <u>uranium</u>, which are not ▸(8) <u>renewable resources</u>. Living without ▸(9) <u>electrical power</u> is not feasible as long as everything in our lives depends on ▸(10) <u>electricity</u>, but (11) <u>entire world</u> will be in (12) <u>big crisis</u> if (13) <u>ignorance regarding renewable energy</u> continues. (14) <u>Renewable energy</u>, including (15) <u>solar energy</u>, (16) <u>wind energy</u>, (17) <u>hydro energy</u>, and (18) <u>biomass energy</u>, need (19) <u>more attention</u> from (20) <u>scientists</u>.

---

(3) Using Other Determiners with Nouns

Determiners are words that function as adjectives to limit or qualify the meaning of nouns. In addition to articles, nouns may be identified by other determiners that function in ways similar to articles, such as demonstrative pronouns, possessive nouns and pronouns, numbers (both cardinal and ordinal), and other words indicating amount or number order.

Close-up: Using Other Determiners with Nouns

- **Demonstrative pronouns** (*this, that, these, those*) communicate the following:
  1. the relative nearness or farness of the noun from the speaker's position. Use *this* and *these* for things that are near, *that* and *those* for things that are far: *this* book on my desk, *that* book on your desk; *these* shoes on my feet, *those* shoes in the closet.
  2. the number of things indicated. Use *this* and *that* for singular nouns, *these* and *those* for plural nouns: *this* (or *that*) flower in the vase; *these* (or *those*) flowers in the garden.
- **Possessive nouns and pronouns** (*Ashraf's, his, their*) show who or what the noun belongs to: *Maria's* courage, *everybody's* fears, the *country's* natural resources, *my* personality, *our* groceries.
- **Cardinal numbers** (*three, fifty, a thousand*) indicate the quantity of the noun: *seven* continents, *twelve* apples, *a hundred* lakes.
- **Ordinal numbers** (*first, tenth, thirtieth*) indicate in what order the noun appears among other items: *third* planet from the sun, *first* date, *tenth* anniversary.
- Words other than numbers may indicate **amount** (*many, few*) or **order** (*next, last*) and function in the same ways as cardinal and ordinal numbers: *few* opportunities, *last* chance.

48c Using Prepositions

See 20f

In English, prepositions (such as *to, from, at, with, among,* and *between*) link noun phrases to other parts of a sentence. Prepositions convey several different kinds of information:

- Relations to **time** (*at* nine o'clock, *in* five minutes, *for* a month)
- Relations to **place** (*in* the classroom, *at* the library, *beside* the chair) and **direction** (*to* the market, *onto* the stage, *toward* the freeway)
- Relations of **association** (go *with* someone, the tip *of* the iceberg)
- Relations of **purpose** (working *for* money, dieting *to* lose weight)

(1) Commonly Used Prepositional Phrases

In English, the use of prepositions is often idiomatic rather than governed by grammatical rules. In many cases, therefore, learners of English as a second language need to memorize which prepositions are used in which phrases.

In English, some prepositions that relate to time have specific uses with certain nouns, such as days, months, and seasons:

- *On* is used with days and specific dates: *on* Monday, *on* September 13, 1977.
- *In* is used with months, seasons, and years: *in* November, *in* the spring, *in* 1999.
- *In* is also used when referring to some parts of the day, as in the following cases: *in* the morning, *in* the afternoon, *in* the evening.
- *At* is used to refer to other parts of the day: *at* noon, *at* night, *at* seven o'clock.

Close-up: Difficult Prepositional Phrases

The following phrases (accompanied by their correct prepositions) sometimes cause difficulties for ESL writers:

according *to*	*at* least	relevant *to*
apologize *to*	*at* most	similar *to*
appeal *to*	refer *to*	subscribe *to*
different *from*		

(2) Pronouns in Prepositional Phrases

Both native and nonnative English speakers sometimes have difficulty choosing which pronoun should follow a preposition. The pronoun that is the object of a preposition should be in the <u>objective case</u>.

See 21a–b

Would you like to go to a movie with <u>me</u>? (not "Would you like to go to a movie with *I*?")

Would you like to eat lunch with Felix and <u>me</u>? (not "Would you like to eat lunch with Felix and *I*?")

Just between you and <u>me</u>, I think you won the contest. (not "Just between *you* and *I*, I think you won the contest.")

Exercise 48.4

An ESL student in a composition class wrote the following paragraphs as part of a paper about her experiences learning to write in English. In several cases, she chose the wrong prepositions. The student's instructor has underlined the misused prepositions. Your task is to replace each underlined preposition with a correct preposition. (In some cases, there may be more than one possible correct answer.) If you have trouble, consult a dictionary, and look up a noun or verb that is part of the phrase in question.

My first experience writing ▶(1) <u>of</u> English took
place ▶(2) <u>at</u> my early youth. I don't remember what the
experience was like, but I do know that I have improved
my writing skills since then. The improvement stems from
various reasons. One major impact ▶(3) <u>to</u> my writing was
the fact that I attended an American school ▶(4) <u>of</u> my
country. This helped a lot because the first language
▶(5) <u>to</u> the school was English. Being surrounded (6) <u>in</u>
English helped me improve both my verbal skills and my
writing skills. Another major factor that helped me
develop my English writing skills, especially my grammar
and vocabulary, was reading novels.

(7) <u>At</u> the future, I plan to improve my writing
skills in English by participating (8) <u>to</u> several
activities. I plan to read more novels so I can further
develop the grammar and vocabulary skills that will help
me earn my degree. I also plan to communicate verbally
with native speakers and to listen (9) <u>at</u> public
speeches (such as the president's state of the union
address), which usually contain rich vocabulary. But my
main plan is to keep writing more papers and discussing
my writing (10) <u>to</u> my instructor. The more I write, the
more confident I will become and the more my writing
will improve. And there is always room for improvement.

48d Understanding Word Order

Word order is extremely important in English sentences. For example, word order may indicate which word is the subject of the sentence and which is the object, or it may indicate whether the
sentence is a question or a statement.

(1) Standard Word Order

Like Chinese, English is an "SVO" language, one in which the most
typical sentence pattern is "subject-verb-object." (Arabic, by contrast, is an example of a "VSO" language.) If you deviate from
the SVO pattern, you may not communicate your ideas clearly.
There are times, however, when writers in English do deviate from
the SVO pattern. For information on some of these instances, **see
48d2–6.**

(2) Word Order in Questions

Word order in questions can be particularly troublesome for speakers
of languages other than English because there are so many different
ways to arrange words when questions are formed in English.

Close-up: Word Order in Questions

- To create a **yes/no question** from a statement using the verb *be*, simply move the helping verb so it precedes the subject.

  Rasheem is researching the depletion of the ozone layer.

  Is Rasheem researching the depletion of the ozone layer?

- To create a **yes/no question** from a statement using a verb other than *be*, use a form of the auxiliary verb *do* before the subject, and do not invert the subject and verb.

  Does Rasheem want to research the depletion of the ozone layer?

  Do Rasheem's friends want to help him with his research?

  Did Rasheem's professors approve his research proposal?

- You can also form a question by adding a **tag question** (such as *won't he?* or *didn't I?*) to the end of a statement. If the verb of the main statement is *positive*, then the verb of the tag question is *negative*; if the verb of the main statement is *negative*, then the verb of the tag question is *positive*.

  Rasheem is researching the depletion of the ozone layer, isn't he?

  Rasheem doesn't intend to write his dissertation about the depletion of the ozone layer, does he?

- To create a **question asking for information**, use **interrogative** words (*who, what, where, when, why, how*), and invert the order of the subject and verb (note that *who* functions as the subject of the question in which it appears). Do not move the helping verb to precede the subject.

  Who is researching the depletion of the ozone layer?

  What is Rasheem researching?

  Where is Rasheem researching the depletion of the ozone layer?

(3) Word Order in Imperative Sentences

Imperative sentences state commands. It is common for the subject of an imperative sentence to be left out because the word *you* is understood to be the subject: "Go to school"; "Eat your dinner." Therefore, the word order pattern in an imperative sentence is often "verb-object," or "VO."

(4) Word Order with Direct and Indirect Quotations

Direct quotations use the exact words that the original writer or speaker used; consequently, the order of the words in a direct quotation cannot be changed. However, you can vary the placement of the **identifying tag,** the phrase that identifies the writer or speaker you are quoting. The identifying tag can be placed **before, in the middle of,** or **after** the quotation. (Note that direct quotations are always placed within quotation marks.)

> He said, "Before I return the shoes to the department store, I must find the receipt." (identifying tag before the quotation)

> "Before I return the shoes to the department store," he said, "I must find the receipt." (identifying tag in the middle of the quotation)

> "Before I return the shoes to the department store, I must find the receipt," he said. (identifying tag after the quotation)

With **indirect quotations,** which summarize what the speaker or writer said, quotation marks are not used. Because you are simply reporting to your audience what the speaker or writer said, not quoting directly, you may change the words the speaker or writer used so long as you retain the original meaning of the source. With indirect quotations, it is often necessary to change the order of the words as well as the pronouns and the verb tenses used in the source.

> **Direct quotation:** "Before I return the shoes to the department store, I must find the receipt."

> **Indirect quotation:** He said that he needed to find the receipt for the shoes before he could return them to the department store.

(5) Position of Adjectives and Adverbs

Adjectives and adverbs are modifiers that describe or provide additional information about other words in a sentence. Adjectives provide information about nouns, and adverbs provide information about verbs, adjectives, and other adverbs.

Adjectives generally describe nouns. A book might be *large* or *small, red* or *blue, expensive* or *cheap.* Unlike adjectives in other languages, English adjectives change their form only to indicate degree (*fast, faster, fastest*). In English, adjectives do not have to agree in number or gender with the nouns they describe.

See 20d, Ch. 23

Adverbs in English are easily identified; nearly all end in *-ly* (*calmly, loudly, rapidly*), except for a small number of "intensifiers," such as *very, rather,* and *quite.* Adverbs generally describe verbs. A person may walk *slowly* or *quickly, shyly* or *confidently, elegantly* or *clumsily.* Adverbs may also modify adjectives (*very* blue eyes, *truly* religious man) or other adverbs (answer *rather* stupidly, investigate *extremely* thoroughly).

See 20e, Ch. 23

In English, adjectives usually appear **before** the nouns they describe. In English, one would say, "*Red and black cars* are involved in more accidents than *blue, green, or white cars.*"

Adverbs may appear **before** or **after** the verbs they describe, but they should be placed as close to the verb as possible: not "I *told* John that I couldn't meet him for lunch *politely,*" but "I *politely told* John that I couldn't meet him for lunch" or "I *told* John *politely* that I couldn't meet him for lunch." When an adverb describes an adjective or another adverb, it usually comes *before* that adjective or adverb: "The essay has *basically* sound logic"; "You must express yourself *absolutely* clearly." Never place an adverb between the verb and the direct object.

Incorrect: Rolf drank *quickly* the water.

Correct: Rolf drank the water *quickly* (or, Rolf *quickly* drank the water).

(6) Order of Adjectives

A single noun may be described by more than one adjective—sometimes even by a list of adjectives in a row. Given a list of three or four adjectives, native English speakers would arrange them in a sentence in the same order. If shoes are to be described as *green* and *big*, numbering *two*, and of the type worn for playing *tennis*, native speakers would say, "two big green tennis shoes." Generally, the adjectives most important in completing the meaning of the noun are placed closest to the noun.

Close-up: Order of Articles, Adjectives, and Other Words

- Articles (*a, an, the*), demonstrative pronouns (*this, that, these, those*), or possessive nouns or pronouns (*his, our, Maria's, everybody's*)
- Amounts (*one, five, many, few*) and order (*first, next, last*)
- Personal opinions (*nice, ugly, crowded, pitiful*)
- Sizes and shapes (*small, tall, straight, crooked*)
- Ages (*young, old, modern, ancient*)
- Colors (*red, blue, dark, light*)
- Nouns that compound to form a noun phrase (*soccer* ball, *cardboard* box, *history* class)

Exercise 48.5

Write five original sentences in which two or three adjectives describe a noun. Be sure that the adjectives are in the right order.

48e Using Pronouns

Any English noun may be replaced by a <u>pronoun</u>. For example, *doctor* may be replaced by *he* or *she, books* by *them,* and *comput*er by *it.* The English language uses more pronouns than most other languages. (Note that a pronoun, like the noun it replaces, must <u>agree</u> with the verb in number.)

(1) Pronoun Reference

<u>Pronoun reference</u> is very important in English sentences, where the noun the pronoun replaces (the **antecedent**) must be easily identified. In general, then, you should place the pronoun as close as possible to the noun it replaces so the noun to which the pronoun refers is clear. If this is impossible, it is best to use the noun itself instead of replacing it with a pronoun.

> **Unclear:** When Tara met Emily, she was nervous. (Does *she* refer to Tara or Emily?)
>
> **Clear:** When Tara met Emily, Tara was nervous.
>
> **Unclear:** Stefano and Victor love his DVD collection. (Whose DVD collection—Stefano's, Victor's, or someone else's?)
>
> **Clear:** Stefano and Victor love Emilio's DVD collection.

(2) Pronoun Placement

Never use a pronoun immediately after the noun it replaces. For example, do not say, "Most of my classmates they are smart"; instead, say, "Most of my classmates are smart." The only exception to this rule occurs with an **intensive pronoun,** which ends in *-self* and emphasizes the preceding noun or pronoun: "Marta *herself* was eager to hear the results."

(3) Indefinite Pronouns

Unlike **personal pronouns** (*I, you, he, she, it, we, they, me, him, her, us,* and *them*), **indefinite pronouns** do not refer to a particular person, place, or thing. Therefore, an indefinite pronoun does not require an antecedent. **Indefinite pronoun subjects** (*anybody, nobody, each, either, someone, something, all, some*), like personal pronouns, must <u>agree</u> in number with the sentence's verb.

    has
Nobody ~~have~~ failed the exam. (*Nobody* is a singular subject and requires a singular verb.)

(4) Appositives

Appositives are nouns or noun phrases that identify or rename an adjacent noun or pronoun. An appositive usually follows the noun it explains or modifies but can sometimes precede it.

> My parents, Mary and John, live in Louisiana. (*Mary and John* identifies *parents*.)

NOTE: The <u>case</u> of a pronoun in an appositive depends on the case of the word it describes.

If an appositive is *not* necessary to the meaning of the sentence, use commas to set off the appositive from the rest of the sentence. If an appositive *is* necessary to the meaning of the sentence, do not use commas.

> His aunt Trang is in the hospital. (*Trang* is necessary to the meaning of the sentence because it identifies which aunt is in the hospital.)

> Akta's car, a 1994 Jeep Cherokee, broke down last night, and she had to walk home. (*a 1994 Jeep Cherokee* is not necessary to the meaning of the sentence.)

(5) Pronouns and Gender

A pronoun must agree in **gender** with the noun to which it refers.

> My *sister* sold *her* old car.

> Your *uncle* is walking *his* dog.

NOTE: In English, most nonhuman nouns are referred to as *it* because they do not have grammatical gender. However, exceptions are sometimes made for pets, ships, and countries. Pets are often referred to as *he* or *she*, depending on their sex, and ships and countries are sometimes referred to as *she*.

Exercise 48.6

There are no pronouns in the following passage. The repetition of the nouns again and again would seem strange to a native English speaker. Rewrite the passage, replacing as many of the nouns as possible with appropriate pronouns. Be sure that the connection between the pronouns and the nouns they replace is clear.

> ▶The young couple seated across from Daniel at dinner the night before were newlyweds from Tokyo. ▶The young couple and Daniel ate together with other guests of the inn at long, low tables in a large dining room with straw mat flooring. ▶The man introduced himself immediately in English, shook Daniel's hand firmly, and, after learning that

Daniel was not a tourist but a resident working in Osaka, gave Daniel a business card. ►The man had just finished college and was working at the man's first real job, clerking in a bank. ►Even in a sweatsuit, the man looked ready for the office: chin closely shaven, bristly hair neatly clipped, nails clean and buffed. After a while the man and Daniel exhausted the man's store of English and drifted into Japanese.

The man's wife, shy up until then, took over as the man fell silent. The woman and Daniel talked about the new popularity of hot springs spas in the countryside around the inn, the difficulty of finding good schools for the children the woman hoped to have soon, the differences between food in Tokyo and Osaka. The woman's husband ate busily. From time to time the woman refilled the man's beer glass or served the man radish pickles from a china bowl in the middle of the table, and then returned to the conversation.

48f Distinguishing Commonly Confused Words

A number of word pairs in English have similar meanings. These word pairs can be confusing to nonnative English speakers because the ways in which the expressions are used in sentences are different although their meanings may be similar.

No and Not

No is an adjective; *not* is an adverb. Therefore, use *no* with nouns, and use *not* with verbs, adjectives, and other adverbs.

She has <u>no</u> desire to go to the football game.

Sergio's sisters are <u>not</u> friendly.

Too and Very

Too is an intensifier. It is used to add emphasis in a sentence and to indicate excess.

It is <u>too</u> cold outside to go swimming.

Very is also an intensifier. It means greatly or intensely, but not to excess.

It was <u>very</u> cold outside, but not cold enough to keep us from playing in the backyard.

Even , Even If, and Even Though

When used as an adverb, *even* is used to intensify or indicate surprise.

Greta felt <u>even</u> worse than she looked.

<u>Even</u> my little brother knows how to figure that out!

Even if is used in a sentence where there is a condition that may or may not occur.

Even if it rains tomorrow, I'm going to the park.

Even though is similar in meaning to *although*.

Even though Christopher is a very fast runner, he did not make the national track team.

A Few/A Little and Few/Little

A few and *a little* mean not much, but some or enough. *A few* is used with count nouns. *A little* is used with noncount nouns.

We have a few screws remaining from the project.

There is a little bit of paint left in the can.

Few and *little* mean a small number—there are some, but perhaps not as much as one would like.

Few singers are as talented as Kelly.

I have little hope that this situation will change.

Much and Many

Both *much* and *many* mean "a great quantity" or "to a great degree." Use *much* to modify noncount nouns: "much experience"; "much money." Use *many* to modify count nouns: "many people"; "many incidents."

Most of, Most, and The Most

Most and *most of* have similar meanings. *Most of* means "nearly all of something." Use *most of* when the noun that follows is a specific plural noun. When you use *most of*, be sure to use the definite article *the* before the noun.

Most of the children had cookies for dessert.

Most is used for more general observations and means nearly all.

Most houses in the United States have electricity.

The most is used for comparing more than two of something.

Thomas has the most jellybeans.

Pedro is the most experienced of the engineers.

Some and *Any*

Some denotes an unspecified amount or quantity that may be part of a larger amount. It can modify both count and noncount nouns: "some water"; "some melons." *Any* indicates an unspecified amount, which may be none, some, or all. It can modify both count and noncount nouns: "any person"; "any luggage."

48g Understanding Spelling, Punctuation, and Capitalization

In English, spelling, punctuation, and capitalization are important because all three help readers to understand your meaning.

(1) Spelling

Misspelled words can confuse and distract readers. <u>Spelling</u> in English is not perfectly phonetic and sometimes may seem illogical. In many languages that use a phonetic alphabet or syllabary, such as Japanese, Spanish, or Persian script, words are spelled as they are pronounced. In contrast, spelling in English may be related more to the history of the word and its origins in other languages than to the way a word is pronounced. Therefore, learning to spell correctly is often a matter of memorization, not sounding out the word phonetically. For example, "ough" is pronounced differently in the words *tough*, *though*, and *thought*. In addition to memorizing the spelling of words, you can use your computer's spell checker to help you, but remember that spell checkers do not identify all misspelled words.

See
Ch. 35

(2) Punctuation

<u>Punctuation</u> provides readers with hints to the meaning a writer is trying to convey. Since punctuation rules vary from language to language, it is important to learn how punctuation is used in American English.

See
Pt. 5

(3) Capitalization

Different languages have different rules for <u>capitalization</u>; in fact, in the writing systems of some languages, capitalization does not exist at all. English has very specific rules for the use of capital letters, and when a writer violates them, it can distract or confuse a reader.

See
Ch. 36

Exercise 48.7

An ESL student in a composition course wrote the following paragraph as part of a paper about his experiences learning to write in

English. Rewrite the paragraph, correcting errors in spelling, punctuation, and capitalization.

▶My first experience started when I was studying english as a second language in Collage, I had to write essays as part of the course. ▶The teacher assigned us to write about something such as Winter, football games or living in the dessert. ▶It is not so hard to write about these things, but I did not have the necesary tools for arranging the information in my mind. ▶Therefore when I submitted my assignment, I got a low grade. However the teacher did not write enough comments on my paper when he corrected it. I remember one day when he asked the class to write about new technology. I spent a long time writing in order to turn in a high-quality essay. In the end I got a c and he wrote at the end of my paper "you need to work harder". That made me so disapointed; I knew I had a very long way to go to improve my writing.

Glossary of Usage

This glossary of usage lists words and phrases that writers often find troublesome and explains how they are used.

ESL Tip

For a list of commonly confused words that present challenges for ESL writers, **see 48f.**

a, an Use *a* before words that begin with consonants and words with initial vowels that sound like consonants: *a* person, *a* historical document, *a* one-horse carriage, *a* uniform. Use *an* before words that begin with vowels and words that begin with a silent *h*: *an* artist, *an* honest person.

accept, except *Accept* is a verb that means "to receive"; *except* as a preposition or conjunction means "other than" and as a verb means "to leave out": The auditors will *accept* all your claims *except* the last two. Some businesses are *excepted* from the regulation.

advice, advise *Advice* is a noun meaning "opinion or information offered"; *advise* is a verb that means "to offer advice to": The broker *advised* her client to take his attorney's *advice*.

affect, effect *Affect* is a verb meaning "to influence"; *effect* can be a verb or a noun—as a verb it means "to bring about," and as a noun it means "result": We know how the drug *affects* patients immediately, but little is known of its long-term *effects*. The arbitrator tried to *effect* a settlement between the parties.

all ready, already *All ready* means "completely prepared"; *already* means "by or before this or that time": I was *all ready* to help, but it was *already* too late.

all right, alright Although the use of *alright* is increasing, current usage calls for *all right*.

allusion, illusion An *allusion* is a reference or hint; an *illusion* is something that is not what it seems: The poem makes an *allusion* to the Pandora myth. The shadow created an optical *illusion*.

a lot *A lot* is always two words.

among, between *Among* refers to groups of more than two things; *between* refers to just two things: The three parties agreed *among* themselves to settle the case. There will be a brief intermission *between* the two acts. (Note that *amongst* is British, not American, usage.)

amount, number *Amount* refers to a quantity that cannot be counted; *number* refers to things that can be counted: Even a small *amount* of caffeine can be harmful. Seeing their commander fall, a large *number* of troops ran to his aid.

an, a   See **a, an.**

and/or   In business or technical writing, use *and/or* when either or both of the items it connects can apply. In college writing, however, avoid the use of *and/or.*

as . . . as . . .   In such constructions, *as* signals a comparison; therefore, you must always use the second *as:* John Steinbeck's *East of Eden* is *as* long *as* his *The Grapes of Wrath.*

as, like   *As* can be used as a conjunction (to introduce a complete clause) or as a preposition; *like* should be used as a preposition only: In *The Scarlet Letter,* Hawthorne uses imagery as (not *like*) he does in his other works. After classes, Fred works *as* a manager of a fast food restaurant. Writers *like* Carl Sandburg appear once in a generation.

at, to   Many people use the prepositions *at* and *to* after *where* in conversation: *Where* are you working *at*? *Where* are you going *to*? This usage is redundant and should not appear in college writing.

awhile, a while   *Awhile* is an adverb; *a while,* which consists of an article and a noun, is used as the object of a preposition: Before we continue, we will rest *awhile* (modifies the verb *rest*); Before we continue, we will rest for *a while* (object of the preposition *for*)

bad, badly   *Bad* is an adjective, and *badly* is an adverb: The school board decided that *Huckleberry Finn* was a *bad* book. American automobile makers did not do *badly* this year. After verbs that refer to any of the senses or after any other linking verb, use the adjective form: He looked *bad.* He felt *bad.* It seemed *bad.*

being as, being that   These awkward phrases add unnecessary words, thereby weakening your writing. Use *because* instead.

beside, besides   *Beside* is a preposition meaning "next to"; *besides* can be either a preposition meaning "except" or "other than" or an adverb meaning "as well": *Beside* the tower was a wall that ran the length of the city. *Besides* its industrial uses, laser technology has many other applications. Edison invented not only the lightbulb but the phonograph *besides.*

between, among   See **among, between.**

bring, take   *Bring* means "to transport from a farther place to a nearer place"; *take* means "to carry or convey from a nearer place to a farther place": *Bring* me a souvenir from your trip. *Take* this message to the general, and wait for a reply.

can, may   *Can* denotes ability; *may* indicates permission: If you *can* play, you *may* use my piano.

capital, capitol   *Capital* refers to a city that is an official seat of government; *capitol* refers to a building in which a legislature meets: Washington, DC, is the *capital* of the United States. When we were there, we visited the *Capitol* building.

center around   This imprecise phrase is acceptable in speech and informal writing but not in college writing. Use *center on* instead.

cite, site   *Cite* is a verb meaning "to quote as an authority or example"; *site* is a noun meaning "a place or setting"; it is also a shortened form of *Web site:* Jeff *cited* five sources in his research paper. The builder cleared the *site* for the new bank. Marisa uploaded her *site* to the Web.

climactic, climatic   *Climactic* means "of or related to a climax"; *climatic* means "of or related to climate": The *climactic* moment of the movie occurred unexpectedly. If scientists are correct, the *climatic* conditions of Earth are changing.

coarse, course   *Coarse* is an adjective meaning "inferior" or "having a rough, uneven texture"; *course* is a noun meaning "a route or path," "an area on which a sport is played," or "a unit of study": *Coarse* sandpaper is used to smooth the surface. The *course* of true love never runs smoothly. Last semester I had to drop a *course*.

complement, compliment   *Complement* means "to complete or add to"; *compliment* means "to give praise": A double-blind study would *complement* their preliminary research. My instructor *complimented* me on my improvement.

conscious, conscience   *Conscious* is an adjective meaning "having one's mental faculties awake"; *conscience* is a noun that means the moral sense of right and wrong: The patient will remain *conscious* during the procedure. His *conscience* would not allow him to lie.

continual, continuous   *Continual* means "recurring at intervals"; *continuous* refers to an action that occurs without interruption: A pulsar is a star that emits a *continual* stream of electromagnetic radiation. (It emits radiation at regular intervals.) A small battery allows the watch to run *continuously* for five years. (It runs without stopping.)

could of, should of, would of   The contractions *could've, should've,* and *would've* are often misspelled as the nonstandard constructions *could of, should of,* and *would of.* Use *could have, should have,* and *would have* in college writing.

council, counsel   A *council* is "a body of people who serve in a legislative or advisory capacity"; *counsel* means "to offer advice or guidance": The city *council* argued about the proposed ban on smoking. The judge *counseled* the couple to settle their differences.

couple, couple of   *Couple* means "a pair," but *couple of* is often used colloquially to mean "several" or "a few." In your college writing, specify "four points" or "two examples" rather than using "a couple of."

criterion, criteria   *Criteria,* from the Greek, is the plural of *criterion,* meaning "standard for judgment": Of all the *criteria* for hiring graduating seniors, class rank is the most important *criterion*.

data *Data* is the plural of the Latin *datum*, meaning "fact." In everyday speech and writing, *data* is often used as the singular as well as the plural form. In college writing, use *data* only for the plural: The *data* discussed in this section *are* summarized in Appendix A.

different from, different than *Different than* is widely used in American speech. In college writing, use *different from*.

discreet, discrete *Discreet* means "careful or prudent"; *discrete* means "separate or individually distinct": Because Madame Bovary was not *discreet*, her reputation suffered. Atoms can be broken into hundreds of *discrete* particles.

disinterested, uninterested *Disinterested* means "objective" or "capable of making an impartial judgment"; *uninterested* means "indifferent or unconcerned": The American judicial system depends on *disinterested* jurors. Finding no treasure, Hernando de Soto was *uninterested* in going farther.

don't, doesn't *Don't* is the contraction of *do not; doesn't* is the contraction of *does not.* Do not confuse the two: My dog *doesn't* (not *don't*) like to walk in the rain. (Note that contractions are generally not acceptable in college writing.)

effect, affect See **affect, effect.**

e.g. *E.g.* is an abbreviation for the Latin *exempli gratia*, meaning "for example" or "for instance." In college writing, do not use *e.g.* Instead, use "for example" or "for instance."

emigrate from, immigrate to To *emigrate* is "to leave one's country and settle in another"; to *immigrate* is "to come to another country and reside there." The noun forms of these words are *emigrant* and *immigrant:* My great-grandfather *emigrated from* Warsaw along with many other *emigrants* from Poland. Many people *immigrate* to the United States for economic reasons, but such *immigrants* still face great challenges.

eminent, imminent *Eminent* is an adjective meaning "standing above others" or "prominent"; *imminent* means "about to occur": Oliver Wendell Holmes Jr. was an *eminent* jurist. In ancient times, a comet signaled *imminent* disaster.

enthused *Enthused*, a colloquial form of *enthusiastic*, should not be used in college writing.

etc. *Etc.*, the abbreviation of *et cetera*, means "and the rest." Do not use it in your college writing. Instead, use "and so on"—or, better yet, specify exactly what *etc.* stands for.

everyday, every day *Everyday* is an adjective that means "ordinary" or "commonplace"; *every day* means "occurring daily": In the Gettysburg Address, Lincoln used *everyday* language. She exercises almost *every day*.

everyone, every one *Everyone* is an indefinite pronoun meaning "every person"; *every one* means "every individual or thing in a particular group": *Everyone* seems happier in the spring. *Every one* of the packages had been opened.

except, accept   See **accept, except.**

explicit, implicit   *Explicit* means "expressed or stated directly"; *implicit* means "implied" or "expressed or stated indirectly": The director *explicitly* warned the actors to be on time for rehearsals. Her *implicit* message was that lateness would not be tolerated.

farther, further   *Farther* designates distance; *further* designates degree: I have traveled *farther* from home than any of my relatives. Critics charge that welfare subsidies encourage *further* dependence.

fewer, less   Use *fewer* with nouns that can be counted: *fewer* books, *fewer* people, *fewer* dollars. Use *less* with quantities that cannot be counted: *less* pain, *less* power, *less* enthusiasm.

firstly (secondly, thirdly, . . .)   Archaic forms meaning "in the first . . . second . . . third place." Use *first, second, third* instead.

further, farther   See **farther, further.**

good, well   *Good* is an adjective, never an adverb: She is a *good* swimmer. *Well* can function as an adverb or as an adjective. As an adverb, it means "in a good manner": She swam *well* (not *good*) in the meet. *Well* is used as an adjective with verbs that denote a state of being or feeling. Here *well* can mean "in good health": I feel *well*.

got to   *Got to* is not acceptable in college writing. To indicate obligation, use *have to, has to,* or *must*.

hanged, hung   Both *hanged* and *hung* are past participles of *hang*. *Hanged* is used to refer to executions; *hung* is used to mean "suspended": Billy Budd was *hanged* for killing the master-at-arms. The stockings were *hung* by the chimney with care.

he, she   Traditionally *he* has been used in the generic sense to refer to both males and females. To acknowledge the equality of the sexes, however, avoid the generic *he*. Use plural pronouns whenever possible. **See 19e2.**

hopefully   The adverb *hopefully*, meaning "in a hopeful manner," should modify a verb, an adjective, or another adverb. Do not use *hopefully* as a sentence modifier meaning "it is hoped." Rather than "*Hopefully*, scientists will soon discover a cure for AIDS," write "*I hope* scientists will soon discover a cure for AIDS."

i.e.   *I.e.* is an abbreviation for the Latin *id est*, meaning "that is." In college writing, do not use *i.e.* Instead, use its English equivalent.

if, whether   When asking indirect questions or expressing doubt, use *whether*: He asked *whether* (not *if*) the flight would be delayed. The flight attendant was not sure *whether* (not *if*) it would be delayed.

illusion, allusion   See **allusion, illusion.**

immigrate to, emigrate from   See **emigrate from, immigrate to.**

implicit, explicit   See **explicit, implicit.**

imply, infer   *Imply* means "to hint" or "to suggest"; *infer* means "to conclude from": Mark Antony *implied* that the conspirators had murdered Caesar. The crowd *inferred* his meaning and called for justice.

infer, imply   See **imply, infer.**

inside of, outside of   *Of* is unnecessary when *inside* and *outside* are used as prepositions. *Inside of* is colloquial in references to time: He waited *inside* (not *inside of*) the coffee shop. He could run a mile in *under* (not *inside of*) eight minutes.

irregardless, regardless   *Irregardless* is a nonstandard version of *regardless.* Use *regardless* or *irrespective* instead.

is when, is where   These constructions are faulty when they appear in definitions: A playoff is (not *is when*) an additional game played to establish the winner of a tie.

its, it's   *Its* is a possessive pronoun; *it's* is a contraction of *it is*: It's no secret that the bank is out to protect *its* assets.

kind of, sort of   *Kind of* and *sort of* to mean "rather" or "somewhat" are colloquial and should not appear in college writing: It is well known that Napoleon was *rather* (not *kind of*) short.

lay, lie   See **lie, lay.**

leave, let   *Leave* means "to go away from" or "to *let* remain"; *let* means "to allow" or "to permit": *Let* (not *leave*) me give you a hand.

less, fewer   See **fewer, less.**

let, leave   See **leave, let.**

lie, lay   *Lie* is an intransitive verb (one that does not take an object) meaning "to recline." Its principal forms are *lie, lay, lain, lying*: Each afternoon she would *lie* in the sun and listen to the surf. *As I Lay Dying* is a novel by William Faulkner. By 1871, Troy had *lain* undisturbed for two thousand years. The painting shows a nude *lying* on a couch.

   Lay is a transitive verb (one that takes an object) meaning "to put" or "to place." Its principal forms are *lay, laid, laid, laying*: The Federalist Papers *lay* the foundation for American conservatism. In October 1781, the British *laid* down their arms and surrendered. He had *laid* his money on the counter before leaving. We watched the stonemasons *laying* a wall.

like, as   See **as, like.**

loose, lose   *Loose* is an adjective meaning "not rigidly fastened or securely attached"; *lose* is a verb meaning "to misplace": The marble facing of the building became *loose* and fell to the sidewalk. After only two drinks, most people *lose* their ability to judge distance.

lots, lots of, a lot of   These words are colloquial substitutes for *many, much,* or *a great deal of.* Avoid their use in college writing: The students had many (not *lots of* or *a lot of*) options for essay topics.

man   Like the generic pronoun *he*, *man* has been used in English to denote members of both sexes. This usage is being replaced by *human beings, people*, or similar terms that do not specify gender. See **19e2**.

may, can   See **can, may**.

may be, maybe   *May be* is a verb phrase: *maybe* is an adverb meaning "perhaps": She *may be* the smartest student in the class. *Maybe* her experience has given her an advantage.

media, medium   *Medium*, meaning "a means of conveying or broadcasting something," is singular; *media* is the plural form and requires a plural verb: The *media* have distorted the issue.

might have, might of   *Might of* is a nonstandard spelling of the contraction of *might have* (*might've*). Use *might have* in college writing.

number, amount   See **amount, number**.

OK, O.K., okay   All three spellings are acceptable, but this term should be avoided in college writing. Replace it with a more specific word or words: The lecture was *adequate* (not *okay*), if uninspiring.

outside of, inside of   See **inside of, outside of**.

passed, past   *Passed* is the past tense of the verb *pass; past* means "belonging to a former time" or "no longer current": The car must have been going eighty miles per hour when it *passed* us. In the envelope was a bill marked *past* due.

percent, percentage   *Percent* indicates a part of a hundred when a specific number is referred to: "*10 percent* of his salary." *Percentage* is used when no specific number is referred to: "a *percentage* of next year's receipts." In technical and business writing, it is permissible to use the % sign after percentages you are comparing. Write out the word *percent* in college writing.

phenomenon, phenomena   A *phenomenon* is a single observable fact or event. It can also refer to a rare or significant occurrence. *Phenomena* is the plural form and requires a plural verb: Many supposedly paranormal *phenomena* are easily explained.

plus   As a preposition, *plus* means "in addition to." Avoid using *plus* as a substitute for *and:* Include the principal, *plus* the interest, in your calculations. Your quote was too high; moreover (not *plus*), it was inaccurate.

precede, proceed   *Precede* means "to go or come before"; *proceed* means "to go forward in an orderly way": Robert Frost's *North of Boston* was *preceded* by an earlier volume. In 1532, Francisco Pizarro landed at Tumbes and *proceeded* south.

principal, principle   As a noun, *principal* means "a sum of money (minus interest) invested or lent" or "a person in the leading position"; as an adjective, it means "most important"; a *principle* is a noun meaning a rule of conduct or a basic truth: He wanted to reduce the *principal* of the loan. The *principal* of the high school is a talented administrator.

Women are the *principal* wage earners in many American households. The Constitution embodies certain fundamental *principles.*

quote, quotation   *Quote* is a verb. *Quotation* is a noun. In college writing, do not use *quote* as a shortened form of *quotation:* Scholars attribute these *quotations* (not *quotes*) to Shakespeare.

raise, rise   *Raise* is a transitive verb, and *rise* is an intransitive verb—that is, *raise* takes an object, and *rise* does not: My grandparents *raised* a large family. The sun will *rise* at 6:12 this morning.

real, really   *Real* means "genuine" or "authentic"; *really* means "actually." In your college writing, do not use *real* as an adjective meaning "very."

reason is that, reason is because   *Reason* should be used with *that* and not with *because,* which is redundant: The *reason* he left is *that* (not *because*) you insulted him.

regardless, irregardless   See **irregardless, regardless.**

respectably, respectfully, respectively   *Respectably* means "worthy of respect"; *respectfully* means "giving honor or deference"; *respectively* means "in the order given": He skated quite *respectably* at his first Olympics. The seminar taught us to treat others *respectfully.* The first- and second-place winners were Tai and Kim, *respectively.*

rise, raise   See **raise, rise.**

set, sit   *Set* means "to put down" or "to lay." Its principal forms are *set* and *setting:* After rocking the baby to sleep, he *set* her down carefully in her crib. After *setting* her down, he took a nap.

Sit means "to assume a sitting position." Its principal forms are *sit, sat,* and *sitting:* Many children *sit* in front of the television five to six hours a day. The dog *sat* by the fire. We were *sitting* in the airport when the flight was canceled.

shall, will   *Will* has all but replaced *shall* to express all future action.

should of   See **could of, should of, would of.**

since   Do not use *since* for *because* if there is any chance of confusion. In the sentence "*Since* President Nixon traveled to China, trade between China and the United States has increased," *since* could mean either "from the time that" or "because." To be clear, use *because.*

sit, set   See **set, sit.**

so   Avoid using *so* as a vague intensifier meaning "very" or "extremely." Follow *so* with *that* and a clause that describes the result: She was *so* pleased with their work *that* she took them out to lunch.

sometime, sometimes, some time   *Sometime* means "at some time in the future"; *sometimes* means "now and then"; *some time* means "a period of time": The president will address Congress *sometime* next week. All automobiles, no matter how reliable, *sometimes* need repairs. It has been *some time* since I read that book.

sort of, kind of See **kind of, sort of.**

stationary, stationery *Stationary* means "staying in one place"; *stationery* means "materials for writing" or "letter paper": The communications satellite appears to be *stationary* in the sky. The secretaries supply departmental offices with *stationery*.

supposed to, used to *Supposed to* and *used to* are often misspelled. Both verbs require the final *d* to indicate past tense.

take, bring See **bring, take.**

than, then *Than* is a conjunction used to indicate a comparison; *then* is an adverb indicating time: The new shopping center is bigger *than* the old one. He did his research; *then*, he wrote a report.

that, which, who Use *that* or *which* when referring to a thing, use *who* when referring to a person: It was a speech *that* inspired many. The movie, *which* was a huge success, failed to impress her. Anyone *who* (not *that*) takes the course will benefit.

their, there, they're *Their* is a possessive pronoun; *there* indicates place and is also used in the expressions *there is* and *there are; they're* is a contraction of *they are:* Watson and Crick did *their* DNA work at Cambridge University. I love Los Angeles, but I wouldn't want to live *there*. *There* is nothing we can do to resurrect an extinct species. When *they're* well treated, rabbits make excellent pets.

themselves; theirselves, theirself *Theirselves* and *theirself* are nonstandard variants of *themselves*.

then, than See **than, then.**

till, until, 'til *Till* and *until* have the same meaning, and both are acceptable. *Until* is preferred in college writing. *'Til*, a contraction of *until*, should be avoided.

to, at See **at, to.**

to, too, two *To* is a preposition that indicates direction; *too* is an adverb that means "also" or "more than is needed"; *two* expresses the number 2: Last year we flew from New York *to* California. "Tippecanoe and Tyler, *too*" was William Henry Harrison's campaign slogan. The plot was *too* complicated for the average reader. Just north of *Two* Rivers, Wisconsin, is a petrified forest.

try to, try and *Try and* is the colloquial equivalent of the more formal *try to*: He decided to *try to* (not *try and*) do better. In college writing, use *try to*.

-type Deleting this empty suffix eliminates clutter and clarifies meaning. Found in the wreckage was an *incendiary* (not *incendiary-type*) device.

uninterested, disinterested See **disinterested, uninterested.**

unique Because *unique* means "the only one," not "remarkable" or "unusual," never use constructions like "the most unique" or "very unique."

until   See **till, until, 'til.**

used to   See **supposed to, used to.**

utilize   In most cases, replace *utilize* with *use* (*utilize* often sounds pretentious).

wait for, wait on   To *wait for* means "to defer action until something occurs." To *wait on* means "to act as a waiter": I am *waiting for* (not *on*) dinner.

weather, whether   *Weather* is a noun meaning "the state of the atmosphere"; *whether* is a conjunction used to introduce an alternative: The *weather* will improve this weekend. It is doubtful *whether* we will be able to ski tomorrow.

well, good   See **good, well.**

were, we're   *Were* is a verb; *we're* is the contraction of *we are:* The Trojans *were* asleep when the Greeks attacked. We must act now if *we're* going to succeed.

whether, if   See **if, whether.**

which, who, that   See **that, which, who.**

who, whom   When a pronoun serves as the subject of its clause, use *who* or *whoever;* when it functions in a clause as an object, use *whom* or *whomever:* Sarah, *who* is studying ancient civilizations, would like to visit Greece. Sarah, *whom* I met in France, wants me to travel to Greece with her. To determine which to use at the beginning of a question, use a personal pronoun to answer the question: *Who* tried to call me? *He* called. (subject); *Whom* do you want for the job? I want *her.* (object)

who's, whose   *Who's* means "who is" or "who has"; *whose* indicates possession: *Who's* going to take calculus? *Who's* already left for the concert? The writer *whose* book was in the window was autographing copies.

will, shall   See **shall, will.**

would of   See **could of, should of, would of.**

your, you're   *Your* indicates possession; *you're* is the contraction of *you are*: You can improve *your* stamina by jogging two miles a day. *You're* certain to be the winner.

Answers to Selected Exercises

Answers are provided here for exercise items marked with a ▶ throughout the text.

Exercise 3.1 (p. 31)
1. An announcement, not a thesis.
2. A subject, not a thesis. Gives no indication of essay's focus or direction, let alone writer's position.
3. A subject, not a thesis. Why should it be avoided? What coast? What kind of development? What constitutes overdevelopment?
4. No position indicated. What aspects will be considered? What patterns of development might be used? What standards of judgment will be used?
5. A good start, but "but it has a number of disadvantages" is not specific enough.

Exercise 5.4 (p. 79)
1. A. Give specific examples; exemplification. The paragraph could be developed further by exemplification—that is, by giving examples of words that came into the English language from computer terminology, from popular music, from politics, and from films or TV. If enough examples are given, the paragraph can be expanded into an essay.

Exercise 6.1 (p. 86)
1. F
2. O
3. F
4. O
5. F

Exercise 6.4 (p. 96)
Rewritten statements will vary. Here are the logical fallacies.
1. *Post hoc* fallacy
2. Argument to the person; sweeping generalization
3. Argument to the person
4. Equivocation
5. Begging the question

Exercise 13.1 (p. 154)
1. <u>Isaac Asimov</u> first <u>saw</u> science fiction stories (do) in the newsstand of his parent's Brooklyn candy store.
2. <u>He</u> <u>practiced</u> writing (do) by telling his schoolmates (io) stories (do).
3. <u>Asimov</u> <u>published</u> his first story (do) in *Astounding Science Fiction*.
4. The magazine's <u>editor</u>, John W. Campbell, <u>encouraged</u> Asimov (do) to continue writing.

5. The young <u>writer</u> <u>researched</u> scientific principles (do) to make his stories more accurate.

Exercise 13.2 (p. 157)
1. IC
2. DC
3. P
4. IC
5. IC

Exercise 14.1 (p. 159)
1. The average American consumes 128 pounds of sugar each year; therefore, most Americans eat much more sugar than any other food additive, including salt.
2. Many of us are determined to reduce our sugar intake; consequently, we have consciously eliminated sweets from our diets.
3. Unfortunately, sugar is found not only in sweets but also in many processed foods.
4. Processed foods like puddings and cake contain sugar, and foods like ketchup and spaghetti sauce do too.
5. We are trying to cut down on sugar, yet we find limiting sugar intake extremely difficult.

Exercise 14.2 (pp. 160–61)
1. Many high school graduates who are out of work need new skills for new careers.
2. Although talented high school students are usually encouraged to go to college, some high school graduates are now starting to see that a college education may not guarantee them a job.
3. Because a college education can cost a student more than $100,000, vocational education is becoming increasingly important.
4. Because vocational students complete their work in less than four years, they can enter the job market more quickly.
5. Nurses' aides, paralegals, travel agents, and computer technicians, who do not need college degrees, have little trouble finding work.

Exercise 15.1 (p. 163)
Answers will vary. Here is one revision.
The first modern miniature golf course, built in New York in 1925, was an indoor course with eighteen holes. As the game caught on, entrepreneurs Drake Delanoy and John Ledbetter built one hundred fifty more indoor and outdoor courses; Garnet Carter, who made miniature golf a worldwide fad with his elaborate miniature courses, later joined with Delanoy and Ledbetter to build more courses.

Exercise 15.2 (p. 165)
Answers will vary. Here is one revision.
In surveying two thousand Colorado schoolchildren, Dr. Alice I. Baumgartner and her colleagues at the Institute for Equality in Education found some

startling results. They asked, "If you woke up tomorrow morning and discovered that you were a (girl) (boy), how would your life be different?" The answers were sad and shocking.

Exercise 15.3 (p. 166)
Answers will vary. Here are some possibilities.
1. When he was a very young child, Momaday was taken to Devil's Tower, the geological formation in Wyoming that is called Tsoai (Bear Tree) in Kiowa, and given the name Tsoai-talee (Bear Tree Boy). (adverb clause)
2. In the Kiowa myth of the origin of Tsoai, a boy playfully chases his seven sisters up a tree, which rises into the air as the boy is transformed into a bear. (prepositional phrase)

Exercise 16.1 (p. 168)
Listening to diatribes by angry callers or ranting about today's news, the talk radio host spreads ideas over the air waves. (climactic order)
Every day at the same time, the political talk show host discusses national events and policies, the failures of the opposing view, and the foibles of the individuals who espouse those views. (beginning)
Listening for hours a day, some callers become recognizable contributors to many different talk radio programs. (beginning)
Other listeners are less devoted, tuning in only when they are in the car and never calling to voice their opinions. (beginning)

Exercise 16.2 (p. 169)
1. Because criminals are better armed than ever before, police want to upgrade their firepower.
2. A few years ago, felons used small-caliber, six-shot revolvers—so-called Saturday night specials.

Exercise 16.3 (p. 170)
1. A. However different in their educational opportunities, [both Jefferson and Lincoln as young men became known to their contemporaries as "hard students."] (periodic)
   B. Both Lincoln and Jefferson as young men became known to their contemporaries as "hard students," however different their educational opportunities.

Exercise 16.4 (p. 172)
Answers will vary. Here is one revision.
Many readers distrust newspapers and magazines; they also distrust what they hear on radio and television. Of these media, newspapers have been the most responsive to audience criticism. Some newspapers even have ombudsmen, who listen to reader complaints and act on these grievances.

Exercise 16.5 (p. 173)
Answers will vary. Here is one revision.
Jack Dempsey, the heavyweight champion between 1919 and 1926, had an interesting but uneven career. Many considered him one of the greatest boxers of

all time. Dempsey began fighting as "Kid Blackie," but his career didn't take off until 1919, when Jack "Doc" Kearns became his manager. Dempsey won the championship when he defeated Jess Willard in Toledo, Ohio, in 1919. Dempsey immediately became a popular sports figure; President Franklin D. Roosevelt was one of his biggest fans.

Exercise 17.1 (p. 175)

Answers will vary. Here is one revision.
The shopping mall is no longer so important to American culture. In the 1980s, shopping malls became gathering places where teenagers met, walkers came to get in a few miles, and shoppers looking for selection (not value) went to shop. Several factors have undermined the mall's popularity. First, today's shopper is interested in value and is more likely to shop in discount stores or bulk-buying warehouse stores than in the small, expensive specialty shops in large shopping malls.

Exercise 17.2 (pp. 176–77)

For different reasons, people today are choosing a vegetarian diet. Strict vegetarians eat no animal foods; lactovegetarians eat dairy products but no meat, fish, poultry, or eggs; and ovolactovegetarians eat eggs and dairy products but no meat, fish, or poultry. Famous vegetarians include George Bernard Shaw, Leonardo da Vinci, Ralph Waldo Emerson, Henry David Thoreau, and Mahatma Gandhi. Like them, people today have become vegetarians for good reasons.

Exercise 17.3 (pp. 178–79)

Some colleges that have supported fraternities for many years are reevaluating the fraternities' positions on campus. Opposing the fraternities are students, faculty, and administrators, who claim that fraternities are inherently sexist and, therefore, are unacceptable in coed institutions that offer equal opportunities. Many members of the college community see fraternities as elitist as well as sexist and favor their abolition.

Exercise 18.1 (p. 181)

1. After he completed his engineering degree, Manek returned to India [to visit his large extended family] and [to find a wife].
2. [Unfamiliar with marriage practices in India] and [accustomed to American notions of marriage for love], Manek's American friends frowned on his plans.

Exercise 18.2 (p. 183)

1. The world is divided between those who wear galoshes and those who discover continents.
2. World leaders, members of Congress, and American Catholic bishops all pressed the president to limit the arms race.

Exercise 19.2 (pp. 186–87)

Answers will vary. Here are some examples.
1. deceive, mislead, beguile
2. antiquated, old, antique

3. pushy, assertive, goal-oriented
4. pathetic, unfortunate, touching
5. cheap, inexpensive, economical

Exercise 19.3 (pp. 187–88)
Answers will vary. Here is one revision.
Part-time jobs I have held include waiting tables, landscaping, and selling stereo equipment. Each of these jobs requires strong communications skills. In my most recent position, I sold automobile stereos.

Exercise 19.5 (p. 192)
Answers will vary. Here are some examples.
forefathers, ancestors
man-eating shark, carnivorous shark
manpower, workforce
workman's compensation, worker's compensation
men at work, workers
waitress, server
first baseman, first base
congressman, representative
manhunt, search

Exercise 21.1 (p. 205)
1. he; it is the subject of the sentence
2. me; it is the direct object

Exercise 21.2 (p. 207)
1. Herb Ritts, who got his start by taking photographs of Hollywood stars, has photographed world leaders, leading artistic figures in dance and drama, and a vanishing African tribe.
2. Tim Green, who once played for the Atlanta Hawks and has a law degree, has written several novels about a fictional football team.

Exercise 21.3 (p. 209)
1. the expedition
2. Lewis and Clark

Exercise 22.1 (pp. 212–13)
sold, sneaked

Exercise 22.2 (p. 213)
1. set
2. laying

Exercise 22.3 (pp. 217–18)
1. give
2. have read
3. established
4. becoming
5. had made

Exercise 22.4 (p. 219)
performed, challenged, were, was

Exercise 22.5 (pp. 220–21)
The Chinese invented rockets about AD 1000. They packed gunpowder into bamboo tubes and ignited it by means of a fuse. Soldiers fired these rockets at enemy armies and usually caused panic. In the thirteenth century, England's Roger Bacon introduced an improved form of gunpowder. As a result, soldiers used rockets as a common—although unreliable—weapon in battle.

Exercise 22.6 (p. 221)
Answers will vary.
The Regent Diamond is one of the world's most famous and coveted jewels. The 410-carat diamond was discovered by a slave in 1701 in an Indian mine. [Emphasis is on the diamond rather than on who discovered it.] Over the years, it was stolen and sold several times. [Emphasis is on what happened rather than on people.]

Exercise 23.1 (p. 223)
A popular self-help trend in the United States today is subliminal tapes. These tapes, with titles like *How to Attract Love, Freedom from Acne,* and *I Am a Genius,* are intended to solve every problem known to modern society—quickly and easily. The tapes are said to work because their "hidden messages" bypass conscious defense mechanisms. The listener hears only music or relaxing sounds, like waves rolling slowly and steadily.

Exercise 23.2 (p. 224)
Answers will vary. Here are some possibilities.
1. David seemed tired.
   Jerry was anxious.
   Lienne appeared happy.
   Maggie is depressed.
   Chris remained confident.

Exercise 23.3 (p. 226)
1. difficult/more difficult/most difficult
2. eccentric/more eccentric/most eccentric
3. confusing/more confusing/most confusing
4. bad/worse/worst
5. mysterious/more mysterious/most mysterious

Exercise 24.1 (p. 228)
1. F
2. F
3. CS
4. F
5. F

Exercise 24.2 (pp. 229–30)
The drive-in movie came into being just after World War II, <u>when both movies and cars were central to the lives of many young Americans.</u> Drive-ins

were especially popular with teenagers and young families during the 1950s, <u>when cars and gas were relatively inexpensive</u>. Theaters charged by the carload, <u>which meant that a group of teenagers or a family with several children could spend an evening at the movies for a few dollars</u>. In 1958, when the fad peaked, there were more than four thousand drive-ins in the United States, <u>while today there are fewer than three thousand</u>.

Exercise 24.3 (p. 231)
Most college athletes are caught in a conflict <u>between their athletic and academic careers</u>. Sometimes college athletes' responsibilities on the playing field make it difficult for them to be good students. Often, athletes must make a choice <u>between sports and a degree</u>. Some athletes would not be able to afford college <u>without athletic scholarships</u>. Ironically, however, their commitments to sports (training, exercise, practice, and travel to out-of-town games, for example) deprive athletes <u>of valuable classroom time</u>. The role of college athletes is constantly being questioned.

Exercise 24.4 (p. 232)
Answers will vary. Here is one revision.
Many food products have well-known trademarks, <u>identified by familiar faces on product labels</u>. Some of these symbols have remained the same, while others have changed considerably. Products like Sun-Maid Raisins, Betty Crocker potato mixes, Quaker Oats, and Uncle Ben's Rice use faces <u>to create a sense of quality and tradition and to encourage shopper recognition of the products</u>. Many of the portraits have been updated several times <u>to reflect changes in society</u>.

Exercise 24.5 (pp. 233–34)
Answers will vary. Here is one revision.
Until the early 1900s, communities in West Virginia, Tennessee, and Kentucky were isolated by the mountains that surrounded them, <u>the great chain of the Appalachian Mountains</u>. Set apart from the emerging culture of a growing America and American language, these communities retained a language rich with the dialect of Elizabethan English and with hints of a Scotch-Irish influence. In the 1910s and '20s, the communities in these mountains began to long for a better future for their children. The key to that future, as they saw it, was education.

Exercise 24.6 (pp. 234–35)
Answers will vary. Here is one revision.
As more and more Americans discover the pleasures of the wilderness, our national parks are feeling the stress. Wanting to get away for a weekend or a week, hikers and backpackers stream from the cities into nearby state and national parks. They bring with them a hunger for wilderness <u>and very little knowledge about how to behave ethically in the wild</u>. They also do not know how to keep themselves safe. Some of them think of the national parks as inexpensive amusement parks. Without proper camping supplies and lacking enough food and water for their trip, they are putting at risk their lives and the lives of those who will be called on to save them. One family went for a hike up a desert canyon with an eight-month-old infant <u>and their seventy-eight-year-old grandmother</u>.

Exercise 25.1 (p. 238)

Answers will vary. To illustrate the various responses, each sentence below is fol-
lowed with the four possible types of correction. You should balance the types of
choices in a piece of writing rather than adhering to a single method of correction.
Entrepreneurship is the study of small businesses, college students are embracing it enthusiastically.

1. businesses. College students
2. businesses; college students
3. businesses, and college students
4. Entrepreneurship, the study of small businesses, is being embraced enthusiastically by college students.

Many schools offer one or more courses in entrepreneurship these courses
teach the theory and practice of starting a small business.

1. entrepreneurship. These courses
2. entrepreneurship; these courses
3. entrepreneurship, and these courses
4. entrepreneurship, which teach the theory and practice of starting a small
   business.

Students are signing up for courses, moreover, they are starting their own businesses.

1. courses. Moreover,
2. courses; moreover,
3. courses, and, moreover,
4. Students who sign up for courses are even starting their own businesses.

One student started with a car-waxing business, now he sells condominiums.

1. business. Now
2. business; now
3. business, and now
4. One student, who started with a car-waxing business, now sells condominiums.

Exercise 25.2 (p. 239)

1. Several recent studies indicate that many American high school students
   have a poor sense of history; this is affecting our future as a democratic
   nation and as individuals.
2. Surveys show that nearly one-third of American seventeen-year-olds cannot identify the countries the United States fought against in World War
   II, and one-third think Columbus reached the New World after 1750.
3. Several reasons have been given for this decline in historical literacy, but
   the main reason is the way history is taught.
4. Although this problem is bad news, the good news is that there is increasing agreement among educators about what is wrong with current methods of teaching history.
5. History can be exciting and engaging, but too often it is presented in a
   boring manner.

Exercise 26.1 (p. 244)

1. C
2. C

3. Neither Western novels nor science fiction <u>appeals</u> to me.
4. Stage presence and musical ability <u>make</u> a rock performer successful today.
5. C

Exercise 26.2 (p. 247)

1. The core of a computer is a collection of electronic circuits that <u>is</u> called the central processing unit.
2. Computers, because of advanced technology that allows the central processing unit to be placed on a chip, a thin square of semiconducting material about one-quarter of an inch on each side, <u>have</u> been greatly reduced in size.
3. No error
4. Pressing keys on keyboards resembling typewriter keyboards <u>generates</u> electronic signals that are input for the computer.
5. Computers have built-in memory storage, and equipment such as disks or tapes <u>provides</u> external memory.

Exercise 27.1 (p. 249)

1. He wore his <u>almost</u> new jeans. [He wore his nearly new jeans.]

   He <u>almost</u> wore his new jeans. [He decided at the last minute not to wear his new jeans.]

2. He had <u>only</u> three dollars in his pocket. [Besides the three dollars, he had nothing else in his pocket.]

   <u>Only</u> he had three dollars in his pocket. [He alone had this amount of money in his pocket.]

Exercise 27.2 (p. 250)

1. The bridge <u>across the river</u> swayed <u>in the wind</u>.

2. The spectators <u>on the shore</u> were involved <u>in the action</u>.

3. <u>Mesmerized by the spectacle</u>, they watched the drama unfold.

4. The spectators were <u>afraid of a disaster</u>.

5. <u>Within the hour</u>, the state police arrived <u>to save the day</u>.

Exercise 27.3 (pp. 250–51)

1. The lion, <u>watching Jack</u>, paced up and down in its cage, ignoring the crowd.

2. <u>Nervous yet curious</u>, Jack stared back at the lion.

Exercise 27.4 (p. 251)

1. She realized after the wedding that she had married the wrong man.
2. *The Prince and the Pauper* by Mark Twain is a novel about an exchange of identities.

Exercise 27.5 (pp. 252–53)
1. The people in the audience finally quieted down when they saw the play was about to begin and realized the orchestra had finished tuning up and had begun the overture.
2. Expecting to enjoy the first act very much, they settled into their seats.

Exercise 27.6 (p. 254)
1. Writing for eight hours a day, she publishes a lengthy book every year or so.
2. As an out-of-state student without a car, Joe had difficulty getting to off-campus cultural events.
3. To build a campfire, one needs kindling.
4. With every step we took upward, the trees became sparser.
5. Because I am an amateur tennis player, my backhand is weaker than my forehand.

Exercise 28.1 (pp. 256–57)
1. C
2. Women went to work in the fabric mills of Lowell, Massachusetts, in the late 1800s; and their efforts at reforming the workplace are seen by many as the beginning of the equal rights movement.
3. Farm girls from New Hampshire, Vermont, and western Massachusetts came to Lowell to make money and to experience life in the city.
4. The factories promised the girls decent wages and promised their parents that their daughters would live in a safe, wholesome environment.
5. Dormitories were built by the factories to ensure a safe environment for the girls.

Exercise 28.2 (pp. 257–58)
Answers will vary. Here are some possibilities.
1. Implementing the "motor voter" bill has made it easier for people to register to vote.
2. They won the game because she sank the basket.

Exercise 28.3 (p. 259)
Answers will vary. Here are some possibilities.
1. Inflation is a decline in the purchasing power of currency.
2. Hypertension is elevated blood pressure.

Exercise 28.4 (p. 260)
1. Opportunities in technical writing are more promising than those in business writing. (illogical comparison)
2. Technical writing is more challenging than business writing. (incomplete comparison)

Exercise 29.1 (pp. 263–64)
1. Julius Caesar was killed in 44 BC.
2. Dr. McLaughlin worked hard to earn his PhD.

Exercise 29.2 (p. 265)
1. He wondered whether he should take a nine o'clock class.
2. The instructor asked, "Was the Spanish-American War a victory for America?"

Exercise 30.1 (p. 266)
1. The Pope did not hesitate to visit Cuba, nor did he hesitate to meet with President Fidel Castro.
2. Agents place brand-name products in prominent positions in films so that the products will be seen and recognized by large audiences.

Exercise 30.2 (p. 267)
1. Seals, whales, dogs, lions, and horses are all mammals.
2. C

Exercise 30.3 (p. 269)
   While childhood is shrinking, adolescence is expanding. Whatever the reason, girls are maturing earlier. The average onset of puberty is now two years earlier than it was only forty years ago. What's more, both boys and girls are staying in the nest longer. At present, it is not unusual for children to stay in their parents' home until they are twenty or twenty-one, delaying adulthood and extending adolescence.

Exercise 30.4 (p. 271)
   The Statue of Liberty, which was dedicated in 1886, has undergone extensive renovation. Its supporting structure, whose designer was the French engineer Alexandre Gustave Eiffel, is made of iron.

Exercise 30.5 (pp. 272–73)
1. Kermit the Frog is a Muppet, a cross between a marionette and a puppet.
2. The common cold, a virus, is frequently spread by hand contact, not by mouth.
3. C
4. C
5. The submarine *Nautilus* was the first to cross under the North Pole, wasn't it?

Exercise 30.6 (pp. 274–75)
1. India became independent on August 15, 1947.
2. The UAW has more than 1,500,000 dues-paying members.
3. Nikita Khrushchev, former Soviet premier, once said, "We will bury you!"
4. Mount St. Helens, northeast of Portland, Oregon, began erupting on March 27, 1980, and eventually killed at least thirty people.
5. Located at 1600 Pennsylvania Avenue, Washington, DC, the White House is a popular tourist attraction.

Exercise 30.7 (pp. 275–76)
1. According to Bob, Frank's computer is obsolete.
2. Da Gama explored Florida; Pizarro, Peru.

3. By Monday, evening students must begin preregistration for fall classes.
OR
By Monday evening, students must begin preregistration for fall classes.
4. Whatever they built, they built with care.

Exercise 30.8 (p. 278)
1. A book is like a garden carried in the pocket.
2. Like the iodine content of kelp, air freight is something most Americans
   have never pondered.

Exercise 31.1 (pp. 278–79)
During the 1950s movie attendance declined because of the increasing popularity of television. As a result, numerous gimmicks were introduced to draw audiences into theaters. One of the first of these was Cinerama; in this technique
three pictures were shot side by side and projected on a curved screen. Next
came 3-D, complete with special glasses; *Bwana Devil* and *The Creature from the
Black Lagoon* were two early 3-D ventures. *The Robe* was the first picture filmed
in Cinemascope; in this technique a shrunken image was projected on a screen
twice as wide as it was tall.

Exercise 31.2 (pp. 279–80)
Answers will vary. Here are some possibilities.
1. The Aleutians lie between the North Pacific Ocean and the Bering Sea,
   where the weather is harsh; for example, dense fog, 100-mile-per-hour
   winds, and even tidal waves and earthquakes are not uncommon.
2. These islands constitute North America's largest network of active volcanoes; still, the Aleutians boast some beautiful scenery, and they are relatively unexplored.

Exercise 31.3 (pp. 280–81)
1. The history of modern art seems at times to be a collection of "isms":
   Impressionism, a term that applies to painters who attempted to depict
   contemporary life by reproducing an "impression" of what the eye sees;
   Abstract Expressionism, which applies to artists who stress emotion and
   the unconscious in their nonrepresentational works; and, more recently,
   Minimalism, which applies to painters and sculptors whose work reasserts
   the physical reality of the object.
2. Although the term *Internet* is widely used to refer only to the World Wide
   Web and email, the Internet consists of a variety of discrete elements, including newsgroups, which allow users to post and receive messages on an
   unbelievably broad range of topics; interactive communication forums,
   such as blogs, discussion forums, and chat rooms; and FTP, which allows
   users to download material from remote computers.

Exercise 31.4 (pp. 282–83)
Barnstormers were aviators who toured the country after World War I, giving people short airplane rides and exhibitions of stunt flying; in fact, the name
barnstormer was derived from the use of barns as airplane hangars. Americans'
interest in airplanes had all but disappeared after the war. The barnstormers

helped popularize flying, especially in rural areas. Some were pilots who had flown in the war; others were just young men with a thirst for adventure.

Exercise 32.1 (p. 285)
1. Addams's
2. The popularity of *A Room of One's Own*

Exercise 32.2 (p. 286)
1. It's; you're
2. Who's
3. They're; their
4. Who's
5. its

Exercise 32.3 (p. 287)
1. *x*'s and *o*'s
2. *R*'s

Exercise 32.4 (p. 288)
1. Schaefers'; ours
2. colleges; outsiders
3. its
4. yours
5. favorites

Exercise 33.1 (p. 290)
1. Few people can explain what Descartes's words "I think, therefore I am" actually mean.
2. Gertrude Stein said, "You are all a lost generation."

Exercise 33.2 (p. 295)
1. "Kilroy was here" and "Women and children first" are two expressions *Bartlett's Familiar Quotations* attributes to Anon.
2. C; indirect quotation
3. "The answer, my friend," Bob Dylan sang, "is blowin' in the wind."
4. The novel was a real thriller, complete with spies and counterspies, mysterious women, and exotic international chases.
5. The sign said, "Road liable to subsidence"; it meant that we should look out for potholes.

Exercise 34.1 (p. 297)
1. Books about the late John F. Kennedy include the following: *A Hero for Our Time; Johnny, We Hardly Knew Ye; One Brief Shining Moment;* and *JFK: Reckless Youth.*
2. Only one task remained: to tell his boss he was quitting.

Exercise 34.2 (pp. 298–99)
1. Tulips, daffodils, hyacinths, lilies—all these flowers grow from bulbs.
2. St. Kitts and Nevis—two tiny island nations—are now independent after 360 years of British rule.

Exercise 34.3 (p. 300)
1. During the Great War (1914–1918), Britain censored letters written from the front lines.
2. Those who lived in towns on the southern coast (like Dover) could often hear the mortar shells across the channel in France.

Exercise 34.4 (p. 303)
Answers will vary. Some possibilities follow.
1. "When I was eighteen . . . my mother told me that when out with a young man I should always leave a half-hour before I wanted to."
2. "When I was eighteen or thereabouts, . . . I recognized the advice as sound, and exactly the same rule applies to research."

Exercise 34.5 (p. 303)
1. Mark Twain (Samuel L. Clemens) made the following statement: "I can live for two months on a good compliment."
2. Liza Minelli, the actress/singer who starred in several films, is the daughter of Judy Garland. [For emphasis, dashes may replace the commas.]
3. Saudi Arabia, Oman, Yemen, Qatar, and the United Arab Emirates—all these are located on the Arabian Peninsula.
4. John Adams (1735–1826) was the second president of the United States; John Quincy Adams (1767–1848) was the sixth.
5. The sign said, "No tresspassing [*sic*]."

Exercise 35.1 (p. 310)
1. rec ei pt
2. var ie ty
3. caff ei ne
4. ach ie ve
5. kal ei doscope

Exercise 35.2 (p. 311)
1. surprising
2. surely
3. forcible
4. manageable
5. duly

Exercise 35.3 (p. 312)
1. journeying
2. studied
3. carrying
4. shyly
5. studying

Exercise 36.1 (pp. 318–19)
1. Two of the Brontë sisters wrote *Jane Eyre* and *Wuthering Heights,* nineteenth-century novels that are required reading in many English classes that study Victorian literature.

2. It was a beautiful day in the spring—it was April 15, to be exact—but all Ted could think about was the check he had to write to the Internal Revenue Service and the bills he had to pay by Friday.
3. Traveling north, they hiked through British Columbia, planning a leisurely return on the cruise ship *Canadian Princess.*
4. Alice liked her mom's apple pie better than Aunt Nellie's rhubarb pie, but she liked Grandpa's punch best of all.
5. A new elective, Political Science 30, covers the Vietnam War from the Gulf of Tonkin to the fall of Saigon, including the roles of Ho Chi Minh, the Viet Cong, and the Buddhist monks; the positions of Presidents Johnson and Nixon; and the influence of groups such as the Student Mobilization Committee and the Vietnam Veterans against the War.

Exercise 37.1 (p. 322)

1. I said <u>Carol</u>, not <u>Darryl</u>.
2. A *deus ex machina*, an improbable device used to resolve the plot of a fictional work, is used in Charles Dickens's novel <u>Oliver Twist</u>.
3. He dotted every <u>i</u> and crossed every <u>t</u>.
4. The Metropolitan Opera's production of <u>Carmen</u> was a <u>tour de force</u> for the principal performers.
5. C

Exercise 38.1 (p. 325)

1. One of the restaurant's blue-plate specials is chicken-fried steak.
2. Virginia and Texas are both right-to-work states.
3. He stood on tiptoe to see the near-perfect statue, which was well hidden by the security fence.
4. The five-and-ten-cent store had a self-service make-up counter and many up-to-the-minute gadgets.
5. The so-called Saturday night special is opposed by pro-gun-control groups.

Exercise 39.1 (pp. 328–29)

1. The committee meeting, attended by representatives from Action for Children's Television (ACT) and the National Organization for Women (NOW), Senator Putnam, and the president of ABC, convened at 8 a.m. on Monday, February 24, at the YWCA on Germantown Avenue.
2. An economics professor was suspended after he encouraged his students to speculate on securities issued by a corporation under investigation by the Securities and Exchange Commission (SEC).
3. Benjamin Spock, the MD who wrote *Baby and Child Care,* was a respected doctor known throughout the United States.
4. C [if this sentence can be defined as "technical writing"]
5. The Reverend Dr. Martin Luther King Jr., leader of the Southern Christian Leadership Conference (SCLC), led the famous Selma, Alabama, march.

Exercise 40.1 (pp. 331–32)

1. C [*1984* is a book title.]
2. C

3. In a control group of 247 patients, almost 3 out of 4 suffered serious adverse reactions to the new drug.
4. Before the Thirteenth Amendment to the Constitution, slaves were counted as three-fifths of a person.
5. The intensive membership drive netted 2,608 new members and additional dues of over five thousand dollars.

Exercise 42.1 (p. 364)

You are encouraged to try to find the information in more than one source. Here are some possibilities.

1. *Book Review Index*
2. *Consumer Information Catalog* or *Monthly Catalog of U.S. Government Documents* will list available publications.
3. *Dictionary of American Biography, Encyclopedia Americana, Webster's Biographical Dictionary*
4. Catalog
5. *The Encyclopedia of Associations* lists organizations by subject; there are several with the word *wolves* in the title.

Exercise 42.2 (pp. 365–66)

1. Informative source for thesis. Although published in 1968, its issues remain relevant today.
2. Acceptable source for basic facts.

Exercise 48.1 (p. 476)

1. asked
2. had
3. decided
4. travels
5. spent
6. do
7. decide

Exercise 48.2 (p. 482)

1. months
2. C
3. C
4. C
5. rules

Exercise 48.3 (p. 484)

1. The
2. the
3. C
4. C
5. C
6. C
7. C
8. C

9. C
10. C

Exercise 48.4 (pp. 486–87)
1. delete *of*
2. in
3. on
4. in
5. in

Exercise 48.6 (pp. 492–93)

The young couple seated across from Daniel at dinner the night before were newlyweds from Tokyo. The young couple and Daniel ate together with other guests of the inn at long, low tables in a large dining room with straw mat flooring. The man introduced himself immediately in English, shook Daniel's hand firmly, and, after learning that <u>he</u> was not a tourist but a resident working in Osaka, gave <u>him</u> a business card. The man had just finished college and was working at <u>his</u> first real job, clerking in a bank. Even in a sweatsuit, the man looked ready for the office: chin closely shaven, bristly hair neatly clipped, nails clean and buffed.

Exercise 48.7 (pp. 495–96)

My first experience started when I was studying <u>E</u>nglish as a second language in <u>college</u>. I had to write essays as part of the course. The teacher assigned us to write about something such as <u>w</u>inter, football games, or living in the <u>desert</u>. It is not so hard to write about these things, but I did not have the necessary tools for arranging the information in my mind. Therefore, [add comma] when I submitted my assignment, I got a low grade.

Credits

This page constitutes an extension of the copyright page. We have made every effort to trace the ownership of all copyrighted material and to secure permission from copyright holders. In the event of any question arising as to the use of any material, we will be pleased to make the necessary corrections in future printings. Thanks are due to the following authors, publishers, and agents for permission to use the material indicated.

Text and Illustrations

p. 371: Figure 43.3. Reprinted by permission of Google Inc.

p. 380: Excerpt from "Freedom of Hate Speech?" by Phil Sudo from *Scholastic Update* magazine. Copyright © 1992 by Scholastic Inc. Reprinted by permission of Scholastic Inc.

p. 403: "a song in the front yard" by Gwendolyn Brooks. Reprinted by Consent of Brooks Permissions.

Photos
Part Openers

p. 9: © Keith Brofsky/Photodisc Green/Getty Images

p. 113: © Taxi/Getty Images

p. 333: © Photodisc Red/Getty Images

p. 473: NASA Goddard Space Flight Center

Icons

Computer tips, p. iv: © Keith Brofsky/Photodisc/Getty Images

Checklists, p. iv: © John Coletti

Close-up boxes, p. iv: © Photodisc/Getty Images

Print sources, p. iv: © Simon Battensby/Stone/Getty Images

ESL tips, p. iv: NASA Goddard Space Flight Center

Photos

p. 143: Figure 11.5. Courtesy of Deb Martin

Index

Note: Page numbers in blue refer to definitions.

☐ Do you have a personal organizer? a calendar? Do you use them regularly?

☐ Have you set up a comfortable study space?

☐ Have you made a study schedule?

☐ Have you joined a study group?

☐ Have you read your course syllabi and orientation materials carefully?

☐ Are you attending classes regularly and keeping up with your assignments?

☐ Do you take advantage of your instructors' office hours?

☐ Do you participate in class?

☐ Do you participate in college life?

☐ Do you know where to get help if you need it?

☐ Do you know how to use your college library? Do you use it?

☐ Are you satisfied with your level of technological expertise? Do you know where to get additional instruction?

☐ Are you trying to make contacts and find mentors?

☐ Do you see yourself as a lifelong learner?